An Intergovernmental View of American Government

Pragmatic Federalism

Parris N. Glendening
Mavis Mann Reeves

2nd Edition

Pragmatic Federalism

Pragmatic Federalism

An Intergovernmental View of American Government

Second Edition

Parris N. Glendening
Mavis Mann Reeves

University of Maryland
College Park

Palisades Publishers
Pacific Palisades, California 90272

For our fathers
Raymond G. Glendening
and
Fletcher Wills Mann
because they believed in us

Second edition, Copyright © 1984
by Palisades Publishers

Library of Congress Catalog Card Number 83–062328
International Standard Book Number 0–913530–36–0

Library of Congress Cataloging in Publication Data

Glendening, Parris N.
  Pragmatic federalism.

  Includes bibliographical references and index.
  1. Federal government—United States.   2. Intergovernmental fiscal relations
—United States.   I. Reeves, Mavis Mann.   II. Title.
JK325.G57   1984   321.02'3'0973   83–62328
ISBN 0–913530–36–0 (pbk.)

Palisades Publishers
P.O. Box 744, Pacific Palisades, CA 90272-0744

Cover art by Larry Belliston and Kurt Hanks

Printed in the United States of America

CONTENTS

v

4   STATE-LOCAL RELATIONS: STRONG INTERDEPENDENCE   125

5   NATIONAL-LOCAL RELATIONS: DYNAMIC FEDERALISM   170

6   FINANCING THE FEDERAL SYSTEM   213

PREFACE TO
SECOND EDITION

THE favorable response to the first edition of this book encouraged us to revise it for a new edition. The updating and revision have been extensive because the pace of change in intergovernmental relations has been swift. Often changes made in the early chapters had to be revised again before the updating of the remainder was completed.

Again, we are grateful to the many people who provided assistance. John Bollens, Henry Schmandt, Loren Waldman, and Joseph Zimmerman deserve our special thanks. Their comments gave us guidance for the revisions. We appreciate equally the help of most of the staff of the Advisory Commission on Intergovernmental Relations. Without them, the revision would not have been so thorough or so accurate. We would single out especially David R. Beam, Timothy J. Conlan, Albert J. Davis, Bruce D. McDowell, Albert J. Richter, Jane F. Roberts, and David B. Walker for the information and critical comments they provided and Lynn Schwalje for other help. Ben and Andree Reeves again served as critical readers and editors and Margaret Wrightson, Georgetown University, was especially helpful with Chapter 5. Pat Bowle continued to provide bibliographic assistance for this edition.

Frances Anne Glendening and Ben Reeves probably deserve the highest praise, however. They put up with us through it all.

P.N.G.

M.M.R.

College Park, Maryland

CHAPTER 1

THE DYNAMICS OF INTERGOVERNMENTAL ACCOMMODATION

Dear Congressman:

I want you to help me. I am having all kinds of trouble getting my kids to school. I live here at the mouth of Piney Creek close to Foreman. The school board won't send the bus any closer than two miles because the road is so bad. Theres mud puddles in it deep enough to fish in and the school bus driver say he aint going to drive over it. I called the county and they claimed it wasn't their responsibility and for me to see the state highway department. I wrote them and they come and throwed a load of gravel on it and said it wasn't no use to fix it until the creek was dredged because the floods would ruin it again. I dont know who has to dredge the creek. Some said it was the core of engineers. Can you get something done? It's bad weather for little children to walk two miles to school.

Ans. soon.

Henry Wooton

THIS letter illustrates the complications faced by citizens when they attempt to sort through the multiplicity of public jurisdictions in the United States in an effort to solve a problem. Such complications are the price Americans pay for the numerous layers of government under which we live and for the pragmatism we have exhibited in dividing functions among them. The existence of multiple governments and our penchant for assigning functions such as highway maintenance to the state transportation department in some instances, to counties, towns, or townships in others, and to some combination of these in another group of states complicates the lives of citizens trying to get a problem solved. At the same time, citizens may profit from a welcome diversity, a diversity reflected in the more stringent laws on abortion, alcohol, and marijuana in some states than in others, for example. The individual who disagrees strongly with one way of doing things has the option of moving elsewhere.

The Henry Wootons of this world are not always conscious of the impact of this multiplicity of governmental jurisdictions and the relations among them on their lives. Some may be unaware that they live in a nation where the functions of government may be divided among several jurisdictions or shared by several. They blame their frustrations in dealing with government on red tape, bureaucratic maze, or public officials who are not doing their job or who do not care. They are unaware that their frustrations frequently result from their positions in a welter of governmental jurisdictions, all ministering to their needs and all requiring their support.

Nevertheless, according to a Harris poll, most American citizens recognize the existence of the three levels of government and have preferences among them for the performance of governmental functions.[1] Not surprisingly, they see achieving peace in the world and controlling inflation as proper activities for the national government. In addition, they see Washington as the best place for taxing incomes, making taxes fair to everyone, and dealing with consumer protests against high prices. To a substantially lesser degree, citizens would give the national government responsibility for gun control, combatting air and water pollution, and providing adequate health services.

Most people feel that states should retain obligations for improving colleges, building better highways, and preventing motor vehicle accidents. They believe local governments should provide police protection, collect trash, keep the streets clean, provide zoning for housing, and deal with the problems of traffic congestion and big rock concerts. Other activities, such as providing low cost housing, getting rid of corrupt politicians, combatting drug abuse, integrating schools, handling racial demonstrations, and taking care of people on welfare should be shared by two or more levels of government. This does not mean, of course, that functions will necessarily be allocated entirely in line with public preferences. Other factors besides public opinion affect public policy. Most of the above functions are, in fact, shared by more than one government level.

The governmental system appears to be in constant flux as to which level of government should perform which function. The trend of recent years seems to be an effort to assign functions downward from the national level to the states and upward from local governments to the states. If this continues, states should become more and more important in the federal system.

82,000 GOVERNMENTS

The frustrated citizen trying to get a road built or a sewer repaired probably is not conscious of how many governments there are in the United States—82,688 according to the most recent Census of Governments.[2] As Table 1-1 shows, most of these are local governments, including 3,041 counties, 19,083 municipalities, 16,748 townships (including New England towns), 15,032 independent school districts, and 28,733 nonschool special districts. The total number has declined over the last four decades despite a substantial increase in the number of municipalities and an almost four-fold rise in special districts. Almost all the decrease results from a reduction in the number of school districts, a product of the school consolidation movement. The number of townships is also somewhat smaller. Nevertheless, the remaining thousands of local jurisdictions fragment the delivery of public services and increase the frustrations of citizens, such as Henry Wooton, who are trying to penetrate the maze of governments. At the same time, they offer more opportunity for citizen access to government decision-makers.

These myriad local governments were not established all at once, but were largely created one by one as the need arose. Nor are they usually regarded as conflicting entities. They serve as additional mechanisms for accomplishing public purposes.

In most of the nation, the county traditionally was the local juris-diction relied on to administer state laws on the local level. In many instances, however, its limited functions, designed primarily for rural areas, were not adequate to deal with the problems created by dense settlements. Consequently, local citizens generated the incorporation of municipalities to provide supplemental services or advantages, to be financed by addi-tional taxes on municipal residents. Townships, on the other hand, which are subdivisions of counties, provided a means for county governments to ensure community control of such important activities as education, highways, and relief for the poor.

Both in the majority of the states where counties were important juris-dictions and in New England where the town was the vital unit, problems often overflowed the boundaries of established governments. The mismatch

TABLE 1-1
GOVERNMENTAL JURISDICTIONS IN THE UNITED STATES, 1942–1982

Types of government	1942*	1952*	1962	1972	1982
Total	155,115	116,806	91,237	78,269	82,688
U.S. government	1	1	1	1	1
State governments	48	50	50	50	50
General local governments	38,189	37,061	38,185	38,552	38,872
Counties	3,050	3,052	3,043	3,044	3,041
Municipalities	16,220	16,807	18,000	18,517	19,083
Townships**	18,919	17,202	17,142	16,991	16,748
Other local governments	116,878	79,695	53,001	39,666	43,765
School districts	108,579	67,355	34,678	15,781	15,032
Nonschool special districts	8,299	12,340	18,323	23,885	28,733

*1952 data adjusted to include units in Alaska and Hawaii that were reported separately prior to statehood in 1959. Comparable data not available for 1942.

**Includes New England towns.

Source: Adapted from U.S. Bureau of the Census, *1972 Census of Governments: Governmental Organization,* Vol. 4, p. 23; *1982 Census of Governments, Governmental Units in 1982, Preliminary Report No. 1.*

of jurisdictions and problems often led to the creation of special districts, individually designed to provide service to the population of the affected areas.

Local governments are not spread uniformly throughout the United States. Nine states have nearly half of them (46 percent). Illinois has more than 6,000, Pennsylvania over 5,000, and California, Kansas, Minnesota, Nebraska, New York, Ohio, and Texas more than 3,000 each. The average number for a state is 1,653. Looking at averages can distort one's view, however, because Illinois has more than 6,000 while Hawaii has only 19. Even taking into account the fact that Hawaii is much smaller than Illinois, this means that one level of government—the state—is performing more functions in Hawaii or that Hawaiian citizens are getting only a small fraction of the state and local services provided in Illinois for its citizens. It also means that each citizen in Illinois is likely to live under the jurisdiction of more governments than his or her counterpart in Hawaii.

In addition to the governments included in the Census count, there are a number of other governmental organizations serving regional needs. Often the citizen has little contact with these, but they are nonetheless important in the American system. Although federal financial support was withdrawn recently from eight of the nine multistate regional organizations for economic development, the federally created Appalachian Regional Commission, encompassing 13 states, is still functioning, and three others have incorporated as interstate agencies supported by member states. Other interstate organizations have been established through the adoption of interstate compacts or agreements. The Port Authority of New York and New Jersey is an example of this type of organization. Furthermore, local governments in almost all metropolitan areas in the nation have joined in the establishment of councils of government or regional councils. These institutions promote voluntary cooperation in the solution of areawide problems. There are other substate organizations as well, many of them inspired by federal requirements attached to financial assistance. Examples are area agencies on the aging, water quality planning agencies, and others —such as alcoholism authorities in Texas—found in only one state. Most of them operate separately from the general local governments in the same area, further confusing the citizen as to who does what. A list is in Table 1–2.

At the same time, substantial interaction is present among these governmental organizations and it often requires action of more than one to accomplish some purpose. In fact, the administration of the public's business is more often intergovernmental than not. A significant portion of all public management is intergovernmental management. This situation frequently bewilders citizens and frustrates public managers.

TABLE 1-2
PUBLIC MULTI-JURISDICTIONAL REGIONAL
ORGANIZATIONS, 1983

MULTI-STATE REGIONAL ORGANIZATIONS*

8 Federally Initiated Organizations for Economic Development
Appalachian Regional Commission
5 Former Title V Commissions Now Formally Reconstituted by States**
Council of Ozarks Governors, Inc.
Council of Four-Corners Governors, Inc.
Great Lakes Governors' Council, Inc.
New England Governors' Conference, Inc.
Southwest Border Conference Association, Inc.
2 Former Title V Commissions in Transition
Old West Regional Commission
Pacific Northwest Regional Commission

3 Interstate River Basin Commissions***
Missouri Basin States Association, Inc.
Ohio River Basin Commission
Upper Mississippi States Association, Inc.

58 Interstate or Federal-Interstate Compact Organizations
2 Federal-Interstate Compact Organizations
Delaware River Basin Commission
Susquehanna River Basin Commission
56 Other Interstate Compact Organizations: Examples
Education Commission of the States
Gulf States Marine Fisheries Commission
Ohio River Valley Water Sanitation Commission
Republican River Compact Commission
Kansas City Area Transportation Authority
Port Authority of New York and New Jersey
Southern Regional Education Board
Western Interstate Nuclear Board
New England Higher Education Compact

7 Interstate Agreement Agencies
Southern Growth Policies Board
New England Governors' Conference, Inc.
Midwest Governors' Conference
Council of Northeastern Governors (CONEG)
Southern Governors' Conference
Western Governors' Conference
Western Governors' Policy Office (WESTPO)

TABLE 1-2 Continued

1932 SUBSTATE REGIONAL ORGANIZATIONS (other than special districts)

675 General purpose organizations: Examples

Councils of governments
Regional planning councils
Economic development districts
Planning district commissions

1257 Special Purpose Organizations: Examples

Community action agencies
Area agencies on the aging
Health system agencies
Criminal justice planning agencies
Water quality planning agencies
Regional mental health organizations in Connecticut
Alcoholism authorities in Texas
Metropolitan Transportation Commission in California

---

*The reader is cautioned that many of these organizations are in a period of transition. Some are in the process of abolition and others are being merged.

**The former Coastal Plains Commission merged into the Southern Growth Policies Board.

***These replaced the federally initiated and financed Title II river basin commissions. The Great Lakes Basin Commission turned over its assets to the Great Lakes Commission, an interstate compact organization concerned with transportation and commerce, and the New England Governors' Conference, Inc. took on responsibilities previously handled by the New England River Basins Commission. The activities of the Pacific Northwest Basin Commission ceased; however, informal meetings of state representatives continue.

Source: Compiled from U.S. Bureau of the Census, *1977 Census of Governments: Regional Organizations;* Council of State Governments, *Interstate Compacts and Agencies, 1981 Edition* (Lexington, Ky.: 1981); U.S. Advisory Commission on Intergovernmental Relations, *Multi-State Regionalism Revisited,* Report A-66 (Washington, D.C., 1979); ACIR, *The State and Local Roles in the Federal System,* Report A-88 (1982:); U.S. Water Resources Council, *Water Resource Coordination Directory* (Washington, D.C., 1979); and updated by information from various sources including *The Federal Register,* John Whisman of the Governors' Council on Regional Development, Bruce McDowell, U.S. Advisory Commission on Intergovernmental Relations, and Joel Frisch, U.S. Geological Survey. Regional organizations were not included in the 1982 Census of Governments.

Not only must citizens find their way through a maze of governmental units and subordinate agencies, but also when they wish to vent their ire on public officials, they must locate the responsible culprits from among a portion of the almost 500,000 elected officeholders in the nation. No wonder that frustration over the complexity of the system is often followed by exasperation over difficulties in pinpointing responsibility. Who, for example, does Henry Wooton, the writer of our opening letter, blame for his situation? The school board that refused to send the school bus further? The county commissioners who said it "wasn't their responsibility?" The governor who did not get the state highway department to act? The President, responsible for the Corps of Engineers? Or the member of Congress who has ended up with the problem? Understandably, Wooton is confused. Moreover, even if he solved the problem for the moment, he might be even more perplexed if he moved to another state because no nationwide answer exists to these questions.

Functions assigned to counties in one state may be performed by cities or towns in a second and at the state level in a third. To complicate matters further, local jurisdictions with the same name—such as towns or townships—may not be the same in different states. And even if an official wanted to help, he or she might be stymied by a lack of cooperation from officials of another jurisdiction.

DISTRIBUTION OF FUNCTIONS AMONG GOVERNMENTS

Functions of government once were fairly clearly divided among national, state, and local levels, although the national government undertook fewer activities. It concentrated primarily in areas of national defense, governance of territories, control of the currency and economic matters, regulation of foreign and interstate commerce, and the operation of the postal service. In general, states were responsible for higher education, health and hospitals, regulating to protect the public health, safety, and morals of the citizens, corrections, state courts, business regulation, and establishing and empowering local governments. Local units had jurisdiction over maintenance of law and order, local roads, schools, water and santitation, fire protection, and what public welfare there was.

Today, governmental activities are shared to a far greater degree, and almost all major functions have more than one provider.[3] Even in the clearly national function of defense, the state National Guard units, which are state military organizations unless called into the federal service, help bolster the defense establishment. And although fire protection is the *only* major function for which local governments provide more than 55 percent of the funding, both states and the national government have significant roles in fire protection. In 1979 the national government was involved in more than 50 intergovernmental programs affecting local fire protection.[4] Moreover, it now dominates the funding of welfare services and participates heavily in other activities previously the province of state and local governments.

Citizens in some nations do not face so difficult a task of determining which government handles which function. It is a problem peculiar to federal governments, and perhaps even more so to the United States than to most other federal systems because of substantial state power based in constitutional provisions, uncentralized political parties, and the support state and local governments enjoy in public opinion.

THE FEDERAL ARRANGEMENT

The present federal arrangement was designed when the United States Constitution was written in 1787. It emerged from the protracted negotiations by the delegates from the 13 new states. Because of a need for a common defense and for some order to the commercial and financial disarray that existed, the delegates were willing to trade some of the authority their states possessed under the Articles of Confederation—our first constitution—for the advantages of a common attack on a few problems. Like delegates to constitutional conventions everywhere, they struck the best bargain they could at the time.

The result was a federal arrangement that divided powers of government between the states and a new national government. Unlike the Articles, which provided for a central government consisting simply of a Congress that dealt only with state governments in domestic matters, the new constitution established a national government that could exercise its powers directly on the people throughout the country. Each state was to employ its authority in a smaller geographic portion of the nation.

Although the delegates may have thought they had been explicit in the division of powers when they wrote the proposed constitution, by the time it was adopted they disagreed about the kind of bargain they had struck. Some thought of it as *federal*, although they used it in the sense we would use *confederal* today—to mean a loose league of states with these jurisdictions giving the central government whatever powers they thought it needed. While it would not be as powerless an organization as the United Nations, which is the leading current example of a confederation, the bulk of the authority would rest with the states. Others believed they had established a much stronger national government with state authority in most areas still preserved. Even various numbers of *The Federalist Papers* conflicted or were vague (perhaps purposefully so) in their exposition of what that document meant.[5] These were essays written by Alexander Hamilton, James Madison, and John Jay under the pseudonym, *Publius,* to encourage ratification of the new constitution in New York.

Patrick Henry may have expressed some of the confusion of the period when he declared:

> We are told that this government, taken collectively, is without example; that it is national in this part, federal in that; in the brain it is national, in the stamina federal; some limbs are federal, some national; it is federal in conferring powers, it is national in retaining them; it is not to be supported by the states, the pockets of individuals are to be searched for its maintenance.[6]

No wonder there have been conflicting interpretations of American federalism ever since.

Today, different authorities emphasize various aspects of federalism. Some have stressed its contractual and legal status, while others have characterized it by its pragmatic and procedural nature. William H. Riker regards it as a bargain between prospective national leaders for the purpose of aggregating territory and raising taxes and armies. He regards a constitution as federal if: (1) two levels of government rule the same land and people; (2) each level has at least one area of action in which it is autonomous; and (3) there is some guarantee (even though merely a statement in the constitution) of the autonomy of each government in its own sphere.[7] Daniel J. Elazar also sees federalism as contractual. Separate polities are able to maintain their political integrity within an overarching political system by "contractually distributing power among general and constituent governments in a manner designed to protect the existence and authority of all."[8]

Richard H. Leach views federalism as a process and disagrees with those who regard it as a system of power distribution. He writes:

> It is a misconception to view American federalism as a power system. Despite common usage, power is not exercised systematically in the United States. Indeed, it is probably wrong to use the suffix "ism" for federalism, for the danger is always present that it will be read to mean adherence to a system rather than a process which is all its use should imply. "System" suggests a regularly interacting group of power units, a power network, which performs its functions in a steady flow. That simply is not descriptive of federalism. Units there are aplenty, and interactions in great quantity, but there is nothing regularized about it, nor is there a steady flow of output. Power in the federal system moves irregularly, in spurts even as water overcomes obstacles and flows on again until it meets another. It is characterized by disorder and seldom moves twice in precisely the same way to accomplish its objectives.[9]

Michael D. Reagan distinguishes between old-style and new-style federalism. The former is "a legal concept, emphasizing a constitutional division of authority and functions between a national government and state governments, with both levels having received their powers independently of each other from a third source—the people." The latter he defines as "a political and pragmatic concept, stressing the actual interdependence and sharing of functions between Washington and the states, and focusing on the mutual leverage that each level is able to exert on the other."[10]

We incorporate both pragmatic and contractual dimensions, regarding *federalism in the United States as an arrangement whereby: (1) the same territory and people are governed by two levels of government, both of which derive their authority from the people and both of which share some functions and exercise other functions autonomously; (2) the existence of each level is protected from the other; and (3) each may exert leverage on the other. Basic to this arrangement are the spirit of self-restraint in interfering with the powers of the other and concern for maintaining the arrangement.* At the same time, we agree with Leach that American federalism lacks many systematic attributes and with Reagan as to its pragmatic nature. We see it as characterized by extensive interdependence and by an ongoing struggle for power among governments. It is flexible, fluid, and pragmatic.

A FEDERAL ARRANGEMENT MODIFIED BY INTERGOVERNMENTAL RELATIONS

Since adopted, the Constitution and the federal arrangement it included have undergone constant modification. This ability to adjust to changing needs and times probably has been the major reason why both have endured for two centuries. The federal arrangement, in particular, has achieved flexibility by relying on a network of intergovernmental relations that permits choices to be made pragmatically—that is, on the basis of whatever option appears to solve the problem best at a given time. These relations have included the local governments as well as the states despite the fact that the smaller jurisdictions were not partners to the original bargain. Still not theoretically or technically a part of the federal arrangement, local governments are integral factors in its operations today because of the important responsibilities they shoulder in implementing major state and federal programs that these governments choose not to administer directly. In discussing local governments and other community organizations, James L. Sundquist and David W. Davis declared in *Making Federalism Work:*

. . . the effectiveness of the execution of federal programs depends crucially upon the competence of community institutions to plan, initiate, and coordinate. The federal contribution of money, ideas and leadership . . . is indispensable, but . . . it is at the community level that the offerings must be . . . turned into concrete undertakings.[11]

Without the massive body of intergovernmental relations that exist—not only between the national government and the states and among the states, but state-local, federal-local, and inter-local as well—American federalism would not work. It is our thesis that these relationships are dynamic, that is, they are in constant change. As each problem involving more than a single governmental jurisdiction arises, it is dealt with in a pragmatic fashion; an individual solution is devised for it without reference to any general theory of intergovernmental relations. This may require a national-state interaction in a certain instance, a state-local one in another, or an interlocal one in a third, or indeed it may involve interface among people in all these governments at the same time. It could include financial assistance, advice, or the creation of a new special district, among other things. A similar problem arising elsewhere in the nation, or five years later, may be handled in another way.

Intergovernmental relations constantly change and adjust. They are at once cooperative, competitive, conflicting. Above all they are pragmatic and dynamic, tailored to and changing with the need and the times. They breathe life into the operations of American federalism. Hence, the title of this book is *Pragmatic Federalism,* and its contents deals with the relationships among people employed in governments of all classifications.

Characteristics of Intergovernmental Relations

Intergovernmental relations were traditionally thought of in terms of federalism; however, the term now has a broader meaning, although in the United States the relations occur in a federal setting. A pioneer in the study of intergovernmental relations, William Anderson, used the phrase to designate an important body of activities or interactions occurring between governmental units of all types and levels within the federal system.[12] It could certainly be applied to relationships within nonfederal systems and to polities other than the United States.[13]

Both Anderson and Deil S. Wright, who also has worked at defining the term, emphasize that the concept of intergovernmental relations has to be understood in terms of human behavior. Wright says, ". . . strictly speaking, then, there are no intergovernmental relations, there are only relations among the officials in different governing units." He further characterizes intergovernmental relations as "continuous, day-to-day patterns of contact, knowledge, and evaluations of the officials who govern."[14]

Informal as well as formal interactions are involved. The scope of inter-governmental relations, Wright continues, extends to all public officials—administrators as well as elected executive, legislative, and judicial officers—and it encompasses political, economic, and administrative interactions as well as legal ones. To this the present authors would add that inter-governmental relations include the attitudes of public officials, an idea implicit in the definitions of Anderson and Wright. These attitudes, behavior, and interactions of the people involved must be seen in the light of the environment in which public officials operate, including all the constraints and stimuli within that environment as well as those imposed from the outside.

Then, for the purposes of this book, *intergovernmental relations are the interactions, attitudes, and behavior of both elected and appointed officials and bureaucrats of two or more governmental jurisdictions functioning in their public capacities. The relations reflect their environment—their historical, cultural, legal, organizational, financial, political, and geographical settings. They may occur on both horizontal and vertical planes. Not only are the federal relationships of the national government and the states included, but so are the interstate, state-local, interlocal, and national-local relations. They must be understood in the context of American federalism.*

Horizontal and Vertical Relations

Intergovernmental relations may be divided into two categories, horizontal and vertical. Horizontal relations occur among equals, such as state with state, county with county, and township with township. In these relationships, there is ordinarily no legal compulsion for officials to interact because neither exercises authority over the other. Encouragement for them to do so, however, may come from the state or national government in the form of requirements for grants-in-aid or other provisions.

Proximity is often a major factor in horizontal relationship because officials in jurisdictions bordering each other frequently find it necessary to cooperate to solve a problem affecting both. Officials of other jurisdictions may have no relationships at all, except, perhaps, as they convene at national meetings. For the most part, personnel in units operating horizontally expect noninterference from each other, and they at least hope for cooperation in solving mutual problems.

Vertical relationships are more complex and diverse. They occur between officials of larger or more central governments and geographically smaller constituent units. The element of legal authority of one jurisdiction over another may be involved. The federal relationship between the national government and the states was considered earlier in this chapter. In contrast to that is the unitary relationship between the states and their local units, an arrangement whereby the larger jurisdiction determines the powers of the smaller ones unilaterally with state officials often exercising some administrative supervision over local personnel. Although the absolute legal control of the state is somewhat modified by political and other resources of the localities, determination of what local officials legally may do rests with the state.

In their vertical relations with larger jurisdictions, officials of smaller units seek autonomy, financial assistance, and policies with which they agree. Those in central jurisdictions look to the constituent units for administrative assistance in program implementation, and for responsibility for certain functions, such as law enforcement, which can be undertaken better in a smaller geographic area.

Relations between some jurisdictions are difficult to classify because of the diversity that exists both among and within states. As far as counties and municipalities (cities, towns, boroughs, and villages) are concerned, county officials normally have no authority over municipal governments, although they may provide countywide services to the municipal citizenry. Consequently, their relationships are likely to be of a horizontal nature, those of equals. Some states, nonetheless, allow counties to determine certain aspects of municipal affairs. County officials may be able to control the incorporation of new municipalities, determine boundary changes, and affect other aspects of municipal activity. In a number of instances the same governmental jurisdiction may constitute both a city and a county. Generalizations are risky because of the differences in state laws and practices applying to city-county relationships. In some states, enactment of special local legislation applying to only one situation further diversifies the arrangements.

Similar variations exist in relations between counties and other local units. Generally, townships are likely to be subject to some county authority since they are county subdivisions. Consequently, the relations are vertical. When it comes to school districts and other special districts, however, diversity is pronounced. This is because of the many variations in the administration of public elementary and secondary education. Some states have established independent school districts with separately elected officials who administer the schools and levy taxes for their support. Others have dependent school districts that are responsible for school operation, but that must rely on municipal or county authorities for local funding. Elsewhere, general local government jurisdictions, such as cities, counties, towns, or townships, run the schools just as though they were another department of the government. As a consequence of this American ingenuity for designing local governments and prescribing their relations, it is often necessary to examine a particular situation before coming to conclusions as to the basic relationships.

Factors Stimulating Intergovernmental Relations

It is a truism to state that no government operates in a vacuum, but obviously some are involved in intergovernmental interactions to a greater degree than others. What stimulates intergovernmental relations? Contributing factors vary with the government and activity concerned. A list of major factors include (1) spatial proximity; (2) legal requirements; and (3) financial assistance of one jurisdiction to another.[15]

Proximity plays a major role, especially in respect to horizontal relations. It stands to reason that New York and California are not likely to be engaged in boundary disputes or controversies over air pollution with one another. Texas and Louisiana, on the other hand, may need to reach accommodation on many matters; and certainly Kansas City, Kansas, and Kansas City, Missouri, have mutual problems to resolve simply because they are neighbors. Proximity also affects vertical relations. Research suggests that states or localities near Washington, D.C. interact with the national government more than do those further away.[16] Part of this may be a factor of personal acquaintance. Bureaucrats from surrounding jurisdictions know national officials, and this personal relationship promotes official interactions.

Legal requirements contained in constitutions, statutes, and court decisions, and the executive orders or administrative regulations and guidelines promulgated to effectuate them, often require government officials to interact. Provision for rendition of a fugitive from one state to another necessitates intergovernmental contact between personnel of the state desiring the return of the fugitive and those of the state to which he fled. State laws mandate certain actions by local officials in the conduct of elections. Court decisions may require national agency approval of local school desegregation plans. National statutes or guidelines provoke joint activities among officials within a region. A recent study identified 39 federal programs that supported substate regional organizations in such functional areas as transportation, health planning, and economic development.[17]

Financial assistance from one level of government to another, particularly from the national government to the states, often has been a primary stimulant for intergovernmental relations. All national grants-in-aid require some intergovernmental action by the receiving government, be it the filing of a grant application, the submission of reports on the use of the money, or one of myriad other actions. It would be a mistake, however, to regard financial aid as the catalyst in all intergovernmental relations or necessarily as the most important factor. A case study of low-income housing in Montgomery County, Maryland, for example, found that the county waited 27 years after grant availability to take advantage of federal housing money. Thus, neither the legal provision nor the availability of funds stimulated intergovernmental interaction in housing in this instance. More important were environmental factors such as population growth, rising housing costs, and shifts in public attitude concerning the provision of housing. These developments produced demands on the county government, which responded by creating a local housing authority and moving into the provision of low-income housing.[18]

The same variables that determine the existence of intergovernmental relations are important in their tone. Once established, relations among the people involved may be harmonious or abrasive, competitive or complimentary, frequent or occasional. These elements are difficult to quantify, but seemingly relations are smoothest when the individuals involved have compatible goals, are personally acquainted, and when both have a knowledge of the particular area and problems. Officials of one jurisdiction mildly distrust those of another and, although goals are the same, differences develop over how to administer a program. Each jurisdiction's officials are concerned with maintaining its viability. They operate in a political culture and environment distinct from any other. Each group has a unique constituency to please.

The communications and interactions among governments in the United States are the focus of this book. When so many governments exist, understanding the relations among them is essential to comprehending how the American system works. One who looks only at the national government, state government, or local government, sees only part of the picture, understands only part of the workings of the system. Behind and between these governments lies a whole network of activities and relationships among the millions of individuals who people the thousands of governments in the United States, what Senator Edmund S. Muskie called the ''hidden dimension'' of American government.[19] This book seeks to bring these activities and relationships out into the light, to expose the unseen side of American government.

FACTORS CONTRIBUTING TO CHANGE

Regardless of the sources of their stimulation, intergovernmental relations undergo constant change and adjustment. New circumstances place new stresses on the political system. Numerous factors, including catastrophic events, demographic changes, and technological developments, alter the political arrangements.

Cataclysmic Events

Cataclysmic events, such as depression, war, or riots, often require shifts of government functions from one level to another, usually from a smaller to a large level, to provide swift and comprehensive action. The Depression of the 1930s, for example, saw a welfare system that had formerly relied almost entirely on private support, with local units furnishing county poor farms and orphanages and occasional emergency relief, shifted to the states with a strong input of national public assistance. In some states, additional functions, such as schools and roads, also became state activities while in other instances states joined localities in their support.

Every war in which the United States has been engaged altered the intergovernmental picture, frequently by producing a centralizing effect. The frustrating experience of trying to coordinate the diverse training, equipment, and performance of the various state militias during World War I, for instance, resulted in the National Guard Act of 1921 that authorized national financing for uniform training, equipment, and operations of these units. The G.I. Bill offering education to World War II veterans in lieu of the usual bonus, brought the national government into direct contact with state (and private) colleges and universities in the administration of these veterans' benefits. Moreover, the crush of college enrollments stimulated by the G.I. Bill led to other national programs with an intergovernmental impact. Financial assistance for college dormitories is an example.

Riots and other civil disorders, such as those occurring in the late 1960s and early 1970s, precipitated extensive changes in the provision of urban services. The national government acted to assuage the discontent existing in the large cities and provided funds for both rebuilding riot-scarred areas and social programs.

Growing and Migrating Population

Population changes have had a major impact in altering relationships. Since 1920 when the growing number of Americans living in urban areas tipped the balance and the United States first became an urban nation, three continuing movements of population have substantially altered the demographic makeup of the country: (1) movement to urban areas; (2) shifts within urban areas to the suburbs; and (3) migration to the "Sunbelt."

Urbanization and Suburbanization. The massive trek from the farms to the cities transformed the nation from predominantly rural to overwhelmingly urban in less than three decades, with almost three-fourths of the population now residing in urban areas. This urbanization was followed by movement within urban areas from the central cities to the suburbs. The accelerated suburbanization in the 1950s and 1960s meant that by 1980 more people lived in suburbs than in either rural areas or central cities. The latter, in fact, lost population. Both of these changes produced a great increase in the representation of urban areas at all levels of government, particularly after the judicial spur of fair apportionment in the 1960s. Moreover, suburbanization sometimes separated the poorer, nonwhite, and ethnic citizens of the central city (except in the South and Southwest) from the wealthier, overwhelmingly white suburbs, and both parochialism and conflict increased. New municipalities were formed, adding to the separateness of various groups and making problem solving for metropolitan areas more difficult.[20]

During the 1970s, Americans, particularly young whites, began to desert large metropolitan areas for small municipalities, further diminishing the political power of large cities; nevertheless, the nation remains largely urban and metropolitan. Still, urbanization has meant more effective urban demands on the national government—demands that have accelerated national-local interface, often bypassing the states. The pressures of urban growth have also been felt by the states, and some have reacted by granting broader powers and increased financial assistance to localities.

Migration to the Sunbelt. The third trend was the movement of the highly mobile American people to the southern and western states, especially those of the "Sunbelt." Population growth in these areas exceeded that of any other region between 1970 and 1980, and the population center of the nation continued its move west. Figure 1–1 shows this development.

It is important to understand the magnitude of the population shifts behind the percentages of changes. California's population, for instance, increased from fewer than 3.5 million in 1920 to almost 20 million in 1970. After that, the rate of growth slowed; nevertheless, the population grew by another 3.7 million by 1980. This is almost as though the entire population of Kentucky had moved to California in the decade of the 1970s! Although the numbers were not so great, Nevada's population grew by 63.5 percent, Arizona's by 53.1 percent, and Florida's by 43.4 percent in the 1970s. Florida had 3 million more people in 1980 than in 1970, an increase about equal to the population of either Connecticut or Oklahoma.

Population shifts brought changes in political power and an intensification of regional conflicts. Representation in Congress altered. Since the number of seats in the House of Representatives is determined by law, every state's portion is recomputed after each decennial census. Consequently, some states gain and some lose seats. For example, the reapportionment of seats following the 1980 census resulted in the Mountain states, which had a population increase of 37.1 percent, picking up 5 congressional seats while the East lost 7. Since a change in representation in the Congress also modifies votes in the Electoral College, the regions that

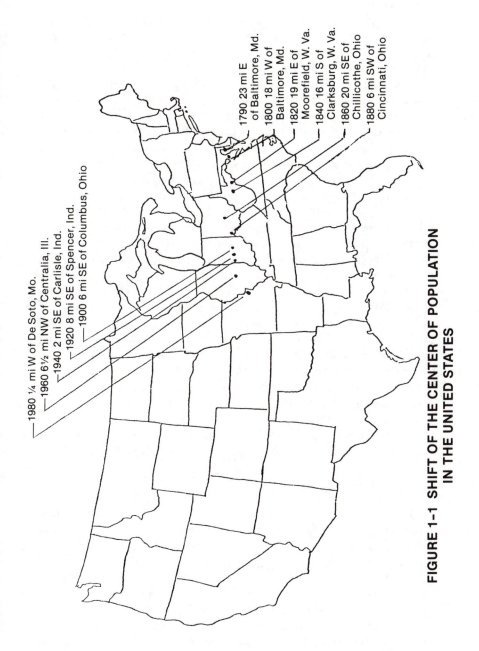

1790 23 mi E of Baltimore, Md.
1800 18 mi W of Baltimore, Md.
1820 19 mi E of Moorefield, W. Va.
1840 16 mi S of Clarksburg, W. Va.
1860 20 mi SE of Chillicothe, Ohio
1880 6 mi SW of Cincinnati, Ohio

1980 ¼ mi W of De Soto, Mo.
1960 6½ mi NW of Centralia, Ill.
1940 2 mi SE of Carlisle, Ind.
1920 8 mi SE of Spencer, Ind.
1900 6 mi SE of Columbus, Ohio

FIGURE 1-1 SHIFT OF THE CENTER OF POPULATION IN THE UNITED STATES

gained seats also got a stronger voice in the selection of the President and Vice President.

Other ramifications of population shifts are important as well. States with diminishing proportions of the total population experienced a slower growth in financial resources from both their own resources and their proportionate share of intergovernmental aid. At the same time, the income of the people of these areas diminished, sometimes requiring outside aid to deal with the difficulties created by unemployment. The growth areas had problems, too. They were faced with rising demands for services that often outstripped revenues to pay for them. The lag between the time a service or facility is needed and the time it can be provided creates stresses on the system. If a new subdivision is constructed and families with 500 children move there, many of those youngsters immediately require school buildings and teachers and cannot wait for construction and training to take place. The inability of one level of government to meet such needs is likely to result in city or county officials of the area involved making demands on state or national officials for assistance. This has been graphically evident in connection with the immigration of Cuban refugees into the Miami area.

The transient nature of the population in itself has consequences for intergovernmental relations because it increases the interdependence of all governments horizontally. Policy outputs from one state often "spill over" to another. For example, untrained laborers do not always stay in the areas where training is poor but move to other jurisdictions and raise the unemployment rate there. Or the better-supported welfare programs in one state may attract the indigent of others, thus stimulating officials of the receiving jurisdiction to agitate for a national welfare program. Further, this constant movement may increase the orientation of citizens to the national government because this is the only public unit in which they consistently reside as they wander nomadically from state to state.

Technological Development

Technological developments modify the balance in society, thus creating stresses in the social system that produce demands on government. For instance, mass production of the automobile permitted the affluent to move away from downtown areas of cities and avoid a share of the problems existing there. At the same time, the automobile increased the range of criminal activity so that apprehending fleeing offenders might require the cooperation of several governments. In another development, air conditioning permitted the massive growth in the southern states that otherwise would not have been as likely without it. Moreover, it encouraged Congress to remain in Washington, D.C. during the summer months, allowing more time for creation of government programs. Television, of course, exerts tremendous impact on all levels of government and on their relationships. Not only does it provide a homogenizing influence on the nation, but also a devisive one as it exhibits for all to see the disparities in American society. This creates pressures for remedial measures by whatever government has the resources—usually the national government. Television, furthermore, along with newspapers and radio, educates the public in pressure group techniques and stimulates citizen action.

Other Factors

A rise in the age level also contributed to change in intergovernmental relations. With the advent of the birth control pill, the birth rate dropped precipitously. Consequently, as the baby boom children of the 1940s and 1950s reached maturity, the average age of the population moved upward. Fewer schools for the young and more facilities for the aging were needed.

More recently, the energy shortage, precipitated by actions of the Organization of Petroleum Exporting Countries (OPEC), fed an inflation already underway. The resulting price increases and rising taxes provoked popular imposition of tax and spending limits in many places and, in general, encouraged efforts to cut back public spending and stem government growth. California led off a "taxpayers revolt" with the adoption of Proposition 13, which limited local property taxes, and the tax cutting fervor quickly spread to some other states. An unintended result was a greater degree of governmental centralization as the state assumed formerly local responsibilities.

The 1980 election of a conservative President and United States Senate majority hastened retrenchment efforts on that plane. Such cutbacks are resisted, of course, by the groups that have relied on government support of the programs they favor. In time of retrenchment, higher levels of government tend to mandate that lower levels perform functions, usually without any financial reimbursement. The result may be a change in the assignment of governmental functions and continuing adjustments on all levels to accommodate the changes.

FACTORS IMPEDING CHANGE

Drastic alterations in governmental systems rarely occur except as a result of crisis. Most change is incremental and the system has time to adjust to it without severe stress. This is true of intergovernmental relations as well. Modifications in the general pattern have taken place, and they have generally been adopted piecemeal. Adjustments could be managed a little at a time. The exceptions occurred with the replacement of the Articles of

Confederation by the present Constitution, altering substantially the balance between the central government and the states, and during the Depression of the 1930s when the economic situation necessitated an upward shift of functions to larger governmental jurisdictions. The Reagan administration appears to have touched off another series of dramatic changes by moving to reduce spending, cut federal growth, ease regulations, and devolve some functions of government to the state and local levels.

Numerous factors operate to impede change. Existing legal provisions in constitutions and statutes serve to keep things the same. Constitutional provisions are especially difficult to modify, requiring a popular vote in all states except Delaware and sometimes stipulating approval by a majority greater than a plurality of those voting on the issue. Revision of the national constitution necessitates action by both the Congress and the states and is often a long drawn out process. Court decisions are likely to follow the rule of *stare decisis,* thus relying on previous decisions. Law is a conservative force in most situations.

Bureaucratic resistance based on fear of loss of status in a new situation, habit, or simply the inertia of large organizations supports the status quo. Pressures of entrenched interest groups reenforce the existing arrangements because those with access to government are reluctant to have to establish it anew. Existing boundary lines, especially those of states, also impede change since they are difficult to alter. Those who advocate the abolition of states are not cognizant of the reservoir of power there, not to mention the deep-seated loyalties states engender from their citizens. Local boundaries inspire similar loyalties in some instances and provide protection from higher taxes, different service levels, and social problems existing in adjacent areas. All these things, along with general conservatism toward change and the demands for on-going public services, erect obstacles that slow the change process.

HOW CHANGE OCCURS

Incremental though it may be, change over time can produce substantial modifications in intergovernmental arrangements. It emanates from accumulated pressures produced by events as well as demographic, economic, and other inputs into the environment, and by individuals, usually organized into groups. Adapting their techniques to the prevailing value system and public opinion, interest groups exert pressures on the legislatures, executives, bureaucracies, and through judicial branches of all levels of government to achieve their goals. Many have federal-type organizations corresponding to the American governmental system. They apply their pressure where they have the most leverage, a condition varying with the issue or the group. Elected officials also respond to the verdicts of the citizens at election time and to their opinions reported in the polls or expressed by letter, telephone, telegram or in person. Some of them assume entrepreneurial roles in promoting government action.[21] They themselves pressure each other. And bureaucrats, because of their expertise and continued presence, can exert powerful influence from within.

The aggregation of sufficient pressures, from whatever source, forces public officials to act. Incremental action deflates the pressure and may actually deter major reform. A problem has to approach crisis proportions to compel fundamental change.[22] The civil rights struggle and the efforts to control environmental pollution are pertinent examples in this connection. Certainly blacks had suffered from discrimination since the Colonial period, but sustained pressure for reform produced fundamental changes only twice, at the time of the Civil war and in the middle of the twentieth century. Environmental pollution existed for a long time before conditions deteriorated enough that sufficient sentiment for change surfaced, and then the energy shortage and pressures for fewer regulations mitigated its force.

It should be understood that not all the action, or the pressure to act, relates to the adoption of legislation. Changes in administrative regulations, personnel, or organization can substantially modify public policy, and knowledgeable interests operate with that in mind. Note, for instance, the effect of the Reagan administration's cutback of funds for certain programs previously enacted by Congress—an action accomplished by executive fiat and not by legislation. Another illustration is a decision by the national Office of Management and Budget that Prince George's and Montgomery counties, Maryland, should have the activities of their planning boards (parts of a bi-county agency) included in determining their revenue-sharing allotments, resulting in an increase of several million dollars for each of them. Such a decision afforded these counties the pleasant job of adjusting to more revenue while local units elsewhere faced the sad duty of making do with less.

Judges also contribute to the shifting relations among governments. They always have been the arbiters of intergovernmental change, sometimes through the settlement of disputes between the states, and often through cases not raising intergovernmental questions directly but whose impact stimulates alterations in intergovernmental arrangements. Probably no better example of the latter exists than *Brown* v. *Board of Education of Topeka*[23] that, in requiring desegregation of schools, also set off a chain of events and decisions that gave the national government a powerful club (withholding of funds) over local school districts.

Change in the governmental system, whatever its cause, requires a corresponding adjustment. This is true of the relations among governments as well as of other aspects of the system. And it is true of minor shifts in routine as well as of major shifts. A study of intergovernmental relations in housing found, for example, that changing a form so that a checkmark could be substituted for a comment altered the route of intergovernmental communications. More important changes, such as a national requirement for review of certain local projects by a regional agency, precipitated the creation of new governmental agencies (i.e., councils of government or regional councils) to perform this function and produced an entirely new pattern of interactions.[24] New inputs into the system modify the existing arrangements with consequent adjustment all along the line.

EMERGING PATTERNS

Government Growth Followed by Retrenchment

Even the casual observer of American government can hardly fail to perceive its growth in recent years. On all levels, governments were spending more, employing more people, and taking on new functions. Expenditures for all governments in the United States as a percentage of the gross national product (GNP) multiplied three and one-half times between 1929 and 1982, rising almost tenfold for every man, woman, and child in the United States.[25] In the late 1970s, however, the rate of spending slowed and the outlook for the 1980s is for increasingly contracting services to the private sector as governments respond to popular pressures for reduced taxing and spending.

Space exploration and nuclear energy development are exciting new activities; however, more mundane although important functions such as consumer protection provide good examples. Several national agencies protect consumers, and all 50 states have such organizations, mostly created in the late 1960s or early 1970s.[26] Some large cities and counties even have separate counterparts. Government's concern for the consumer came recently to the American scene; *caveat emptor*—let the buyer beware—was the motto of both the vendor and government, for the most part, for generations.

Some expansion of public functions on the state and local levels resulted from national legislation, particularly grant-in-aid statutes. Grant programs either stimulated or required the offering of new or enlarged services, the creation of additional agencies, and the hiring of more personnel. Examples include legal services for the poor, establishment of "black lung" clinics for disabled coal miners, and Title IX provisions for equal athletic programs for women. Other programs pursued by the states and localities were designed to meet demands of their own citizens. Innovative ones, such as consumer protection, sometimes were later adopted and promoted by the national government.

Increased Governmental Interactions

The growth of governmental activities, coupled with improved communication and burgeoning problems requiring multijurisdictional action for solution, accelerated governmental interactions. These cannot be counted precisely because of the seemingly endless number of routes through which they could occur. Nevertheless, more grants-in-aid to more governments through more agencies are evidence of the expansion. In addition, the growth of intergovernmental organizations and agencies, such as the Advisory Commission on Intergovernmental Relations (ACIR)— a national agency in which all levels of government and the public are represented—and the more frequently scheduled meetings of public officials from more than one jurisdiction testify to their expansion.

More Cooperation

Greater intergovernmental cooperation accompanied the increased interactions. This is evident in many ways—the growth of interstate compacts and other agreements, the development of new regional organizations on interstate, substate, and metropolitan-area bases, and national legislation such as the Intergovernmental Cooperation Act and the Intergovernmental Personnel Act. Others are the proliferation of state agencies to provide assistance for local governments, consolidation of functions on an interlocal basis, more state financial aid to localities, and, until 1982, an increase in national financial and other assistance to state and local governments.

More Regional Organizations

Increased cooperation, along with problems not confinable to existing jurisdictional boundaries, spawned governmental jurisdictions covering larger geographic areas. This may be seen in the development of regional organizations such as the Appalachian Regional Commission, in the patterns of statewide substate district systems that developed rapidly for awhile, and in the sporadic but persistent efforts at metropolitan governmental reorganization. The emphasis was on cooperative and coordinated development rather than on governments with coercive capabilities.

Expanded Intergovernmental Aid

In the fiscal field over about the last half century, intergovernmental financial aid from nation to states and localities, and from states to local governments expanded in amount and purpose. National fiscal assistance multiplied manyfold, its emphasis shifted, the methods of delivery diversified, and its administration improved. Both the number and total dollar amount of federal grants-in-aid grew, and the proportion of state and local revenues received from the national government expanded. The addition of general revenue sharing made the smaller jurisdictions even more dependent on the national bounty. Periodically some observers argue that revenue sharing, with its relatively unrestricted provision of fund for localities, will establish a tripartite federal system by upgrading localties and decreasing their dependence on the states through giving them revenue sources the states cannot control. Recent cutbacks in federal funds, however, may increase local reliance on state government bounty and growing state control.

Emphasis in the national grant program fluctuates. The earlier trend of assisting states and localities with their priorities gave way during the 1960s to an emphasis on national choice. With this change the national government made use of the states and local governments to advance some national programs, so that to some extent the states and localities became "handmaidens" of the central government, to use Roscoe C. Martin's term. With the advent of the new manpower programs and other efforts to develop block grants and to devolve authority in the period since 1966, a more mixed pattern emerged.

Increased Conflict Among Governments

The rise in governmental interactions also generated greater conflict among governments. This is especially true of national-state relations. Never totally benign and often characterized by contests for power, the relationship, beginning in the late 1970s, shifted from the primarily cooperative one in effect since the 1930s, to one more regulatory in nature. Regulations imposed by direct congressional mandate, grant-in-aid conditions, and by the courts resulted in public recriminations, court cases, and other adversary moves, indicating strained relations between the two levels of nation and the states.

Stronger competition between states and their local units and between cities and counties developed as well. Localities, fortified by some direct federal grants-in-aid and particularly by general revenue sharing funds, are competing against the states in the national political arena. In contrast to past practices, representatives of local governments now appear before congressional committees urging that the states be bypassed in the financing and administration of certain national programs. Also, representatives of local public-interest groups are consulted on national regulations and guidelines for administering grant-in-aid programs.

City-county conflict developed in some states as both units tried to occupy the dominant local government position. In New England, especially in Connecticut where counties were abolished, it has been a losing battle for the counties. In other states, such as Maryland, the paramount position of counties has been reenforced by restrictions on the incorporation of new municipalities and by legislation giving counties responsibility for overseeing functions both units perform, such as planning for water and sewer systems.

Creation of New Local Governments

As a result of continuing urbanization and the spread of metropolitan areas outward from the central city—for a hundred miles in some instances —new types of local governments and new forms of old ones are developing that have consequences for intergovernmental relations. The rise of new suburban municipalities with limited functions and the increase in the number of urban counties, which resemble cities in organization and function, require adjustment of other jurisdictions, such as central cities, who have to deal with them. These suburbs and counties block boundary extensions of existing cities and compete for revenue-sharing funds and other financial assistance. They also demand representation on intergovernmental agencies.

State Resurgence

After a long period of despair, there is evidence of a resurgence of states as strong partners in the federal system. Although the pattern is uneven, through constitutional revision, executive reorganization, and legislative, judicial, and financial reform, states in general have upgraded almost every aspect of their structures. Administrative procedures have been improved as well and political processes made more open.[27] Their governors and legislatures are a new breed of officials who speak with louder voices. States well may develop as the only jurisdictions of sufficient size to administer metropolitan areas, although obviously even they are not large enough to encompass some metropolitan areas that transcend state boundaries.

Pragmatic Intergovernmental Relations

The most dominant pattern emerging from intergovernmental change is that of pragmatic intergovernmental relations within the federal system— a constantly evolving, problem-solving attempt to work out solutions to major problems on an issue-by-issue basis, resulting in modifications of the federal and intergovernmental systems. The government receiving the most pressure from citizen demands or possessing the greatest resources may undertake an activity. Later a shift may be made to another jurisdiction. As each shift or modification occurs, adjustments are made to accommodate to it, and more change is created. The very elasticity of the arrangement helps to maintain the viability of the American system. Both federalism, in its more limited definition, and the broader concept of intergovernmental relations, then, must be understood in terms of their pragmatic nature.

NOTES

1. U.S. Senate Committee on Government Operations, Subcommittee on Intergovernmental Relations, *Confidence and Concern: Citizens View American Government: A Survey of Public Attitudes* (Washington, D.C.: U.S. Government Printing Office, 1973), Vol. 1, pp. 236–240.

2. U.S. Bureau of the Census, *1982 Census of Governments: Governmental Units in 1982,* Preliminary Report No. 1, (Washington, D.C.: U.S. Government Printing Office, 1982).

3. Advisory Commission on Intergovernmental Relations, *The State and Local Roles in the Federal System* (Washington, D.C.: 1981), chap. 2. Hereafter, this agency will be cited as ACIR. All ACIR reports are published by the Commission unless otherwise indicated.

4. ACIR, *The Federal Role in Local Fire Protection,* A–85 (Washington, D.C.: U.S. Government Printing Office, 1980), p. 7.

5. See: Alexander Hamilton, James Madison, and John Jay, *The Federalist* (New York: The American Library of World Literature, Inc., 1961), Nos. 9 (Madison) and 39 (Hamilton), for example. See, also, Martin Diamond, "What the Framers Meant by Federalism," in *A Nation of States,* 2nd edition, edited by Robert Goldwin (Chicago: Rand, McNally and Co., 1974), pp. 25–42.

6. *Debates,* collected and revised by Jonathan Elliot (Philadelphia: 1791), Vol. 4, p. 9.

7. William H. Riker, *Federalism: Origin, Operation, Significance* (Boston: Little, Brown and Co., 1964), p. 11.

8. Daniel J. Elazar, *The Principles and Practices of Federalism: A Comparative Historical Approach* (Philadelphia: Center for the Study of Federalism, Temple University, n.d.), p. 3. See his *American Federalism: A View From the States,* 2nd ed. (New York: Thomas Y. Crowell Company, 1972), chap. 3, on the American federal system as a partnership. Both Elazar and Stephen Schechter emphasize the role of the states as polities, or "distinct political societies," and give strong recognition to their political role. See Elazar, "The Rebirth of Federalism: The Future Role of the States in the Federal System," *Commonsense,* Vol. 4, No. 1 (1981), pp. 113–146, and Schecter, "The State of American Federalism: 1981," *The Publius Annual Review of American Federalism,* edited by Stephen Schechter (Washington, D.C.: The University Press of America, forthcoming). See also Schechter and Elazar, *The*

Role of the States as Polities in the American Federal System (Philadelphia: Center for the Study of Federalism, Temple University, 1982).

9. Richard H. Leach, *American Federalism* (New York: W.W. Norton and Company, 1970), pp. 58–59. See also his "Federalism: A Battery of Questions," in *The Federal Polity*, edited by Daniel J. Elazar, a special edition of *Publius: The Journal of Federalism*, Vol. 3, No. 2 (Fall, 1973), pp. 11–47.

10. Michael D. Reagan, *The New Federalism* (New York: Oxford University Press, 1973), p. 3. Several authors discuss federalism in *The Federal Polity*. See also K.C. Where, *Federal Government* (4th ed.: New York: Oxford University Press, 1964).

11. James L. Sundquist with David W. Davis, *Making Federalism Work* (Washington, D.C.: The Brookings Institution, 1969), p. 243.

12. William Anderson, *Intergovernmental Relations in Review* (Minneapolis: University of Minnesota Press, 1960), p. 3. This is the tenth in an important series directed by Anderson and Edward W. Weidner on intergovernmental relations in Minnesota. Another pioneer was W. Brooke Graves whose *American Intergovernmental Relations* (New York: Charles Scribner's Sons, 1964) is a standard, although somewhat dated, reference in the field.

13. Jesse Burkhead, "Federalism in a Unitary State: Regional Economic Planning in England," *Publius*, Vol. 4, No. 2 (Summer, 1974), pp. 39–61.

14. Deil S. Wright, "Intergovernmental Relations: An Analytical Overview," *The Annals*, Vol. 416 (November, 1974), p. 2. See also two other articles by Wright, "Intergovernmental Relations in Large Council-Manager Cities," *American Politics Quarterly*, Vol. 1, No. 2 (April, 1972), pp. 151–153, and "Intergovernmental Relations and Policy Choice," *Publius*, Vol. 5, No. 4 (Fall, 1975), pp. 1–6.

15. Some other significant stimulating factors are: (1) structural organization of governmental units; (2) voluntary agreements; (3) compatibility of goals; (4) issues; (5) environment, including the density and spread of population and the attitudes and perceptions of public officials; (6) tenure of personnel; (7) personalities of public officials and bureaucrats; (8) personal acquaintance of governmental figures; (9) political realities including support in public opinion for interactions; (10) interest group activity which may both draw together officials from various jurisdictions and pressure individual governments to interact; and, (11) the development stage of a program or project. See Mavis Mann Reeves, "Change and Fluidity; Intergovernmental Relations in Housing in Montgomery County, Maryland," *Publius* Vol. 4, No. 1 (Winter, 1974), pp. 5–44.

16. Ibid.

17. Jerome M. Stan and J. Norman Reid, *Federal Programs Supporting Multicounty Substate Regional Activities: An Overview* (U.S. Department of Agriculture, Economics, Statistics, and Cooperatives Service, 1980).

18. Reeves, op. cit.

19. *Problems of Federal-State-Local Relations*, Hearing before the Subcommittee on Intergovernmental Relations of the Committee on Government Operations, U.S. Senate, 87th Congress, 2nd Session, September 18, 1962, p. 4.

20. For discussions of suburbanization and its effects, see, among others: Earl M. Baker, ed. *The Suburban Reshaping of American Politics*, Vol. 5, No. 1, *Publius*

(Winter, 1975). Note especially Baker's introductory essay, "The Suburban Transformation of American Politics: The Convergence of Reality and Research," pp. 1–14; and Thomas P. Murphy and John Rehfuss, *Urban Politics in the Suburban Era* (Homewood, Il.: The Dorsey Press, 1976).

21. ACIR, *An Agenda for American Federalism: Restoring Confidence and Competence*, A–86, (Washington, D.C.: June, 1981), pp. 13–14.

22. See Parris N. Glendening and Mavis Mann Reeves, "The Future of State and Local Government and American Federalism," in Reeves and Glendening, *Controversies of State and Local Political Systems* (Boston: Allyn and Bacon, Inc., 1972), pp. 471–483.

23. 374 U.S. 483 (1954).

24. Parris N. Glendening, "The Federal Role in Regional Planning Councils," *The Review of Regional Studies*, Vol. 1, No. 3 (Spring, 1971–72), pp. 93–115.

25. ACIR, *Significant Features of Fiscal Federalism, 1982-83 Edition*, Report M–135 (Washington, D.C.: April, 1983), p. 12.

26. *Book of the States, 1980-81* (Lexington, Ky.: Council of State Governments, 1980), p. 459.

27. ACIR, *State and Local Roles in the Federal System*, chap. 3. See also Mavis Mann Reeves, "Look Again at State Capacity: The Old Gray Mare Ain't What She Used to Be," *American Journal of Public Administration*, Vol. 16 (Spring, 1982), pp. 74–89.

CHAPTER 2

NATIONAL-STATE RELATIONS: EVOLVING FEDERALISM

THE states and the national government have maneuvered for position and power since the formation of the Union. At one time their relationships were so brittle that they could be shattered by the Civil War. At other times they have been marked by the smooth cohesion of a defense effort. But most of the time they have been somewhere in between. Currently they reflect the pragmatic give-and-take of governments adjusting to an increasingly urbanized and technological society facing financial retrenchment on all levels.

SHIFTING NATIONAL AND STATE ROLES

Before the adoption of the Constitution, the states and localities performed most functions of government in the United States. The threat of cities as "third partners in the federal system" had not been voiced. One of the major trends since that time has been the increasing activities of the national government—Many think at the expense of the states.

Under the original allocation of power the states had all the powers except what the Continental Congress had assumed, and they gave up very little authority with the adoption of the Articles of Confederation. There was no way for the national government to go but "up" in the acquisition of power. Little by little over the years it expanded its role in the federal partnership. Through congressional action, court decisions, constitutional amendment, presidential initiatives, and custom and usage, the activities and authority of the national government grew.

The growth of national power is hardly open to argument; but the loss of state power is subject to debate. Although some commentators and politicians regard the expansion of the national role as being at the expense of the states, the fact is that the states, too, are doing more, spending more, and employing more people, and so are local governments. If the total functions of American government are viewed as fixed, an increase in the portion of one government automatically decreases the shares of the others. If, on the other hand, governmental functions are viewed as undergoing expansion at all levels, this may not necessarily be true. Figure 2–1 illustrates this point by use of the traditional pie.

In the first pie, one sees an *arbitrarily* assumed original division of powers. Pie 2 shows what happens under a concept where the amount of governmental power remains static. As N (national) increases, S (State) and L (local) get smaller. Pie 3 illustrates approximately the same division of powers as Pie 1, but with a bigger pie, which includes part of the area of total activities previously private or those not performed at all.

We believe this is what is happening in the United States—the powers of all governments are increasing. This does not mean that private activities are necessarily on the decrease, but it does mean that the sphere of government in general is larger. The compass or range of human activities has expanded within both the public and private sectors, albeit unevenly, and some functions have contracted. In an era of expansion of governmental activities, abandonment of a public function or activity often goes unnoticed; nevertheless, the contraction of government control, sometimes at judicial instigation, in the area of morals, such as divorce, birth control, and homosexuality, is impressive.

FIGURE 2-1 CONTRASTING VIEWS OF GROWTH
IN GOVERNMENTAL POWERS

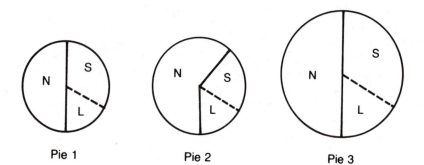

Pie 1   Pie 2   Pie 3

THE FORGING OF FEDERALISM

American political institutions did not spring full blown from the writing of the present United States Constitution, but owe much of their form and substance to the 167 years of the Colonial period. During this time Anglo-Saxon traditions of law were established, recognizing a government of laws and the rights of man, particularly the rights of Englishmen. It was then, too, that local governments were created of necessity, most bearing distinctive hallmarks of their British heritage; and many cities and counties existed before the states. The experiences of the Colonial period produced a host of ideas that shaped the subsequent development of American ideas of government—fear of the executive, trust of the legislature, and judicial supremacy. Basic governmental institutions and relation- the British Crown, but also were jealous and distrustful of each other. Some wars of the period encouraged temporary cooperation, but at the time of the American Revolution, the colonies were held together by little more than a desire to be independent of British rule. Commenting on the "forging of Federalism," Carl Swisher wrote:

> A common hate can bring temporary unity and co-operation, but it offers no guarantee of survival of togetherness. Our pattern of federal relations was a product of a forging process; it was to be forged not merely by the traumatic experience of the Revolution but also in the crucible of continuing struggle after the adoption of the Constitution, with the Supreme Court as one of the major instruments of the forging process.[1]

At the Outset

Several attempts at union were made in the period before independence. The New England Confederation (1643–1684) provided a valuable precedent, but eventually it came to naught because of the serious conflicts among its members. Benjamin Franklin presented a plan of union to the Albany Congress in 1754; nine of the colonies met in the Stamp Act Congress in New York in 1765 and declared that act unconstitutional and asked for its repeal.

In 1772, Samuel Adams originated his Committees of Correspondence among the colonies and within a year a complete network of committees existed. Numerous scholars have pointed out that these groups performed many functions of modern political parties. As basic organizers of the rebellion, the committees exchanged information and ideas, elected the Continental Congress, and provided an agency through which its decisions were enforced. In addition, they constituted an extra-legal system growing up alongside British institutions.

The Continental Congresses, the First in Philadelphia in 1774 and the Second in the same city in 1775, were looked upon as temporary, having been created to function in emergency situations. The First arranged to join in a non-importation, non-exportation, and non-consumption agreement extending throughout the colonies that was enforced by the committees of correspondence. The Second assembled shortly after the battle of Lexington and Concord. It was in itself a revolutionary body, because the British Ministry had sent letters to the governors to prevent election of members.

The Declaration of Independence, which it finally agreed upon in 1776, establisihed a new nation, subject, of course, to the successful conclusion of the war. It endowed the colonies with sovereignty—both internally and externally—so that the future actions of the Congress had the sanction of law. The Declaration raised a question which has intergovernmental consequence to this day. Was one nation created by this declaration, or were 13 of them thus established? If only one government were created then it alone had the authority to declare war, send ambassadors, and make treaties: if 13, then all could. The wording of the document was ambiguous enough that states rights advocates could call attention to one group of selected phrases and nationalists to others. W. Brooke Graves made this comparison:

States' Rights	Nationalists
Emphasized that these United Colonies are and of right ought to be free and independent states. . . . "They have full power to levy war, conclude peace, and contract alliances, establish commerce, and do all other acts and things which independent states may of right do."	Stressed statement that Declaration was made "in the name and by the authority of the good people of these colonies" by "the representatives of the United States of America, in general Congress assembled."[2]

During the time from the Declaration of Independence until the adoption of the present Constitution in 1789 several significant events bearing on the forging of federalism occurred—adoption of the first state constitutions, agreement to the Articles of Confederation with the expansion of central government powers under them, attempts at revision of the Articles through the Annapolis Convention, and finally the Constitutional Convention of 1787 in Philadelphia.

Relations Under the Articles of Confederation

The United States had no constitution until 1781 when it adopted the Articles of Confederation. In the interim the Continental Congress continued to be the official organ of government. The Articles established a very loose confederation, not a national government at all, because "Each state retained its sovereignty, freedom, and independence, and every power, jurisdiction and right . . . not . . . expressly delegated" to the Congress. They made very little change in existing government structure, establishing a unicameral congress as the sole instrument of government. It was quite weak, being elected by the state legislatures annually. Each state sent from two to seven delegates whom it paid and could recall. Voting was by states with each state possessing one vote. Attendance of nine states was required for a quorum that sometimes was difficult to achieve. Congress was given many powers the British government exercised during the Colonial period and all its powers were explicitly stated; none was implied. It could declare war, conclude peace, conduct foreign relations, requisition revenue and soldiers from the states, and build a navy. It could borrow money, emit bills of credit, settle disputes among the states, establish a postal system, regulate weights and measures, create courts for limited purposes, and appoint committees and officials. It had no way to compel compliance, however, and at least nine states had to concur for action, except for amendment of the Articles, which required a unanimous vote.

At a time such as the present, when government reaches into almost every aspect of daily life, it is difficult to imagine a government operating with such a frugality of institutions and paucity of powers unless one looks at the United Nations or regional councils of government, which in many respects markedly resemble the operation of the United States under the Articles. But at the time of adoption each state regarded itself as sovereign; conflicts and jealousies among the states and fear of a strong central government were such that it is amazing that any agreement was reached at all. Like the U.N. and regional councils, the Congress had no relations with individuals but dealt only with states. It was unable to enforce its requisitions for money. It could ask for anything, but had no way to compel compliance. But it did serve as a transition to a stronger form of government, one not politically acceptable when the Articles were adopted.

At the time of their inception, the Articles were the kind of arrangement desired by the people, but it became apparent almost immediately that they were not working well. Problems with the currency (resulting from the lack of a uniform medium of exchange with each state circulating its own money), inability of the Congress to enforce its requisitions on the states so it could pay its debts and deal with both British and state violations of the peace treaty, difficulties of negotiating trade agreements with other nations, and trade conflicts among the states all demonstrated the weakness of the central government and brought on demands for change. Eventually the Virginia legislature adopted a resolution calling on the states to send delegates to Annapolis to discuss uniform trade regulations.

The Annapolis Convention was significant for recommending that another convention be held in Philadelphia for the purpose of considering changes in the Articles. Attendance at Annapolis indicated the lack of enthusiasm with which the states regarded efforts to improve their relations. Delegates from five states attended, four other states appointed delegates who failed to appear, and the remaining four states, including Maryland, the host state, took no action.

THE PHILADELPHIA CONVENTION

Attendance was better in Philadelphia in 1787, although some delegates were a long time in arriving, and Rhode Island did not name any representatives. The Convention moved almost immediately from its narrow focus on revision of the Articles to a general consideration of a whole new governmental arrangement. Several plans for the central government were offered at the Convention.

The Virginia Plan, presented by Edmund Randolph, expressed the views of large states, which wanted a strong central government and representation in the Congress based on population. It would have established three branches of government with the national legislature having the power "to negative" all state laws not in agreement with the Constitution and with the power to use force, if necessary, against any state failing to fulfill its duty under the document. The central government would have been authorized to admit new states and to guarantee a republican form of government to each state.

The New Jersey Plan, put forward by William Paterson, also would have strengthened the powers of the central government but not so drastically as the Virginia Plan. Supported by the smaller states, it proposed to limit the national government to a unicameral congress whose members were to be elected by state legislatures with each state being granted one representative. The executive under this proposal was to be an executive council chosen by the Congress. The council would select a supreme court which would serve during good behavior. The New Jersey Plan contained some provisions especially important for intergovernmental relations. All acts of Congress and all ratified treaties were to be the supreme law of the land, state laws conflicting with national laws would be forbidden, and the national government would have the power to use force against the states.

Alexander Hamilton and Charles Pinckney also presented plans, but neither had much influence on the final outcome. Both would have strengthened the central government.

After extensive debate and conflict that almost wrecked the possibility of any agreement, a compromise arrangement, known as the Connecticut

Compromise, was adopted which set out the current structure and representation in the Congress and laid the foundation for the present federal system of American government. Each state was to be represented equally in the United States Senate and on the basis of its population in the House of Representatives. Votes in the Electoral College were apportioned in the same fashion, and state action was required to amend the Constitution.

The Congress, in operation since acceptance of the Articles of Confederation, received the proposed Constitution from the Convention in 1787 and soon forwarded copies to the state legislatures. Debates over the advisability of adopting it continued for two years before New York approved the document. The necessary nine states had ratified by June, 1788, but neither New York nor Virginia had acted and, without them, the new government had little chance of success. New York's location split the country, and Virginia was the most populous state. Finally, by November, 1789, both had agreed—the New York Convention by three votes—and the Constitution went into effect. North Carolina and Rhode Island ratified shortly thereafter.

The great debates that occurred over the ratification of the Constitution brought forth a substantial amount of literature, published in pamphlets and in the press. Richard Henry Lee's *Letters from the Federal Farmer to the Republican* were probably the best attack on the new document, the most telling point being its lack of a bill of rights. The defense came from Alexander Hamilton, James Madison, and John Jay. Their *Federalist Papers,* published in New York newspapers, have been cited as classics in political science.[3] As impressive and influential as these papers and other documents were, they probably were not as influential as the support of both Washington and Franklin for ratification.

ENLARGING THE PARTNERSHIP

While the 13 colonies became the charter members of the Union, the remainder of the states have entered in various ways, all depending on action by Congress, which has the constitutional authority to admit new states. Thirty were admitted from territorial status, the procedures differing slightly between the "incorporated" and "unincorporated" territories. The distinction between them is not sharply defined, but incorporated territories were the ones on which Congress had conferred some powers of local government. Four areas had been parts of existing states and were admitted as states by simple acts of admission: Kentucky and West Virginia were formerly part of Virginia, Maine was fashioned from Massachusetts, and Vermont was once part of New York. Texas, which was an independent entity prior to its annexation, came in under a joint resolution setting out its enabling act. California was an unorganized area subject to the authority of the United States Army.[4]

Congress, as the admitting agency, has authority to impose conditions on a propective state before its admission; but once the state is in the Union it is equal with all others in the political powers it may exercise. This question arose in *Coyle* v. *Smith*,[5] which involved the admission of Oklahoma. The act of Congress under which Oklahoma came into the Union stipulated that the state capital should be temporarily located at Guthrie and should not be changed before 1913 and that meantime no public money should be appropriated for the erection of capital buildings. The admission ordinance further provided for the irrevocable acceptance of the conditions by the constitutional convention of the state. Such acceptance was made; nevertheless, in 1910 Oklahoma passed an act removing the capital to Oklahoma City and appropriating money for buildings. In a case contesting this action, the U.S. Supreme Court ruled that Oklahoma could not be so restricted and said, "The power is to admit 'new states into *this* Union.' 'This Union' was and is a union of states equal in power, dignity, and authority, each competent to exert that residuum of sovereignty not delegated to the United States by the Constitution itself." Nevertheless, the United States may enter into binding contracts with entering states which do not destroy political equality.

Political as well as legal controversies have occurred over the admission of states, and some territories have had to wait as long as sixty-two years, as in the case of New Mexico. Possibly the greatest controversy centered on the admission of Kansas and Nebraska, which became entangled with the slavery issue.

Controversy also raged around the admission of Hawaii because of racial issues and because of the fear of the Democrats that its admission would add two Republicans to the Senate and a Republican to the House of Representatives. This party controversy was finally compromised when Alaska and Hawaii were admitted in close succession in the belief that the former would be Democratic and the latter Republican. Interestingly, immediate tendencies were in the opposite direction.

On entering the Union, states begin a permanent relationship. They may not withdraw. This was effectively settled at Appomattox Court House, but in *Texas* v. *White* (1869)[6] the Supreme Court, faced with the question of whether Texas ever had been out of the Union, reenforced the verdict of the Civil War with some ringing rhetoric on the nature of the Union:

> The Union of the states was never a purely artificial and arbitrary relation. It began among the colonies, and grew out of common origin, mutual sympathies, kindred principles, similar interests and geographical relations. It was strengthened by the necessities of the war and received definite form, and character, and sanction from the Articles

of Confederation. By these the Union was solemnly declared to be perpetual. And when these Articles were found to be inadequate to the exigencies of the country, the Constitution was ordained to "form a more perfect union." It is difficult to convey the idea of indissoluble unity more clearly than by these words. What can be indissoluble if a perpetual union made more perfect is not? When Texas became one of the United States she entered into an indissoluble relation. All the obligations of perpetual union and all the guarantees of republican government in the Union attached at once to the state. Considered therefore as a transaction under the Constitution, the ordinance of secession, adopted by the convention and ratified by a majority of the citizens, and all the acts of her legislature intended to give effect to that ordinance were absolutely void. Texas continued to be a state.

GENERAL DISTRIBUTION OF POWERS

What kind of a national-state arrangement was provided by the Constitution of 1789? Many aspects of it were left vague and have precipitated conflict ever since. How intense the conflict is a matter of disagreement. It is likely to fluctuate from time to time and even from issue to issue. Certainly the states have not always seen eye to eye on states' rights and even the governor and legislature of the same state often disagree. The separation of powers on the national level provides the potential for divergent presidential and congressional opinions, especially in periods when the two branches of government are controlled by different parties.

The Constitution sets out the general distribution of powers and, theoretically, that distribution should remain the same at all times, subject to amendment. Nevertheless, the interpretation of that document by the Supreme Court, under its authority to review all legal actions brought before it, has been so liberal as to allow Congress to change the distribution almost unilaterally (subject always to control by the electorate). Congress has not been reluctant to use its powers, and the role of the national government in providing programs has expanded step by step.

Delegated Powers

Essentially what the Constitution does is to grant to the national government certain *delegated* powers and to *reserve* to the states all those powers not granted to the national government, unless their exercise by the states is constitutionally restricted or denied. Among the powers delegated to the national government are those of declaring war, making treaties, coining money, regulating interstate commerce, and taxing. Others are establishing rules of naturalization, providing for an army and a navy, establishing post offices and post roads, governing the District of Columbia, providing for courts, and many more. Some of these powers, such as declaring war and coining money, are exclusive with the national government; others, such as taxing and building roads, are exercised concurrently with the states. Some powers are denied to one and not the other and some to both.

But to describe the distribution of powers in this way is to oversimplify the framework of federalism as it has developed over the years. Through constitutional amendment, court interpretation, congressional action, and custom and usage the relationship has undergone constant change. Moreover, this relationship is still in the process of modification. This is particularly evident as provisions affecting individual liberties are interpreted so as to expand national powers to protect individual rights against state interference. Federalism is still being forged.

Implied v. Reserved Powers

The Tenth Amendment specifically provides for reserved powers for the states. It declares: "The powers not delegated to the United States by the Constitution, nor prohibited by it to the States, are reserved to the States respectively, or to the people." Nonetheless, the Supreme Court's development of the doctrine of implied powers, gave the national government a means for expanding the powers delegated to it. In *McCulloch* v. *Maryland* (1819),[7] the Court held that Congress could exercise whatever means were "necessary and proper" to carry out its delegated powers. This case arose when the national government established a United States bank and the state of Maryland levied a tax on the banknotes issued by the Baltimore branch. A question arising in the case was whether Congress had the authority to establish a bank since the Constitution made no mention of it in setting out the powers delegated to the national government. The Court held that the central government had the implied power to establish a bank under its power to control the currency. The Court said, in effect, that if the purpose of the congressional action were within the authority granted to it by the Constitution, Congress could choose whatever means it saw fit to implement its power. Furthermore, a state could not tax a federal instrumentality.

States' Rights and National Supremacy

The Tenth Amendment appears to specify explicitly the reserved powers of the states. Despite this straightforward statement, the Supreme Court has declared it not to limit the national power but to reiterate "A truism that all is retained which has not been surrendered."[8] In effect, then, the Tenth Amendment can be construed to read: "The powers not delegated *or implied* to the United States by the Constitution, nor prohibited by it to the States, are reserved to the States respectively or to the people." This leaves the states with the residual powers—those that remain after the determination of the scope of national power.

The Court nevertheless recently declared in *Fry* v. *United States* (1975),[9] that the Tenth Amendment was not without significance. It said: "The Amendment expressly declares the constitutional policy that Congress may not exercise power in a fashion that impairs the States' integrity or their ability to function effectively in a federal system. . . ." Later, the Burger Court, in a series of cases ranging from the legality of state severance taxes to the condition of jails, reinforced the concept of the Tenth Amendment as an affirmation of state reserved powers.[10]

Does the grant of power to the national government withdraw it from the states? There is no general answer to this question. The Court has to act as arbiter in each case in controversy. Under the Constitution states share, in some instances, powers delegated to the Congress. States may, for example, exercise some powers over interstate commerce, and state courts share national power to naturalize aliens. The operation of a post office, on the other hand, is an exclusively national function, as are certain aspects of interstate commerce. Sometimes state statutes prevail in a field of national power until they are superseded by national legislation. Along this line, state laws on bankruptcy were recognized until Congress enacted a national bankruptcy law. If Congress repeals this legislation, any state laws still on the statute books would be revived.

The supremacy clause of the Constitution makes it clear that in the event of conflict the national government is supreme. In Article VI, Section 2, the Constitution reads:

> This Constitution, and the laws of the United States which shall be made in pursuance thereof, and all treaties made, or which shall be made under the authority of the United States, shall be the supreme law of the land; and the judges of every State shall be bound thereby, anything in the Constitution or laws of any State to the contrary notwithstanding.

Placed in the Constitution because of the fear of excessive state power this clause contributed to the growth of national power through both legislation and treaties. By making national laws on a matter within congressional jurisdiction superior to those of the states, it has sometimes operated to push state governments out of fields of activity.

Neither the national government nor the states may expand their activities to the extent of destroying the federal system. In *McCulloch* v. *Maryland* the Court denied Maryland's right to tax the national bank, indicating that a state may not tax a national instrumentality because the power to tax is the power to destroy. If Maryland could tax the bank a reasonable amount, it could tax it out of existence, reasoned the Court. The state could then tax to excess the mails, customhouses, courts, and other national means employed to carry on activities, thus destroying the national government. The indestructability of both the states and the Union was set out in *Texas* v. *White*. Other constitutional protections also are provided to the states.

Constitutional Limitations on the States

The most effective limitations on the activities of the states are their own inabilities to act, for one reason or another, and the exercise of authority by Congress that sometimes displaces state action. The Constitution imposes effective limitations, nonetheless, some designed to strengthen the hand of the national government against the state and some to protect individual liberties. Both types have served to deter state action and have occasionally forced unwanted activities on the states.

Restraints designed to fortify the national government involve finance and foreign relations. National control of the currency is protected by prohibitions against states coining money, emitting bills of credit, or making anything but gold or silver coin legal tender in payment of debt. Neither may then levy duties on tonnage, nor impose any duties on imports or exports, except what may be necessary for executing inspection laws, a matter subject to congressional control.

To insure national dominance over foreign relations and war making, states are forbidden to enter into any treaty, alliance, or confederation, or grant letters of marque or reprisal. They may not keep troops of war in peacetime (except a militia) or engage in war unless in such actual danger of invasion as will admit no delay. Compacts with a foreign power require congressional consent. Despite these restrictions, activities of state governments directly influence foreign relations, sometimes to the chagrin and embarrassment of the United States. Refusal of some states to pay off bonds sold to finance internal improvements following the War of 1812 and loans for reconstruction after the Civil War caused international controversy until 1934 when the Principality of Monaco brought suit against Mississippi for payment. The Supreme Court ruled that it had no jurisdiction over cases against a state without that state's permission.[11]

More troublesome instances have occurred. One took place in Louisiana in 1891 when state authorities refused to take action when several Italian nationals were lynched. A second transpired in California in 1906 when Japanese nationals were segregated in schools despite treaty obligations of the United States and Japan. A third developed in 1935 when Americans hauled down a Nazi flag from a German ship and then the local magistrate dismissed charges against five of them with language offensive to the Nazi regime. Certainly state failures to afford full civil liberties to blacks, some of which have inadvertently been applied to diplomats and citizens of African and South Asian nations, made international cooperation more difficult for the national government and adversely affected the image of the United States in large parts of the world.

Other restraints on the states deal with the protection of individual rights. A few of these limitations, such as the prohibition against enacting ex post facto laws and bills of attainder and impairing the obligation of contract, appear in the original Constitution; others have been added by amendment. The Bill of Rights (first eight amendments), proposed by the First Congress, was so worded as to restrict the Congress and not the states, but successive court interpretations through the years have applied most of the bill of rights to the states. In addition, the Civil War amendments impose important restraints. The Thirteenth prohibits slavery and the Fifteenth prohibits the states or the national government from denying the vote to any citizen on account of race, color, or previous condition of servitude. Other amendments restrict state control of national elections and voting.

Important as these amendments are, they have not involved nearly so much litigation as the Fourteenth Amendment. It defines citizenship to include all persons born or naturalized in the United States and subject to the jurisdiction thereof. It further prohibits the states from making or enforcing any law that abridges the privileges or immunities of the citizens of the United States, or denies any person life, liberty, or property without due process of law, or of the equal protection of the laws. The due process and the equal protection clauses have served as substantial restraints on the states.[12] The former is the umbrella under which most of the Bill of Rights has been applied to the states by the courts. The latter has been the basis of the school desegregation, busing of students to achieve racially-balanced schools, reapportionment, and voting rights decisions. All these have constrained the freedom of the states to run their schools as they please or to manage elections in whatever way they see fit.

Other State Limitations

Too much emphasis can be placed on constitutional restrictions and court rulings in national-state relations. Other very real limitations operate on the states at the same time. These constraints rest in a political culture varying from state to state and often within a state. They restrict states in their ability to act in concert even though certain general beliefs seem to prevail throughout the country.[13] Even when states agree, they sometimes have difficulties making their voices heard, because no one can speak for all of them. The various public interest organizations, such as the National Conference of State Legislatures and the National Governors' Association, attempt to do this although it can hardly be on an everyday, sustained basis to the same extent that the President speaks for the national government. When state delegations in Congress try to voice the views of their states, they are often divided by party, sectional, or economic interests.

States lack the visibility of the national government in the news media, and often when the spotlight is focused on them it is for their failures rather than their successes. This lack of visibility is evident in a nationwide survey of how up-to-date people perceive themselves to be about what is going on in national, state, and local governments. Table 2–1 summarizes this survey, which was conducted under the auspices of a Senate subcommittee.

State governments cannot command the resources available on the national level. In addition, their actions are sometimes subject to the initiative or referendum and, when these are invoked, the people frequently take advantage of the only chance they get to vote against more government and higher taxes. Moreover, catastrophic events may dissipate state resources and force them to rely on national munificence.

Some state inability to act results from past patterns and "sunk" costs— or money already invested—in activities previously begun. Another factor is a shortage of funds, partially as a result of the national government

TABLE 2-1

HOW PEOPLE RATE THEMSELVES ON HOW UP TO DATE THEY ARE ON WHAT IS GOING ON IN GOVERNMENT, BY LEVEL OF GOVERNMENT

Question: How would you rate yourself on how up to date you are on what is going on in the federal government in Washington?
. . . on what is going on in state government in your state capitol?
. . . on what is going on in your local government?

	Excellent	Pretty good	Only fair	Poor	Positive	Negative
Knowledge of national government	6%	34%	42%	18%	40%	60%
Knowledge of state government	3	24	49	24	27	73
Knowledge of local government	8	35	38	19	43	57

Source: Adapted from U.S. Senate, Committee on Government Operations, Subcommittee on Intergovernmental Relations, Confidence and Concern: Citizens View American Government, A Survey of Public Attitude (Washington, D.C.: Government Printing Office, 1973), part 2, pp. 451–455. Survey conducted by Louis Harris and Associates.

drawing off large portions of potential tax resources through the income tax and partially from increased demands for more and better services by larger populations. State citizens often are unwilling to impose any more taxes on themselves.

Caught in a vise between local cries for assistance and national prodding to administer more and more programs under the grant-in-aid system, the states in the past often seemed unable to move off dead center and act to solve the burgeoning problems that faced them. State structures and procedures ill-equipped them to act decisively and responsively. Constitutions were outmoded with about one-third having been adopted more than 100 years before. They were overly specific and unduly restrained state policy makers. Governors were weak, reflecting the popular distrust of a strong executive. Structures of the executive branch, the legislature, and the courts often impeded speedy or even deliberative actions. Legislatures, for example, were malapportioned, overrepresenting rural areas in many instances. Moreover, they met rarely and did not have the staff support needed for dealing with complicated problems. In the past two decades, however, states have engaged in such a flurry of reform that their organizations and operations have been transformed. As one of us wrote elsewhere about states, "The Old Gray Mare, She Ain't What She Used To Be."[14]

Guarantees to the States

The Constitution guarantees certain rights to the states. As pointed out earlier, they are admitted on an equal basis with every other state, and this equality is reenforced by a section of the amending clause that prohibits amending the Constitution to deprive a state of its equal representation in the Senate. It is doubtful if there is an unamendable clause in the Constitution, but the question is moot because there has never been a serious move to deny this equality of representation. The territorial integrity of states is also protected, as new states may not be formed out of existing states without the consent of the legislatures of the states concerned. Even the Civil War did not prevent compliance with this restriction when the western counties of Virginia refused to secede from the Union and a new state was formed. West Virginia was admitted as a separate state in 1863, after a legislature, composed of representatives of counties loyal to the Union and recognized by the United States as the reconstructed legislature of Virginia, gave its consent to dissolution of bonds with Virginia.

One of the more important but amorphous guarantees is that of a republican form of government for each state. In a strict classical interpretation, republican government means representative government (as contrasted to direct democracy) and no person has a vested interest in office, that is, by blood or title. Over the years since its early Greco-Roman usage the term has become much less precisely defined. The Constitution does not define it, and the courts have refused to do so, by labeling it as a "political question" to be answered by Congress when it seats representatives of a state.

In an interesting case involving the "Dorr Rebellion" in Rhode Island, the question of whether the state had a republican form of government arose after the President had decided to call out the militia to aid the state in suppressing the insurrection. The Court was faced with a possible constitutional crisis if it then decided that the state government, toward which the rebellion was directed and in support of which the President had acted, was not a republican form of government as guaranteed by the Constitution. The Court adroitly decided that this was not a judicial question but a political one. Chief Justice Taney wrote:

> . . . when the senators and representatives of a State are admitted into the council of the Union, the authority of the government under which they are appointed, as well as its republican character, is recognized by the proper constitutional authority. And its decision is binding on every other department of the government, and could not be questioned in a judicial tribunal.[15]

Thus if Congress seats the representative of a state, the state is deemed to have a republican form of government. The Court again refused to rule on the question of a republican form of government in a case challenging Oregon's mixture of direct citizen participation through the initiative and referendum with legislative representation. The question was to be answered by the Congress when it seated the representatives of the state.[16]

The Second Amendment protects the right of states to maintain a militia for use within their boundaries, and for many years some states refused to allow their militias to be used outside the state. Today the state militia is known as the National Guard, and the national government pays for much of its support and determines minimum requirements. Nevertheless, the militia remains under the command of the governor, unless called into the national service by the President.

Even though the states have National Guard units, they may receive help from national military forces in the event of an invasion or a domestic uprising. The guarantee of protection against foreign invasion indicates the distrust by the original states of the new national government, as it is difficult to imagine how a state could be invaded without a simultaneous invasion of the United States. This protection, as well as assistance in putting down domestic violence, is at the discretion of the President as commander in chief of the armed forces acting under congressional delegation of authority; and he may or may not send troops on the request of a state legislature or governor. He also has authority to send national troops into a state to protect national property or activities or to enforce an order of the national courts, even over the protest of a governor. Two instances of such occurrences were in the Pullman strike in Chicago in 1894 and in the school desegregation conflict in Little Rock, Arkansas, in 1957.

Because of the controversies involving trade at the time of its adoption, the Constitution guarantees that the ports of a state shall not be the subject of discrimination. This has been interpreted to mean that tariff levies shall be uniform throughout the nation, and the vessels of one state shall not be required to enter, clear, or pay duty in another. These were common practices in the early period of the Republic and contributed to the abandonment of the Articles of Confederation.

The Eleventh Amendment, by removing from the jurisdiction of the national courts cases brought against a state by citizens of another state, guarantees that a state may not be sued by a private citizen in these courts. This amendment followed the outcry resulting from the early Supreme Court decision in *Chisholm* v. *Georgia* (1793)[17] in which a decision against the state was rendered. The amendment may protect the state against suits by private citizens entirely since the only place left to sue would be in the courts of that state. If the state consitution or legislature does not extend the jurisdiction of the state courts to such cases, the only remedy is legislative action.

State immunity from suit by private citizens in the national courts is not absolute. Recently the Supreme Court has been whittling away at it. According to the ruling in *Fitzpatrick et al* v. *Bitzer, Chairman, State Employees Retirement Commission* (1976),[18] national courts may entertain otherwise impermissible suits by private citizens against states. This is done in the context of their being the "appropriate means" selected by Congress for the enforcement of certain other constitutional sections, such as the Fourteenth Amendment provision for due process or equal protection of the laws. In a related area, liability of elected state officials for their actions, the Court recently reduced the immunity of these individuals from suit.

Obligations of the States

Without the states, the Union could not operate; and, if they did not exist, some other subdivisions would have to be created on either political or administrative lines. The Constitution places certain responsibilities upon the states. They are required to elect representatives and senators to the Congress, to name electors to choose the President and Vice President of the United States, and to consider amendments to the Constitution. Congress may increase these obligations as long as it does not require states to act outside their field of authority. Congress has not been reluctant to take advantage of this possibility, and often state and local officials are used to enforce national laws. The states have taken on an increased role in national security, for example, both in providing National Guard units for service in foreign military engagements since World War I and in training Reserve Officers' Training Corps students at land grant colleges. The military draft, until its abolition, was enforced to a great extent through state officers.

In less dramatic areas, too, state officials have enforced national laws. In banking, civil rights enforcement, environmental protection and intergovernmental health programs, to mention only a few, substantial dependence has been placed on the states. Increasingly, the national government has relied on them for the administration of programs essentially national in character that are financed by federal grants-in-aid.

MODIFYING THE FEDERAL BARGAIN

Congress often has used its implied powers to expand the activities of the national government. This is especially evident in respect to the regulation of interstate and foreign commerce, taxing, and spending, elaboration of treaties, and provision for the national defense.

Commerce Clause

The commerce clause of the Constitution has been mighty in the expansion of national powers. Under this provision, Congress has authority to regulate commerce that affects more than one state and with foreign countries. Broad judicial interpretation of "commerce" enabled extension of national activities into fields once believed to be the exclusive realm of the states. In addition to the actual sale of goods across state lines, Congress has regulated the production of goods intended for interstate commerce, such as those produced in prison industries or by child labor. It has invoked the commerce clause to prohibit certain crimes, such as kidnapping and white slavery (interstate transportation of individuals for immoral purposes) that it would be unable to deal with otherwise. It also has regulated labor-management disputes and protected the civil rights of black citizens to access to public transportation and accommodations and to jobs under the guise of regulating commerce. These are only a few of the broad uses of this important power.

Taxing and Spending

It may be argued that the power to tax and spend for the general welfare has been the most useful to Congress in altering the balance of national-state powers. Congress invokes its authority to tax as a constitutional base to regulate in areas traditionally controlled by the states. Also, its spending through grants-in-aid to state and local governments enables it to control assisted activities through the threat to withdraw funds. It is important to stress that fiscal arrangements contributed to the cooperative nature of the federal system and simultaneously provided broader opportunities for friction. The national government increased its bounty with one hand and imposed restrictions on its use with the other. These restrictions ran the gamut of state activities, reaching down into what were once considered the bastions of state and local powers—education, law enforcement, land use, and welfare services.

Treaty Power

The treaty-making power has been used to broaden the base of national power. Interpretation of the supremacy clause of the Constitution allowed Congress to undertake functions to effect treaties that it might otherwise have had no authority to perform. For instance, Congress enacted a law pursuant to a 1916 treaty with Great Britain in which the two nations agreed on closed seasons on the killing of migratory birds flying between the United States and Canada. The Supreme Court upheld the law although a previous national statute regulating the killing of migratory birds had been held unconstitutional by lower national courts before the enactment of the treaty. In the same case, the Court recognized the inherent powers of the national government to act in matters of national concerns in which every civilized government is empowered to act. These include war powers, control over foreign relations, ability to acquire territory, and authority to exclude and deport aliens. Acquisition of national power by prescription —that is, by exercising it over a long period without challenge—has also been recognized by the Court.[19]

Defense Powers

In an era when civilization can be destroyed in its entirety by the push of a button, it is not surprising that the authority to provide for the national defense carries with it almost unlimited power. Defense powers have been used to do all kinds of things that at first glance would not seem closely related to protecting the citizens. For example, Congress has used the defense clause of the Constitution as a basis for constructing dams, producing and selling electricity, financing the interstate highway system, aiding college students, and requiring young men to register for possible military service.

During wartime, national actions expand even more. The national government may find it necessary to marshal the total resources of the country to destroy the war-making capacity of the enemy. In the past, for instance, Congress has authorized the rationing of gasoline, food, clothing, and raw materials needed for production.

The President is the primary figure in the exercise of the war powers under which the national government has almost unlimited authority to direct the lives and requisition the property of its citizens. President Lincoln suspended the writ of *habeas corpus,* a fundamental safeguard against arbitrary imprisonment, during the Civil War, and President Franklin D. Roosevelt interned American citizens of Japanese origin living on the West Coast during World War II. In an era when war is no longer "declared" but ordered by the executive, when the military capacity to destroy civilization completely is at hand and might be used arbitrarily, and when constant defense readiness becomes a way of life, national activities that were expanded during the existence of an official state of war do not shrink entirely when hostilities cease. The President can make war if not declare it. The question of the legitimacy of the chief executive committing American troops abroad without congressional consent—a power past presidents have exercised—is still unresolved.

Other Factors in National Government Expansion

In using its implied powers to enlarge its scope of action, Congress has not hesitated to enact legislation superseding state statutes or mandating state and local activities. Moreover, through the use of financial assistance, it has, in a sense, "bought" state power, diffusing national influence through almost every aspect of subnational government. For the most part, these developments have been concentrated in the period since 1930.

The Supreme Court has participated actively in the evolution of the federal system. Prior to 1937, the Court showed little reluctance to strike down both national and state actions in the sphere of social regulation. This was especially true of the 50 years from 1875 to 1925, a period of great social experimentation by the states. It can be argued that this led to a shift in demands for action—a shift that concentrated pressures at the national level rather than on the states and generated a later willingness (after 1937) to allow both national and state actions in the social sphere. Nevertheless, despite the circuitous path taken by the Court, the end reached to date is an increasingly strong national role. Many years ago Professor Oliver P. Field commented in the following vein:

> The Supreme Court of the United States has been as impartial an umpire in the national-state disputes as one of the members of two opposing teams could be expected to be. This is not to impugn the wisdom or the fairness of the Supreme Court, but it is to say that the Supreme Court has been partial to the national government. . . . The

States, as members of the federal system have had to play against the umpire as well as against the national government itself.

*   *   *

This increase in Federal power and this place of dominance of the national government in the Federal system, has been aided by the Supreme Court. For the time being, such changes do not necessarily mean that the states lose power, although they have already lost position, so far as the Federal system is concerned.[20]

National powers expanded very little through constitutional amendment because most amendments are restrictive rather than additive. The Sixteenth Amendment has special significance, however. By permitting national taxation of incomes, it provided the financial means for the national government to expand its activities, especially through grants-in-aid. Furthermore, in recent cases dealing with individual liberties, the Fourteenth Amendment's due process and equal protection of the laws clauses have been interpreted so as to expand the central government's control over state and local actions.

THEORIES OF AMERICAN FEDERALISM

Scholars have never agreed on the nature of American federalism. Debates as to the kind of national-state arrangement the Constitution established occurred in the course of the drafting of that document, continued during the struggle for its ratification, reached the status of armed conflict with the Civil War, and are today at the forefront of arguments about the New Federalism.

In general, theories of federalism can be designated as competitive or cooperative. The competitive theories see the states and the national government as two opposing forces struggling to maintain their position and powers. Richard H. Leach has set out three models in the competitive category—nation-centered federalism, state-centered federalism, and dual federalism.[21] In recent years, theories of cooperative federalism that perceive the national and state governments in a mutually-assisting partnership have attained prominence.

Nation-Centered Federalism

Central to the theory of nation-centered federalism is the idea that the Constitution emanated from the people of the United States as a whole rather than from the states. Furthermore, the national government is the repository of the most important powers and responsibilities. Proponents of this theory argue that the Union existed before the states or the Constitution. They contend that it was formed by the Articles of Association in 1774, continued by the Declaration of Independence, and made perpetual by the Articles of Confederation. Then, the preamble to the Constitution explicitly stated that "We the people of the United States . . . in order to form a more perfect union . . . do ordain and establish this Constitution of the United States."

The nation-centered theory originated with Alexander Hamilton and is set out in his numbers of *The Federalist*. It was enunciated by Chief Justice John Marshall in *McCulloch* v. *Maryland* when he wrote that the national government "is the government of all; its powers are delegated by all; it represents all, and acts for all." Abraham Lincoln continued the tradition in his *First Inaugural Address,* declaring the Union to be older than the Constitution and noting that the Constitution was established "to form a more perfect union."

State-Centered Federalism (or States' Rights)

Proponents of the state-centered theory stress the dominance of the states and seek to guard against the enlargement of national government power. They believe that the powers of government are limited and that any increase at one level takes power away from the other. They hold that the Constitution resulted from state action. It was states that were represented in Philadelphia and that ratified the completed Constitution.

First expressed in the Virginia and Kentucky resolutions of 1790, the theory was developed further by Thomas Jefferson and John C. Calhoun. More recently, President Ronald Reagan stated in his 1981 *Inaugural Address* that "the states created the federal government through the Constitution."

During the first century of the Union's existence the doctrine of states' rights served as a source of bitterness and conflict. In more contemporary times, the states' rights philosophy is still very much alive. Now, however, it is perceived by many of its advocates as a positive force which has helped to: (1) maintain the federal bargain; (2) prevent total centralization of political and governmental powers; and (3) develop the responsibilities of the states.

To understand the durability of the states' rights philosophy, it is necessary to appreciate the pre-eminent position of the states at the time of the forming of the nation. For 150 years before the American Revolution, the colonists had as the focus for loyalty and identity the individual colony or the Crown. As tensions with England mounted, the main identification was transferred to the respective colony. The emphasis was on being a Virginian, New Yorker, or Pennsylvanian. With the dissolution of the relationship with Great Britain, it was state loyalties that were intensified, not allegiance to a new central government. The competition among states and among regions during the first 75 years of the Republic served to heighten these feelings of state identification. Such loyalties reenforced the states' rights position that often relied on the devices of threatened secession, nullification, or imposition.

Secession. A voluntary withdrawal from a union is known as secession. The definition suggests a peaceful dissolution. Proponents of secession of Quebec from Canada, for example, assume that the process would be nonviolent. Nevertheless, as is sadly obvious, secession, whether or not successful, is rarely a peaceful process. Fratricidal wars over the "perpetuality of the union" are commonplace throughout the world.[22] The recent bloody secession efforts in Pakistan and Nigeria, the former successful and the latter not, suggest the high costs of such efforts.

Hans Kelsen observes in his monumental work, *Allgemeine Staatslehre,* the widely held theory that peaceful secession from a confederation is possible under certain conditions, but secession from a federal union is never possible.[23] Although this distinction is logically and legally untenable, Kelsen notes that it has been argued for centuries by students of federalism. This was a major distinction made in the early debates about the American arrangement. Did the states retain their sovereignty in a type of confederal agreement among equal sovereigns, and therefore retain the right to determine their continued association with the Union? Or did they give up that sovereignty in "order to form a more perfect union?" Theorists such as John C. Calhoun, Jefferson Davis, Bernard J. Sage, and Alexander H. Stephens argued the first of these two points. Calhoun, for one, hoped that a serious threat of secession would be sufficient to force compromise on the Union to avoid dissolution.

Although in the end the question of secession became a southern issue, that course of action had been proposed by other groups. The earliest effort was the attempt to form the Northern Confederation (1803), and the most famous, other than the Civil War, was probably Aaron Burr's infamous action designed to end the Union.[24] As W. Brooke Graves points out at the conclusion of his review of secession, "While sentiment for union evolved rather slowly, separatist sentiment was easily stimulated."[25] These earlier efforts aside, the question of the indestructibility of the Union, and in theory the question of the location of the sovereign, were settled by the Civil War. Although most observers would agree with Graves' comment, "It would seem clear that a State has no right, under any circumstances, to withdraw from the Union,"[26] a few contemporary theorists still argue that a state, primarily through the guarantees of the Tenth Amendment, possesses the right of secession.[27]

As a final comment on the use of the secession, the question should be asked: What changes in the federal agreement occurred because of the use of this extreme instrument of states' rights? An early and generally prevailing view is that the Civil War was a great centralizing event for the Republic and some scholars still hold to this view. We went into that conflict as a rather loosely formed confederation, it is argued, and emerged as a relatively centralized Union. Recent studies, however, suggest that this may not have been the case. Daniel Elazar argues that very little actually changed as a direct result of the War.[28] The Union was preserved, some economic issues were temporarily settled or set aside, and the blacks were emancipated, although kept in a condition of near bondage for many decades thereafter. Certainly these were not radical changes considering the violence of that conflict. As Elazar observes:

> The most intriguing thing about the Civil War is that American federal-ism emerged from it intact as a system and substantially as it was before the war began. It is all the more intriguing when one stops to consider that whatever the composite of causes leading to war, it was the existence of federalism . . . that gave the Southern secessionists the form through which to mount their rebellion and the arguments by which to justify it.[29]

The reasons for the continuation of substantially the same federal agreement range from the maintenance of the same forms of government throughout the conflict—state governments were unchanged and the Confederacy was amazingly similar in structure to the Union—to the reappearance of the Supreme Court as a major defender of federalism after the excesses of Reconstruction. Of major importance was ''the deeply imbedded political consensus of the American people, North and South, which is founded on commitment to the federal principle.[30] The net result, according to Elazar, was that

> The existence of federalism prevented the victorious North from con-fronting the defeated South with an ''either-or'' proposition, namely, demanding that the Southerners accept reunification on the North's terms alone or forever be denied their rights as Americans, this despite the desire of some Northern radicals to do just that. The existence of federalism made it possible for the South to accept those minimal terms which the North could not help but demand—abjuration of seces-sion and slavery and minimal recognition of the Negroes' civil rights while retaining much of its own way of life and regaining the right to be the master of its future.
> More specifically, the fact that the Southern states were left intact allowed Southerners to reidentify with the Union which had humbled them, destroyed their institutions and property, and killed their sons, without accepting the Northern interpretation of the meaning of the war.[31]

A similar aftermath was recorded for the more recent Biafran secession attempt from Nigeria. Of that conflict, one study concludes that "its resolution has not only reaffirmed Nigerian unity but its unity on a federal basis."[32]

Nullification. Many people who have stressed that the republic is a union of sovereign states have advanced the concept of nullification. That is, as a sovereign, a state may declare a national law null and void and therefore not binding upon its citizens. Nullification, like other mechanisms of more extreme states' rights views, has traditionally been associated with the South and its pre- and post-Civil War struggle with questions of racial equality. Interestingly, nullification was first advanced in New England, and when first expounded by a southern state it was over economic, not racial, issues.

In the southern example the state of South Carolina was objecting to trade and tariff policies it believed to be enriching the northern states at the expense of the South. Nullification had been alluded to earlier by both Virginia and Kentucky in their protest of the Alien and Sedition Acts of 1798. The Kentucky Resolutions noted that the Federalist-inspired Acts were "altogether void and of no force." In point of fact, some states' rights advocates supported the more extreme doctrine of secession but rejected nullification. Alexander H. Stephens argued, for instance, that a sovereign state had the right to leave the Union, but if it elected to stay, it must abide by the collective legitimate decisions since to do otherwise would be too dysfunctional to the federal agreement.[33]

John C. Calhoun was the main apologist for the doctrine of nullification. His views were based on the firmly held conviction that the Union was composed of individual sovereign entities that were autonomous and equal as a result of the break with England, and who did not give up that sovereignty upon entering the Union. Therefore, the Constitution was but a statement of a compact among states—not individuals. As a condition of that compact the sovereign states retained the right to review the actions and laws of the central government and, if need be, to declare them "null and void" and not binding on the people of the state. Calhoun's perception of the federal arrangement was unlike earlier definitions. As one student of his work summarizes,

> Calhoun declared the central government of the United States to be a federal government in contradistinction to a national government on the one hand and to a confederacy on the other. It was federal and not national because it was a government of states united in a political union, not a government of individuals socially united by what was usually called a social compact.[34]

In defense of this position Calhoun observed that the colonies had each case one vote to approve the Declaration of Independence and the Articles of Confederation, and in both proposing and ratifying the Constitution states voted as units, casting a single vote apiece. That is, the states were acting as single sovereign entities. Calhoun, one of the few American original political theorists, advanced his major theories in his *Disquisition on Government* and *Discourse on the Constitution and Government of the United States,* both of which still serve as basic references for advocates of nullification.

Interposition. A milder form of state resistance to national action is found in the doctrine of interposition. This concept holds that a state may place (interpose) itself between its citizens and actions of the national government so as to prevent the enforcement of a perceived illegal or unjust national action. In this milder instance the state need not actually declare the national law "null and void." It merely interposes its authority and resources to prevent effective enforcement.

As in the case of nullification, the act of interposition finds its basis in a dual-federalism orientation to the federal agreement stressing state sovereignty and residual powers. Associated with the doctrines of secession and nullification, interposition today is primarily linked with the South, the Civil War, and post-World War II resistance to integration. The doctrine, however, has most often been invoked by nonsouthern states and for non-racial issues. Massachusetts, for example, adopted a report against the embargo legislation associated with the War of 1812, stating in part, "Whenever the national compact is violated, and the citizens of this state are oppressed by cruel and unauthorized laws, this legislature is bound to interpose its power, and wrest from the oppressor its victim."[35] Similar positions were taken by Rhode Island over the same controversy, by Connecticut over the use of that state's militia in the War of 1812, by Virginia and Kentucky over the Alien and Sedition Acts, and by Pennsylvania over the extent of national judicial power, to name some instances.

The overtness and direct challenge to the maintenance of the system of actions taken under the doctrines of secession and nullification make them ineffective. Interposition, on the other hand, while dysfunctional to a smoothly functioning federal system, has been relatively effective. The reason is that interposition often does not call for a direct confrontation, but rather a nebulous and more subtle interposing of state authority. One study goes so far as to assert that "from its early history to this date, interposition has always succeeded in the hands of a Governor or a State court that has had the desire and the courage to use it with determination."[36] While this view is obviously extreme and untrue, the doctrine has been effective. Witness the long delays created by southern states' use of interposition to delay effective integration. On issues of this type, victory may not lay in a total reversal of national policy but in protracted delays.

It is often thought that the doctrines of nullification and interposition are exhausted mechanisms of the nineteenth century. This is not so as the following statement of nullification and interposition, adopted in 1950 by the Alabama Legislature, illustrates.

RESOLVED By The Legislature of Alabama, Both Houses Thereof Concurring:

That until the issue between the State of Alabama and the General Government is decided by the submission to the states, pursuant to Article V of the Constitution, of a suitable constitutional amendment that would declare, in plain and unequivocal language, that the states do surrender their power to maintain public schools and other public facilities on a basis of separation as to race, the Legislature of Alabama declares the decisions and orders of the Supreme Court of the United States relating to separation of races in the public schools are as a matter of right, null, void, and of no effect; and the Legislature of Alabama declares to all men as a matter of right, this State is not bound to abide thereby; we declare, further, our firm intention to take all appropriate measures honorably and constitutionally available to us, to avoid this illegal encroachment upon our rights, and to urge upon our sister states their prompt and deliberate efforts to check further encroachment by the General Government, through judicial legislation, upon the reserved powers of all states.[37]

Statements of nullification and interposition generally received widespread support in the South during this period as illustrated by the signatures on the famous "Southern Manifesto." Congressional delegations from 11 southern states signed that document of resistance to school integration.

The general bankruptcy of these mechanisms did not lead to the total decline of the states' rights philosophy. It is often forgotten that many modern theorists still subscribe to earlier views that stress that dominant position of the states and their crucial residual powers. James J. Kilpatrick, a leading contemporary states' rights advocate, observes that

It is astonishing how many persons in public life never have grasped— or even thought about—the origin and abiding location of political power in the United States. This power now flows from fifty identical springs, filling fifty separate but identical reservoirs. And whatever powers may be vested, now or hereafter, in the central government, these powers must flow upward from the State reservoirs. The flow never goes the other way. If beginning students of the Constitution were asked to understand one truth only of their government, they could not do better than to begin with this. *The Constitution acts upon the States in a prohibitory fashion only.*[38] (Emphasis in original)

Dual Federalism

Even while advocates of nation-centered federalism and state-centered federalism argued, and in a sense fought the Civil War over their differences, the seeds of the doctrine of dual federalism were being planted. This concept, to some extent a compromise between the other theories, had its beginnings in the decisions of the Taney Court before the Civil War, although the term came into prominence through the writings of Edward S. Corwin during the early part of the present century. It holds that the national government and the states each are sovereign in certain spheres and that between them exists an area of activity into which neither can go. The two are basically equal. In Corwin's words:

> Sovereignty in the United States was divided between two centers, the States and the National Government, both of which operated over a common territory and a common citizenship for distinct purposes; each of which was completely equipped with the organs necessary for the discharge of its functions and neither of which was dependent upon or subordinate to the other, save in one particular which did not alter the theory of the system. For while an organ of the National Government, the Supreme Court, construed the Constitution finally, yet it did so under the Constitution which recognized the sovereignty and independence of the States within the range of their powers.[39]

Thus, the doctrine of dual federalism: (1) sees a clear demarcation between the powers of the two levels of government; (2) stresses the reserved powers of the states as well as a limited, strict interpretation of the delegated powers to the national government; and (3) holds that the distribution of powers under the federal arrangement can be altered only by formal amendment to the Constitution. Further, the delegated powers of the central government are to be understood as if the Tenth Amendment used the term "expressly delegated," even though that terminology was explicitly rejected by the 1780 Congress that drafted this amendment.

Matured during the post-Civil War period, the doctrine of dual federalism was in full flower in the last quarter of the nineteenth century and judicial reliance on it continued until the mid-1930s. One of the most explicit statements of a Tenth Amendment-based dual federalism is found in the 1917 case of *Hammer* v. *Dagenhart*.[40] In this decision the Court invalidated Congress' attempt to prohibit interstate shipment of items made by children. Noting that the legislation involved the powers reserved to the states, the Court wrote that "in interpreting the Constitution, it must never be forgotten that the nation is made up of states to which are entrusted the powers of local government. *And to them and to the people the powers not expressly delegated to the national government are reserved.*" (Emphasis added). The Tenth Amendment was still being invoked in this manner for the important New Deal decisions of *A.L.A. Schecter Poultry Corporation* v. *United States* (1935),[41] *United States* v. *Butler* (1936),[42] and *Carter* v. *Carter Coal Company* (1936).[43]

The Court's reliance on the dual federalism doctrine was welcomed particularly by corporations that wanted to avoid regulation at either level of government. Its supporters were not limited to business interests, nonetheless. It prevailed as the generally-accepted theory of national-state relations until the 1930s and still enjoys substantial public support, especially in the South.

During the 1936–1942 period, however, the Court began to back away from the dual federalism concept. Fighting for its survival in its existing form in the face of Roosevelt's court-packing plan and mounting public criticism, the Court made a series of decisions beginning with the *Social Security Act* cases[44] that undid the judicial endorsement of dual federalism based on the Tenth Amendment.

Cooperative Federalism

Dual federalism has been replaced to a substantial degree by doctrines of cooperative federalism. In these, prominent scholars of American federalism propound the theory that the relationship of the national government and the states has continually functioned on a cooperative basis. Morton Grodzins, whose work *The American System* is the bible of cooperative federalism, reasoned that the American government was a "single mechanism" in which the powers and functions of nation and state were intermeshed in a "marble cake," an analogy adopted from Joseph E. McLean, rather than in a "layer cake" fashion as proponents of dual federalism claimed.[45]

Historic Cooperation Theory. Elazar presents evidence in *The American Partnership* that cooperation existed from the early days of the Republic. He examined the activities of Virginia, New Hampshire, Colorado, and Minnesota during the nineteenth century, particularly as they related to internal improvements, finance, and education, and concluded that the American system has always been a partnership. He wrote:

> . . . The American federal system has been fundamentally a cooperative partnership of federal, state, and local governments since the early days of the Republic. Within a dualistic structural pattern, the governments of the United States have developed a broadly institutionalized system of collaboration, based on the implicit premise that virtually all functions of government must be shared by virtually all governments in order to fulfill the demands of American democracy for both public service and private access. More specifically, the evidence presented . . . indicates that the relative balance between the federal government and the

states has not significantly shifted over the past one hundred and seventy-five years.[46]

Elazar cites many examples of cooperation. Some are informal cooperation between the second Bank of the United States and the various states in the development of a national monetary system, cooperation between the Army Corps of Engineers and state and local authorities in the construction and maintenance of river and harbor improvements and shared responsibility for implementing parts of a jointly produced state-federal plan for internal transportation and communications systems. Others are reimbursement of states for money spent on behalf of the national government for defense purposes, and grants-in-aid in the form of land grants, grants of material, cash grants based upon land sales, and direct cash grants.

This political scientist sees American federalism as evolving over three historical periods, identified by the forms of intergovernmental collaboration predominant in each. The first period encompasses the formative years of the Republic and the federal system, beginning with the convening of the second Continental Congress in 1775 and lasting until the Mexican War. The basic procedure for cooperation during this time was outlined in the Articles of Confederation and refined under the Constitution. The chief vehicles of intergovernmental collaboration were the joint-stock company for long-term projects such as the Dismal Swamp Canal, and the cooperative survey carried out with the use of national technicians by the states. Thus, national services-in-aid were provided to the states.

The second period began during Jackson's administration and was marked by the use of the land grant as the predominant means of cooperation. The highlight was the Land Grant College Act of 1862 that provided land grants to all states. This period lasted until the end of the nineteenth century. The third period, which started about 1913, is regarded as the era of cooperative federalism. During this time cooperation was refined to the extent that many believed it began with this period.[47] Other scholars have adopted the cooperative view.

Cooperation Not The Historic Pattern? As is usual in such complicated matters, all scholars are not in agreement, however. For example, Harry N. Scheiber disputes this analysis in his *Condition of American Federalism: An Historian's View*.[48] Scheiber grants that occasional instances of cooperation did exist, but denies that this was the general pattern. He contends, instead, that American federalism has gone through a series of stages before emerging to its existing state. He defines the first period, extending from 1790 to 1860, as one of "rivalistic state mercantilism" in which "dual federalism, involving effective separation of powers, became the basic framework for a pervasive rivalism among the individual states and among local communities within the States."[49] The power center gradually shifted to a period of "centralizing federalism" from 1860 to 1933. During this time the national government gradually preempted functions formerly lodged in the states.

The third period was the "New Deal and new federalism" era from 1933 to 1941 when the shaping of modern cooperative federalism occurred. There was a dramatic centralization of powers as the national government moved to respond to the crisis of the Depression and the Supreme Court overturned landmark cases. Scheiber's final period dates from 1941 to 1966, the latter date being when the study was published. World War II began to involve state and local officials in national activities, such as the military draft and rationing. The years after this war committed the national government to growing welfare programs as the states found difficulty in maintaining their traditional levels of services. There also came a renewal of emphasis upon intergovernmental effort, a significant increase in grants-in-aid, and important shifts in purposes for which grants are distributed.

Creative Federalism. One of the more distinctive theories of cooperative federalism—creative federalism—was first advanced by Nelson Rockefeller in lectures at Harvard in 1962[50] and subsequently adopted by President Lyndon B. Johnson. This theory recognizes local governments and private organizations, as well as the national and state governments, as centers of power. All should work together to solve the problems facing the nation before they become critical. It recognizes that different combinations of these power centers may work on different problems. Johnson applied the creative federalism theory in a pragmatic way. He regarded the inclusion of local government and private organizations as an enabling combination of forces and was not so interested in who should bear responsibility for government actions as in getting problems solved.[51]

New Federalism. Although most Americans may not think in these terms, the survey data used throughout this book indicate a continued strong support for decentralization of functions and a viable federalism, meaning strong states and localities. The stress on the positive part of the states' rights philosophy is found in the "New Federalism" approach as developed during the Nixon administration. Emphasis was on: (1) decentralizing national power; (2) returning functions and responsibilities to the states and localities where local options could prevail and adequate administration occur; and (3) increasing the financial viability of state and local governments, especially through the use of general and special revenue sharing. The philosophy of the New Federalism comes through in President Nixon's remarks upon signing the State and Local Fiscal Assistance Act of 1972 (general revenue sharing) in Philadelphia:

> As we sign this historic document . . . today, we are carrying on the work which started here in Independence Square—where independence was declared, where the Constitution was written, and where the Bill

of Rights was formally added to the Constitution. . . . They came here in the 18th century to establish the federal system. We return here in the 20th century to renew the federal system. They came here to create a balance between the various levels of government. We come here to restore that balance. . . . This program will mean both a new source of revenue for state and local governments—and a new sense of responsibility.

New Federalism, then, is a positive embodiment of an early often negative states' rights doctrine.[52] It is more a mode of operation than a distinct political philosophy. As former White House staff member William Safire noted at the time:

> A sea-change in the approach to the limitation of centralized power—part of what is "new" in the New Federalism—is that *"States' rights" have now become rights of first refusal.* Local authority will now regain the right to meet local needs of its citizens. States' rights are now more accurately described as States' duties; this is a fundamental change in Federalism, removing its great fault without undermining its essential local-first character. . . . [53] (Emphasis in original.)

In stressing the positive responsibilities aspect of states' rights, the New Federalism moved the philosophy from a reliance on dual federalism to a view that emphasizes a viable, balanced system relying on cooperative interaction of all levels of government.

The doctrine of New Federalism received the enthusiastic endorsement of the Reagan administration. Harking back to the emphasis of dual federalism, the President waited no longer than his inaugural address to announce his intention "to demand recognition of the distinction between the powers granted to the Federal Government and those reserved to the states and to the people." Subsequent events provided evidence of his support for devolution of responsibilities to the states. Among other actions, he endorsed the transfer of certain social programs to the states and moved to implement a number of proposals put forward by leaders of the "sagebrush rebellion," a coalition of states' rights advocates seeking to end federal control of lands in the West. Moreover, federal administrative and cabinet personnel choices reflected this philosophy. The Reagan administration's efforts to consolidate programs and to reassign the functions within the federal system appeared to be attempts to engender a revolution in American federalism.

Pragmatic Federalism

We borrow from all of the theories above in trying to formulate our own hypotheses as to how American federalism works, although we find none of them completely accurate in reflecting operations under the federal arrangement. We stipulate that:

1. Pragmatism characterizes operations under the federal arrangement in the United States. The approach is a problem-solving one without any special effort to work out solutions in accordance with any particular philosophic view of federal, state, or local responsibilities. Each problem is dealt with in turn and similar problems have a variety of solutions in different parts of the nation or at different times.

2. As a result, the national government and the states are increasingly interdependent. This interdependence creates higher tension levels in the political arena at the same time that shared administrative and program activities are on the rise.

3. The national government has become the dominant partner—legally, financially, and progammatically—under the federal arrangement; nevertheless, states still retain important political powers and governmental functions that make them a necessary part of the partnership.

4. Although not true partners to the federal arrangement, local governments have become increasingly crucial to its operations. Moreover, they have grown in political power and thus exert more influence on the workings of federalism.

5. The federal arrangement in the United States is undergirded by a web of intergovernmental relations that enables it to function and that is constantly adjusting in response to pragmatic actions. At any point in time, federalism can be understood in the context of current intergovernmental relations.

EVOLVING FEDERALISM

Regardless of one's theories about the operation of American federalism, there can be little argument over the fact that the national-state partnership established in 1789 has changed markedly since that time. The ongoing adjustments in the federal bargain favored the national government although the states' position remained important.

Court interpretations of the Constitution played a major part in these adjustments. Early on, the United States Supreme Court developed the doctrine of implied powers that enabled the Congress to exercise any authority that could be "reasonably implied" from its enumerated powers. Congress subsequently joined in a liberal interpretation of its authority, relying especially on the commerce, taxing and spending, defense, and treaty powers as the bases for its actions.

Other forces also were at work. Several wars centralized power at the national level and presidents were able to act without many of the usual constraints. Formal constitutional changes were less important overall than either judicial or congressional initiatives, although the Sixteenth Amendment as well as the Fourteenth formed the basis of later national expansion.

The states resisted what they regarded as usurpation of their rights, both through political action by their representatives in the Congress and by formal legislative acts. Southern efforts at secession were thwarted by the Union army, and movements to nullify fell before the courts. The nation arrived at the federalism divide of the 1930s with a system of dual federalism under which the functions of the national government were increasing but were still fairly distinct from those performed by the states. The almost revolutionary changes that occurred in American federalism after that date are discussed in Chapter 3.

NOTES

1. Carl Swisher, "The Supreme Court and the Forging of Federalism, 1789–1864," *Nebraska Law Review,* December, 1960, p. 4.

2. Adapted from W. Brooke Graves, *American Intergovernmental Relations* (New York: Charles Scribner's Sons, 1964), p. 51. This section draws heavily from Graves.

3. See, for example, Charles Beard and Mary Beard, *A Basic History of the United States* (New York: New Home Library, 1944), p. 136.

4. This account follows Graves, pp. 94–95.

5. 221 U.S. 559, L.Ed., 858 (1911).

6. 7 Wall, 700 (1869).

7. 4 Wheat, 316 (1819).

8. U.S. v. Darby Lumber Company, 312 U.S. 100 (1941).

9. 421 U.S. 547 (1975).

10. On severance taxes, see Commonwealth Edison v. Montana, 453 U.S. 1981. Docket No. 80–581, in which the Court ruled Montana's severance tax was not a restraint on interstate commerce. State authority to double-cell prisoners was upheld in Rhodes v. Chapman, 49 LW 4677 (June 15, 1981). See also Pennhurst State School v. Halderman, No. 79–1404 (1981) in which the Court ruled that Pennsylvania was not required to meet standards set out in a federal "Bill of Rights" for the mentally retarded.

11. Monaco v. Mississippi, 29 U.S. 313 (1934). See W. Brooke Graves, *American State Government* (Lexington, Mass.: D.C. Heath & Co., 1953) for elaboration on the topic of states in foreign relations.

12. Historically the Fourteenth Amendment's role has been equally if not more important in the economic sphere in preventing populist attempts to control the implications of the Industrial Revolution at the state level. Thus our economic and industrial systems were maintained as national systems.

13. See Daniel J. Elazar, *American Federalism: A View from the States* (New York: Thomas Y. Crowell Co., 1966) for a discussion of different state cultural patterns and Donald J. Devine, *The Political Culture of the United States* (Boston: Little, Brown and Co., 1972) for a discussion of belief systems.

14. Mavis Mann Reeves, "Look Again at State Capacity: The Old Gray Mare Ain't What She Used to Be," *American Journal of Public Administration*, Vol. 16 (1982). For a detailed discussion of state reform by the same author, see Advisory Commission on Intergovernmental Relations, *The State and Local Roles in the Federal System* (Washington, D.C.: Government Printing Office, 1981), chap. 3. The public is clearly aware of some of this change. See Parris N. Glendening, "The Public's Perception of State Government and Governors," *State Government*, Vol. 53, No. 3 (Summer, 1980), pp. 115–120. For strong defenses of the states, see: Terry Sanford, *Storm Over the States* (New York: McGraw-Hill Book Co., 1967) and Ira Sharkansky, *The Maligned States*, 2nd ed. (McGraw-Hill Book Co., 1978).

15. Luther v. Borden, 7 How. 1, 41, 12 L.Ed. 581 (1849).

16. Pacific States Telegraph and Telephone Company v. Oregon, 223 U.S. 118 (1912).

17. 2 Dall 419 (1793).

18. Fitzpatrick v. Bitzer, 427 U.S. 445 (1976). See, also: Owen v. City of Independence, Mo., 48 L.W. 4389 (1980), and Maine v. Thiboutot, 48 L.W. 4859 (1980). For an extensive discussion of the Court and the states, see A.E. Dick Howard, "The States and the Supreme Court," *Catholic University Law Review*, Vol. 31, No. 3 (Spring, 1982). This article is part of a symposium on "State and Local Government Issues before The Supreme Court."

19. U.S. v. Midwest Oil Company, 236 U.S. 459 (1915); Inland Waterways Corp. v. Young, 309 U.S. 517 (1940).

20. "States v. Nation and the Supreme Court," *American Political Science Review*, April, 1934, pp. 233, 244–45.

21. Richard H. Leach, *American Federalism* (New York: W. W. Norton & Co., 1970), pp. 10–24.

22. For an interesting discussion of the reasons for the dissolutions of federal arrangements, see Thomas M. Franck, ed., *Why Federations Fail: An Inquiry Into the Requisites for Successful Federalism* (New York: New York University Press, 1968).

23. For a discussion of Kelsen's complex but critical theories on federalism, see Sobei Mogi, *The Problem of Federalism: A Study in the History of Political Theory*, Vol. II (London: George Allen and Unwin Ltd., 1931), pp. 965–1056.

24. A good review of several early attempts to secede is found in Edward P. Powell's *Nullification and Secession in the United States* (New York: G.P. Putnam's Sons, 1898).

25. Graves, *American Intergovernmental Relations*, p. 127.

26. Ibid., p. 126.

27. See, for example, M.B. Holifield, "Secession: A Right Reserved to the States," *Kentucky State Bar Journal* (September, 1954), pp. 160–173; and H.N. Morse, "Study in Legalities of Doctrines of Nullification and Secession," *Journal*

of the Bar Association of the District of Columbia, March, 1950, pp. 130–142, and April, 1950, pp. 182–193.

28. Daniel J. Elazar, "Civil War and the Preservation of American Federalism," *Publius,* Vol. 1 (1971), pp. 39–58.

29. Ibid., pp. 39–40. Elazar's evaluation of the limited impact of the Civil War focuses on the constitutional and, to a lesser extent, political structure of the American system. Not addressed are the major fiscal, social, and functional changes growing out of that conflict. Most observers would agree that in these areas, at least, the Civil War had a major impact on the American system.

30. Ibid., p. 51.

31. Ibid., p. 55. Concerning the last point, Elazar facetiously notes that "Given the popular response to Confederate symbols in the intervening century, the South may even have won the war of myth and interpretation."

32. John A. A. Ayoade, "Secession Threat as a Redressive Mechanism in Nigerian Federalism," *Publius,* Vol. 3 (Spring, 1973), p. 74.

33. Alexander H. Stephens, *A Constitutional View of the Late War Between the States,* 2 vols. (Philadelphia: 1868, 1870). See especially Vol. I, pp. 421ff.

34. For an excellent summary of these interpretations, see Walter Hartwell Bennett, *American Theories of Federalism* (University of Alabama Press, 1964), p. 132.

35. Quoted in ibid., p. 103.

36. Drew L. Smith, *Interposition: The Neglected Weapon* (New Orleans: Federation of Constitutional Government, 1959) as quoted in Graves, *American Intergovernmental Relations,* p. 115.

37. Alabama Legislature, Act No. 42, February 2, 1950. See also Mississippi Legislature, Senate Concurrent Resolution No. 125, February 29, 1956, and the statement of Congressman John Bell Williams of Mississippi before the U.S. House of Representatives, January 25, 1956.

38. James Jackson Kilpatrick, "The Case for 'States' Rights'," in Robert A. Goldwin, ed., *A Nation of States: Essays on the American Federal System* (2nd ed.; Chicago: Rand McNally and Co., 1974), p. 97.

39. Edward S. Corwin, *National Supremacy* (New York: Henry Holt and Co., 1913), pp. 108–109.

40. 247 U.S. 251 (1918).

41. 295 U.S. 495 (1935).

42. 297 U.S. 1 (1936).

43. 298 U.S. 23 (1936).

44. Steward Machine Co. v. Davis, 301 U.S. 548 (1937) and Helvering v. Davis, 301 U.S. 619 (1937) are sometimes referred to as the Social Security cases. See also, Graves v. New York ex rel. O'Keefe, 306 U.S. 466, 486 (1939), and U.S. v. Darby 312 U.S. 100 (1941).

45. Morton Grodzins, *The American System: A New View of Government in the United States,* edited by Daniel J. Elazar (Chicago: Rand McNally and Co., 1966). For McLean's usage, see Joseph E. McLean, *Politics is What You Make It,* Public Affairs Pamphlet, No. 181 (Washington, D.C.: Public Affairs Press, April, 1952), p. 5. The authors are indebted to E. Lester Levine for pointing out the origin of the analogy.

46. *The American Partnership: Intergovernmental Cooperation in the Nineteenth Century* (Chicago: University of Chicago Press, 1962), p. 297.

47. Ibid., pp. 312–317.

48. A Study submitted by the Committee on Government Operations, Subcommittee on Intergovernmental Relations, U.S. Senate, 89th Congress, 1966. Now out of print his heavily documented study is most readily available in Mavis Mann Reeves and Parris N. Glendening, *Controversies of State and Local Political Systems* (Boston: Allyn and Bacon, Inc., 1972), pp. 64–92.

49. Ibid., p. 69.

50. Nelson A. Rockefeller, *The Future of Federalism* (Cambridge, Mass.: Harvard University Press, 1962).

51. Leach, pp. 76–77.

52. For further analysis of New Federalism, see: Leigh E. Grosenick, ed., *The Administration of the New Federalism: Objectives and Issues* (Washington, D.C.: American Society for Public Administration, 1973); "The New Federalism: Theory, Practice, Problems," special report of *National Journal,* March, 1973; Richard P. Nathan, "The New Federalism versus the Emerging New Structuralism," *Publius: The Journal of Federalism,* Vol. 5, No. 3 (Summer, 1975), pp. 111–129; and especially, "The Publius Symposium on the Future of American Federalism," ibid., Vol. 2, No. 1 (Spring, 1972), which reprints a collection of papers written by four members of the Nixon administration: William Safire, Tom Huston, Richard Nathan, and Wendell Hulcher. For a discussion of the differences between the Nixon and Reagan "New Federalisms," see Deil S. Wright, "New Federalism: Recent Varieties of an Older Species," *American Journal of Public Administration,* Summer, 1982. This article is part of a symposium on intergovernmental relations edited by Beth Walter Honadle.

53. Publius Symposium, p. 99. See also Zell Miller's "A New Definition of States' Rights," *State Government,* Vol. XLVIV (Winter, 1976), pp. 31–33. Miller speaks of states' rights not "as an abstract notion of political science or as a code word for something else, but a new division of responsibilities among levels of American government—a vital idea whose time has arrived." (p. 32.)

CHAPTER 3

NATIONAL-STATE RELATIONS: CHANGE AND ACCOMMODATION

THE coming of the New Deal in the 1930s launched a new era in American federalism. With the onset of the Great Depression and the Franklin Roosevelt administration's effort to solve the resulting economic problems, the nation embarked on a different course. It was a direction that, with starts and stops, altered the face of federalism. In contrast to the pattern of incremental change that had marked most of the history of the United States, 50 years after the inauguration of the New Deal—especially the two decades beginning in the 1960s—saw rapidly accelerating changes in the federal arrangement and its accompanying intergovernmental relations. By 1980, these changes had modified both the federal bargain itself and the entire operation of American government, leading to efforts by the Reagan administration to recast the face of federalism when it took office in 1981.

The most important of the developments of the four decades from Franklin Roosevelt to Jimmy Carter include: (1) unprecedented expansion of the national government's functional role in the federal system; (2) the increasingly regulatory stance of the national government; (3) the states' emergence as major intergovernmental managers of both federal and state assistance programs while remaining significant political partners; (4) the rise of local governments, especially cities, as strong powers in the federal system; (5) intergovernmentalization of almost all governmental functions;

(6) an increase in the breadth and frequency of intergovernmental interactions; (7) burgeoning administrative problems that impeded the operations of the governmental system; and (8) a changed political environment. These developments resulted in a complex web of intergovernmental relations underpinning a constantly changing federal bargain and the governments designed to implement it. The growth of local power is discussed in Chapter 5; attention here is directed to the other developments.

EXPANSION OF THE NATIONAL ROLE

The growth of national influence in American government at all levels did not come about overnight. The central government took on new functions gradually over the years, paralleling to some degree the growth of the nation and the economy. Particularly during periods of war and economic crises, its activities expanded until, by the beginning of the Great Depression of the 1930s, it was engaged in a wider variety of functions than ever before. In addition to its original responsibilities for national defense, control of the currency, conduct of foreign relations, and providing postal service, it had assumed major obligations in other areas. Among other things, it promoted economic development and forest conservation and emerged as an important regulator of communications, banking, and railroads. Furthermore, it had initiated an embryonic grant-in-aid system as well, aimed at assisting states in solving some of the problems facing them. Grants later became a major mechanism for expanding national influence.

Grants-in-aid are gifts, usually with strings attached, from one level of government to another. They appeared early in our history as federal lands to be used for public schools were authorized for states by the Land Ordinance of 1785. After that, grant programs were initiated only intermittently until the 1930s although they had become a standard practice with the enabling act admitting Ohio to the Union in 1803. Early grants involved relatively small transfers of funds or property. Their primary purposes were to help states solve problems that faced them or, as in the case of the school lands, to encourage states to follow a particular course of action. Consequently, they took the form of categorical grants awarded for specific purposes.

New Deal Developments

With the advent of the New Deal, national growth accelerated. Federal agencies proliferated so rapidly that jokes developed about the "alphabet agencies" such as the AAA (Agricultural Adjustment Administration), NRA (National Recovery Administration), PWA (Public Works Administration), CCC (Civilian Conservation Corps), and WPA (Works Progress

Administration), so called because they usually were referred to by their initials. Some of othe legislation establishing the new agencies fell before the axe of a supreme court that, early in the New Deal period, declared them unconstitutional encroachments on the reserved powers of the states. Others, such as the WPA, PWA, and CCC, were abandoned as the need for jobs disappeared with rearmament and the military draft for World War II.

The granting of financial assistance to the states became more frequent and more bountiful. Rather than provide for direct national administration of its policies when the nation's economic system dictated haste in getting national funds into the economy, Congress often opted to give money to state and local governments for implementation of its programs. Frequently the grants were in areas of activity regarded as reserved to the states, and they supplemented ongoing state support of the programs.

Sixteen continuing grant-in-aid programs were adopted during the years from 1933 through 1938.[1] The Social Security Act of 1935, the most successful and enduring of the New Deal legislation despite the controversy it provoked at the time, established the foundation of the nation's welfare program. In addition to the Old Age and Survivors Insurance Program that is now generally referred to as Social Security, the law provided grants for old age assistance, aid to the blind, maternal and child health, and aid to dependent children. Provision was made for unemployment compensation as well.

The easing of constitutional restraints after 1937 by a more liberal court provided the national government a clear field for expansion to the extent that such policies received popular support. Thereafter, federal officials were relatively unfettered by constitutional constraints as they moved the central government into other functional areas. For a 40-year period not a single act of Congress was declared unconstitutional on the grounds that it violated states' rights. Particularly important as far as congressional use of grants-in-aid was concerned was the Supreme Court's decision in *United States* v. *Butler* (1936) that, although it invalidated the AAA, enunciated the position that Congress' power to spend for the general welfare was separate from the legislative powers enumerated in the Constitution and therefore spending was not restricted to these purposes.[2]

Post-War Growth at a Slower Rate

The nationalization of governmental functions waned during World War II and its immediate aftermath, grew moderately in the Eisenhower years of the 1950s, and exploded with the ebullience President Lyndon B. Johnson brought to the White House in the 1960s. Like a snowball rolling down hill, it picked up momentum until national influence permeated all levels and types of government.

The immediate post-war period of the Truman administration witnessed important national initiatives to assist subnational governments with airport construction (1946), subsidized housing (1947), and urban renewal (1949). During the 1950s, federal programs continued to accumulate at a moderate pace despite the declared intention of President Eisenhower to cut down some federal activities and turn over some responsibilities to the states.

Although Eisenhower named a Commission on Intergovernmental Relations (Kestenbaum Commission) in 1953 and established a Joint Federal-State Action Committee in 1957 in hopes of reversing the trend toward nationalization, it did not stop. The latter group agreed to lodge with the states full responsibility for the performance of certain functions, cut off national financial assistance that had supported them, and give the states some fiscal resources to pay for them. It recommended state action in vocational rehabilitation, maintenance of minimum standards in disaster assistance, atomic energy promotion and regulation, and urban renewal. States were to receive up to 40 percent of the national telephone tax to alleviate the financial strain of these activities. Despite presidential transmission of these recommendations to the Congress, no action was taken. Even state reaction was less than enthusiastic.[3] The growth of the federal role continued. Most notable during this period was the adoption of the National Defense Highway Act of 1956 that authorized federal funds on a nine-to-one matching basis for the construction of the interstate highway system.

A Burst of Growth with Johnson

Even the experience of the New Deal had not prepared the country for the explosion of national activities that came with the Johnson Administration in 1963. Congress and the White House vied for the lead in promoting federal assistance programs. The same can be said of both major parties, although Democrats perhaps had greater philosophical disposition in this direction. When Johnson took office in 1963, there were 160 federal grant programs authorized by Congress. By the end of 1966, the number had reached 379. Most of these were categorical grants, providing funds for narrow purposes such as strengthening education in mathematics. Nevertheless, the pioneering block grant legislation, the Partnership for Health Act (1966), which consolidated a number of categorical grants into a broader, comprehensive public health services grant, and the Omnibus Crime Control and Safe Streets Act of 1968, providing funds for law enforcement, initiated the block grant concept during this period. Block grants are made for broader purposes than categoricals (e.g., crime control instead of police equipment) and allow recipients more latitude in their uses. The dollar amount of federal assistance fattened during this period as well, rising from approximately $8.6 billion in 1963 to almost $13.0 billion by 1966.[4]

Continued Growth During the 1970s

Federal expansion continued in the decade of the 1970s, although the rate of growth decelerated somewhat. Despite President Nixon's efforts to apply the principles of the New Federalism and devolve responsibilities to the states, grant problems continued to proliferate during his tenure. The Nixon-supported general revenue sharing (GRS) program, under which a portion of the National income tax was shared with state and local general governments (cities, towns, townships, and counties) on an entitlement basis (meaning that the jurisdictions received the funds on the basis of a formula without having to apply for them) was enacted in 1972. Complementary proposals for special revenue sharing (similar to, but somewhat broader than, block grants) did not survive congressional scrutiny.

Grant programs continued to multiply under Presidents Ford and Carter, both of whom were more concerned with other aspects of public policy than with national-state functional assignments, although President Carter worked to improve intergovernmental management. By 1981 when the Reagan administration took office, more than 600 federal programs had been adopted to provide assistance to state and local governments, according to U.S. Office of Management and Budget (OMB) estimates.[5] A count by the Advisory Commission on Intergovernmental Relations of programs actually funded, however, placed the figure at 534 as of January, 1981.

The two decades between 1960 and 1981 witnessed the greatest expansion in federal assistance programs for state and local governments in the nation's history. A total of 440 new programs were added during this period, almost quadrupling the number available in 1962. Despite the development of two new types of federal aid mechanisms—block grants and general revenue sharing—the tendency was toward increasingly specialized categorical programs. The Department of Education alone had responsibility for 158 separate programs, according to its Secretary,[6] although probably only about 100 of them were funded.

Reagan and Attempts at Reversal

When the Reagan administration came to office in 1981, it found hardly any function of state or local government ineligible for federal financial assistance. The national treasury supplied funds in major areas such as social services, manpower training, environmental protection, energy conservation, community development, education, health services delivery, medical care for the indigent, economic and regional development, and mass transportation, to mention only a few. In addition, it yielded to the tendency to deal with less weighty, primarily local problems.

Within six months of taking office, the Reagan administration moved to delete some grant programs, consolidate others into block grants, and reduce funds for others. It also eliminated some of the regulations accompanying them. Much of the early action took place in the process of budget reconciliation; consequently, it is not yet clear whether the principal purpose was to devolve activities to the states as a tenet of the New Federalism or was simply one means of trimming the national budget or terminating altogether government involvement in some functions. In any event, it was a major change in federal assistance provisions and presaged a massive readjustment in the system.

In the first round of change, nine block grants were created or revised, superseding 77 categoricals. Four of the blocks were for health, three for social services and cash payments for the poor, and one each for education and community development. All nine go to the states, expanding the state role and reducing the local role in the overall federal grant system. In addition, all nine blocks allow the recipient governments more discretion overall, although individual characteristics of some programs sometimes contradict this. Only one, Primary Health Care, requires a prior federal agency approval of an application or a statement of intended use. Although the new arrangements were not as comprehensive as the Reagan administration proposals and differ markedly in some respects, they provide substantially more state discretion than the programs they replaced.

Dimensions of National Growth

In addition to the heightened national role in financing state and local governments, the growth of the national government is reflected in other dimensions: (1) the multiplicity of functional areas in which it is involved; (2) the larger number of governments with which it interacts; (3) the deeper penetration of its influence in state administrations; and (4) the growing financial dependence of state and especially local governments on its largesse. The result is a far more incestuated American government than once was the case.

Multiplication of National Functions. As a result of the additive effects of grant authorizations, the national government now participates in almost every governmental activity. It has taken on important responsibilities in functional areas once considered the sphere of state and local governments— health, welfare, employment security, manpower training, environmental protection, occupational and highway safety, and consumer protection, to name a few. What is more, it has tried to solve problems that might be

regarded as the work of local governments, as exemplified by the following
list of already enacted programs:

school security	bridge replacement and rehabilitation
urban gardening	rat control
pothole repair	education of gifted children
noise control	alcohol abuse
home insulation	arson
urban park facilities	homemaker and residential repair
meals-on-wheels	services for the elderly
jellyfish control	development of bikeways
snow removal	solid waste disposal
police disability payments	aid to museums
aquaculture	runaway youths
displaced homemakers	art education
	rural fire protection[7]

Broader Reach to More Governments. One of the side effects of the
proliferation of federal assistance programs and, particularly the institution
of general revenue sharing and direct grants to local governments, has been
the participation of more jurisdictions in the grant-in-aid programs. The
original grants were given to states. During the Depression of the 1930s,
aid began to go directly to local governments as well. Not all local jurisdictions were eligible to receive it, however, and not all of those that were
eligible applied.

In 1972, Congress enacted the Federal Domestic Assistance Act providing general revenue sharing funds originally to both state and local
governments, although states were later deleted as participants. These funds
were largely unrestricted as to expenditure purpose and were forwarded
to the general governments that received them without the necessity for
application. Consequently, more and more local jurisdictions participated
in Federal programs, although other national legislation contributed as
well.

Deeper Penetration of National Influence. Because of the greater specialization of categorical grant programs and their broader functional
spread, as well as the increasing national tendency to regulate activities
of state and local governments, the federal influence penetrates deeper
into state administrations. States have not been hesitant to apply for the
assistance Congress provides. Consequently more state agencies are involved
in the aid process and subject to its conditions. Responses to the University
of North Carolina's American State Administrators Project surveys indicate
that 78 percent of the state agencies reported receiving grant monies in
1978, up from 63 percent in 1974. Furthermore, in excess of one-third of
the recipients got aid from three or more national government agencies.[8]

Greater Fiscal Dependency. The growth of federal assistance increased the dependence by state and especially local governments on outside funds to the point where the latter could be thought of as "welfare dependents." Federal aid as a percentage of the monies state and local governments raised from their own sources grew from 11.4 percent in 1954 to 31.7 percent in 1978. Most of this went to the states, but these governments passed through almost 20 percent of it to their local jurisdictions.[9] After 1978, federal aid as a percentage of the funds states and localities raised themselves began to decline and had dropped to 25.4 percent by 1982— still a significant amount.

Reasons for National Government Growth

National government growth has been fed by more sophisticated technology that increased the geographical area of problems at the same time that it improved the means of dealing with them. The explosion in communications technology, to the point where anyone anywhere can view the same telecast or hear the same broadcast simultaneously (and from the viewpoint of the same broadcaster), affected in a homogenizing way the attitudes of the American public. Constant crises occurred on either the international or economic fronts. Several wars and increased international responsibilities expanded national activities and powers enormously. Skyrocketing population growth created at once new problems and new demands on government. The nation became increasingly accustomed to a national government that promised to respond when other governments did not. All these developments contributed to the reversal of the situation existing at the outset of the Republic and substituted for constitutional federalism a pragmatic federalism that adjusts anew for each problem, particularly in the administrative sense.

The national government moved into new fields, not in a conscious effort to increase its power at state expense, but, in part, as a consequence of public demands for solutions to pressing problems. William Anderson pointed to a little realized fact when he wrote in 1960:

> Here is no power assault on the states by the national government, but instead the actions of numerous individual candidates for Congress and members of Congress trying to meet the demands of their constituents in the only way they can, by promising to work for national action and national aid—for they obviously cannot promise action by state governments.[10]

In other instances, individuals or groups promoted federal involvement. Recent studies of federal growth in seven functional areas by the Advisory

Commission on Intergovernmental Relations (ACIR) point up the differences in the ways the national government became a participant in each case. Sometimes, as reflected in Table 3-1, the push for national involvement came from within the government and federal action was advocated by the President, the Congress, the bureaucracy, or stimulated by court decision. In others, interest groups or external factors such as major events, public opinion, elections, political parties, the media, or environmental influences assumed a more important role. Nevertheless, the Congress was a major promoter in all areas, and individual members often acted as entrepreneurs, initiating and pushing programs that were not at the outset sought by substantial portions of the public or strong interest groups.[11]

Sometimes the national programs developed step by step from small or accidental beginnings. Others came on the scene more suddenly, although the sperm of their creation may have been around for a long time. A stream of national policy, such as defense, provided the incubation in some instances while in other cases parentage could be traced to several policy areas.

GROWTH OF A NATIONAL REGULATORY ROLE

Although the national government long has regulated private activities to some extent, beginning in the 1960s, it expanded its regulatory thrust to include state and local governments. Early actions by the Reagan administration slowed this trend, but, up until that time, there had been a precipitous increase in the national penchant to regulate state and local governments or to use them as regulators of the private sector. The tendency was particularly strong during the decade of the 1970s. See Figure 3-1.

A list of major statutes of intergovernmental regulation appears in Table 3-2. Most of the regulations imposed show a proclivity to substitute the "stick" of mandates (or requirements) for the "carrot" of fiscal assistance as a device for ensuring state compliance with national goals.

David R. Beam prepared the following typology of intergovernmental regulations:

Program type	Description	Major policy areas employed
Direct orders	Mandate state or local actions under the threat of criminal or civil penalties	Public employment, environmental protection
Crosscutting requirements	Apply to all or many federal assistance programs	Nondiscrimination, environmental protection, public employment, assistance management

TABLE 3-1
MAJOR ACTORS AND FORCES IN POLICY DEVELOPMENT AND GROWTH

	Functional Fields—ACIR Case Studies						
	Public assistance	Elementary & secondary education	Higher education	Environment	Unemployment	Libraries	Fire protection
Internal policy actors							
Congress	X	X	X	X	X	X	X
President		X			X		
Interest groups		X		X		X	X²
Bureaucracy				x	x		x
Courts		X		X			
External policy actors							
Public opinion	X¹			X			
Elections							
Political parties					X		
Press	X¹			X			
Environmental influences							
Demographic & social trends	X	X	X				
Dislocations (war, depression)	X		X	X	X		

¹Food stamps only

²Interest groups were crucial in the creation of the U.S. Fire Administration only.

Source: Advisory Commission on Intergovernmental Relations, *An Agenda for American Federalism: Restoring Confidence and Competence,* Report A-86 (Washington, D.C.: June, 1981), p. 105.

FIGURE 3-1 THE GROWTH OF MAJOR PROGRAMS OF INTERGOVERNMENTAL REGULATION, BY TYPE OF INSTRUMENT, BY DECADE, 1930-1980

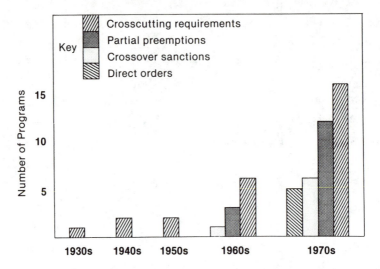

Source: Prepared by Timothy J. Conlan for Advisory Commission on Intergovernmental Relations, *Regulatory Federalism: Policy, Process, Impact, and Reform* (Washington, D.C.: forthcoming).

Program Type	Description	Major policy areas employed
Crossover sanctions	Threaten the termination or reduction of aid provided under one or more specified programs unless the requirements of another program are satisfied	Highway safety and beautification, environmental protection, health planning, handicapped education
Partial preemptions	Establish federal standards, but delegate administration to states if they adopt standards equivalent to the national ones	Environmental protection, natural resources, occupational safety and health, meat and poultry inspection

Direct Orders

A study of five states by Catherine Lovell and her associates at the University of California, Riverside, identified 223 direct federal orders.[12] Almost all of these had been imposed since 1960 and the overwhelming majority after 1970. Only eight direct orders appeared before 1960.

TABLE 3-2
MAJOR STATUTES OF
INTERGOVERNMENTAL REGULATION,
1960-80

1964 Civil Rights Act (Title VI)	1974 Safe Drinking Water Act
1965 Highway Beautification Act	Hazardous Materials Transportation Act
Water Quality Act	
1967 Wholesome Meat Act	National Health Planning and Resources Development Act
1968 Civil Rights Act (Title VIII)	Emergency Highway Energy Conservation Act
Architectural Barriers Act	
Wholesome Poultry Products Act	Family Educational Rights and Privacy Act
1969 National Environmental Policy Act	Fair Labor Standards Act Amendment
1970 Occupational Safety and Health Act	1975 Education for All Handicapped Children Act
Clean Air Amendments	Age Discrimination Act
1972 Federal Water Pollution Control Act Amendments	1976 Resource Conservation and Recovery Act
Equal Employment Opportunity Act	1977 Surface Mining Control and Reclamation Act
Education Act Amendments (Title IX)	1978 National Energy Conservation Policy Act
Coastal Zone Management Act	Public Utility Regulatory Policy Act
1973 Flood Disaster Protection Act	
Rehabilitation Act (Section 504)	Natural Gas Policy Act
Endangered Species Act	

Source: David R. Beam, "Washington's Regulation of States and Localities: Origins and Issues," *Intergovernmental Perspective*, Vol. 7, No. 3 (Summer, 1981), p. 9.

Although direct legal orders are employed less frequently than conditions of aid, they constitute an effective means of national control. Civil or criminal penalties against the offending government or its officials can be imposed by the courts if compliance is not forthcoming. Examples of these mandates are provisions of the Equal Employment Opportunity Act prohibiting job discrimination by state and local governments on the basis of race, color, sex, religion, or national origin.

Grant-in-Aid Conditions

Regulations attached to grants may require planning, establish accounting and auditing standards, prescribe administrative procedures, or set out performance standards, among a host of other things. Each program has its unique set of conditions, often referred to as vertical conditions, with which state and local governments must comply to receive federal funds. State officials often object to these regulations, particularly those that interfere with their administrative options in implementing programs. They feel regulations multiply the number of participants in decision-making, thus slowing and complicating the process.

Cross-over Sanctions. In the past, compliance with the regulations was encouraged by the enticement of additional funds or enforced by threats to cut off federal aid from the particular grant program involved. Beginning with the Highway Beautification Act of 1965, however, Congress added another stick—that of holding back funds from *other* grant programs—called cross-over sanctions. In regard to highway beautification, Congress sought to control outdoor advertising along interstate highways, control that in the past had been encouraged by bonuses for state compliance. Since many states did not take advantage of the bonus funds, Congress then provided for a withholding of 10 percent of *all* national highway construction funds going to the noncomplying state. Subsequently, other federal assistance statutes included the same device. For instance, the Energy Conservation Act of 1974, in an attempt to cut fuel consumption, prohibited the Secretary of Transportation from approving *any* highway construction projects in states with speed limits in excess of 55 miles per hour. Use of this tactic reached its zenith with the Health Planning and Resources Development Act that threatened states that did not participate in health planning with the loss of funds in 41 other health assistance programs as well as in the one provided by the act.

As David R. Beam points out, the element of *compulsion* is the distinguishing feature under the newer regulations. Formerly, conditions attached to federal aid programs were regarded as part of a contractual arrangement to cooperate between coequal levels of government. Regulation could be avoided by the expedient of refusing to participate in the program to which the regulations were attached. Under some current arrangements, that option is not available. The state can be coerced through other programs.[13]

Crosscutting Regulations. Even more pervasive and intrusive in state administration are the *horizontal or crosscutting regulations* that apply generally to federal assistance programs including general revenue sharing. Beginning in the mid-1960s, Congress enacted conditions, presumably to achieve ''national purposes,'' and expanded them to the entire range of federal aid programs. Appended largely at the time the programs were extended for an additional period of time, the regulations reflect the pressures exerted on the Congress by the growing number of interest groups concentrated in Washington. Office of Management and Budget inventoried the crosscutting regulations in 1980 and found 36 applying to various social and economic issues and 23 additional administrative and fiscal requirements.[14] The regulations stipulate that states receiving federal funds must ensure that these monies are administered so as to prevent (and redress) discrimination, protect the environment and historical, architectural, and cultural resources, involve citizens in program development and implementation, and protect and advance the economy, among other things. A list of objectives of crosscutting requirements is set out in Table 3–3. Grant recipients must comply with all of the general requirements as well as with general administrative and fiscal guidelines and any conditions accompanying specific grants they are administering. Otherwise, they may lose federal funds.

Regulations that are conditions of grants-in-aid may be specified in the statutes authorizing the grants or appropriating money for them. More likely, however, the federal agencies administering the programs write them as they prepare and issue the guidelines and regulations expanding on the congressionally set conditions. These sometimes run to hundreds of pages. They are published in the *Federal Register*. After an appropriate period of time for comment and objection, guidelines and regulations may be revised. In any event, the final draft will be republished and have the force of law. Regulations codified by subject matter are set out in the *Code of Federal Regulations*.

Partial Preemption

A third regulatory development uses the partial preemption technique. This differs from past federal practices in which the national government often took over totally from the states one of its constitutionally enumerated functions that they were performing in the absence of federal entry into the field. State regulation of bankruptcy and the establishment of maximum interest rates are examples of this. States formerly controlled both of these activities. Then Congress, exercising its constitutionally delegated powers to regulate bankruptcy and control the currency, enacted legislation superseding the state statutes. If the federal laws are repealed, the state laws again take effect providing they are still on the books.

Reprinted with permission of *U.S. News & World Report*.

TABLE 3-3
OBJECTIVES OF CROSSCUTTING
SOCIOECONOMIC POLICY REQUIREMENTS
APPLICABLE TO FEDERALLY-ASSISTED ACTIVITIES

Related to Human Resources

Prohibit discrimination because of race, color, national origin, or age

Prohibit discrimination because of sex in education programs

Prohibit discrimination because of race, color, religion, sex, and national origin in sale, rental and financing of housing

Prohibit discrimination against handicapped

Ensure access to public facilities by handicapped

Prohibit discrimination against alcohol abusers by hospitals

Prohibit discrimination against drug abusers by hospitals

Prohibit discrimination in construction employment because of race, color, religion, sex, and national origin

Give preference to Indians in assistance that benefits Indians

Encourage women's business enterprise

Protect human research subjects

Prohibit use of lead base paint

Pay construction workers prevailing wage (Davis-Bacon)

No sweat shops allowed: pay workers for overtime

No illegal deductions or kickbacks from wages earned in construction

Related to Animals and Natural Resources

Provide humane treatment of research animals

Eliminate damage to environment

Clean up waterways

Protect drinking water sources

Synchronize state/federal efforts to clean up air

Clean up air

Protect endangered species

Protect floodplains

Protect wetlands

Protect from loss caused by floods

Maintain fish and wildlife resources

Protect historical, archaeological, and cultural resources

Protect wild and scenic rivers

Protect and enhance coastal resources

Preserve (or account for) archaeological remains in construction

Related to Economy

Protect U.S. shipping

Protect U.S. air transport

Encourage employment of resources in labor surplus areas

Source: Adapted from Executive Office of the President, Office of Management and Budget, *Managing Federal Assistance in the 1980s: Working Papers,* Vol. 1 (Washington, D.C.: June, 1980), pp. A-2-12 to A-2-14. A few objectives have been combined.

Partial preemption works differently, however. When it is used, Congress delegates administrative responsibility for a certain function, such as controlling water pollution, to state or local governments providing they conduct the administration according to certain nationally determined standards. If a state does not establish regulations acceptable to the responsible federal agency, then that agency will do so. If the agency's regulations are not enforced by the state, then the national government can assume jurisdiction over the function. This technique was employed in the Water Quality Act of 1965.

Through the use of partial preemption, the national government can mobilize the resources of state and local governments for the implementation of its programs and the enforcement of its regulations. The Clean Air Act of 1970 mandated that states devise effective plans for implementing and enforcing national air quality standards. Under this statute, states can be required to change their transportation policies (convert to mass transit, for example) or regulate private individuals (require emission controls on automobiles), among other things.[15] Mel Dubnick and Alan Gitelson point out that underlying the national government's mobilization of state resources through technical, financial, or other forms of assistance is "the ability of national officials to formally and officially 'draft' those resources into the national service." They add, "We call this *legal conscription.*"[16]

Compulsion Replaces Negotiation

Because of the element of compulsion included in the more recent national legislation, all three techniques—direct orders, grant-in-aid conditions, and partial preemption of state functions—impose a stronger regulatory control over state activities than was the case before 1960. Prescription and compulsion have replaced the negotiation that previously was the prevailing norm in national-state relations.

Furthermore, the use of states as enforcers of national rules and goals is a cheap way of evidencing congressional support for certain problems. In the place of money that in the past was Washington's antidote for problems, in time of retrenchment "Congress uses sticks instead of carrots in legislating against problems."[17]

In addition, the use of states as enforcers of national policies is an inexpensive way for the national government to regulate in terms of both finances and political costs. State, rather than federal, employees are used to administer the regulations, thus avoiding the political and financial costs of a larger bureaucracy and leaving the states with the onus of being the regulator. Some might call it nationalization through the back door.

THE GROWING ROLE OF THE STATES

Just as the role of the national government has evolved over time, so has that of the states. Traditionally, state contributions to American government have been many and important, and today, despite the growth of the national government's role, the states contribute more than ever before. The states' original roles have been supplemented by their assumption of responsibility for financing and administering large programs on behalf of the national government as well as on their own initiative.

Counterweights Against Centralization

As full partners in the federal system and as the repositories of the reserved powers under the Constitution, states always have provided the major resistance to the centralization of powers in the hands of the central government. Although many factors contribute, their ability to act as balance wheels and preserve the federal arrangement rests largely on their political power in a system characterized by multiple power bases. This pluralism in American politics is undergirded by an uncentralized political party system that leaves the bulk of the political power back in the states and communities rather than in Washington. National party organizations must depend on the state parties for most of their strength. Other political activities of the states add to their power bases. Under the Constitution they have the basic responsibility for enfranchisement of voters and administration of elections, although in recent years there has been a nationalizing trend in these respects. Moreover, states have loud voices in presidential nominating conventions and in the Electoral College. The governors of states (individually and collectively), as well as their legislatures, attract attention when they speak out on public issues. States have a final gun behind the door in both proposal and ratification of constitutional amendments. Two-thirds of them can petition Congress to call a national constitutional convention for the purpose of proposing an amendment, and it takes three-fourths of the states to ratify amendments. In exercising their political powers, states have represented strongly their differing electorates.

Mechanisms for Diverse Policy Choices

States have performed, and still perform, other important functions, too. Their existence as major policy makers has permitted diverse public choices in the adoption of different policies for different states. The legislature of one state may provide for public funding of abortions while that of another may not. Capital crimes can be punished by death in some states while life terms are the maximum sentences in others. Provisions relating to divorce, Sunday closings, gambling, and prostitution differ across the country, to cite only several areas where policies vary. Arkansas and Louisiana opted to require the teaching of biblical creationism along with the theory of evolution in their public schools, for example, although other states do not.

Major Public Service Providers

In another role, states are major providers of public services. Most of the policy choices, administration, and funding for the criminal justice system, health and hospitals, transportation, higher education, and business regulations through commercial codes come from the states. For instance, 96 percent of all cases are tried in state courts, and state colleges and universities enroll more than 9 million students, the bulk of those who attend institutions of higher education.[18] Citizens also depend on states for protection of the public health, safety, welfare, order, and convenience, for the states are the primary exercisers of the police (or regulatory) power. Furthermore, they are the cauldrons of ideas for innovative public policies often adopted by other states or the national government.

Responsibilities for Local Governments

Important among state activities has been the exercise of their responsibilities concerning local governments. These jurisdictions are not recognized under the national constitution and depend on the states for life itself. The states create them, participate in the design of their governments, authorize them to act, supplement their revenues, and supervise their activities to some extent.

THE STATES' EMERGENCE AS INTERGOVERNMENTAL MANAGERS

Although states still perform their traditional functions, they have emerged as major intergovernmental managers during the last two decades. They are now involved more than ever before as intergovernmental bankers, regulators, and administrators. Not only do they provide from their own treasuries the bulk of outside funds going to local governments, but they ar the chief recipients and disbursers of federal financial assistance as well. They receive and spend national monies for programs administered at the state level and pass federal grant funds through to their local governments.

States have always done these things to some degree. Recently, however, their responsibilities in this connection have intensified, partially as a result of federal requirements and partially on their own initiatives. Before the

1960s states directed some federal assistance programs. Today, the national government depends on them for the management of an even greater number of nationally assisted, and in some cases heavily state-matched, programs. In many instances management responsibilities have been undertaken willingly, and sometimes eagerly. At other times the burdens were imposed from above and with little regard for the extensive variety that marks state-local systems throughout the nation.

In statute after statute and regulation after regulation, the national government has imposed new management duties on the states. These have been especially notable in education, environmental protection, and health. In education, for example, Title I of the Elementary and Secondary Education Act (1965). The law, which provided federal funds for the education of disadvantaged children, required states to direct local school agencies (1) in their determination of which schools among eligible areas containing high concentrations of low-income families would receive Title I services and (2) in their design of programs for eligible children. Subsequent amendments augmented the state's management role. State agencies received responsibility for monitoring and enforcing the federally supported programs even in states where state agencies had not exercised this kind of authority before. Regular inspections of the practices of local school districts were required, and the state was made responsible for ensuring that an audit was conducted every two years.

Furthermore, Section 504 of the Rehabilitation Services Act of 1973, which prohibits discrimination against the handicapped, vested in state educational agencies the responsibility for guaranteeing that all local jurisdictions administering educational programs comply. If the states do not carry out their management responsibilities under this act, and even *one* local jurisdiction falls short, the U.S. Department of Education has authority to cut off national educational funds to the state and to all school districts within it.[19] By federal fiat, the state education agency has exchanged its "helper's hat" for a police officer's uniform.[20]

The states themselves bear the responsibility for the growing number of regulations they have attached to both state and federal funds going to local governments. As these have risen, so have their duties in monitoring local performance and enforcing compliance.

GALLOPING INTERGOVERNMENTALIZATION

A major consequence of the national government's growth is the intergovernmentalization of almost every functional area. It is no wonder that Henry Wooton is confused as to which government should fix the roads so his children can get to school. Practically no activity is confined to one government anymore. From employment security to housing and from highways to parks, many governments take a hand.

Some comprehension of the extent of intergovernmentalization can be gleaned from Table 3–4 that shows the breakdown of general expenditures of the national government on the one hand and state and local governments on the other for a number of functional classifications. Notice that although the national governments spends more for defense and international relations, the postal service, space research and technology, and public welfare, and state and local governments spend more for education, health and hospitals, highways, and natural resources, that both levels contribute to the support of many functions. Even in areas where the expenditures of one level appear nonexistent or are infinitesimal, it may be involved in other ways. The role of the states in defense, for example, does not show up in an expenditure table.

Although general fire protection is not dealt with in Table 3–4, statistics on expenditures and employment show it almost entirely as a local government activity. And so it is. Nevertheless, both states and the national government have important functions relating to it. The National Bureau of Standards' Fire Research Center does important work relating to building materials, flammable fabrics, and chemicals. State fire marshals or fire agencies enforce state fire laws, conduct training, or assist local departments.

INCREASE IN INTERGOVERNMENTAL INTERACTIONS

Another important development in the period from 1930 to 1980 was an increase in the breadth and frequency of intergovernmental intercourse, an outgrowth providing fertile soil for both conflict and cooperation. A substantial portion of such increase resulted from the expansion of the national grant-in-aid programs. As more and more governments received federal assistance, as the number of programs grew, and as more state agencies became involved, the necessity for interaction among officials on the respective levels intensified.

The growing national regulatory thrust undoubtedly engendered a rise in interactions among officials as well. Similarly, state attachment of regulations for local officials to follow heightened encounters of state and local officials.

Another manifestation of increased contacts deserves attention. Requirements for participation in federal programs stimulated the creation of councils of government and other cooperative regional bodies on the local level. Areawide networks of local governments and state-local bargaining were promoted as well. The networks are informal arrangements drawing together local governments so they may bargain from a position of strength.

TABLE 3-4
GENERAL EXPENDITURES BY GOVERNMENT LEVEL
AND FUNCTION, 1980
(In billions of dollars)

Function	National	State and local
Total, all functions	$446.6	$368.3
National defense and international relations	149.5	x
Postal service	18.2	x
Education	23.5	133.2
Highways	9.9	33.3
Public welfare	47.7	45.6
Health and hospitals	14.6	32.2
Natural resources	31.4	5.5
Housing and urban renewal	12.2	6.1
Space research and technology	4.9	x
Air transportation	3.2	2.5
Social insurance administration	4.4	2.0
Interest on general debt	61.3	14.7
Other and combined	66.0	92.3

x Not applicable

Source: U.S. Department of Commerce, Bureau of the Census, *Governmental Finances 1981*, as reported in *Statistical Abstract of the United States, 1981*, p. 278.

ADMINISTRATIVE PROBLEMS

The national government's increasingly assertive role in financing, regulating, and stimulating state and local governments in the 50 years between 1930 and 1980 had major ramifications for the administration of the public's business. Coupled with the more active stance states took in regard to banking, regulating, and even assuming the functions of their local governments, it intergovernmentalized almost every function and created management problems on all levels. Increasingly, although the national government provides few services directly, it relies on state and local governments to carry on most functions in accordance with conditions imposed by the national level.

What this has meant is that matters that once might have been dealt with easily by one agency have become more complex. Decisions are delayed, costs rise, frustrations increase as every major point is negotiated by officials on two or more levels. A dozen administrators might have to sign off on a decision rather than just one. It also meant that the Henry

Wootons of the nation experienced difficulties in locating the provider of a needed service. Above all it made fixing accountability for governmental sins of commission or omission almost impossible. The buck could always be passed to another level.

One authority on intergovernmental relations calls the end result an "ominously overloaded federal-state-local network" that is almost dysfunctional.[21] While not all observers would go this far—one, in fact, refers to this as the "henny penny school of federalism"[22] in reference to the nursery story—there is widespread concern with the complexity and confusion in the present administrative arrangements. It is obvious that the national government cannot supervise effectively the activities of thousands of subnational governments. Approximately 800,000 to 900,000 federal administrators and employees are responsible for running programs administered by approximately 12 million state and local civil servants operating under thousands of separate personnel and administrative systems.

Difficulties Magnified

The problems that arise from such a situation are many and too complex to discuss in detail here. Nevertheless, it should be noted that when the administration of public programs becomes overly intergovernmentalized, the magnitude of any problems is intensified. The hundreds of programs—often duplicating and overlapping and sometimes conflicting—magnify difficulties that would be hard enough to deal with under a limited fiscal aid system.

Uniform Standards Hard to Implement

In addition, major administrative difficulties may be created when, in a nation as large and diverse as the United States, the central government attempts to impose uniform standards and requirements for all parts of the country and all types of governments. National administrators often ignore, or are ignorant of, the remarkable diversity in state and local governments. They assume that all states, cities, counties, and towns have similar functions and operate in the same fashion. Many are unaware of the differences in state-local relations from state to state. Moreover, they sometimes write guidelines for program administration that go beyond statutory requirements. Even when they do not, the standards and uniform requirements imposed tend to be detailed and rigid, especially as to administrative procedures. Consequently, subnational administrators experience difficulties applying them to their individual situations.

Conflict of Laws and Purposes Reduces Supervisory Capacity

In other instances, national requirements often conflict with state laws, placing the state officials in a precarious position. Perhaps more important, federal and state purposes are not always in agreement so that each set of officials is working toward a different end. The availability of national monies frequently changes state priorities and skews the budget. Unless the legislature reappropriates federal funds coming into the state, state supervision over the spending of those dollars may be undermined. Moreover, as Hale and Palley point out, state agencies dependent on federal funds were more likely to "end run" the governor by directly requesting the legislature to approve more funds than the governor recommended and to ask for additional funds to continue national programs.[23]

Undercutting of Central Coordination

Because most national assistance comes in the form of categorical grants allotting funds for one purpose, it often undermines efforts of state and local political officials to provide general supervision of their governments. Roadblocks are placed in the way of overall planning and coordination by federal programs that encourage specialists to operate outside the control of the chief administrator. If health or highway funds, for example, come in large part from outside the jurisdiction, the loyalty of the health or highway administrator may go to the source of the money. At least, he or she can operate somewhat more independently of the governor, mayor, or county executive. About half (48 percent) of state administrators responding to a 1978 survey perceived supervision by the governor and legislature to be less in federally financed activities.[24]

Even under the best of circumstances, one administrator may be intent on building highways to the detriment of the department concerned with parks. With separate plans for the two types of activities and difficulties of central coordination increased by national funds and requirements, the outcome may be a mishmash rather than a well-planned endeavor.

Categorical grants also encourage the creation of one-purpose planning bodies, such as water quality boards or health system planning agencies. Since each set of grant requirements is individually designed, it may be impossible to combine any of the many agencies that must be established because of special requirements. A health board might require the participation of health service specialists while other types of representation might be specified for a community action agency.

In addition to stimulating and often mandating the creation of single-purpose planning agencies, categorical grants sometimes encourage the establishment of single-purpose special districts. While these are useful in solving particular problems, they aggravate the problems of overall management by increasing the number of jurisdictions involved in negotiations over service provisions.

Other Difficulties

Federal mandates and requirements also create other problems. Executive branch reorganization may be impeded by national specifications that a single agency be designated to administer a program. Paperwork balloons as applications must be filed, reports completed, and procedures enforced. Substantial administrative time and money are devoted to these ends. State administrative officials find their workloads increased as they must prepare designs for managing funds passed through to local governments and work to ensure accountability. The necessity for dealing with numerous officials complicates management difficulties, whether the state is on the receiving or allocating end of the regulatory and funding process.

CHANGED POLITICAL ENVIRONMENT

Fifty years of changes in the United States have altered the political environment in which governments operate. Although these alterations are manifested in many ways, three aspects stand out prominently: (1) the changing representation in the Congress, state legislatures, and other representative bodies; (2) the rise of single-issue interest groups, and (3) weakened political parties. Also deserving mention is the inclusion of private organizations as regular providers of government services, a development discussed in Chapter 5.

Changing Representation in the Federal System

The debates of the Philadelphia Convention revealed one of the concerns of a federal system—equitable representation. The issue of small-state, large-state representation in Congress was settled by the Connecticut Compromise providing for equal representation in the Senate and representation on the basis of population in the House of Representatives. Other issues, such as who is eligible to vote for representatives, how they are apportioned, and the equitability of the districts from which they are selected, have remained to plague us. The handling of these issues illustrates both the continuing evolution of the American federal system and the pragmatic fashion in which decisions concerning the allocation of functions of government are made.

Early suffrage requirements were very restrictive. At the time of the ratification of the Constitution, approximately 3 percent of the population was eligible to vote. By the time of the Civil War, the nation had moved from a position of limited franchise to the point that practically all free adult males could participate in the selection of public officials for all levels of government. Religious requirements were the first to go, followed by those of property ownership. Blacks in the states of the Old Confederacy did not vote, while those elsewhere in the nation experienced little difficulty. Although a few women voted in school board elections, another 60 years had to pass before the franchise was extended to women on a nation-wide basis. A number of taxpaying provisions remained until the present century, and numerous localities still allow only property owners to vote in bond or tax millage referenda.

Black Enfranchisement. The end of racial and sexual restrictions in the election of representatives was not easily achieved. The painfully slow extension of the suffrage to blacks in some states had its roots in historical and cultural factors. Nevertheless, the existence of a federal system of government, under which differing public values as to who should vote were allowed full play, undoubtedly retarded voting equality.[25] Some states demonstrated remarkable ingenuity in circumventing constitutional prohibitions against discrimination.

Following the Civil War, Congress enacted a series of laws, including the submission of the Fifteenth Amendment, to ensure the right to vote for all male citizens. They were aimed primarily at the recently freed blacks. As a result of narrow judicial interpretation, congressional amendments to those acts stimulated by post-Civil War presidential politics, and public reactions to the excesses of Reconstruction, these laws passed into gradual impotence leaving the question of franchise again entirely to the states.

Two-thirds of a century later new activities began in this field. The first major recent changes occurred through interest group and court actions. In the case of *Smith* v. *Allwright* (1944), the very effective "white primary" was outlawed as a violation of the equal protection of the laws clause.[26] Later in response to growing public pressure and after bitter controversy, Congress passed the Civil Rights Act of 1957. Thus, for the first time in almost 80 years, the national government moved to enforce universally the basic voting rights of the Constitution, which some states and localities had consistently abridged. Increasing public concern, prompted by marches, protests, and television coverage that exposed the discrimination for all to see, brought adoption of the Twenty-Fourth Amendment. It outlawed the requirement of a poll or capitation tax payment as a prerequisite for voting in national elections in the handful of states that still used it. Subsequently, the prohibition was extended to state elections by a U.S. Supreme Court ruling in *Harper* v. *Virginia Board of Elections* (1966).

With the Civil Rights Acts of 1960 and 1964 and the Voting Rights Act of 1965, the national government moved step-by-step into an area of traditional state operation as it sought to extend further and more aggressively the national protection of voting rights.[27] Of particular importance was the establishment of national "referees" or "examiners" to register citizens in areas where the courts find "patterns or practice" of voting discrimination.

The success of these actions is shown in table 3–5 that depicts a major increase in voter registration for blacks in the affected states during the period before and immediately after the enactment of the Voting Rights Act. Note in particular the Mississippi figures. Overall in the seven states, there was a 21.9 percent increase in black registration and a decline of amost 8 percent in white registrants, a reduction of the point spread between the two races of 29.8. Some of this balancing is, of course, a product of recent black political activism as well as of legal change. The consequences are a dramatic increase in black voting turnout to the point where it sometimes exceeds that of whites, a growing number of black elected officials, particularly on the local level, and a greater responsiveness to minority pressures by all representatives.

Other Franchise Extensions. Just as the extension of voting rights for blacks progressed unevenly with advances and regressions, and with the

TABLE 3-5
VOTER REGISTRATION BY RACE IN THE SOUTHERN STATES COVERED BY THE VOTING RIGHTS ACT: 1964 VERSUS 1971-72.

	1964 Percent registered		1971-72 Percent registered	
	White	Black	White	Black
Alabama	70	23	81	57
Georgia	75	44	71	68
Louisiana	81	32	80	59
Mississippi	70	7	72	62
North Carolina	97	47	62	46
South Carolina	79	39	51	48
Virginia	56	46	61	54
TOTAL—7 states	76	35	68	57

Source: Testimony of J. Stanley Pottinger, Assistant Attorney General, Civil Rights Division, U.S. Department of Justice. Hearings before the Subcommittee on Civil and Constitutional Rights, U.S. House of Representatives, on Extension of the Voting Rights Act. Ninety-Fourth Congress, First Session, March 5, 1975 (Washington: Government Printing Office, 1975), Serial 1, Part 1, p. 243.

national government making inputs at some times and not at others, so has the affording of rights to vote for representatives to other groups. The struggle to gain national recognition of voting rights for women was long. Although widows voted for school board members in Kentucky in the 1850s and Montana sent Jeanette Rankin to Congress in 1917, the Women's Suffrage Amendment was not ratified until 1920, which was 50 years after the Black Suffrage Amendment. Once the amendment took effect in 1920, however, women experienced little difficulty exercising their franchise, although until 1982 their turnout was slightly less than that of men. This reluctance to ''exercise their flabby franchise'' to the same degree as men probably resulted from a socialization process that discouraged political participation by women. The idea that political activity by women was ''unfeminine'' and that men should make political decisions for the family still persists in some areas. Rather like a woman sitting at a bar, female political participation ''wasn't done'' in some places.

The suffrage was expanded further in 1971 when the minimum age for voting in national elections was fixed at 18 by the Twenty-Sixth Amendment. Prior to this amendment's ratification, most states had set the voting age at 21, although Alaska, Georgia, Hawaii, and Kentucky had lower minimum age requirements. Subsequently, the minimum age for voting in state and most local elections was fixed by the respective states at 18.

Lastly, a series of relatively minor state and local limitations to registration and voting in states and localities has been struck down by the courts or legislated out of existence by the Congress and the state legislatures. Registration and voting regulations are still state functions, but as three prominent observers have noted, the changes described above ''have moved the U.S. toward a nationally defined electorate.''[28]

The Reapportionment Controversy

Apportionment refers to the allocation of legislative seats. In the United States the intention was for the national House of Representatives and houses of representatives of state legislatures to be based on population, generally meaning nearly equal population. Many states employed modifications of the national representation model and apportioned their senates on factors other than population, normally geographic units such as the county or town. Local representative bodies, when elected by districts that were not areawide, were almost always required to take population into account.

State legislatures have the responsibility to redraw congressional and state legislative district boundaries to reflect population changes reported in the decennial national census. For many years, rural-controlled state legislatures often failed to enact representation plans and, when they did, they drew district boundaries in a manner designed to maximize their own rural interests. The great population growth and movement of the early part of the current century further aggravated the situation so that by the 1940s the system of representation had become "locked in" to extreme malapportionment.

As urban voters sought equal representation they found a generally closed system. The malapportioned national and state legislatures would not act, and the more sympathetic executives were powerless to offer relief. The state courts for a variety of political and legal reasons offered only occasional and partial relief, while the national courts passed over the whole controversy as being a "political question" to be settled by the legislative branches of government. In the 1946 case of *Colegrove* v. *Green,* the Supreme Court declared that the courts "ought not to enter this political thicket."[29]

The Colegrove "political thicket" precedent stood until 1962. In that year the Supreme Court stepped in to alleviate the growing disparities in the representation system. In the case of *Baker* v. *Carr*[30] the Court pointed out that population of districts from which members of the Tennessee House of Representatives were elected ranged from 42,298 to 2,340 and that counties with less than 40 percent of the state's population could elect more than three-fifths of the members of that chamber. Similar and in many cases more extreme disparities existed in other states. The Court rejected the Colegrove guidelines by noting that "the mere fact that the suit seeks protection of a political right does not mean it presents a political question. Such an objection 'is little more than a play upon words'."[31] With this statement the national courts entered a period of aggressive intervention designed to bring equal representation to the federal system.

One year later, giving evidence that equal standards were to apply throughout the country, the Supreme Court outlawed the "county-unit system" in *Gray* v. *Sanders.*[32] As employed in Georgia and a half dozen other states, the county-unit system provided that the candidate receiving the highest vote in a county garnered one unit vote. In addition, the person with the most unit votes, regardless of total popular votes, was the victor. The Court refused to accept this "winner take all" approach at the state level.

In 1964, the Supreme Court held in *Reynolds* v. *Sims*[33] that both houses of the state legislature must be apportioned on the basis of equal population. The long-established "little federal system," in which one house was apportioned on a basis other than population, was no longer acceptable. The very structure of the state legislature, the Court ruled, must be changed. In the same year, the justices declared that congressional districts must be based on equal population. In *Wesberry* v. *Sanders* the Court declared that Georgia, and by precedent other states, must equalize the population of congressional districts.[34] The "one man, one vote" requirement was extended to general-purpose local governments in the case of *Avery* v. *Midland County, Texas.*[35]

The complete long-range impact of these actions is still uncertain.[36] Despite predictions to the contrary, major and immediate public policy changes have not resulted from the court actions. Intergovernmentally, two major changes are noticeable. First, urban areas are now fairly represented at all levels of government. In the past much of the bypassing of the states and the development of national-local ties was justified on the basis of control of state assemblies by anti-urban rural legislators. The increased state representation of urban interests has led in many cases to a weakening of Washington-city bonds and to a new vitality and responsiveness of the states. Second, the court decisions clearly established the principle of national judicial review and intervention in the federal system's apportionment schemes, an activity that before 1962 was almost exclusively a function of state legislatures.

The reapportionment controversy did not die with the decade of the 1960s, and it is a continuing source of conflict. Battles raged in many states following the 1980 census, particularly in states subject to the condition imposed by the Voting Rights Act of 1965 that any changes in district lines required approval of the Attorney General of the United States. In Virginia, for example, the controversy involved both political parties, the legislature, the governor, the U.S. Attorney General, the federal courts, and regional and racial interests before it was finally settled.

The Rise of Single-Issue Interest Groups

In a circular fashion, the demands produced by an ever larger, more mobile, urban, and increasingly technocratic society have generated greater national responsiveness to perceived needs. This, in turn, promoted a proliferation of interests better equipped to make demands on the government.[37] Particularly in the last two decades, Congress responded generously to claims upon its largesse, especially as far as urban areas and the disadvantaged were concerned. As each program was created, a constituency developed around it, sometimes funded directly with national monies, as was the case, for instance, with organizations for the aging and the poor. These groups then stepped up their demands, and were often rewarded by a Congress that recognized both a threat if these wants went unattended and an opportunity to build support by acting to sate the thirst for national funds.

With each organization's success, other interests were encouraged to mobilize. Groups representing single issues, such as "right to life," antinuclear power, and environmental protection, developed a sophisticated approach to pressure politics, an approach members of Congress resisted at their peril. The associations learned to use public opinion polls, attract the attention of the electronic media in various ways, and resort to the courts. They established political action committees, known as PACs, to collect and distribute campaign funds. Efforts to achieve results in Congress by such practices as supporting the attachment of special interest provisions to unrelated legislation, focusing publicity on a recalcitrant member, and preparing hit lists for advocates to vote against became commonplace. No member wanted to be tarred by the environmentalists as one of the "dirty dozen," for example.

Breakdown of Party Discipline

Part of the success of the single interests can be attributed to the breakdown of political party discipline both inside and outside the Congress. Party discipline has never been so strong in the United States as in European parties and should not be expected to be under our system. Nevertheless, it has been weakened in recent years primarily as a result of the capacity of candidates to run their own campaigns independently of the party organization—thus reducing the party's control of the nominating process —and because of changes within the Congress.

Campaigns became more candidate oriented because the services formerly provided by political parties were available for hire or purchase in the marketplace. Candidates with sufficient funds could employ pollsters to measure their success, direct mail services to raise funds, and managers to run the campaign. They could get into private homes through the electronic media. With the decline in their usefulness, party leaders lost what control they had of campaigns and candidates. Consequently, the party could not use the strength engendered by coalition building to protect its members in the Congress by insulating them from single interest pressures.

Similarly, in the Congress the seniority system began to disintegrate, committee chairpersons lost authority to the committee membership, and subcommittees emerged as prime fashioners of legislation. Rules were liberalized to open up the process. Weakened parties were unable to act as shields for their members. Where, in the past, the member could plead the necessity for adhering to the party position, party loyalty began to evaporate. The result was a political environment without many of the traditional constraints that had blocked much legislation but with a plethora of uncompromising single-issue groups prepared to stake everything on the adoption of their positions. The older, multi-interest groups continued to influence national policies, but few were looking out for the general interest.

Results of the Changes

These developments affected governmental operations on all levels. Generalists, trying to coordinate all aspects of government policy and achieve what they considered an overall good, found it necessary to engage in hand-to-hand combat with the one-issue groups or else yield to their demands. Often it was easier to buy off segments of the population with policies they championed than it was to risk incurring their wrath.

One result was that policy determination agendas at all levels changed. Many matters formerly dealt with by state and local legislatures were promoted to the national arena. Groups found it easier to influence one Congress than 50 state legislatures. They learned to assemble a whole series of discrete local problems to produce a large enough number of them to support the claim that they were "national problems." This worked in getting programs with respect to teen-age pregnancies, abandoned children, potholes, and the need for bicycle paths, for example.

Tactics such as this are difficult to deal with because there is no general agreement as to what are national problems or even on the criteria for making the determination. Moreover, it is easier in many instances to push a knotty problem to another level than to risk the consequences of trying to solve it at home. It is often difficult to discuss some problems on the basis of which level of government should deal with them. Strong advocates do not entertain the idea that solutions should be sought on a state-by-state basis.

LIMITATIONS ON THE GROWTH OF NATIONAL POWER

The national role has not grown unhindered and unopposed. There are constitutional limitations on its expansion, especially in the Bill of Rights.

Judicial Actions

Court rulings have restrained the national government in some instances, although the courts generally tend toward liberal interpretations of national authority. The first Supreme Court decision limiting Congress' delegated powers since the 1930s was handed down in *Oregon* v. *Mitchell* in 1970. In this case, the Court held that congressional lowering of the minimum voting age to 18 in state elections exceeded its powers.[38] Subsequently, the Twenty-Sixth Amendment accomplished the same result. Again in 1976, in *National League of Cities* v. *Usery*,[39] the Court restrained national action. This time it ruled that congressional exercise of the power to regulate commerce did not extend to the authority to require state and local governments to pay minimum wages to their employees.

Grass-Roots Philosophy

Other limitations operate at the same time, some perhaps more important than the constitutional constraints. There is, in the first place, the philosophical bent of the American people for decentralization. Dating back to the Jeffersonian model of an agrarian republic is a widely-respected belief in the wisdom of small, self-governing rural communities, sometimes referred to as "grass-roots." As Roscoe Martin put it, "One who rejects or ignores a grass-roots incantation does so at his peril, for the public mind does not entertain the alternative of grass-roots fallability."[40]

Public Opinion

National public opinion polls show a trust of state and local governments that serves to restrain, to some extent, the expansion of the national role.[41] Results of a 1981 Gallup poll appear in Figure 3–2. Note that the states

FIGURE 3-2 FAVORABLE VIEWS OF THE STATES

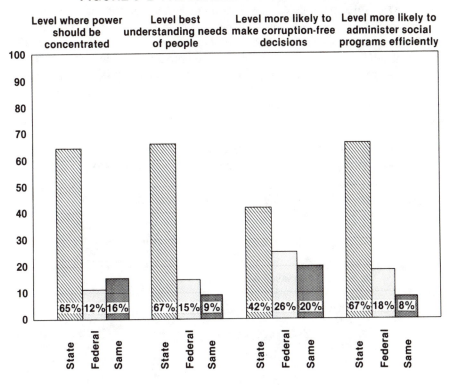

Source: Compiled from the Gallup Poll, September 18–21, 1981.

are viewed more favorably than the national government on all the issues. On the other hand, the national government usually came out somewhat ahead in opinions about which level of government gave the most for the money.[42] Despite this, results of a 1982 ACIR survey, shown in Table 3–6, clearly show that citizens would prefer to reduce national power. This is a reversal of public opinion in the middle of the Great Depression of the 1930s. In 1936, a total of 56 percent of those queried preferred a concentration of power in the national government. By 1981, the states were preferred by a 64 to 36 percent majority.[43] It should be remembered that responses to questions of this type are not always consistent and that in some specific policy areas support for national performance is substantial. Officials on all three levels came out with identical scores in a 1978 Harris poll. Eighteen percent of the respondents reported "a great deal of confidence" in people running institutions on all three levels.[44]

Past Actions

Past actions further serve to constrain national expansion. A constituency of interests that has access to the decision makers and resists change is built up around services performed at one of the other levels of government. With the increased professionalism in more functional areas, however, this factor would seem to have more leverage in opting for transfer of an activity to the national level than for keeping it with the states. In fact, the Reagan administration met substantial resistance in its efforts to transfer decisions about federally aided programs from the national to the state level.

TABLE 3–6
CITIZENS' VIEWS OF FEDERAL POWER: 1982

Question: Which of These Statements Comes Closest to Your View About Government Power Today?

	Percent of U.S. Public	
	1978	1982
The federal government has:		
1. Too much power.	38	38
2. About the right amount of power.	18	18
3. Should use its powers more vigorously.	36	30
4. No opinion.	8	14

Source: U.S. Advisory Commission on Intergovernmental Relations, *Changing Public Attitudes on Governments and Taxes,* Report S–11 (Washington, D.C.: 1982), p. 6.

Political Parties

Very real constraints exist in the political party and electoral system. Anyone who has spent much time in Washington knows that the real basis of political power is back in Sacramento, Austin, Columbus, or Chicago. National officials, from the President on down, depend upon state centers of political power for their support—particularly as they relate to campaign activities. The center is not necessarily the state capital but it does include state and local party organizations and the vote that comes from throughout the nation. Were this not so, such substantial amounts of time would not be spent by national figures, when they are out of the nation's capital, visiting governors, party officials, and other political leaders, and speaking before party-oriented groups. This does not mean that all states present unified power bases. Often they are honey-combed with factions. But with their local components they exert a powerful force in national affairs.

Representatives and senators in Congress are particularly sensitive to state and local supportive structures. They may receive some help from the national committees of their parties, or even more from the concerned national congressional or senatorial campaign committee, but they rely more heavily on the party organization within their state or district. This is not to say that they do not often set up their own campaign committees or sometimes operate independently of the state and local party organization. It does mean that they try not to alienate the party organization, for the relationships maintained within the constituency are crucial to the success of the candidate.

A state party is often in a position to influence voting by members of the U.S. House or Senate for political purposes back home. This influence extends not only to legislative issues, but also to votes that approve presidential appointments, elect the President and Vice President when no majority develops in the Electoral College, impeach and remove civil officers on conviction, and fill a vacancy in the office of the Vice President (as in the selections of Gerald Ford and Nelson Rockefeller). Constituency public opinion, as expressed by party leaders as well as by citizens themselves, can often be determinative on all of these actions.

What must be kept in mind when considering the effect of party as a limitation on national power, or on any other aspect of American government, is the confusing complexity that exists within the system, both as its organization appears on paper and as it functions. Parties display unpredictable degrees of autonomy and cohesion. Argument among scholars continues as to whether the uncentralized nature of American political parties maintains the federal bargain as William H. Riker contends or whether the federal system contributes to an uncentralized party organization as put forth by David Truman.[45]

State Options

State choices often limit the spread of national power and influence. State governments frequently serve as managers of federal assistance programs, and in this capacity they can exercise options as to how these programs are administered or, in fact, as to whether they are administered in their jurisdictions at all. Not all states participate in all grant-in-aid programs and their decisions to use or not to use assistance affect the extent of national influence accompanying the program. Even when states elect to participate, they may exert their considerable political influence and bargain with federal officials to get more favorable terms. They can and frequently do, drag their feet in complying with national mandates or else comply halfheartedly. For example, in response to a federal requirement that states impose and enforce a 55 mile per hour speed limit in order to qualify for federal highway funds, Nevada enacted legislation providing for a five dollar fine for violation of the limit, an obvious snub to national policy.

Controversies over state compliance with federal grant requirements are frequent. In such cases the federal agency is faced with withholding federal funds, bargaining with state officials, or letting the requirements remain unenforced. Most of the time it bargains because neither of the other alternatives will get the national program administered in the face of state intransigence. This happened in 1981 when the U.S. Department of Education yielded on some of its requirements in a long-standing dispute with North Carolina over further integration of its institutions of higher education. The national threat to cut off $90 million in aid was unable to alter the state's resolve to control its own education system. The compromise saw national officials yielding more than the state,[46] although a change from a Democratic to a Republican administration in Washington may have been a factor.

STATE REACTION TO NATIONAL GROWTH

A growing national presence produced a mixed reaction from the states. Although federal financial assistance is welcomed and even sought much of the time, the old fear of federal encroachment on states' rights still prevails.

Gubernatorial Militance

The voices of state governors became quite loud in expressing opposition to national expansion. Governor Bruce Babbitt of Arizona, a liberal Democrat, told the National Governors' Association in 1980:

Today . . . the Federal system is in complete disarray. Congress has lost all sense of restraint. The Congress no longer even asks the question that preoccupied Hamilton and Madison: "Is this legislative proposal an appropriate function for the federal government?"

It is long past time to dust off the Federalist Papers and to renew the debate commenced by Hamilton, Madison, and Jay.

- They would ask not only whether a proposal is a good program, but also "Is this a *Federal* function?"
- They would ask, "Is it the role of the National Congress to fund programs for jelly-fish control? A comprehensive program for rat control? Grants to local libraries?"
- They would ask, "Is it appropriate to have a national program that buys typewriters, desks, guns and patrol cars for local police agencies across the entire continent?"
- They would certainly ask how the Federal Government has come to be so deeply involved in that most uniquely local of all American institutions, the public school.
- And, they would ask how we have allowed their most original creation, a carefully layered system of separate units with specified functions to become scrambled into one undifferentiated governmental omelette.
- They would ask what happened to the concept of enumerated powers in Article I, and why the 10th Amendment, reserving powers to the states, is a hollow shell.

If the states are to have a future, the process of sorting out and separating must begin now. We must devise ways to unscramble the omelette and reconstitute a layered Federal system in which each level of government has its own flavor, shape and function.[47]

The governors, described by one writer as "distressed and angered by a continued erosion of authority to the Federal Government,"[48] unanimously called on the President and Congress to convene a national commission on federalism to propose legislative and constitutional changes assigning certain functions to the national government and others to the states. The functions each level would perform were not specified in the resolution, although many governors wanted the national government to assume responsibility for welfare and leave education, transportation, and crime control to the states.

Much of the state wrath was directed at national orders, regulations, and the guidelines and requirements accompanying national grants-in-aid. Another governor, Christopher Bond of Missouri, commented on this point, saying:

There's been a continued growth in the federal government. The cumulative effect of all the little nitpicking things, the regulations, the hassle, has become substantial.[49]

By the next meeting of the National Governors' Association in August, 1981, the governors were more concerned with financing the programs turned over to the states at the Reagan administration's behest. Governor George Busbee of Georgia, chairman of the Association, reiterated a previously announced gubernatorial position when he told the meeting:

> Federalism must be a two-way street. . . . State and local officials are willing to take on greater responsibilities if there is a carefully conceived plan to sort out appropriate roles for each level of government and to balance those with adequate resources. In the absence of such a consensus, further efforts to shift new responsibilities to state and local governments will meet with firm resistance from the states.[50]

Obviously concerned about the Reagan administration's cuts in national financial assistance and the prospect of having to pick up abandoned programs, the governors adopted a resolution reflecting their concerns and offering, in effect, to bargain with the national government over the reassignment of functions between the two levels. The resolution said, in part:

> The governors reiterate their strong belief that the so-called 'safety-net' programs—such as welfare and Medicaid—have been, are and should continue to be primarily a federal responsibility. We will continue to resist . . . any effort to shift Medicaid or Aid to Families with Dependent Children in any way. . . . We offer to work with the administration and Congress toward a phased-in reduction of federal support in the areas of education, law enforcement and transportation in return for increased federal responsibility for income security programs. . . .[51]

The governors were concerned also with the impact of federal tax reductions on state tax collections. Although state taxes are imposed independently of national income taxes, many state income tax rates are pegged to national rates. Consequently, a cut in federal taxes reduces state collections as well. New York state estimated its losses at $100 million in the first year after the 1981 legislation reducing the federal income tax.[52] Some states are reluctant to cut state rates loose from federal levies or to increase taxes because it might place them at a disadvantage in competing for business and industry.

Changes in Structure and Policies

States responded to the growth of national activity and especially to the lure of the fisc (money) by gearing their governmental policies and machinery to maximize their opportunities. Legislatures passed enabling statutes permitting them to take advantage of national assistance and shifted appropriations and policy emphasis to programs receiving national

—from *Herblock On All Fronts* (New American Library, 1980)

financial support. Recent administrative reorganizations demonstrate a tendency to establish state structures that correspond to the national departments. For example, several states have replaced highway departments with departments of transportation that handle varied transportation modes and resemble the national model. In addition, there has been a proliferation of planning and substate regional organizations encouraged by national grants.

Establishment of Washington Liaison Offices

State responses to a growing national role also have included increases in efforts to influence the national government through lobbying. Part of these efforts were channeled through the National Governors' Association and the National Conference of State Legislatures, in which all states participate, and other public interest groups. Another facet of increased lobbying has been the establishment and growth of state liaison offices in Washington that are major channels of information to their states.

Thirty states now maintain liaison offices in Washington. They exist for states in the immediate proximity of the national capitol as well as for more distant states, and are most likely to service the more populous states. Tenure for these establishments is somewhat erratic, and some states have created and later abolished them. Usually a Washington-based extension of the governor's office, their effectiveness depends largely on his or her support.

The Washington offices provide a wide range of services to their states and often to localities within them as well. Among their more important activities are: (1) the collection and distribution of a variety of data to their states, including proposed legislation, regulations, and government actions; (2) provisions of communication and coordination services facilitating the exchange of views between the state and national levels; (3) arrangement of appointments for officials, organizations, and groups within the state with national personnel; (4) service as spokesmen for state interests with congressional staff or executive agency staff; (5) promotion of tourism in the home state through the distribution of brochures and other information; (6) encouragement to out-of-state businesses to locate in the state through provision of information; and (7) arrangement of travel, dining, theater, and lodging reservations for officials journeying to Washington. Not all offices perform all these services.

How much a state benefits from the establishment of a liaison office in Washington remains to be determined. Research indicates that there is little relationship between whether a state operates such an office and its success in influencing national policy. Furthermore, states with these agencies are not among the most successful in receiving national financial assistance. No causal effect should be inferred, however. It may be that the low fiscal success results from the less favored states creating the offices for that reason, or it may be a matter of size, industrialization, or other factors. The offices seem to facilitate intergovernmental relations. For example, Washington offices were in a position to alert their respective states when the Office of Management and Budget decided that private contributions for social services would not be matched by national grants. Furthermore, they help to provide a state counterbalance to local demands on Washington which have been growing an intensity in recent years. The Washington offices work closely with the National Governors' Association.[53]

NATIONAL-STATE CONFLICTS

Students of American federalism are engaged in an ongoing dispute as to whether the nature of the arrangement is one of cooperation or conflict. Considerable evidence supports the view that between 1930 and 1970 the relationship could be termed cooperative even if the two levels had not always worked in harmony. Since that time, relations seem increasingly fractious, as the account of the National Governors' Association meeting, discussed above, indicates. Observers have described current American federalism as "cooptive," "conscriptive," and "regulatory," among other terms that denote lack of harmony.

Controversies between states and the national government frequently are generated by conflicts among private individuals or groups. In the words of Harold Herman and Donald Zauderer, "intergovernmental conflict often reflects calculations by private interests of their success in or potential for 'capturing' alternative government organizations and thus is merely one expression of broader political conflict."[54] Disputes among individuals are raised to a higher arena for settlement.

While earlier surveys of state officials revealed little conflict,[55] more recent polling uncovered substantial amounts. Results of a 1973 nationwide survey by a U.S. Senate subcommittee showed that 40 percent of state officials responding felt that intergovernmental red tape was an important obstacle to doing their jobs. When views of executives were separated from those of legislators, 53 percent of the executives expressed this view.[56] These findings are reenforced by the American State Administrators Project surveys that showed 75 percent of the administrators agreeing that federal aid leads to "national interference in affairs that are the proper domain of the states." Administrators believed that national interference was higher than it should be in program policies, administrative operations, evaluation of results, personnel policies, and organization structures.[57]

Administrative Conflict

Most of the friction occurs in the day-to-day administration of programs because that is where most of the interaction occurs. Not surprisingly,

state administrators resent the regulations and grant conditions that they
see as interfering with their prerogatives. Listen to the voices of state and
local officials who, rather than being grateful for national largesse, are
resentful of its consequences:

The federal government is altering our own priorities!

The federal government allows too little state and local discretion concerning how to meet national objectives!

We must spend too much time (and money) on federal red tape and
paperwork!

Federal assistance is hard to get and administer! It requires too much
grantsmanship!

The federal government mandates too many activities on us without
paying for them! (or with inadequate reimbursement!)

The federal government makes too many decisions affecting state and
local governments, without consulting them!

The federal government shows little capacity in implementing its own
programs, but pretends to possess it with ours! [58]

Two other comments show the tensions. Former Arizona Governor Ruel
Castro said "The way the Feds cut red tape is lengthwise," while former
Secretary of the U.S. Department of Health, Education, and Welfare
David Matthews remarked "My biggest clients are outraged governors." [59]

A study for the National Governors' Association included as the principal areas of conflict: (1) lack of coordination among federal agencies;
(2) encroachment on state authority by the national executive branch; and
(3) regulations that are prescriptive in methodology rather than oriented
toward results. Other major areas were: (4) excessive paperwork requirements; (5) lengthy approval procedures and other administrative practices
that cause serious dislocations and inequities at the state level; and (6) lack
of national coordination and consistency in implementing procedures for
determining indirect costs. [60]

Conflict on Civil Rights

Another important area of conflict between the national government
and the states has involved national protection of civil rights and the states'
exercise of their police power to protect the health, safety, and morals of
their citizens. Climactic in the 1960s with civil rights marches, campus
protests, urban rioting, and strikes of public employees, it posed a problem
difficult of resolution. In an effort to protect the civil rights of the blacks,
Latinos, and the less affluent, the national government resorted to various

means. These consisted of persuasion, legislation, granting money, withholding of funds, court action, appointment of national officials to perform certain activities once performed in the states (i.e., voting registrars), and armed force. Although most states generally complied with national attempts in this area, a few of them turned to counter legislation, resolutions, court action, refusal to accept national funds, and outright defiance. They saw these as appropriate activities to protect the freedom of action and free use of property of their citizens.

An inherent conflict often exists between two civil rights such as the right to a trial by an impartial jury and the right of a free press, both guaranteed by the Constitution from both state and national interference. But when the power of the state to legislate and regulate for the protection of its citizens is introduced, the situation becomes complicated indeed.

Racial integration and law enforcement are probably the most troublesome areas, although the nation has experienced considerable difficulty with abortion, pornography, and other matters. In law enforcement, for example, necessary national court rulings protecting the rights of defendants in criminal cases have sometimes resulted in the release of hardened criminals to prey upon the public. State and local law enforcement officials have been thwarted in their efforts to clear the streets of repeated offenders and thus fulfill their obligations to protect the lives and property of their citizens. Further, the United States Department of Justice occasionally has entered a case as a "friend of the court" in a school desegregation controversy. Also, since the passage of voting rights legislation, the department has instigated cases on behalf of those deprived of their voting rights.

A particular source of resentment in connection with elections has been the authority conferred on the Department of Justice by the Voting Rights Act of 1965 to veto in advance any changes in election laws, districts, or procedures in areas found to have records of past discrimination against minorities. This review is not limited to changes in registration procedures. It also includes approval of city-county consolidations, annexations, at-large versus district election changes, sizes of local governing bodies and terms of office, and congressional, state, and local election district boundaries, to name only some of the points of irritation. Table 3-7 shows the number of reviews processed by the Department from 1965 from 1980.

Notice that provisions apply to parts of states outside the South. A 1981 New York City primary election had to be postponed because changes in representational districts had not been approved by the Justice Department.

This is not to say that the general position of the states has been in opposition to civil rights. Resistance to some national legislation, executive orders, and court decisions regarding rights of minorities and defendants has come from *some* states not in agreement with the national norms of the times. Sometimes the conflicts in law enforcement have occurred over who

TABLE 3-7
VOTING RIGHTS ACT IN ACTION

The following chart shows the number of proposed changes in state election laws submitted to the Justice Department as required by the Voting Rights Act of 1965, and the number of changes to which the Justice Department has objected:

	Proposed election law changes				Justice Department objections
	1965-70*	1971-75	1976-80	Total	
Alabama	16	614	1,085	1,715	72
Alaska[3]	0	0	37	37	0
Arizona[4]	0	201	1,537	1,738	8
California[1]	—	12	683	695	5
Colorado[1]	—	0	233	233	0
Connecticut[3]	—	0	0	0	0
Florida[1]	—	1	167	168	0
Georgia	158	935	1,998	3,091	226
Hawaii[1]	0	0	9	9	0
Idaho[1]	0	0	1	1	0
Louisiana	5	882	1,709	2,596	136
Maine[1]	—	0	3	3	0
Massachusetts[2]	—	0	17	17	0
Michigan[2]	—	0	3	3	0
Mississippi	32	503	654	1,189	78
New Hampshire[2]	—	0	0	0	0
New Mexico[1]	—	0	65	65	0
New York[1]	—	166	326	492	5
Oklahoma[1]	—	0	1	1	0
North Carolina[1]	2	485	711	1,198	62
South Carolina	308	834	1,260	2,402	77
South Dakota	—	0	6	6	2
Texas	—	249	15,959	16,208	130
Virginia	57	1,093	1,780	2,930	14
Wyoming[1]	—	1	0	1	0
Total				34,798	815

*The pre-clearance requirement submissions of proposed election law changes to the Justice Department, was enacted in 1965. The provision was continued through the extensions of the act in 1970 and 1975.

[1]Selected county or counties covered rather than entire state.

[2]Selected town or towns covered rather than entire state.

[3]Entire state covered 1965-68, selected election districts covered 1970-72, entire state covered since 1975.

[4]Selected county or counties covered until 1975, entire state now covered.

—Not covered for years indicated.

Source: U.S. Department of Justice as published in *1981 CQ Almanac* (Washington, D.C.: Congressional Quarterly, Inc., 1982), p. 416.

had jurisdiction, as in President Kennedy's assassination in Dallas where the dispute concerned the removal of his body without going through the required legal processes in Texas. Sometimes the conflict is a contest between the Federal Bureau of Investigation and state police over investigation or criminal custody in a particular case.

Alaska's Discontent

Antagonism toward federal growth and interference became so intense in Alaska that in 1980, the voters called for the creation of a statehood commission to study relations of the state to the United States and to consider whether statehood should be continued. This was the first time in history that a state had taken such action. Alaskans were upset about the restrictions on trade, efforts to limit natural resources revenues, and by the failure of the national government to live up to a promise to turn over to Alaska 103 million acres of land, among other things.

After examining the benefits and liabilities of other forms of association with the United States, the Alaska Statehood Commission found none of them preferable to statehood. In its final report, *More Perfect Union*, issued in 1983, it made several recommendations, however, aimed at strengthening Alaska's position among the other states and increasing interstate cooperation as a buffer to national power.

STATE COMPLIANCE

The question of state compliance with national laws, rules, and regulations, and court decisions has arisen frequently in recent years, spurred by the Warren Court's expansion of individual rights. State authority is sometimes asserted in counterpoise to national action and, because state officials do retain some powers, confrontation can result. Persuasion is the usual device for convincing a state to comply, and it is not always easy to do so. At times when the matter comes before the Court, it tries to sidestep the issue. Samuel Krislov wrote:

> In the face of determined state opposition to a decision the Court followed the same tactics of delay. Rather than risk an affront to their moral authority, the justices have usually accepted half a loaf or even a gesture, assuming that time would produce acquiescence or at least diminish the intensity of opposition. In stressing the continuity of its moral authority even at the risk of foregoing a victory the Court follows the pattern of other institutions like the Catholic Church, which instills respect through its moral standing rather than through the imposition of sanctions. The Court, like the Church, has not sought to challenge and test the limits of its power, preferring to display the impression of power.[61]

Not all showdowns have been averted, and the national government pointedly emphasizes that challenges to the Court's authority will be met. Power has usually been directed at the weakest point in the state armor, that is, subordinates rather than governors; but in the desegregation cases governors were dealt with directly. Because of their defiance of court orders, two governors of Mississippi were found guilty of contempt.

Organized local opinion against the rulings of the Court present the greatest problems. Compliance to law is ordinarily so traditional that disobedience must be created, usually by a forceful leader such as a governor, before it can be sustained. If the governor asserts that "The law will be enforced," prospects for mass disobedience are unlikely. This happened in several states during the desegregation controversy. In West Virginia, Governor William Marland threatened to "fill the jails" with those who attempted to thwart the Court's desegregation orders, and Governor A.B. "Happy" Chandler of Kentucky sent the Kentucky National Guard into Sturgis to see that legal requirements were met. Delaware officials also insisted on enforcement of the ruling. South Carolina, although under pressure, complied. As a consequence, these states had less difficulty with school integration than those in which the governors led public opinion in defying the courts, such as in Georgia, Mississippi, Alabama, and Arkansas. In the more recent conflicts over mandatory busing to achieve racial integration, governors have not promoted resistance. The remarks of other opinion leaders, however, such as Louise Day Hicks of Boston, a former congresswoman, school board member, and city council member, have lent legitimacy to defiance.

Some feeling of legitimacy for state defiance of national action still obtains in the United States and encourages state officials to speak out for their prerogatives. Once a state has defied national authority, it will be easier the second time because the legitimacy of obedience has been devalued. For example, southern forces, never known for complete acceptance of national actions without question, have attacked the Court on grounds other than desegregation. They have criticized the Court for its decisions on prayer in schools and protection of defendants' rights, and on general interference with states' rights in such matters as apportionment. While at one time their position drew broad support, their coalition seems to have disintegrated.[62]

State and local officials are the keys to opposition to court rulings, and they also are the keys to compliance. Sometimes court rulings are simply ignored as in the case of school prayer decisions in religiously homogeneous communities. Connecticut schools recently refused to abandon prayers. In any event, most decisions relative to free speech, holding rallies, and law enforcement are made on the state and local levels. The support or criticism received by officials from citizens of their communities significantly influences public actions.

NATIONAL-STATE COOPERATION

Whether or not one agrees that the national-state relationship has always been cooperative—and we believe a pragmatic federalism has and does exist, with conflict and cooperation varying from function to function, from time to time, and from one official or bureaucrat to another—it must be admitted that, despite apparent increasing conflict, at present substantial cooperation prevails in the administrative aspects of American government at all levels. This cooperation reflects the accommodations government officials have made to public demands for resolving conflict situations and to change. Congress, because of its local constituency orientation, has chosen many times to effectuate a program through state administration rather than by direct administration by the national bureaucracy. The proliferation of grants-in-aid in areas clearly within the constitutional authority of Congress, such as the construction of roads, is firm evidence of this.

It is currently difficult to think of program areas that do not involve both the national and state governments. The day-to-day consultation going on among administrators testifies to the spirit of accommodation that often exists. Many problems are solved or actions expedited by their telephone calls, letters, luncheon meetings, and the somewhat more structured inter-actions in hearings, conferences, and investigations. At the same time, the lobbying efforts of public interest groups bring officials face to face.

Other intergovernmental cooperation occurs through a wide range of devices. Included are emergency aid, the giving of technical advice and assistance, joint use of facilities and personnel, joint enforcement of laws and regulations, legislation supporting the laws of the other level or making an offense on one level an offense on the other. Other devices are the acceptance of joint standards, compacts and other contracts, and national-interstate commissions. Still others are the establishment of commissions on intergovernmental relations, fiscal assistance in the form of grants, loans, and revenue sharing, and national expenditures in the states. Recent intergovernmental cooperation acts, passed by Congress, furthered such cooperation and oiled some "squeak points." Grants-in-aid are the most prominent device through which the national government encourages the cooperation of the states.

Emergency Aid

Emergencies can occur anywhere and, when they do, they often require more personnel and assistance than are at hand. Those on a large scale emanating from natural disasters, such as tornadoes, floods, or earthquakes, usually result in the President declaring the location a "disaster area," making it eligible for wide ranging assistance of all types—from loans at low interest rates to national aid in restoring essential service. Assistance can be denied, of course, as occurred with the infestation of the Mediterranean fruit fly in California. President Reagan refused Governor Jerry Brown's request for disaster assistance on the grounds that the state could handle a problem of that magnitude.

Other emergencies with which the state cannot cope are usually human-made civil insurrections such as strikes, demonstrations, and riots. The nation went through a rash of them during the civil rights and peace protests of the 1960s and early 1970s. State law enforcement officials are often involved, especially in those conflicts widespread enough to affect more than one community. State police are usually sent first to help local officials and then, if they are unable to quell the disorders, the governor will dispatch the national guard. If the guard is otherwise deployed or cannot cope with the situation, the state legislature if in session, or, if not, the governor, will call on the President of the United States for troops.

The President, as commander in chief of the armed forces, has complete discretion as to whether or not he will comply with the request. If he feels that the situation is too much for the state to handle, he may send them. In fact, he may dispatch them to a state on his own initiative if national property needs protection or national activities are subject to interference. This has happened and usually aggravates the relationship between the national government and the state.

Most of the time, however, the state is reluctant to call for help, and the President is reluctant to send it. No governor likes to admit that his administration cannot maintain order, and armed force is not a politically popular device for the President to employ. Even when both of these officials are willing to cooperate, arguments sometimes ensue about jurisdiction, timing, and other matters. Note the controversy between Governor George Romney of Michigan and President Lyndon B. Johnson over that state's request for assistance at the onset of riots in Detroit in 1967. The Governor claimed the president was slow in responding, and the President accused the Governor of delaying the request.

Technical Advice and Assistance

The exchange of technical advice and assistance occurs every day on a multitude of occasions. It involves the transfer of information, aid in developing skills, and the development and transfer of products. Observers are most likely to notice the assistance which goes from the national government to the states and, in fact, this is the route of most of it. But the path runs in both directions and states frequently provide such help to agencies of the national government. Several states, such as Pennsylvania, Connecticut, California, and New York, got into the superhighway business long before the adoption of the national interstate highway program and were in a position to offer substantial advice on its planning and design elements. State officials are often called for advice when new legislation is being drafted, by both the national bureaucracy and the congressional committees concerned, in order that administration of the programs will be smoother. This practice is also likely to be followed in the preparation of guidelines for the administration of national programs.

From the national government may come technical advice in many fields. That offered by the United States Department of Agriculture is wide-ranging and long-standing. Agriculture is a field in which much cooperation exists. Another example of the type of assistance the states can expect is offered by the Department of Housing and Urban Development. That agency maintains an office devoted primarily to providing management assistance to state and local governments in federally-assisted housing programs. The national Office of Personnel Management is empowered by the Intergovernmental Personnel Act of 1970 to furnish both operational and consultative services. That is, this office can refer names for appointment to state jobs from its own register of eligible personnel, engage in joint recruiting and examining with states and localities, and help to train their employees. On a consulting basis, it is authorized to provide service by its own staff, ranging from one day to several months in duration.

A General Accounting Office study of technical assistance reported:

> A significant segment of the State and local sector sees a need for additional Federal technical assistance, *even though a majority of the questionnaire respondents reported that they neither received nor needed much technical assistance from the Federal level.* One of the major concerns of State and local officials is reluctance to get involved with the Federal Government because of the complexities and regulatory problems associated with Federal assistance.[63] (Emphasis added.)

Those who did see a need for greater assistance showed a preference for help in particular functional areas, such as environmental protection, or for technology transfer (i.e., applying research and development to governmental problems) rather than for general management assistance. The latter is directed toward strengthening the capability of state officials to plan, implement, manage, and evaluate their policies, strategies, and programs. It is sometimes referred to as "capacity building."

Not surprisingly, most of the technical assistance received by states went to the executive branch. Approximately 22.5 percent of the respondents for executive agencies indicated receiving a moderate, considerable, or very great amount of national assistance, while fewer than 2 percent of legislative respondents made a similar report.

Joint Use of Facilities

The states and the national government not infrequently engage in the joint use of facilities as well as of personnel. Campuses of state universities were used during World War II for the training of military forces. One entire section of the Chapel Hill campus of the University of North Carolina was blocked off for use in naval pre-flight training and on other parts of the campus both University facilities and faculty were employed in teaching officer candidates for the Army and Navy. This was not an unusual situation.

Even during peacetime the military services may contract with public (or private) universities for the education of selected personnel. This is fairly routine and in addition to ROTC training. The University of Maryland, for example, offers classes at the Pentagon in Washington and at nearby military bases, as well as overseas, as a convenience for military personnel and their dependents. Moreover, in all parts of the country, state national guard units train at U.S. military bases. To cite a nonmilitary example, the United States Department of Agriculture may use state agricultural experiment stations, financed in part from national funds, for agricultural research.

Cooperative Law Enforcement

It is well known that law enforcement agencies of the states often enforce national as well as state laws and that the Federal Bureau of Investigation often assists state and local officials. Other agencies of both the national and state levels also are involved in this kind of cooperation. The states cooperate with the Bureau of the Census in supplying vital statistics. State officials aid in the enforcement of food and drug regulations, meat inspection, and banking laws; and coal mining safety is a cooperative effort of both state and national inspectors. Court cases involving national issues often are tried in state courts, and national courts apply state statutes in certain instances including those involving crimes committed by persons on national enclaves (e.g., national forests or parks) within a state.

Supporting Legislation

Concurrently with joint law enforcement, one level of government may enact laws supporting those of the other jurisdiction; for example, it is a national crime to transport alcoholic beverages into a state where their sale is prohibited. Congress also legislated to cover the interstate aspects of other crimes—use of the mails to defraud, interstate flight to avoid criminal prosecution, kidnapping, and white slavery, for instance. Furthermore, Congress occasionally refers to or adopts the common law of various states; thus, in passing laws relating to ships in interstate or foreign commerce, Congress recognizes laws of several states regarding pilotage.

The use of state election laws for national elections is generally recognized through the absence of national laws covering most procedures, although some national election laws do exist. The states condone national laws by statute and by use, also; for instance, they recognize the United States mails as transmitters of legal documents and use census data for classification of cities. Either the state or national legislatures may adopt standards set by the other if uniform regulation is desirable. In addition, Congress attempts to protect one state from another; for example, national laws on inheritance and estate taxes prevent some states from becoming havens for people wishing to escape these taxes by moving their places of residence.

Cooperation by Contract

The states and the national government enter into all kinds of agreements of a contractual nature, including compacts. Contracts are made on a routine, day-to-day basis. The ordinary variety includes such agreements as national-state contracts on the temporary incarceration of national prisoners in state or local correctional institutions, on national research at a state university, or on the disposal of surplus equipment or real estate. Often land no longer needed for national purposes will be turned over to the state for a nominal fee. All kinds of arrangements of this sort exist between the two levels of government.

Compacts, which are agreements transferring political power, were long used solely as an interstate device, but in recent years, especially in river basin development, the national government has entered as a party to the compact and participates in its administration.

Intergovernmental Organizations: ACIR

Other developments include the creation of national-interstate commissions and the establishment of intergovernmental bodies for the purposes of suggesting solutions for intergovernmental problems and generating harmony. The use of the latter organizations is not new, but the establishment of the Advisory Commission on Intergovernmental Relations (ACIR) in 1959 as a permanent body was innovative, because previous commissions had enjoyed only temporary existence. This *national* agency is composed of public representatives and officials of the executive and legislative branches of national, state, and local governments. It maintains a continuing review of the federal system, makes recommendations for its improvement, and issues reports. The reports provide a wealth of information on the operation of the federal system. ACIR's studies influence public policy in areas such as grant reform and taxation.

Overall, the attempts at intergovernmental cooperation seem to be increasing in scope and intensity. There is growing recognition of the interdependence of national, state, and local agencies as they attempt to determine public policy.

Cooperative Actions to Improve General Relations

Other efforts at cooperation involved enactment of national legislation and issuance of executive orders or Office of Management and Budget circulars specifically aimed at improving relations among all levels of government. Prominent among the statutes have been the law creating the Advisory Commission on Intergovernmental Relations, the Intergovernmental Cooperation Act of 1968,[64] and the Intergovernmental Personnel Act of 1970.[65] Several other statues have been directed toward lessening the burdens of grant-in-aid administration.[66]

The Intergovernmental Cooperation Act provided that state and local viewpoints had to be considered in the design of federal assistance programs and that state officials, upon request, had to be informed about the purpose and amount of national funds given to state and local governments under grant programs. The Intergovernmental Personnel Act focused on overall improvement of state and local personnel management. It provided grants for fellowships, training, and improvement of personnel management systems, for technical assistance in personnel management, for interchange of employees between all levels of governments and with universities, for intergovernmental training in which state and local employees could participate in national training programs, and for cooperative recruiting and examinations among state and local governments. Although some of these activities had been undertaken previously on a piecemeal basis, this was the first comprehensive legislation in this connection.[67] Recent funding reductions undercut its effectiveness.

Most of the executive orders, presidential memoranda, and OMB circulars were designed to implement the legislation. The Carter administration was especially active in trying to improve grant management. Throughout his tenure President Carter worked to solve the problems connected with grant application, reporting, and planning requirements, financial management practices, audit procedures, requirements to fill national goals, and development of federal regulations.[68] Among his other actions was the issuance of an executive order to clarify and simplify regulations and to ensure that they did not impose undue burdens on state and local governments.[69] Despite the good intentions behind these actions, they were insufficient to deal with the problems confronting grant-in-aid administration.[70]

Another national effort to cooperate is illustrated by the establishment of the 10 standard federal administrative regions. The aim was to achieve more uniformity in the location and geographic jurisdictions of national field offices of the various federal agencies and to promote cooperation among agencies and among the national, state, and local governments. Boundaries were drawn and regional office locations established for each of the regions. When agencies established new offices or changed existing ones, they were required to adopt the uniform system. This meant that state and local officials could deal with numerous federal agencies on one trip and not have to go to Charlottesville to see regional officials of one department and Philadelphia to deal with those of another. Regional offices were established in Atlanta, Boston, Chicago, Dallas, Denver, Kansas City, New York, Philadelphia, San Francisco, and Seattle.[71] President Nixon created by executive order a federal regional council for each of the ten regions and required them to improve coordination of the federal grant system and to develop closer working relations among themselves and with state and local governments.[72] After reconstitution by President Reagan in 1981, the councils included the principal regional officials of the Departments of Agriculture, Education, Energy, Health and Human Resources, Housing and Urban Development, Interior, Labor, and Transportation, and the Environmental Protection Agency. Subsequently, however, President Reagan abolished them.

IN RETROSPECT

The events of the half century since the onset of the Great Depression transformed the face of American federalism. The dual federalism that operated at the beginning of the 1930s gave way to a cooperative mode that endured until it was replaced in the 1970s by more conflictive arrangements.

The national influence that permeated American government in this period was often nebulous, indirect, and sometimes unintended. For the most part, however, national actions were directed specifically toward modifying the performance of state and local officials. Whether through court decisions—such as in reapportionment, school desegregation, and abortion regulation—or through the devices of grants-in-aid and attached conditions, regulations, direct orders, federal preemption of areas of state activity, technical advice and assistance, and creation of intergovernmental

organizations, the national government expanded its presence. This modified the pre-depression balance in the American partnership. The result
was a transformation of fiscal and administrative arrangements.

Some observers believe that an entirely new intergovernmental system
emerged.[73] At least one contends that the governmental system has become
overloaded and dysfunctional as a result of the frenzied national entrance
into almost every area of American government.[74] Equally prominent
authorities think the system has an "impressive degree of stability"[75] or
"do not believe that the federal aid system is fundamentally flawed."[76]

In any event, the constant change and accommodation in the federal
arrangement is apparent. As the 1980s got underway, the designs of Reagan's New Federalism for shoring up the position of the states slowed the
movement toward nationalization of American government and promised
another era of change.

NOTES

1. Advisory Commission on Intergovernmental Relations, *Categorical Grants:
Their Role and Design*, Report A-52 (Washington, D.C.: Government Printing
Office), 1978, p. 18. Future references to this agency will be ACIR.

2. 297 U.S. 1 (1936).

3. W. Brooke Graves, *American Intergovernmental Relations* (New York:
Charles Scribners' Sons, 1964), pp. 892–903.

4. ACIR, *Categorical Grants*, p. 35. The law enforcement block grant was
terminated in 1980.

5. Executive Office of the President, Office of Management and Budget,
Managing Federal Assistance in the 1980s, Working Papers, Vol. 1 (Washington,
D.C.: June, 1980).

6. Statement of Secretary of Education Terrel Bell before the President's Committee on Federalism, Washington, D.C., June 23, 1981.

7. Wayne F. Anderson, "Intergovernmental Aid: Relief or Intrusion?" *National
Civic Review*, March, 1980, p. 120.

8. ACIR, *State Administrators' Opinions on Administrative Change, Federal
Aid, Federal Relationships*, Report M-120 (Washington, D.C.: December, 1980),
pp. 2, 27.

9. ACIR, *Significant Features of Fiscal Federalism, 1981-82 Edition*, Report
M-135 (Washington, D.C.: April, 1983), p. 66. See also ACIR, *Recent Trends in
Federal and State Aid to Local Governments*, Report M-118 (Washington, D.C.:
July, 1980).

10. William Anderson, *Intergovernmental Relations in Review* (Minneapolis:
University of Minnesota Press, 1960), p. 169.

11. ACIR, *An Agenda for American Federalism: Restoring Confidence and
Competence*, Report A-68 (Washington, D.C.: June, 1981), p. 105. This is volume
10 of ACIR's major study of *The Federal Role in the Federal System*. Other volumes

are: Vol. 1, *A Crisis of Confidence and Competence;* Vol. 2, *The Condition of Contemporary Federalism: Conflicting Theories and Collapsing Constraints;* Vol. 3, *Public Assistance: The Growth of a Federal Function;* Vol. 4, *Reducing Unemployment: Intergovernmental Dimensions of a National Problem;* Vol. 5, *Intergovernmentalizing the Classroom: Federal Involvement in Elementary and Secondary Education;* Vol. 6, *The Evolution of a Problematic Partnership: The Feds and Higher Ed;* Vol. 7, *Protecting the Evironment: Politics, Pollutions, and Federal Policy;* Vol. 8, *Federal Involvement in Libraries;* Vol. 9, *The Federal Role in Local Fire Protection;* Vol. 11, *Hearings on the Federal Role.* All were published in Washington, D.C., sometimes by the Commission, sometimes by the Government Printing Office. Single copies of these and other ACIR publications are available from the Commission, Washington, D.C. 20575, without charge.

12. Catherine H. Lovell, Robert Kneisel, Max Neiman, Adam Z. Rose, and Charles A. Tobin, *Federal and State Mandating on Local Governments: An Exploration of Issues and Impacts* (Riverside, Cal: Graduate School of Public Administration, University of California, Riverside, 1979), p. 71. For a summary of mandate issues, see Lovell and Charles Tobin, "Mandating—A Key Issue for Cities," *1980 Municipal Year Book* (Washington, D.C.: International City Management Association, 1980), pp. 73–79, and the same authors' "The Mandate Issue," *Public Administration Review,* Vol. 41, No. 3 (May/June, 1981), pp. 318–331.

13. David R. Beam, "Washington's Regulation of States and Localities: Origins and Issues," *Intergovernmental Perspective,* Vol. 7, No. 3 (Summer, 1981), p. 10.

14. Executive Office of the President, *op. cit.*

15. Congressional Budget Office, *Federal Constraints on State and Local Government Actions* (Washington, D.C.: Government Printing Office, 1979), p. 7.

16. Mel Dubnick and Alan Gitelson, "Nationalizing State Policies," in *The Nationalization of State Government,* edited by Jerome J. Hanus (Lexington, Mass.: Lexington Books, 1981), pp. 56–57.

17. Samuel Halperin, "Federal Takeover, State Default, or a Family Problem," in *Federalism at the Crossroads: Improving Educational Policymaking* (Washington, D.C.: Institute for Educational Leadership, The George Washington University, December 1976), p. 19.

18. Case statistics are from the Joint Committee of the Conference of Chief Justices and Conference of State Court Administrators, *Report of the Task Force on A State Court Improvement Act* (Williamsburg, Va.: National Center for State Courts, 1979), p. 5. Educational figures are from the *Statistical Abstract of the United States, 1981* (Washington: U.S. Government Printing Office, 1981).

19. See Edith K. Mosher, Anne H. Hastings, and Jennings L. Wagoner, Jr., *Pursuing Equal Educational Opportunity: School Politics and the New Activists* (New York: Clearing House on Urban Education, Teachers College, Columbia University, 1979), p. 21.

20. See Donald W. Burns, "Federal Involvement in Education," in *Government in the Classroom: Dollars and Power in Education,* edited by Mary Frese Williams (New York: The Academy of Political Science, Columbia University, 1978), p. 51.

21. David B. Walker, "Speaking Points Concerning the Condition of Contemporary Federalism and President Reagan's New Federalism Prescription," ACIR files, June, 1981.

22. Richard P. Nathan, " 'Reforming' The Federal Grant-In-Aid System for States and Localities," *National Tax Journal*, Vol. XXXIV, No. 3 (September, 1981), p. 323. The reference to Henny Penny is erroneous. It was Chicken Little who ran around proclaiming that the sky was falling. For an argument that intergovernmental relations have not grown so complex that the lay public cannot understand them and are impressively stable, see Thomas J. Anton, "The New Federalism in Illinois," *Illinois Issues*, March, 1982, pp. 7–8.

23. George E. Hale and Marion Lief Palley, *The Politics of Federal Grants* (Washington, D.C.: Congressional Quarterly Press, 1981), p. 105.

24. ACIR, *State Administrators' Opinions*, p. 51.

25. See William H. Riker, *Federalism: Origin, Operation, Significance* (Boston: Little, Brown and Co., 1964), pp. 143–44.

26. 321 U.S. 649 (1944). See also United States v. Classic, 313 U.S. 229 (1940).

27. See Richard P. Claude, "Nationalizing Electoral Process Standards: Is An Obituary for States Rights Premature?" *Idaho Law Review*, Vol. 13, No. 3 (Summer, 1977), pp. 373–402.

28. Marion D. Irish, James W. Prothro, and Richard J. Richardson, *The Politics of American Democracy*, 7th ed. (Englewood Cliffs, N.J.: Prentice-Hall, Inc., 1981), p. 253.

29. 328 U.S. 549 (1946). The decision was not based solely on the "political thicket" issue. In the several opinions written for the case, reference also was made to lack of jurisdiction, standing to sue, inability to offer remedy, and the delicacy of national-state relations. The "political question," however, was picked up by national and state courts as the precedent to be followed in their future deliberations.

30. 369 U.S. 186 (1962).

31. Ibid.

32. 372 U.S. 368 (1963).

33. 377 U.S. 533 (1964).

34. 376 U.S. 1 (1964).

35. 390 U.S. 474 (1968).

36. For an assessment of some reapportionment impacts, see Timothy J. O'Rourke, *The Impact of Reapportionment* (New Brunswick, N.J.: Transaction Books, 1980).

37. See Hugh Heclo, "Issue Networks and The Executive Establishment," in *The New American Political System*, ed. by Anthony King (Washington, D.C.: The American Enterprise Institute for Public Policy Research, 1978), pp. 45–85. This anthology contains other excellent essays by Samuel H. Beer, Fred I. Greenstein, Samuel C. Patterson, Martin Shapiro, Austin Ranney, Jeane J. Kirkpatrick, Richard A. Brody, Leon D. Epstein, and Anthony King.

38. 400 U.S. 112 (1970).

39. 426 U.S. 833 (1976).

40. Roscoe C. Martin, *Grass Roots* (University, Alabama: University of Alabama Press, 1957), p. 5.

41. For examples, see Mavis Mann Reeves and Parris N. Glendening, "Areal Federalism and Public Opinion," *Publius*, Vol. 6, No. 2, pp. 135–167; the *Washington Post*, May 9, 1974, p. A-1 for results of a University of Michigan Institute for Social Research Survey; and William Watts and Lloyd A. Free, *State of the Nationa, III* (Lexington, Mass.: Lexington Books, 1978), p. 30.

42. ACIR, *1982 Changing Public Attitudes on Government and Taxes,* Report S–11 (Washington, D.C.: 1982), p. 2. See Chapter 6 of this book for a table setting out the figures for each year.

43. George Gallup, "Reagan's New Federalism Strikes Responsive Chord with Public," *The Gallup Poll,* October 18, 1981, p. 2.

44. Hospital Care in America: *A National Opinion Research Survey of Consumers, Government Officials, and Health Care Community Attitudes,* April, 1978, p. 8.

45. Riker; David B. Truman, "Federalism and the Party System," in *Federalism: Mature and Emergent,* ed. by Arthur W. MacMahon (New York: Russell and Russell, Inc., 1962), pp. 113–136.

46. *New York Times,* June 21, 1981, p. A22.

47. Remarks by Governor Bruce Babbitt to the National Governors' Association, Denver, Col., August 4, 1980.

48. John Hebers, "Governors Ask Realignment of State and Federal Powers," *New York Times,* August 6, 1980, p. A16.

49. *Washington Post,* March 12, 1981, p. A3.

50. B. Drummond Ayres, Jr., "Georgia Governor Calls on U.S. to Assist States," *New York Times,* August 8, 1981, p. 20.

51. Resolution adopted by the National Governors' Association at the August, 1981 meeting in Atlantic City, N.J.

52. E. J. Dionne, "U.S. Tax Cuts Will Cost New York $100 Million Because of Linkage," *New York Times,* August 9, 1981, p. 1.

53. See Nicholas B. Wilson, "Enhancing Federal-State Relations: State Liaison Offices in Washington," Unpublished Ph.D. Dissertation, University of Maryland, College Park, 1975. See also ACIR, *State-Local Relations Bodies: State ACIRs and Other Approaches,* Report M-124 (Washington, D.C.: March, 1981). For a discussion of state lobbying through public interest groups, see Donald H. Haider, *When Governments Come to Washington* (New York: The Free Press, 1974).

54. Harold Herman and Donald Zauderer, "Intergovernmental Consequences of National Health Planning Policy," a paper presented to the American Society for Public Administration, Phoenix, Arizona, April 12, 1978, pp. 2–3.

55. R. Bruce Carroll, "Intergovernmental Administrative Relations," in *Cooperation and Conflict: Readings in American Federalism,* edited by Daniel J. Elazar, R. Bruce Carroll, E. Lester Levine, and Douglas St. Angelo (Itasca, Ill.: F.E. Peacock Publishers, 1969), pp. 310–311; and Edward R. Weidner, *Intergovernmental Relations As Seen by Public Officials* (Minneapolis: University of Minnesota Press, 1960), pp. 91–96.

56. U.S. Senate Committee on Government Operations, Subcommittee on Intergovernmental Relations, *Confidence and Concern: Citizens View American Government. Survey of Public Attitudes* (Washington, D.C.: Government Printing Office, 1973), Part I, p. 296 (Committee Print).

57. ACIR, *State Administrators' Opinions,* pp. 2, 48.

58. ACIR, Survey forms for 1977 poll.

59. *Ties That Bind . . . HEW National Management Planning Study, 1976* (Seattle, Wash.: U.S. Department of Health, Education and Welfare, Region X, July, 1976), p. 1.

60. National Governors' Conference (now Association), *Federal Roadblocks to Efficient State Government* (Washington, D.C.: February, 1977), Vol. 1, pp. vii–viii.

61. Samuel Krislov, *The Supreme Court and the Political Process* (New York: Macmillan Co., 1965), pp. 145–146.

62. Ibid., p. 148.

63. General Accounting Office Staff, *State and Local Governments' Views on Technical Assistance,* GGD–78–58 (Washington, D.C.: U.S. General Accounting Office, July 12, 1978), p. 25.

64. P.L. 90–577; 82 Stat. 1098.

65. P.L. 91–648; 84 Stat. 1909.

66. See especially *Uniform Relocation Assistance and Real Property Acquisition Policies for Federal and Federally Assisted Programs* (1970), P.L. 91–646; 84 Stat. 1894; *Congressional Budget and Impoundment Control Act of 1974,* P.L. 93–344; 88 Stat. 297; *Joint Funding Simplification Act of 1974,* P.L. 93–510; 88 Stat. 633, 42 USC 4252; *Federal Program Information Act* (1977) 31 USC 1701; and *Federal Grant and Cooperative Agreement Act of 1977,* P.L. 95–244, 41 USC 501.

67. Comptroller General of the United States, *Report to the Congress: An Evaluation of the Intergovernmental Personnel Act of 1970,* FPCD-80-11 (Washington, D.C.: U.S. General Accounting Office, December 19, 1979), p. 4.

68. Office of the White House Press Secretary, "Statement by the President, 9 September 1977."

69. Executive Order No. 12044, "Improving Government Relations," March, 1978.

70. See The White House, *Federal Aid Simplification: White House Status Report, September, 1978* (Washington, D.C.: Government Printing Office, 1978) and Federal Assistance Monitoring Project of the ACIR, "Streamlining Federal Assistance Administration: A Final Report to the President" (mimeographed), November 21, 1978. Advisory Commission on Intergovernmental Relations, *Docket Book, Sixty-Fifth Meeting, December 7–9, 1978,* Washington, D.C., Tab D, pp. 3–9. For a brief summary of these findings, see Parris N. Glendening and Mavis Mann Reeves, "Federal Actions Affecting Local Government: Much Activity, Limited Impact," *Municipal Year Book 1979* (Washington, D.C.: International City Management Association, 1979), p. 29.

71. OMB Circular A–105, *Standard Federal Regions.*

72. Executive Order 11647, February 10, 1972. President Reagan reconstituted the councils in 1981 and broadened their mandate to cooperate with state and local governments. Executive Order 12314, July 22, 1981, *Federal Regional Councils.*

73. ACIR, *Summary and Concluding Observations: The Intergovernmental Grant System: An Assessment and Proposed Policies,* Report A–62 (Washington, D.C.: U.S. Government Printing Office, 1978), pp. 65–78.

74. David B. Walker, "Tackling Dysfunctional Federalism," *Policy Studies Journal,* Vol. 9, No. 8 (Special Issue #4, 1980–81), pp. 1193–1205.

75. Anton, p. 7.

76. Nathan, " 'Reforming' the Federal Grant-in-Aid System for States and Localities," p. 321.

CHAPTER 4

STATE-LOCAL RELATIONS: STRONG INTERDEPENDENCE

IN his attempts to cut through the maze of governments to get his children to school, our friend Henry Wooton, first mentioned at the opening of Chapter 1, may have to take a route different than that to be followed by a resident of another state. No state's local governments are identical to those of any other state, and there is no uniformity among, or often within, states as to which government does what. In some states, a citizen such as Wooton would look to the state highway department for repair of the road. A resident of another might have the gravel to fill the potholes supplied by a local road district or by the county or town. There are similar variations in other activities such as education, sewers, or health services.

STATE-LOCAL FUNCTIONAL PERFORMANCE PATTERNS

Two generalizations can be made about the way states divide functions among governments. In the first place, if one looks at all states across the nation, he or she can see that almost every function is performed by more than one type of government. Even that most local of activities, general fire protection, is an activity of multiple governments in at least two states. The wide range of services that are furnished by more than one type of government can be seen in Table 4–1 that shows which governmental jurisdiction financed more than 55 percent of these activities. Notice that more than half the functions are shared by more than one government in 10 or more states.

TABLE 4-1
DOMINANT SERVICE PROVIDER* BY TYPE OF GOVERNMENT AND FUNCTION, BY NUMBER OF 50 STATES:
1977

	Education	Highways	Public welfare	Hospitals	Health	Police	Fire protection	Sewerage	Other sanitation	Parks & recreation
State	1	39	43	24	30	—	—	—	—	3
County	2	—	1	4	4	—	—	1	1	1
Municipality	—	—	1	—	—	27	48	33	44	24
Townships	—	—	—	—	—	—	—	—	2	—
School Districts	37	—	—	—	—	—	—	—	—	—
Special Districts	—	—	—	1	—	—	—	4	—	2
More than one provider*	10	11	5	21	16	23	2	12	3	20

	Natural resources	Housing/renewal	Airports	Water transport**	Parking	Correction	Libraries	General control	General public buildings
State	48	3	6	16	—	46	2	7	5
County	—	—	9	3	—	1	9	1	8
Municipality	—	16	26	20	47	—	19	—	1
Townships	—	—	—	1	—	—	—	—	—
School Districts	—	—	—	—	—	—	—	—	—
Special Districts	—	21	5	6	1	—	2	—	—
More than one provider*	2	10	4	1	2	3	18	42	36

*A dominant service provider is one that accounts for more than 55% of the direct general expenditure in a particular function. "More than one provider" indicates there is no dominant service provider.

**Only 42 state-local systems exhibited this function in 1967, 40 in 1972, and 47 in 1977.

Source: Derived from U.S. Bureau of the Census, Census of Governments, 1977, *Vol. 4, Governmental Finances, No. 5, Compendium of Government Finances,* Washington, D.C., U.S. Government Printing Office, 1977. Advisory Commission on Intergovernmental Relations, *State and Local Roles in the Federal System* (Washington, D.C.: Forthcoming).

A consequence of this extensive sharing is that superior governments, by providing funds to subordinate jurisdictions, are often able, in effect, to purchase seats in the decisionmaking councils of the smaller governments. Moreover, they can, and do, impose conditions and constraints on local actions. The golden rule of intergovernmental relations applies: he who has the gold makes the rule. The necessity for concurrence by several sets of decisionmakers slows action and fogs accountability to the public. Citizens, such as our friend Henry Wooton, have difficulty knowing where responsibility rests.

A second generalization relates to the level of government likely to perform a function within a state. The states themselves usually bear the major responsibility for highways, public welfare, hospitals, natural resources, and corrections as far as the state-local division is concerned. They also pay the bulk of higher education costs. Municipalities can be expected to engage more often in police and fire protection, sewerage, other sanitation services, parks and recreation, airports, water transports, parking, and libraries. Administrative responsibility for elementary and secondary education is most frequently vested in school districts, and housing districts are the major spenders for shelter. Neither counties nor townships predominate in any activity nationwide although counties in particular spend most of the money that supports a few functions in a few states.

CHARACTERISTICS OF STATE-LOCAL RELATIONS

State and local officials experience all the satisfactions and frustrations in dealing with each other that officials involved in other intergovernmental interactions do. At the same time, certain characteristics that affect the relations of others to a lesser extent mark their intercourse. State and local officials have a high degree of interdependence, strengthened by common traditions, cultures, and economic systems. These may mute cries for change and mitigate the difficulties involved in certain adjustments. The officials work together to influence other governments, particularly the national government. Their constitutional and legal systems bind them closer and often establish formal requirements of intergovernmental interactions. Shared needs enhance their relations and possibly contribute to more stable relations than exist among other governments. A sense of state pride sometimes provides grease for the friction points.

States and localities exert strong influence on each other through numerous instruments of persuasion and coercion. The state possesses an arsenal of legal powers for use with its local jurisdictions, including the power to create and abolish them and to determine their powers. These are supplemented by administrative controls. In addition, the state influences through fiscal controls as well as through the important financial assistance it gives localities. Politically, the state is also potent as it decides on the location of

roads or other public improvements or as economic development is furthered. The governor is the leader of her or his political party in the state
and may use this power as a tool to deal with local officials and party
leaders. The state legislature is nonetheless the most influential body in
local affairs. An eight-state survey by Glenn Abney and Thomas A. Henderson that asked local officials to rank order five institutions—governors, state
legislatures, state bureaucracies, federal bureaucracy, and courts—as to
their impact on local government, found that officials in all eight states
perceived state legislatures to have the most influence. State bureaucracies
ranked second. Moreover, the officials perceived states to have greater
impact on their affairs than the national government.[1]

Localities are not helpless in the face of this legal goliath. They can effectively counter state influence through their delegations in the state legislature, through political party organizations and state associations (such as the
state league of municipalities or counties), and through their votes in
elections for state officers. Local governments have further influence by
lobbying directly, resorting to court action or threatening it, stimulating
public opinion in their behalf, and calling for local home rule. National
financial assistance, especially general revenue sharing, has strengthened
local hands. A closer look at the various aspects of the relationship will
bring the state-local picture into focus.

POLITICAL RELATIONSHIPS

The most pervasive and yet the most nebulous relations between states
and their local governments are political. Interdependence is high, although
the localities probably have the edge in strength.

Local Influence Through the Ballot

Citizens in cities, towns, and counties are also residents and voters in
the states and can exert influence through use of the ballot. By support or
nonsupport for the state elected officials, a locality may vent its displeasure
or approval. Votes of large urban areas can be especially effective in this
respect, and candidates for statewide office hasten to seek support of city
voters and officials. Ballots also may determine issues, as constitutional
amendments and other proposals are subject to referenda. In some states
citizens resort to the initiative to place on the ballot by petition proposed
laws the state legislature has ignored or rejected. Some also can use the
referendum to force a popular vote on already passed legislation, and accept
or reject bond issues for state programs and projects. Occasionally, recall
elections may be used to remove from office before the expiration of their
terms state officials unpopular on the local level. With the exception of the

vote on constitutional amendments and bond issues, these devices are available only in certain states. Where they do exist they offer last-resort opportunities for local counteroffensives against the state.

Local Influence Through Control of Party Organization

The political balance may also be tipped toward localities by local control of political party organization. County executive or central committees are usually the most powerful segments of the party organization. These organs, as well as other parts of the party apparatus—especially the state committee, state convention, and finance committee—may be used to influence the nomination, financing, and electoral support of candidates for state office, favorable or unfavorable to the local position, as well as to mold public opinion.

Richard Lugar, then mayor of Indianapolis, in speaking of the use of the political party in the successful effort to merge Indianapolis and surrounding Marion County in 1970, said,

Each one of us as an office holder or a participant in civic life can find a very high degree of intergovernmental cooperation within one of the two major parties and attempt to influence the dialogue at the congressional level or at the state and local level through that party and offer at least a way of proceeding. At least we have found that to be effective in terms of the Indianapolis situation vis-a-vis the rest of the state of Indiana, because we had to have that support in order to make reforms.[2]

Influence of Party Characteristics

Characteristics of the political party system may be determinative, or at least influential, in state-local relations. The amount of interparty competition within a state; the degree of cohesion in a given party, particularly in the dominant party; and the extent of openness in party operations may affect the influence of one level of government on the other. When strong party competition is present, a state party organization may be more responsive to local demands than if its uncontested position gave it greater freedom to operate autonomously. Since party competition differs from state to state, with some possessing highly competitive parties and others being essentially one-party states, it may bear importantly on the extent of party influence on intergovernmental relations. Similarly, party cohesion may be a significant factor. A strongly unified party may contribute to cooperative relationships while a highly fractionalized organization may stir up rivalries and disputes.

If the state party organization is strongly controlled from one locality, the influence of other areas probably would be reduced. On the other hand, if more than one strong local organization exists, the influence of local units should increase. The ability of citizens to penetrate party councils, whether state or local, and to induce responsiveness to demands may affect state-local relationships on more than one issue.

Local Influence Through Legislative Delegations

State legislatures are composed of representatives of the localities who are interested in their own communities as well as in the state as a whole. A locality may seek their support in its cause and probably get their backing because of the dependent relationship. By combination of blocs of local unit representatives—say, from urban counties—or by control of legislative leadership positions, state statutes affecting the locality can be modified. In states where special local legislation is permitted and state interference with local affairs is likely to be higher, tradeoffs among local delegations are the normal procedure. Usually a unified local delegation has no difficulty getting its proposals relative to that locality adopted and will, in turn, vote for special local measures favored by the representatives of other areas.

Localities may lobby directly with the state or take the less direct route of trying to stimulate public opinion to exert pressure on state officials on their behalf. Each city, for example, may lobby its own representatives or combine with other cities throughout the state in a state municipal association to make demands on all legislators and state elective officials. Counties, towns, and other local units may have similar organizations. Spokesmen for these groups command attention of state officials when they speak with a unified voice for local interests.

Such associations, in addition to performing the usual functions of interest groups, serve as negotiators for their constituent units or candidates. Local opposition, combined under their banners, can sound a death knell for political careers. Furthermore, a few large cities and counties maintain state liaison offices to deal with the state on both political and administrative bases. Also, state advisory commissions on intergovernmental relations have considerable potential for exerting influence.

Local units continue to resort to traditional methods of influencing public opinion, such as adopting resolutions, using communications media, and public speechmaking by officials. Occasionally, a mayor—especially a New York City mayor—proposes that the city secede from the state, a move almost certain to attract press coverage, thus drawing attention to local problems. This device for rallying public opinion is old, dating back at least to 1861 when Mayor Fernando Wood made such a proposal to the Common Council of New York.[3] In their attempts to affect public opinion, localities rely on a prevailing belief in the inherent goodness of local self-government.

Initiatives by the national government, particularly direct grants to cities by passing the states and revenue sharing, shore up local political powers. Operating with some independence of the state because of an outside base of fiscal resources, the localities are bolder in expressing their frustrations and enumerating their needs. Mayors and other local officials can develop programs and consequently political bases independent of the state.

State Political Resources

State governments are not without resources in the political arena. In particular, governors come to the bargaining table with pockets full of favors to dispense or withhold. They often can use them effectively in dealing with local delegations in the legislature, in attracting public support at the polls, or in rallying public opinion to their causes. As their administrations make various decisions—the location of the new highway or bridge, the recipients of state jobs, the legislation to be proposed or supported, the location to be pushed for industrial expansion, the placement of the new prison—governors can make their political presence felt statewide. They usually are the leaders of the state majority party organizations and can use the parties to influence local campaigns. Announced gubernatorial support of a candidate or slate is often sufficient to make others withdraw. The financial resources governors command can be determinative in primary elections.

Legislators, as acknowledged political leaders, also can be influential in local affairs, especially in states permitting special local legislation. As a unit, however, the legislature exerts most of its potency in the legal sphere.

LEGAL RELATIONSHIP

In the realm of legal relationships, interdependence between states and their local units is particularly strong. This is highly evident with respect to local dependence upon the state. Since the United States Constitution makes no mention of local government, the states are the only subnational units it recognizes. This is not to say that localities are unimportant in the national view: a multitude of national-local relationships operates. But, constitutionally, local governments are a part of state governments. Many local units pre-dated the Constitution and the states in which they are located and some, in fact, participated in the establishment of the superior governments. Nevertheless, they are generally regarded as deriving their legal existence from the states and as possessing no "inherent right of local self-government."

State Primacy

Unlike the federal relationship between the national government and the states, the state-local arrangement is a *unitary* one; that is, localities have no powers independent of the state. Cities, counties, towns, townships, school districts, and other units of local government are creatures of the state and under its control. Insofar as local governments collect taxes, provide services, and regulate citizens, they are exercising powers delegated to them by the state.

Unless restricted by the state constitution, the state government is the creator and source of authority for all the local units within its boundaries. Subject to state constitutional limits, the state legislature provides by statute for the creation of local jurisdictions, specifies their form of government, defines their powers, and has the authority to abolish them. This is true even in states allowing municipal or county *home rule*. Some states provide in their constitutions for home rule; that is, the power of the municipality or county to select or draft its charter and exercise broad powers of self-government. Others set out these options in statutes. Even in the constitutional home rule states, the legislatures exercise control over local affairs of statewide importance. Constitutional home rule creates a limited federal arrangement because local powers under this grant are derived from the people of the state and are therefore outside the determination of the state government.

States do not treat all of their local jurisdictions the same. Often considerable variation is present between the authority granted to cities and counties within one state, and frequently large cities may have some powers not granted to smaller municipalities or to towns and villages. These possibilities should be kept in mind.

Dillon's Rule

The grip with which states hold their localities is strengthened by Dillon's Rule, which sets out a strict court construction of grants of authority. Originally applied to municipal corporations, it has been extended to all local governments. The rule states:

> It is a general and undisputed proposition of law that a municipal corporation possesses and can exercise the following powers and no others: First, those granted in express words; second, those necessarily or fairly implied in or incident to the powers expressly granted; third, those essential to the declared objects and purposes of the corporation— not simply convenient but indispensable. Any fair, reasonable doubt concerning the existence of the power is resolved by the courts against the corporation and the power is denied.[4]

When preparing to act, local officials in states that recognize this rule must ask themselves, "Has the state said you can do this?"

Dillon's Rule applies in 46 states, Alaska, Montana, Pennsylvania, and Texas excepted, although New Jersey and Indiana have directed a liberal interpretation of local powers. It operates against change by requiring strict construction of constitutional and statutory provisions relating to local governments. The strictness of the construction depends on the attitudes of judges of the respective state supreme courts. A relaxing trend is indicated, especially in the more urban states. Nevertheless, the legal position of local governments still coincides with that set out for municipal corporations by Judge John F. Dillon, the author of Dillon's Rule, in the case of *Clinton* v. *The Cedar Rapids Railroad Company* (1868). It is as follows:

> The true view is this: Municipal Corporations owe their origin to, and derive their powers and rights wholly from the legislature. It breathes into them the breath of life, without which they cannot exist. As it creates, so it may destroy. If it may destroy, it may abridge and control. Unless there is some constitutional limitation on the right, the legislature might by a single act, if we can suppose it capable of so great a folly and so great a wrong, sweep from its existence all of the municipal corporations in the State, and the corporations could not prevent it. . . . They are, so to phrase it, mere tenants at will of the legislature.[5]

Another view of local powers was enunciated by Judge Thomas M. Cooly of the Michigan Supreme Court in 1871. He held that municipalities had some inherent rights of self-government. State courts in Indiana, Iowa, Kentucky, and Texas followed his lead for awhile, but his view is no longer accepted.[6]

Localities received little help from the federal constitution in regard to their relations with the states. The United States Supreme Court endorsed Dillon's Rule in 1903 in *Atkins* v. *Kansas*[7] and later refused to apply the protection of the due process, equal protection, or contract clauses of the federal constitution in behalf of local governments. The question involving the contract clause, which stipulates that no state shall "impair the obligation of contract," arose in *Trenton* v. *New Jersey* (1923).[8] The city legally acquired from the state the property and franchises conferred by the state to a private water company, including the right to take from the Delaware River all the water needed for municipal purposes. New Jersey later began to charge Trenton for the water. The city went to court claiming the impairment by the state of the city's contract, deprivation of property without the due process of law, and denial of the equal protection of the laws. The United States Supreme Court unanimously ruled against the city on all three grounds holding it to be merely a department of the state government and that the state may grant or withhold privileges as it sees fit.

On the other hand, if state laws conflict with national laws, the state may be prohibited by the supremacy clause of the Constitution from interfering with national grants or licenses to a city to take certain actions to carry out national power. As national activities expand, cities may receive further powers as agents of the national government, sometimes placing them in a conflicting position with the state.

Despite the apparent stringency of Dillon's Rule, local governments frequently are able to rely on their political strength to gain what they want from the legislature. Roscoe C. Martin's observations relative to cities apply to other local governments as well, although to a substantially lesser degree in most instances. Martin wrote:

> The cities are not nearly so supine as Judge Dillon's rule would lead us to believe. Something quite like a federal system has grown up within the states; for while the law calls for state supremacy, practice has produced a considerable measure of municipal autonomy. As a matter of law, the states could of course modify this system in any way they see fit, but in point of fact they find it difficult to abridge any important right enjoyed by the cities. Now and again a state takes punitive action against a city (usually one governed by a political party not in control of the statehouse), but such occurrences are so rare and the storm they provoke so violent as simply to underline the significant change which practice has brought about in Dillon's rule: *de jure* the state is supreme, *de facto* the cities enjoy considerable autonomy.[9]

States have moved to lessen the impact of Dillon's Rule in recent years, as will be discussed later in this chapter. Nonetheless, state impact on local decisions is still strong. Very often a local government's awareness that it lacks a particular power removes options depending on that power from the decisionmaking arena. It passes into the "nondecisionmaking" class, or else the city applies to the state for increased power.

Cities occasionally attempt to use the devices of secession, nullification, and interposition to gain greater freedom from state control. As mentioned earlier, some large cities such as New York have threatened to secede from the parent state, and clusters of "upstate" or "downstate" counties—believing themselves neglected children—at times talk of secession. These pronouncements are principally for propaganda purposes, of course. A more important type of local resistance to state control occurs when localities deliberately enforce state laws, as, for example, those for alcohol or drug control, far more leniently than elsewhere in the state or than intended by the legislators. Similarly, a municipality may try to nullify a state law, as happened with proposals in Ann Arbor, Michigan, and Berkeley, California, to decriminalize state marijuana laws. The use of these devices by local governments is clearly unconstitutional, only sporadically attempted, and of limited effectiveness.

State Constitutional Restrictions on Localities

The general application of Dillon's Rule would appear to eliminate the need for restrictions on local exercise of power because under the rule localities have only those powers specifically delegated to them. Nevertheless, state constitutions contain specific limitation on local freedom of choice. They are aimed at defining local powers and specifying the methods governing how power is to be exercised. Provisions relating to form of government, method of electing officials, listing of duties, and tax and debt limits are frequently found.

Financial restrictions have been particularly inhibitive and have brought forth a wide variety of avoidance techniques. Included are creation of special districts for the performance of certain functions (e.g., sanitary districts for water and sewage disposal), levying of special taxes, and resort to revenue bonds to avoid debt limitations. The restrictions also increased the need to seek aid from higher levels of government when necessary taxing authority was not forthcoming.

Most of these contsitutional limitations were designed to protect the public, but their effect has been to inhibit efforts of localities to meet changing needs. Those preventing or making it difficult to decrease the number of governmental units or increase their size may deter local cooperation or the merger of two or more units. For example, an ACIR study found that 21 state constitutions restrict counties by one or more arrangements. They are (1) freezing the existence of townships or other units smaller than counties; (2) declaring the existence of specific counties; (3) locating county seats; (4) regulating change of county boundaries; and (5) requiring special majorities of the electorate for approval of consolidation or merger.[10]

State statutory restrictions on local units are less important than those of a constitutional nature and usually repeat the more common constitutional denials. Omission of grants of authority may be more damaging to local initiative than restrictive clauses. Nevertheless, statutory provisions can cause substantial conflict.

Special Local Legislation

Some state legislatures control, to a greater extent than others, the internal operations of local governments. This is especially true in states where there are few, if any, state constitutional prohibitions against local legislation applying to one or only a small number of localities. In such states the legislature may enact a law prescribing the salary of a local assessor or the fees to be charged by the justice of the peace in a particular county. Or the legislature may grant the power to levy a certain tax to one city and not to another. In a few states the state legislature enacts annual budgets and tax rates of some communities.

Each legislative session brings local supplicants, hats in hand, to plead for passage of laws to apply only to that jurisdiction. As a consequence, the state legislative representatives from that area are given substantial influence over the internal operations of the area's local governments. This creates two local power bases, forcing the local government authorities to share control with the legislative delegation or even sometimes to assume a position somewhat subordinate to the legislative delegation, as it determines local tax rates and charter amendments and functions on a cooperative basis with other local delegations. In some local jurisdictions the role of the legislative delegation has been formalized to the extent that public hearings are held on the special local legislative program to be presented at the next session of the legislature. Such practices raise the question as to whether the delegation is then part of the local as well as of the state government— or to put it more bluntly, who is in control here?

Most state constitutions contain some kind of prohibition against this type of legislation. These restrictions (1) declare that no special legislation may be enacted where a general law would apply; (2) specifically list matters with which special legislation may not deal (e.g., changing boundaries or amending charters); (3) mandate local request or approval before special legislation may be enacted; or (4) require public laws to be applicable throughout the state. When the constitution provides that no special act may be passed when a general one would be applicable, the legislature cannot legally legislate for one city (or other local unit), if it is possible to handle the matter by a law applying to all cities or all cities in one class. Notwithstanding such prohibitions, many state lawmaking bodies have found it possible to circumvent constitutional intent by classifying cities, usually on a population basis, so that a particular class contains only one city or a small number of cities. Legislation for this class, while written as general legislation, is actually special law. A recent survey by the Advisory Commission on Intergovernmental Relations (ACIR) found widespread use of this technology. A total of 51 percent of the respondents cited its use to circumvent the restriction and enact local legislation.[11]

Authority for Boundary Changes, Control of Adjacent Territory, and Interlocal Agreements

A local government's ability to extend its own boundaries, prevent nearby incorporations, control activities on its borders, and enter into agreements with its neighbors often conditions its competence to deal with local needs. To do any of these things requires state permission. In all states with counties, county boundaries are rarely changed. In fact, many of them are set by state constitutions. Municipalities, on the other hand, frequently annex new territory and expand their perimeters. Nevertheless, only about half the states allow the annexation to be initiated unilaterally by local ordinance or resolution;[12] otherwise, the municipality must wait for citizen petition, or action by the state or some authorized agency. Some states (16) allow cities and counties to consolidate, but in other states, even in the rare instances where consolidation is desired, specific state action is required to permit such mergers. School districts frequently are consolidated by state action, either as related to particular localities or on an overall basis. The Kentucky State Board of Education merged the Louisville and Jefferson County schools in that state after years of vacillation back and forth as to which area desired the merger.

Often municipalities are plagued by the incorporation of areas along their borders into separate municipalities. This prevents central city expansion and fragments control of an economically homogeneous area. Sometimes cities expand between and around these newly created municipalities to the extent that the small units may be completely encompassed by the larger metropolis. This is true in Louisville, Kentucky, where numerous small municipalities are located within city boundaries. To prevent such developments, many states have placed limits on the incorporation of new municipalities. The provisions stipulate a minimum population, although in some instances the figure is so low as to be ineffective in preventing governmental fragmentation in the area. Others specify that new incorporations be located a minimum distance from the existing municipality or require a minimum area or property tax base. More effective are state provisions requiring counties to approve new incorporations or establishing boundary commissions to review both new incorporations and annexations. Seven states have such bodies, legally called by a variety of names.[13] Several others have advisory boundary commissions with no authority to bind local governments to their decisions.

More than two-thirds of the states allow their cities, but rarely any other local governments, extraterritorial jurisdiction. They then can provide services and regulate outside their boundaries. Sewage disposal, water supply, fire protection, and transportation facilities are the most commonly provided services. When it comes to regulation, cities may exercise full police powers in some instances, or impose health and sanitary controls, or exercise miscellaneous regulatory authority in others. While only four states—Alabama, Idaho, North Dakota, and South Dakota—allow cities general control over territory outside their boundaries, others permit them to impose quarantines, to regulate and prohibit cemeteries on their peripheries, and to control refuse disposal and pollution. States often authorize cities to control numerous other practices detrimental to the health and safety of their citizens such as prohibiting or regulating offensive industries such as slaughterhouses, explosive manufacturing, and prostitution.[14]

Often local communities find it expedient to cooperate in the provision of services. This involves interlocal contracts or agreements or the establishment of single- or multiple-purpose regulatory authority with regionwide financing. States often permit these activities, although not all states have conferred the broad authority that local governments regard as necessary.

Broader Delegations of Power

Broader state delegations of power to local jurisdictions long have been advocated, but progress has been incremental and results are limited. Early positive grants of authority took the form of *optional charter legislation*. Under this arrangement the legislature sets out in a statute several possible forms of government from which the localities can choose. For instance, a city may elect to operate under a mayor-council, commission, or council-manager government, and often may select from variations within these forms. Most states have enacted optional charter laws for cities, and nineteen have extended the alternative to counties as well.[15]

Another effort at greater local discretion has involved attempts to divide powers in the state constitution between the general powers perceived as belonging to the state, on the one hand, and local authority on the other. Powers for the localities included authority to levy certain taxes, construct and maintain streets and highways, zone property, inspect restaurants and hotels, collect trash, provide water and sewer services, hold fairs, and control traffic, to mention only some. The legislature, then, cannot deprive a local government of these specific powers. Nevertheless, the courts interpret them strictly using the exclusionary rule; that is, enumeration of certain powers excludes others.

Broader authority has also appeared in constitutional provisions allowing local jurisdictions to draw up and adopt their own charters and to amend them—a grant of authority common referred to as *home rule,* although the term is imprecise. Often these grants have included permission for local governments to manage "local affairs." Nevertheless, many did not contain such authorization, and it was assumed that such power accompanied the charter-making authority. Here, again, the courts are likely to interpret strictly any such general authority. Constitutional home rule progressed by starts and stops and its initial adoption in Missouri in 1875, with the highest interest occurring around 1912, in 1923–24, and during the 1950s. Today forty-one states permit home rule for cities and twenty-seven allow counties the same privilege.[16] Often such power has been eroded by imposition of tax and spending limits or other restrictive devices.

Local governments may exercise even greater authority in a few states that have adopted the *devolution of powers* approach developed by Jefferson B. Fordham, a professor of law, in 1953.[17] Under this arrangement, the state, subject to two exceptions, grants to the locality all authority not specifically denied it by state general law. The exceptions are the ability to enact "civil law governing civil relations" (relations between individuals) and power to define and prescribe punishment for felonies (major crimes). The Alaska Constitution, for example, stipulates that a "home rule borough or city may exercise all legislative powers not prohibited by law or by charter."[18] Devolution of powers, sometimes called "residual powers," shifts the burden of determining the extent of local authority from the courts to the legislature, which has to take positive action to prevent local exercise of authority, and bypasses Dillon's rule by requiring strict construction of *limitations* on local power. In this instance, local officials can ask themselves, "Is there any prohibition against taking this action?"

While a total of 21 states have granted authority to exercise all powers not denied to *some* of their local governments, only Alaska, Montana, and Pennsylvania have adopted the devolution of powers arrangement completely.[19] In addition, Texas, by virtue of a decision of its supreme court, has had it in operation for cities since 1948.[20] Except for Oregon, all the states amending their constitutions in regard to local government since 1953 have set out a general devolution of powers grant but then have imposed specific limitations on local authority.[21] Sometimes these have restrained local action in basic areas—e.g., taxation, indebtedness, control of park lands, and management of elections—with a consequent serious dilution of the general grant.[22]

The quantity of local discretion allowed and exercised by local governments defies exact quantification because of the wide diversity that exists, both among and within states, and because of the difficulties of uncovering all the facets. In Georgia, for example, the state constitution grants discretionary authority only to counties. New Mexico's constitution, on the other hand, gives certain discretionary powers to both cities and counties; however, both must submit their budgets to a state agency for review.[23]

In general, authority can be classified into four categories—structural, functional, personnel, and fiscal. For the most part, the broadest discretion is allowed to local governments in regard to structure and the least in finance. In personnel, the amount granted varies considerably from one function to another. To get some feel for the amount of discretion allowed, after examining legal and other documents, ACIR surveyed local and state officials and other experts about their perceptions as to the amount of discretion local governments legally could exercise in these four categories. The results for cities, counties, and towns in two of the categories, functions and finance, are set out in Table 4-2. Joseph F. Zimmerman devised an index for each type of local jurisdiction—including villages, townships, and boroughs as well as cities, counties, and towns—and then the ACIR staff created a composite index of these for each state. Table 4-3 ranks the states according to this index for all six types of local government together and breaks out cities and counties because of the great weight they carry in the composite.

TABLE 4-2
DISCRETIONARY AUTHORITY BY STATES: 1979

States	Index of cities		Index of counties		Index of towns	
	Functional areas (36)	Finance (13)	Functional areas (8)	Finance (5)	Functional areas (20)	Finance (7)
Alabama						
Alaska	X	X	X	X		
Arizona		X	X	X	X	
Arkansas						
California	X	X			X	X
Colorado						
Connecticut	X		**	**	X	
Delaware	X				X	
Florida	X					
Georgia	X					
Hawaii	–	*				
Idaho	X			•		
Illinois	X	X			X	X
Indiana						
Iowa	X					
Kansas	X					
Kentucky						
Louisiana	X	X	X	X	X	X
Maine	X	X			X	X
Maryland	X				X	
Massachusetts	X				X	
Michigan	X	X				
Minnesota	X		X			
Mississippi	X		X		X	
Missouri	X					
Montana	X		X		X	
Nebraska	X					
Nevada						
New Hampshire	X				X	
New Jersey	X				X	
New Mexico						
New York					X	
North Carolina	X		X		X	
North Dakota	X					
Ohio	X					
Oklahoma	X				X	
Oregon		X				
Pennsylvania	X	X	X	X		
Rhode Island	X		**	**	X	
South Carolina	X	X		X	X	X
South Dakota	X				X	
Tennessee		X				X
Texas	X	X				X
Utah	X				X	
Vermont	X					
Virginia	X	X				
Washington						
West Virginia	X					
Wisconsin	X					
Wyoming						

*There are only four local governments in Hawaii, i.e., County of Hawaii, County of Kauai, County of Maui, and City and County of Honolulu.

**There are no organized county governments in Connecticut and Rhode Island.

Source: 1979 survey by the Staff of the Advisory Commission on Intergovernmental Relations. *The States and Distressed Communities: The 1980 Annual Report.* A Report by the Advisory Commission on Intergovernmental Relations and the Staff of the National Academy of Public Administration, Report M-125 (Washington, D.C.: Advisory Commission on Intergovernmental Relations, May, 1981), pp. 54-55.

TABLE 4-3
STATES RANKED BY DEGREE OF LOCAL
DISCRETIONARY AUTHORITY, 1980

	A. Composite (all types of local units)	B. Cities only	C. Counties only	Degree of state Dominance of fiscal partnership*
1	Oregon	Texas	Oregon	2
2	Maine	Maine	Alaska	2
3	North Carolina	Michigan	North Carolina	1
4	Connecticut	Connecticut	Pennsylvania	2
5	Alaska	North Carolina	Delaware	1
6	Maryland	Oregon	Arkansas	2
7	Pennsylvania	Maryland	South Carolina	2
8	Virginia	Missouri	Louisiana	2
9	Delaware	Virginia	Maryland	1
10	Louisiana	Illinois	Utah	1
11	Texas	Ohio	Kansas	2
12	Illinois	Oklahoma	Minnesota	2
13	Oklahoma	Alaska	Virginia	1
14	Kansas	Arizona	Florida	2
15	South Carolina	Kansas	Wisconsin	1
16	Michigan	Louisiana	Kentucky	2
17	Minnesota	California	California	2
18	California	Georgia	Montana	3
19	Missouri	Minnesota	Illinois	2
20	Utah	Pennsylvania	Maine	2
21	Arkansas	South Carolina	North Dakota	1
22	New Hampshire	Wisconsin	Hawaii	3
23	Wisconsin	Alabama	New Mexico	2
24	North Dakota	Nebraska	Indiana	2
25	Arizona	North Dakota	New York	2
26	Florida	Delaware	Wyoming	2
27	Ohio	New Hampshire	Oklahoma	3
28	Alabama	Utah	Michigan	1
29	Kentucky	Wyoming	Washington	1
30	Georgia	Florida	Iowa	2
31	Montana	Mississippi	New Jersey	3
32	Washington	Tennessee	Georgia	2
33	Wyoming	Washington	Nevada	2
34	Tennessee	Arkansas	Tennessee	2
35	New York	New Jersey	Mississippi	3
36	New Jersey	Kentucky	New Hampshire	3
37	Indiana	Colorado	Alabama	2
38	Rhode Island	Montana	Arizona	2
39	Vermont	Iowa	South Dakota	2
40	Hawaii	Indiana	West Virginia	1
41	Nebraska	Massachusetts	Nebraska	3
42	Colorado	Rhode Island	Ohio	2
43	Massachusetts	South Dakota	Texas	3
44	Iowa	New York	Idaho	2
45	Mississippi	Nevada	Colorado	1
46	Nevada	West Virginia	Vermont	2
47	South Dakota	Idaho	Missouri	3
48	New Mexico	Vermont	Massachusetts	1
49	West Virginia	New Mexico	—	1
50	Idaho	—	—	2

*Key:

   1—State dominant fiscal partner: State share of state-local tax revenues equals 65 percent or more.

   2—State strong fiscal partner: State share of state-local tax revenues from 55–64 percent.

   3—State junior fiscal partner: State share of state-local revenues below 55 percent.

Source: Advisory Commission on Intergovernmental Realtions, *Measuring Local Discretionary Authority*, Report M-31 (Washington, D.C.: 1981), p. 59.

The ACIR survey revealed that nationwide cities received about an equal amount of discretionary authority in government structure and personnel and less discretion in finance. In addition, cities are much more likely to receive more powers than counties in all four categories. The major differences occur in government structure and functions. In most states, cities are subject to few restraints when they want to change their structure or take on new functions. Counties, on the other hand, with a few exceptions have been granted little discretionary authority in these areas. Other data in the survey show that towns in a number of states have discretionary powers either identical or nearly identical to those of cities and that villages in all but a few states have powers similar to those of cities. Townships, on the other hand, typically are awarded little discretionary authority.

The tendency is to look upon the state as the withholder of local power, and much truth is contained in this observation. But it should be noted that, in the past, localities have not rushed to take advantage of home-rule grants. Not a single Wisconsin city or village adopted a charter under home-rule legislation in thirty-five years, and in Maryland only five of the twenty-three counties and Baltimore City (treated as a county under Maryland law) have made use of a 1915 provision permitting county home rule. In similar fashion only six of West Virginia's sixty-eight cities responded to a constitutional home rule grant in the first seventeen years after the adoption of the so-called home rule amendment. Many years later the West Virginia Supreme Court of Appeals held that the amendment did not confer home rule.[24]

Limitations on Legislative Control

The general power of the state legislature over the local jurisdictions in the state is often modified by provisions of the state constitution. This adds another factor to interstate diversity as far as state-local relations are concerned.

Some state constitutions contain extremely lengthy and detailed local government sections. Oklahoma, for instance, has 14 pages on the division of the state into counties,[25] and Maryland includes the structure of the government of the City of Baltimore in its constitution and devotes an entire section to indebtedness.[26] The Maryland provision makes it impossible for either the state legislature or the city to change these provisions without a statewide popular vote on a constitutional amendment. In fact, this was exactly what happened some years ago when Baltimore wanted to construct a parking garage. All Maryland voters who wished could participate in the local decision.

Specific restrictions on state legislative action may prohibit the legislature from doing certain things such as abolishing counties. Similarly, as mentioned above, the constitution may restrict the legislature's ability to enact special local legislation applying to one jurisdiction. Further constitutional limitations on legislative control are imposed by specific lists of enumerated powers for local governments or by general grants of authority to them.

Provisions that neither restrict the state legislature directly nor make grants of authority to local jurisdictions may also limit the legislature. When state constitutions list counties, set out local elective officials, or prescribe the process for granting charters, for example, the state legislature is circumscribed in these matters. Many constitutions, for instance, provide for the election of a sheriff in each county. Despite changes in the form of government and the establishment of county police forces under an appointed chief in some large urban counties, the sheriff remains an elective official but with substantially reduced functions. The office is constitutionally protected from abolition by its inclusion in the state constitution.

The Status of Municipalities

The United States has more than 19,000 local jurisdictions classed by the Bureau of the Census as municipalities. These are cities, towns (New England towns are discussed below), villages, and boroughs (excepting the last named in Alaska that perform the functions of counties). The number increased by 1,083 between 1967 and 1982. Much of the increase came from a steady stream of suburban incorporations, especially in areas surrounding the larger central cities.[27]

All of these jurisdictions legally are *municipal corporations*, created by the authority of the state. Municipal corporations are legal "persons" in the eyes of the law, possessing a legal being over and above the identity of the citizens who compose them or make up their governments. They can exist in perpetuity, even though all the citizens residing there at the time of incorporation die or move away. They are authorized to conduct business in the corporate name, own and dispose of property, contract, and sue and be sued as the "City of _____" rather than as a group of individuals. On the initiative of local citizens, incorporation is sometimes handled by the state legislature, but often the responsibility is given to the courts or to county governing boards.

Municipal corporations differ from other public corporations, such as the Tennessee Valley Authority or the Federal Deposit Insurance Corporation, because they have the "power of local government." That is, they have the authority to adopt local laws, called ordinances. Another difference is that municipalities are created voluntarily at the request of their citizens for their own benefit rather than for the benefit of the citizens of the state as a whole. These two characteristics distinguish them from most counties as well as from most other local governments. These other governments, as quasi-municipal corporations, generally have some, but not all, of the powers of full municipal corporations. The municipal corporations have such powers as are set out in their charters, subject to any constitutional or state statutory provisions.

Every municipality, whether it is city, town, village, borough (except in Alaska), or even counties in some states, has a charter that sets out its boundaries, structure of government, and fundamental powers. These charters are ordinarily state statutes, although the charters for some municipalities may be local provisions adopted under state authority. The charter may be a *special* one designed for that jurisdiction alone and enacted by the state legislature. Or it may be a *general* one set out in the state code of general laws that applies to all municipalities or to all municipalities of a class (usually on a population basis). Many state legislatures follow the *optional charter* system and allow municipalities the option of selecting from one of several the legislature has enacted. Increasingly the states are turning to *home rule* and permitting the municipalities to draft their own charters and adopt them after submission to popular vote. Several charter systems may be in operation in a state.

A survey by the International City Management Association showed the following breakdown in types of charters for municipalities with populations in excess of 5,000—home rule, 38 percent; general charter, 23 percent; classification charters, 10 percent; optional charters, 7 percent, and other legal forms, 6 percent.[28] Larger cities are most likely to use home rule charters, but adoptions are spread throughout population groupings. The Northeast is the only area that has fewer than one-third of its cities with home rule.[29]

The Status of Counties

Counties are the most common, although not the most numerous, units of general local government in the United States. They exist throughout the nation, except in Connecticut, Rhode Island, and the District of Columbia. These two states have retained county boundaries for election purposes and judicial administration but they do not have organized county governments. A similar situation prevails in three counties in South Dakota, and Alaska has 29 census divisions with no organized local government.[30] Counties do not exist in limited portions of other states, such as in the independent cities of Virginia.

In some cities, including Baltimore, Boston, Denver, Honolulu, Indianapolis, Jacksonville, Nashville, New Orleans, New York, Philadelphia, and San Francisco, the municipality operates as a composite city-county, either as the result of city-county consolidation or of separation of the city from the county. Despite these exceptions, only about 12 percent of the nation's population is not served by specially organized county governments.[31] Although actually counties, subdivisions in Louisiana are called "parishes," and in Alaska units performing county functions are known as "boroughs."

Counties vary widely in area, size, government organization, functions, and legal powers.[32] Important responsibilities are vested in them in the South, Midwest, and West, but where they exist in New England they are relatively weak. Governments in rural counties have a very limited range of functions, while the big urban counties of the large metropolitan areas have taken on the complexion of cities in the services they perform. Indeed, much of the literature on local government refers to the "urban county" as if it were a distinctive type of quasi-city, quasi-county form of government.

Counties in most states are involuntary creations existing for the benefit of the state and not for the particular benefit of the citizens within the counties. The typical county administers state laws and does very little ordinance-making on its own. Consequently it is considered a quasi-municipal corporation, not a full municipal corporation. That is, it has some, but not all of the attributes of a full municipal corporation. What it does not have is general authority to enact ordinances. Nor does it ordinarily have a charter. The powers delegated to it by the state are set out in the state constitution and statutes.

To accommodate to recent urbanization trends, counties are increasingly being recognized as units of local self-government with powers of independent action. For example, a 1968 amendment to the Pennsylvania Constitution declares all counties to be municipal corporations. County functions, which traditionally concern public safety, corrections, education, libraries, health, welfare, and highway transportation, have been expanded to include such activities as air and water pollution control, mass transit, parks and recreation, housing, and zoning. These services ordinarily are provided to meet citizen demands, and often are in addition to those required by state law.

As noted earlier, 30 states provide for county home rule to enable counties to adopt charters and to operate more independently. When this occurs the status of counties is then changed so that they can be designated, for all practical purposes, as full municipal corporations because they have charters and are authorized to enact local legislation for the explicit benefit of their own citizens. Constitutional home rule modifies the traditional unitary relationship of the state and the counties and establishes a limited federal arrangement.

Home-rule counties make up a very small percentage of the more than 3,000 counties in the United States. There are only 75 charter counties.[33]

Baker v. *Carr* and subsequent reapportionment decisions of the 1960s provided impetus to the adoption of home-rule charters by reducing the impact of the lightly populated counties in both houses of the state legislatures. These counties, as a consequence, have become increasingly concerned about relying on urban-controlled legislatures to enact legislation affecting their internal affairs. This is the reverse of the earlier situation when urban counties sought to extract themselves from the yoke of rural-dominated legislatures.

The Status of Towns and Townships

The terms "town" and "township" are often confusing because they describe different entities in different places. In most of the nation small urban places are known as towns. They may or may not be incorporated as municipalities and have established governments. In some states they are a class of municipal corporations. In the six New England states, towns differ from both of those just presented. There they include both urban and rural areas. Like counties, they generally blanket the state, one town being immediately adjacent to the next with no intervening distance, except where cities or villages have replaced them or in a few "unorganized areas" where no local government exists at all.

Towns are the principal units of local government in New England. They are particularly well known for the use of the town meeting, which may be composed of all eligible citizens or may be representative in form and which is the town's chief policy forming body. Towns are classed as municipalities in New England constitutions, but their status seems to be more nearly that of a quasi-municipal corporation than full municipal corporations,[34] although many certainly have full municipal status. Their subordination to the state is complete, as exemplified by an action of the state legislature of Connecticut that, despite local opposition, declared that a bridge should be constructed and maintained at the expense of the specially-benefited towns.[35]

Counties in almost half the states are divided into townships with operating governments. Indiana is the only state, however, that uses townships for its entire area and population. In some states—for example, New Jersey, Pennsylvania, and Wisconsin—operating townships include only the territories outside municipalities. Township governments exist mainly in Northeastern and North Central states, but they may be basic units of rural government in other parts of the Midwest, in the Middle Atlantic states, and in a few other places. Because of their involuntary creation and their operation for the benefit of the state in general, townships are viewed as quasi-municipal corporations.

Most townships are small and about three-fifths of them have populations of fewer than 1,000 people.[36] They vary greatly in functions and governmental organization. They seem generally to be losing power and purpose except on the fringes of large urban areas, although some acquired a new lease on life when they received general revenue sharing funds from the federal government. Around larger urban areas, townships are increasing in power and may become full municipal corporations, relatively indistinguishable from cities. Regardless of size, structure, and function, they are in the same relation to the state as other local jurisdictions. They may have a limited (not general) authority to enact ordinances. This means that the state may confer specific power to adopt regulations pertaining to roads and bridges or to the construction of buildings, for example, but does not grant authority to legislate generally on local affairs.

Other Substate Jurisdictions

The state deals with many other substate governmental jurisdictions in its everyday operations. Most of these are special districts created by the state, one or more of its general local governments, or the private initiative of a group of citizens. In the latter instance, approval of some local authority, such as a circuit or district court, is often required. The districts may perform a single function or a combination of several, although over 90 percent engage in only one. Some states use them more freely than others.

Independent school districts comprise the most numerous—approximately 15,000—and the most important type of special districts. Nevertheless, there are almost 29,000 nonschool special district governments of various types in the United States, an increase of almost 3,000 in the five years between the latest two censuses.[37] The latter include fire protection, sanitary, soil conservation, airport, water, and recreation districts. Special districts may have their own taxing and bonding power, or they may be financed by fees for services.

Special districts are independent units of government, enjoying considerable autonomy from other local governments. They may be solely within a county, multicounty, or include parts of counties, towns, and municipalities. Some are interstate. Districts may blanket a state as school districts often do, or they may be confined to one area. Utilization of nonschool special districts has increased greatly in recent years. Many new districts were structured to cope with areawide problems in governmentally fragmented metropolitan areas, while others were established to provide urban services in unincorporated areas or as devices to circumvent tax and spending limits.

Created to deal with special problems, they reflect little uniformity in boundary or function. Some are very large and important, such as the Chicago Sanitary District; others may be concerned with the operation of a single library.

In addition to the state- and locally-created special district governments just discussed, more than 3,000 districts and agencies that are not regarded as independent governments have been established to qualify for national government aid. At least half of them cover more than one county. They include metropolitan-area councils of government, state planning and development districts, and comprehensive health planning agencies.

Also, statewide substate district systems have been established by 40 states.[38] A recent report by the Advisory Commission on Intergovernmental Relations states: "What this means is that there is a new kind of areawide agency proliferation that now is part of the mosaic of substate government . . . the pressure for areawide mechanisms for areawide problems will not fade away."[39]

Multifaceted relationships exist between officials of these subordinate (nonindependent) districts and state officials. State options in the creation, design, continuation, and control of such districts are limited by provisions of congressional statutes setting up requirements for grants-in-aid in some instances and by local and interest group pressures in others. There is a continuing effort to achieve identical boundaries between state-established and nationally sponsored subordinate districts and agencies, and more than one-third are now the same.

The districts mentioned above should be distinguished from local taxing and service districts (areas), with no governmental organizations, and created by local governments to permit service and tax differentials within their boundaries. Another type of nongovernmental district is that established for administrative convenience. Cities frequently have police precincts, fire districts, or other designated areas that they create or abolish at will. These have no independent governing authority.

The existence of thousands of special district governments makes control and coordination of them difficult and undermines general purpose governments. It complicates and makes almost unfathomable the maze of intergovernmental relations, and makes it difficult to know who speaks for the community; nevertheless, they are politically expedient devices in many instances. Sometimes local citizens can unite through a special district to solve a problem or offer a service that otherwise might involve the cooperation of several units of local government. As Daniel J. Elazar points out, special districts may even increase the independence of state and local interests in their relations with the national government by concentrating energy at key points and then letting the districts negotiate with the national agencies. He writes:

> In terms more familiar to the game of poker, the existence of special government institutions is a means of paying the ante that gives interests a right to sit in on the game, a license to negotiate and bargain with other governments and the interests they represent. Once the ante is

paid, the possibilities of coming out ahead are substantially equalized for all players, thus allowing local governments to serve local interests and not just administer national programs.[40]

The Problem of State Mandates

States frequently use their legal authority to mandate local actions, thus creating substantial conflict between the two levels of government. These *state mandates*—that is, state constitutional, legislative, executive, or administrative *requirements* or *limitations* on local government actions— often are regarded as unnecessary interference with their affairs. Moreover, states may impose financial obligations on local jurisdictions without any ameliorating funds or grant of taxing authority.

State officials, on the other hand, may regard the mandates as necessary to ensure that certain important functions are performed throughout the state, that uniform service standards operate, or that desirable social or economic goals are met. In addition, mandates can be used to pass costs along to local governments. Often, however, mandates reflect state legislative responses to private interest groups. For instance, the legislature may impose certain personnel requirements, such as the establishment of pension funds or maintenance of minimum personnel or salary levels, as the result of pressure from local police, firefighter, or teacher unions.

Whatever their derivation or the nobility of purpose associated with them, state mandates complicate the tasks of local officials in governing the community. They add additional elements and thus more complexity to the problems associated with decisionmaking and budgetary control. Moreover, they generate intergovernmental conflict.

Classification. Two of the many possible methods of classifying mandates help to explain the actions involved. A typology of *expenditure* mandates, worked out by the ACIR, sheds light on the reasons for local concern. It distinguishes five major types of expenditure mandates:

rules of the game mandates—relating to the organization and procedures of local government, e.g., the form of government, holding of local elections, and provisions of the criminal code that define crimes and call for certain punishment;

spillover mandates—dealing with new programs or enrichment of existing local government programs in highly intergovernmental areas such as education, health, welfare, hospitals, environment, and nonlocal transportation;

interlocal equity mandates—which require localities to act or refrain from acting to avoid injury to, or conflict with, neighboring jurisdictions, in areas including local land use regulations, tax assessment procedures and review, and environmental standards;

loss of local tax base mandates—where the state removes property or selected items from the local tax base, such as exemption of churches and schools from the property tax, and food and medicine from the sales tax; and

personnel benefit mandates—where the states set salary wage levels, working conditions, or retirement benefits.[41]

Catherine H. Lovell and her associates at the University of California, Riverside, using a more comprehensive definition, worked out a broader typology. It distinguishes mandates as either requirements or constraints and then subdivides these categories. Requirements can be either programmatic, specifying *what* is to be done, or procedural, concerned with *how* it is to be accomplished. The Lovell team emphasizes that to be considered programmatic, the requirement "must be judged as an *end-product* or *objective* in the delivery of some service or the performance of some function."[42] Within the programmatic category may be specifications as to the quality and quantity of the undertaking. The state might, for example, require all local school boards to provide vocational education in all high schools under their jurisdiction. The mandate may not indicate the quality of the vocational education program to be provided, the number of courses to be offered or students to be educated, or the extent of the education offered. The quality could be specified by stipulating the level of education to be reached by the students involved. A quantity mandate, on the other hand, might require a certain number of courses to be offered or specify the number of days a year the education would be provided.

Procedural mandates are directed toward modifying the behavior of local government officials or employees. In regulating the process of how a service is provided, states may require local officials to make reports, plan, keep records, and follow other specific practices. The local health department may be required to devise a plan for the prevention of venereal disease in the locality, prepare a budget setting out the anticipated costs and the revenues necessary to pay them, establish personnel standards to ensure the hiring of competent employees, and operate the personnel program according to a merit system. Record keeping certainly will be mandated and reports on progress required.

Mandates in the form of constraints, on the other hand, limit the discretion of local officials by setting out things they may not do. They are directed most often at financial matters, frequently limiting the kind or amount of local revenues that can be raised or spent.

Some of the mandates are imposed vertically, that is, they are directed at one program or agency. For instance, the state might specify that a police department establish a disability fund for police officers injured on the job. Other mandates, such as requirements for open meetings, might apply to all or most agencies. These are horizontal or cross-cutting mandates, similar to those discussed as imposed by the national government on the states in Chapter 3. In recent years, the horizontal type has become particularly important because they significantly increase the costs of providing public services and change the nature of service provision by adding subsidiary goals and requirements. The addition of a mandate for affirmative action for minorities and women, for example, to all local government hiring means that in selecting police officers or firefighters, for example, the local government must be concerned with redressing past discriminatory practices as well as with employing the most capable personnel. In some instances, the two goals may be incompatible.

Extent of Mandating. The extent of mandating differs from state to state as well as among government functions, types of requirements, and impacts within states. No nationwide data about all classes of state mandates have been gathered. The most extensive survey, that of expenditures by ACIR in 1976, found that in 77 specific program areas examined, almost half of the states (22) had 39 or more mandates requiring local expenditures. Solid waste disposal standards, special education programs, workmen's compensation for local personnel other than police, fire, and educational employees, and provisions related to retirement were the most prevalent.[43]

New York, with 60 of 77 possibilities, California with 52, Minnesota 50, and Wisconsin 50 were the states found most likely to require local expenditures, while the border and southern states imposed the fewest. West Virginia, with only 8, and Alabama with 11 exercised the most self-restraint.[44]

Fiscal Notes and Reimbursement. Local governments object particularly to mandates that impose financial burdens and complain that states often compel local undertakings without consideration of the costs involved. Consequently, more than two-thirds of the states now attach fiscal notes to legislation that requires local governments to engage in certain activities. They estimate the dollar costs involved. Significantly fewer states included fiscal notes with administrative rules.[45]

Having estimated the costs involved, however roughly, states are less inclined to pay them. Fewer than a third of the states authorize reimbursement, and it is unclear as to how much money has been paid out for this purpose. State funds appear to have been spent for mandated functions, nonetheless, even if not in the form of mandate reimbursement. A 1975 survey found that the median figure for the 20 states responding was 75 percent.[46]

ADMINISTRATIVE RELATIONSHIPS

The interactions of states and localities are most often administrative. Because of their dependence on local administrators for carrying out certain programs, state officials exercise substantial supervision of local activities. This administrative oversight has largely replaced the traditional pattern of direct state legislative supervision of local government. The need for flexibility and continuous supervision was beyond the capacity of part-time legislators.

Furthermore, as government became technical, professionals were required to understand its complex details.

The type, area, extent, degree, and effectiveness of state supervision exist in such confusing variation that only the most important can be discussed here. Although all states have established departments of local affairs to coordinate state-local administrative relations, by and large the supervision is on a functional basis. That is, the state department of health supervises local health services, and the state department of assessments oversees local property assessment. Scarcely any field of activity escapes some state supervision, but it tends to be most comprehensive in finance, health, highways, welfare, and education. To some extent supervisory interactions depend upon the distribution of functions among the levels of government. In states where the welfare function has been assumed by the state, for instance, relations in this field may exist only on an inter-mittent basis. In other states where welfare remains a local activity, state supervision of local welfare departments may be prominent in state-local interactions. At the same time, types of supervision may vary between wel-fare and health in the same state. In many states, for example, state depart-ments of health have broad authority over local health departments includ-ing the power to substitute state administration for local management if there is a health emergency. Nevertheless, the state is more likely to use its technical staffs to advise local units.

Techniques

Most state administrative supervision is low-key, relying mainly on persuasive devices and often providing assistance to the locality. Coercion is sometimes used, but most administrators find less rigid techniques more effective on a day-to-day basis. Heavy reliance on coercion effectively sub-stitutes state for local administration. If that is desirable, a transfer of func-tion would afford better results. The administrative techniques range widely, as shown in Figure 4–1, which reflects their increasing coerciveness.

State officials often have an opportunity to influence local actions in informal conferences occurring on a professional, political, or social basis. State and local meetings of the American Society for Public Administration, for example, seethe with informal discussions between state and local bureaucrats who use the occasion to confer in a less structured environment. The governor and a county executive may meet at a political party conven-tion or at a groundbreaking ceremony, or they may belong to the same

FIGURE 4-1 CONTINUUM OF DEVICES FOR STATE
ADMINISTRATIVE SUPERVISION OF LOCALITIES

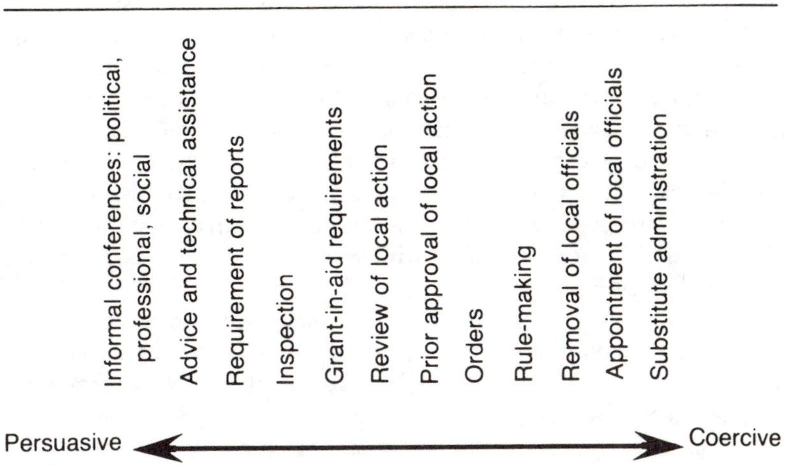

Informal conferences: political, professional, social

Advice and technical assistance

Requirement of reports

Inspection

Grant-in-aid requirements

Review of local action

Prior approval of local action

Orders

Rule-making

Removal of local officials

Appointment of local officials

Substitute administration

Persuasive ◄――――――――――――――――► Coercive

church, lodge, or country club. They may be neighbors or friends who interact often on a social basis. On any of these occasions they may discuss problems of mutual interest. Or they may simply pick up the telephone or write a letter and exchange information. In any case, state officials can use these opportunities to influence local officials. The influence, of course, runs in both directions.

The requirement of reports from the locality to the state, which is one of the mildest forms of supervision, is used extensively. These reports serve a dual purpose—they provide uniform information for the state agency and they focus the efforts of local officials and increase their awareness of what is expected. Sometimes the reports are never read and, once this is realized on the local level, they may be hastily prepared or the requirement ignored.

Inspection of local activities frequently occurs, especially in such functions as hospitals or property assessment. The inspections are often the occasion for consultation and advising as well as for establishing contacts that may prove fruitful at a later date. In some but not all instances the inspector has authority to demand changes. Considerable information can be exchanged at inspection time.

Because of their greater degree of specialization and often professionalism, state bureaucrats are frequently in a position to offer technical assistance. Local administrators, especially in smaller communities, are likely to be generalists or semi-professionals and therefore may not have the skills necessary to deal with some extremely complex problems confronting them. They may look to the officials of state government for aid in establishing pollution standards, designing highways, writing civil service examinations, marketing bonds, and handling many other functions. This assistance may come from bureaucrats in the corresponding department or agency such as a state air pollution expert's aid in establishing local air pollution standards, or from employees of a general agency established to provide assistance.

State agencies, in fact, are principal sources of technical assistance for local governments. In response to a survey by the General Accounting Office, respondents from counties and from cities over 100,000 population indicated that they contacted state agencies for technical aid more frequently than they did federal departments, regional councils, interstate organizations, colleges and universities, state-local associations, or private consultants. Moreover, local officials in general preferred state over federal technical assistance because dealing with their states required less paperwork and presented fewer problems.[47]

Many state colleges and universities are organized to provide technical assistance to local governments. For example, the Institute for Governmental Service at the University of Maryland advises that state's communities on such matters as charter revision and codification of ordinances and undertakes such studies as those on financial administration, personnel, water and sewer rates, and annexation.

North Carolina has gone even further and established an Institute of Government at the University of North Carolina at Chapel Hill that not only supplies technical information and research services but also prepares manuals for local officials on the operation of their offices and conducts training schools and workshops for them. Technical assistance of this sort can serve to upgrade the performance of local bureaucrats and can be a two-way street in the exchange of information. Other states include these activities in state offices for local affairs established as a part of the general administration machinery of the state and not in a university setting.

Some state officials have at their disposal more rigorous controls that can be used if the persuasive devices fail. State statutes may permit state agencies to withhold grants-in-aid to local communities if the conditions concerning them are not met. This action is likely to get results if the sum of money is large enough and the locality is not strongly opposed to the requirement. In addition, state officials may be authorized to review actions taken by local officials (state boards of equalization may review local tax assessments); approve contemplated actions before they are taken (prior approval of a state board of school finance may be required for local school budgets); and issue permits (a state health department permit may be required for liquid waste disposal). They may also license local employees (state departments of education license school teachers and a state housing agency may license local inspectors of modular housing and mobile homes); issue orders (a state water authority may order localities to construct sewage treatment plants), and make rules and regulations (often to set standards in health and safety).

Some states permit the governor or the head of a state agency to remove local officials or employees. In Wisconsin, for example, the governor may remove district attorneys, sheriffs, and other local officials, and in New York all elected sheriffs, county clerks, registers and, excepting New York City, district attorneys may be removed by the governor.[48] The threat of removal may be sufficient to force a resignation, as happened in the celebrated case of the resignation of New York City Mayor James J. Walker when threatened with removal by Governor Franklin D. Roosevelt. Some states go even further and permit governors to appoint local officials on a regular basis. In Maryland, for example,the governor appoints the boards of education for most counties. In Alabama the governor may appoint a special force of inspectors to assist him in locally enforcing state law. Heads of state agencies also may occasionally appoint local administrators, especially in health.

Substitute administration, in which state performance of some local function is temporarily instituted is the ultimate in state control. It is used only in crisis situations. It is most widely authorized in public health emergencies, with most states providing for state takeover of local health services if local officials do not perform satisfactorily, although it probably is employed more frequently in instances of financial crisis when a local government is threatened with bankruptcy. State officials realize that a lowered credit rating for one jurisdiction affects the ratings of both the parent government and that of other local units in the state. When New York City faced insolvency in the mid-1970s, among the actions taken to assist it was the creation of the Emergency Financial Control Board to supervise city finances.[49] Other instances of the use of substitute administration occur when state law enforcement officials supersede local officials in times of crisis or when the state national guard is ordered to take over by the governor in emergencies such as floods, fires, riots, or other situations where local officials cannot handle the problem.

State Offices for Local Affairs

State offices for local affairs, while not new, have proliferated recently and broadened in scope. These are agencies organized for the direct provision of state technical services to localities and for dissemination of information about the availability of services from other agencies. They serve as clearinghouses for information on state and national matters affecting localities and bring the problems faced by local government to the attention of the governor.

The first such office was the Pennsylvania Bureau of Municipal Affairs in the Department of Internal Affairs, created in 1919. Its functions were limited primarily to supervising municipal finance and compiling financial statistics.[50] In a short time a few other states created similar agencies. Not until the late 1950s, however, did states begin to shift emphasis from controlling local governments to providing services for them. The state offices for local affairs established since then are usually non-interfering and constitute state recognition of responsibility for dealing with local—and particularly urban—problems.

All states operate such agencies.[51] Impetus for their general creation came from a study, *The States and the Metropolitan Problem*, by the Council of State Governments to the National Governors' Conference in 1956, recommending that each state establish an agency to determine the needs of urban and nonurban areas. The Governors' Conference, and later the United States Conference of Mayors, the National League of Cities, and the National Association of Housing and Redevelopment Officials endorsed the idea.[52] The national Demonstration Cities and Metropolitan Development Act of 1966 further encouraged the establishment of such state agencies by authorizing grants-in-aid "to assist States to make available information and data on urban needs and assistance programs and activities, and to provide technical assistance to small communities with respect to the solution of urban problems."[53]

Functions of the agencies vary considerably. Joseph Zimmerman groups them into eight categories: (1) advice and information; (2) research and publications; (3) planning and area development; (4) preparation of policy recommendations affecting local governments for the governor; (5) promotion of interlocal cooperation; (6) conducting training programs for local officials; (7) coordination of state services and federal grants, and (8) control functions. Few agencies exercise control functions; those that do regulate financial activities by prescribing forms, revising budgets, approving bond issues, and the like. Recently new functions have been added to the duties of the state offices for local affairs in several states, giving them characteristics of strong, independent operating departments.

State agencies for local affairs appear to be important to local units chiefly as coordinators of national programs. This is most evident from the perspective of officials of the smaller cities who look to them for assistance on these matters and for technical assistance, program evaluation, and financial aid. Larger cities, on the other hand, have their own channels of communication with the national government; moreover, they do not rely on these agencies for technical and financial assistance. They regard state and local affairs agencies as more valuable in the coordination of state programs. Only 129 officials of 838 respondents to a survey of chief administrative officers in cities of more than 10,000 cited state agencies as making significant contributions to local problem solving. This attitude may have resulted from the fact that most state agencies for local affairs were in their infancy at the time of the survey (1969).[54] Responses also indicated that large cities with populations of over 50,000 initiated more contacts with the state agencies, communicating with them about once a week, while smaller cities began less interaction. The state agencies, however, originated contacts with the smaller communities about 25 percent more often than with the larger local jurisdictions.

Perspectives on State Assistance

The effectiveness of the technical assistance local governments receive from the state is unclear. Surveys provide conflicting assessments. The aforementioned General Accounting Office survey, while it did not deal with state offices of local affairs specifically, revealed that three-fourths of those who expressed an opinion had a favorable view of the technical assistance they had received from the state.[55] Looked at from the state level, the assistance was deemed satisfactory as well. A total of 58 percent of the governors gave it this rating in an ACIR survey conducted about the same time. Regarding the perceptions of local officials, however, the latter survey found that state municipal leagues, composed of local officials from throughout the respective states, did not agree. Only 13 percent of the leagues rated it satisfactory while more than two-thirds found it unsatisfactory.[56]

STATE-LOCAL COOPERATIVE MECHANISMS

States have turned to a variety of state-local advisory agencies to deal with the complexities resulting from the intergovernmentalization of most governmental functions. In some instances officials hope that by consulting local administrators and getting their advice before action is taken, they can reduce the friction in state-local affairs. In other cases their efforts have been aimed at reforming local institutions. The advisory agencies supplement the state agencies for local government, discussed previously.

In general, intergovernmental advisory agencies are of two types. States such as New Jersey, Florida, and Texas have established broad-based commissions with sufficient resources to initiate policy recommendations, perform research, and follow up on recommendations. At the other end of the scale, organizations comprised principally of local officials and serving primarily as forums for discussions of intergovernmental problems were created.

State advisory commissions on intergovernmental relations operate in 14 states. These agencies vary in design and function, but they are usually responsible for at least five activities. They (1) serve as a forum for consultation by state and local policy makers; (2) constitute a clearinghouse for information on intergovernmental issues; (3) function as a research agency with capacity to develop research recommendations; (4) become an advocate for these recommendations; and (5) provide technical assistance to state and local agencies in a variety of program areas. Most of them include representatives from various types of local governments, the public, and both legislative and executive branches of state government.[57]

Another type of advisory agency is directed more toward the reform of local institutions and processes. State commissions on local government have been created in a number of states under a variety of titles. These bodies draw into the deliberations both private citizens and local government representatives and approach urban problems from a perspective combining state, local, and nongovernmental concerns.[58] According to Patricia S. Florestano and Vincent L. Marando, these organizations differ from other efforts to reform local government because of their emphasis on a comprehensive policy for the entire state on local reorganization and service delivery. Their use recognizes that current policy, resulting from decades of incremental accumulation of policies, has emerged as "inconsistent and sometimes contradictory."[59] Except for California, Florestano and Marando found surprising consistency among the recommendations of the respective commissions. Not surprisingly, their impact has been slight, suggesting that the proposals lacked political feasibility.

THE STATES AND URBAN PROBLEMS

States were roundly criticized during the 1960s and early 1970s for their failures to deal with the problems facing urban areas. Much of the opprobrium directed at them was deserved. They have, after all, a major voice in determining the viability and vitality of local governments. In their hands rests the only authority enabling local jurisdictions to solve the problems that face them. They play a role in any structural, fiscal, or functional reforms the localities make. If states wish, they can intervene to solve conflicts between local jurisdictions or to restructure local governments. They are important intergovernmental managers for national government financial assistance going to localities. They can use their authority to veto, reduce, or obstruct national aid.

Moreover, states have not always exhibited sensitivity to the problems of their local units. For a long time they failed to deal with difficulties that urban areas, especially large cities, were experiencing as their tax bases shrank, the strain on their resources intensified, and quality of life within them deteriorated. Middle-income whites had fled to the suburbs, leaving the central cities with rising social service loads and less money to pay for them. Inflation, public employee militancy, and inadequate revenue sources, among other factors, intensified the problems, and some large cities, including New York, Cleveland, Detroit, Gary, and Newark, found themselves in dire financial straits.

Smarting from the incessant criticism and inspired by increased urban leverage in reapportioned state legislatures, states began in the decade of the 1970s to display more concern for their urban areas. They moved in many ways to alleviate their difficulties, although not all acted in the same manner or to the same degree. Some granted broader taxing authority to local governments, shared state taxes and receipts, or assumed complete or greater responsibility for such large expenditure items as education and welfare. As discussed earlier in this chapter, general discretionary authority was broadened in some instances. Some tried to target state financial assistance so that instead of being spread somewhat evenly over the state, as had often been the case, it was directed at the most distressed communities.[60] A handful of states authorized the establishment of urban enterprise zones. Under this concept, a distressed geographic area would be targeted for financial incentives to spur economic development. Business locating in the zone might receive tax credits, venture capital loans, property assessment deferments, and other inducements designed to attract developers to the area.

It was long assumed that the national government with its massive urban programs targeted its funds to needy areas better than did the states. Recent research has shown this not to be true. In a study of central cities in standard metropolitan statistical areas, Thomas R. Dye and Thomas L. Hurley found "little empirical support for the idea that the federal government was *more* responsive to the needs of the cities than were the state governments." They discovered that

> . . . on the whole, state grants-in-aid appeared *more* closely associated with urban needs than federal grants-in-aid. . . . This generalization is subject to some exemptions; federal grants-in-aid are more closely associated with public assistance rates, death rates, and aged populations than state grants-in-aid. But even with regard to these indicators of dependent and aged populations, differences between state and federal responsiveness were slight. More importantly, *state* grants-in-aid were more closely associated with size, growth rate, density, age of city, and segregation than *federal* grants-in-aid. Finally, *state* grants-in-aid were negatively associated with resource measures, more so than federal grants-in-aid, suggesting that state grants were more redistributive in their impact among cities than federal grants.[61]

Another study by Fred Tietelbaum and Alice E. Simon examined the the expenditure of combined state grants and federal funds passed through the states to localities as contrasted with federal grants-in-aid going directly to local governments. Combined school district and city budgets for 59 of the nation's largest cities (excluding New York City and Washington, D.C.) were used. Their study indicated that, in general, combined state-federal aid is consistently more responsive to distressed cities than is direct federal aid and becomes more responsive across time.[62]

A study by Robert M. Stein of state aid, aggregated on the national level, to cities of over 25,000 population produced similar results. When Stein replicated the analysis using disaggregated statistics for individual states, however, he could not find a pattern of targeting to needy communities through state aid. His findings suggest that targeting at the aggregate level results from the successful efforts of a small number of states to target funds.[63] Nine states consistently directed their funds to needy areas between 1967 and 1977. They were Minnesota, New Jersey, Michigan, Massachusetts, Wisconsin, California, New York, Iowa, and Ohio. Stein suggests that there are alternative means of dealing with urban problems. Several states have developed comprehensive urban strategies, combining numerous approaches, for this purpose.[64]

LOCAL ASSISTANCE TO STATES

Not all the assistance provided in state-local relations comes from the states. Local governments are frequently in a position to help their states in a number of ways. Their officials often act as state agents in administering state programs because of legal requirements of state statutes—for instance, the county assessing property for state as well as for city and county taxation and local police enforcing national, state, and local laws. Local governments often aid in informal ways, too. The expertise of a local civil servant may provide technical assistance in a state program, or the facilities of the local school system may be used by state highway officials for a meeting to discuss a new transportation program. The city designated as the state capital or a locality that has within its boundaries large state institutions such as a state college or a state university may find itself providing many kinds of services for the state, ranging from parking to the protection of property. There may be little or no recompense for such efforts, except the prestige and commercial advantages of having a state institution located within its boundaries, because state property is exempt from local taxation.

STATE-LOCAL RELATIONS IN FISCAL MATTERS

In financial matters more than in any other realm of state-local affairs the state's attention is likely to be focused on its local units. In this field more assistance, supervision, regulation, and conflict are likely to occur. States and localities share the burden of financing most of the nation's domestic programs and fiscal interactions are prominent in most matters of mutual concern. Their fiscal fates are intertwined.

In the early years, little theorizing took place about state-local fiscal relations, according to the late W. Brooke Graves, a leading authority on the development of intergovernmental relations. The tendency was to act on the basis of certain fundamental assumptions: (1) government itself was a necessary evil and the less we had of it the better; (2) governments should do as little as possible; and (3) taxes should be held to an absolute minimum because money spent by the government did not benefit the community's economic life as did private expenditures. In Graves' words:

> Some changes in these attitudes became noticeable around the turn of the [twentieth] century as government began to expand and assume a more positive role, but by this time, the constitutional and statutory framework, not to mention the psychological climate of the community, had become so fixed and rigid that progress was always difficult and often impossible. Local units found themselves confined in a constitutional and statutory strait-jacket. Limitations applied to the kinds of taxes and the subjects taxed, as well as to the tax rates. Strict limitations were imposed upon the power to contract indebtedness, and no debt could be authorized without approval in a popular referendum, although this is now known to have little or no deterrent effect on the incurring of public debt. These restrictions continued through the end of World War II.[65]

Operating under Dillon's Rule, localities could levy only those taxes authorized by state statute and thus specific restrictions were generally unnecessary to bind them. Furthermore, some states adopted tax limitations, often by constitutional amendment, that imposed a severe financial strain on localities. Taxation in excess of these limits required approval by referendum. When coupled with debt limits and state requirements that localities finance certain functions, little discretion over finance remained with local officials. A constitutional amendment in West Virginia in the 1930s limiting property taxes threw the state into a financial crisis. Reductions of up to two-thirds in property tax revenues (almost the only source of local funds) produced early school closings, dismissal of public employees, and curtailment of vital services. One municipality did not have enough money to operate its water system and another could not pay its police officers. The obvious remedy, an increase in property assessments, was politically infeasible. The assessors were elected by the voters, and it would have been political suicide to increase assessments in the midst of the declining land values of the depression years.

Many restrictions were substantially loosened over the years, most notably with respect to revenue sources. Local governments have been allowed to diversify their revenue systems and many now can impose sales and income taxes as well as levies on property. In addition, local officials have found ways to skirt some restrictions: the increased use of revenue bonds (repaid from the earnings of an enterprise) to finance local projects is an illustration. National grants-in-aid, particularly general revenue sharing, which made available substantial amounts of money for local use, also got localities to some extent out from under the state's fiscal thumb. Never-theless, many constitutional and statutory restrictions on local finance still applied, and recently another round of tax and spending limits swept through many states, limiting local options anew.

State Administrative Supervision Over Local Finance

States exercise substantial administrative supervision over the fiscal activities of their local governments. These run the gamut of the previously-discussed administrative controls. They include, for example, state certifica-tion of assessors, supervision of the assessment of property for taxation and of tax collections, and approval by a state unit of local agency budgets, tax levies (imposition of taxes), and the incurring of debt. Also included are control of the debt procedures such as the marketing and repayment of bonds; supervision of accounting, auditing, and financial reporting practices; and selection of depositories for public funds. Some states require the purchase of certain items for local use, such as school buses, to be made through state agencies.

State fiscal supervision leads to both cooperation and conflict between the state and local levels of government. Technical assistance in many areas of finance, training programs for local officials and employees, and other fields result from state-local cooperation. Despite these benefits, local personnel resent the strictures and red tape involved in following state direction. A recent survey of local officials found that 55 percent of the local administrators regarded "intergovernmental red tape" as a major impediment to doing a good job.[66] Nevertheless, the continuous interface provided by state supervision opens major paths for state-local communi-cations.

State Financial Aid

Local governments have become increasingly more dependent on outside fiscal assistance from the state and national governments. During the past quarter century, aid from both sources grew rapidly. Although state assis-tance did not keep up with the rise in federal aid, it remains the principal source of outside funds for local governments.

Rationale for State Aid. States give financial assistance to local juris-dictions for a variety of reasons. There may be a need for property tax relief for citizens, and shared funds can be used to lower or keep down property taxes, the principal local revenue source. In other instances states may want to equalize resources among jurisdictions, helping communities such as central cities of major metropolitan areas where needs and resources do not match.

Another rationale for state aid is the desire to compensate local governments for tax losses resulting from state exemption of certain kinds of property from taxation. A local government that contains within its boundaries a college or university, for example, cannot collect property taxes from the institution, either because the state owns it or because it has been exempted from taxation by state law. Many kinds of property are excluded, although state laws vary as to which categories. Property belonging to religious, charitable, and educational organizations almost always is exempt, and sometimes that owned by patriotic or veterans groups is taken off the tax rolls as well. Often the state makes homestead exemptions for a certain amount of residential property and also may include household goods and other personal property. The legislature may authorize payments in lieu of taxes to the affected local jurisdiction.

State assistance also may be rationalized on practical grounds. State tax systems can respond more effectively than local ones to local needs for diverse and economically responsible revenue sources because of the superior position of the state to localities in levying and collecting taxes. Moreover, state sharing is often preferable to allowing local diversification of taxes because aid can be extended to a large number of local jurisdictions whose small size, lack of administrative capacity, and meager tax base may make extension of new taxing authority of little value. State assistance also may be preferable to state assumption of the local activity because it permits retention of decentralized authority, leaving control of the function in local hands.

It should be noted that not all state assistance to local governments results from a sense of altruism by state governments. Much of it is produced by pressures that local governments or private citizens bring to bear. Occasionally these even take the form of court actions as in a suit filed against Massachusetts by the city of Boston asking reimbursement of revenues it was losing on tax-exempt property—about 61 percent of the land there.[67] State assumption of a greater share in the financing of public education resulted in part from a 1971 California case, *Serrano* v. *Priest*,[68] that asked for equalization of school expenditures among districts. The subsequent decision by the California Supreme Court requiring equalization of school financing throughout the state stimulated state actions in this direction nationwide.

Aid Diversity. In discussing state financial assistance to local governments, the substantial diversity among the states must be kept in mind. Not only are some local jurisdictions in some states needier than those in others, but state responses differ as to the amount, allocation by function, recipient jurisdictions, and mechanisms for distribution. In states where the state government provides a higher proportion of the services offered by the two levels, or where local governments are allowed a freer hand to tax, less direct aid may be required. For example, Hawaii pays 84.5 percent of the total state-local general expenditures from state sources. Consequently, it may not need to give as much direct fiscal assistance to its local units as states at the other end of the scale—Texas, Nevada, Nebraska and New York—that supply less than half of the state-local expenditures.

In one study a correlation of direct state spending and grants-in-aid for public education (excluding higher education), highways, welfare, and all state functions together revealed a mixed picture. A modest negative relation between state expenditures for highways and welfare and state intergovernmental aid appeared, meaning that states that spent heavily for each of these services tended to rank low among the states in the amount of grants-in-aid provided. For education and the state aggregate functions, however, no systematic relationship, either inverse or direct, was shown.[69]

Functions and Jurisdictions Aided. Education currently receives approximately two-thirds of the state aid funds. In fact, more than half the money spent for education comes from the states. Public welfare, highways, and health and hospitals, in that order, receive the next highest amounts of state money. Note the figures in Table 4-4, adjusted to eliminate federal funds.

The dominance of educational assistance means that all types of local governments do not share equally in the states' largess. School districts receive the largest share, followed by counties, and then municipalities. The degree of local dependence is also in that order as well with school districts receiving $1.05 for every dollar they raise while counties get about 71 cents and municipalities 61 cents.

ADJUSTING RELATIONSHIPS

This chapter has pointed out the highly interdependent nature of state-local relations. Because of the common cultural, political, and economic attributes they share, states and the local jurisdictions within their borders have closer relationships than those among the states, between the states and the national government, or among localities.

Also stressed has been the diversity in the relationships between the states and their local governments. Each state has established its own model of state-local relations and functional assignments. Nevertheless, certain general patterns prevail throughout the nation—general state superiority in a legal sense with localities having only those powers given to them by the state; local political leverage that enables communities to mitigate state control; varying degrees of administrative supervision among and

TABLE 4-4
FUNCTIONAL DISTRIBUTION OF STATE AID TO
LOCAL GOVERNMENT: NOMINAL AND ADJUSTED
FOR FEDERAL PASS-THROUGH, 1976-77
(Millions of dollars)

Category	Nominal	Less pass-through
Education	$36,428	$31,264
Public welfare	9,243	4,272
Highways	3,467	3,235
Health and hospitals	1,411	998
Sewerage	467	453
Urban mass transportation	475	475
Housing urban renewal	294	291
Other general government	—	—
Manpower training	635	—
Older Americans	109	—
Law enforcement	810	342
General local support	5,527	5,527
Other	1,753	1,500
Total	60,619	48,357
Exhibit: Noneducation	24,191	17,093

Source: Advisory Commission on Intergovernmental Relations, *Recent Trends in Federal and State Aid to Local Governments*, Report M-118 (Washington, D.C.: June, 1980), p. 11.

within states; significant amounts of state financial assistance; and a growing reliance on state aid.

State-local relations are changing, just as are relations among other governments. This results partly from alterations at the national level and in part from actions states and localities take themselves and from other forces. Because of recent shifts in national financial assistance practices, states now play an even more dominant role in regard to their localities. Rather than federal funds shoring up local political power as they have in the recent past, they now often enhance the state role as manager of intergovernmental programs and focus local attention on state capitals rather than on Washington, D.C. Meanwhile, state governments have begun to loosen the shackles on the localities, granting more discretion in local affairs, although often increasing financial strictures at the same time. Once having tasted the political power that direct federal aid afforded them, local governments continue to flex their muscles and exert influence in the political arena. Each level continues to joust for position.

NOTES

1. Glenn Abney and Thomas A. Henderson, "Federal and State Impact on Local Governments: The View of Local Officials," A paper presented to the Annual Meeting of the American Political Science Association, Washington, D.C., September 1–4, 1977.

2. *The New Federalism: Possibilities and Problems in Restructuring American Government*, A Conference of the Woodrow Wilson International Center for Scholars (Washington, D.C.: 1973), p. 33.

3. W. Brooke Graves, *American Intergovernmental Relations* (New York: Charles Scribner's Sons, 1964), p. 710.

4. John F. Dillon, *Commentaries on the Law of Municipal Corporations*, 5th ed. (Boston: Little, Brown and Co., 1911), Vol. 1, Sec. 237. Italics in original.

5. 24 Iowa 455, 462, 463 (1868).

6. Council of State Governments, *State-Local Relations* (Chicago: 1946), p. 141.

7. 191 U.S. 207 at 220–21 (1903).

8. 262 U.S. 182 (1923).

9. Roscoe C. Martin, *The Cities and the Federal System* (New York: Atherton Press, 1965), p. 32.

10. Advisory Commission on Intergovernmental Relations, *State Constitutional and Statutory Restrictions Upon the Structural, Functional, and Personnel Powers of Local Government*, Report A–12 (Washington, D.C.: Government Printing Office, 1962), p. 38. In subsequent notes this agency will be cited as ACIR.

11. ACIR, *Measuring Local Discretionary Authority* Report M–31 (Washington, D.C.: 1981), p. 59.

12. ACIR, *State and Local Roles in the Federal System* (Washington, D.C.: 1981), Chapter 6.

13. Alaska, California, Iowa, Michigan, Minnesota, Oregon, and Washington. ACIR tabulation based on Leonard Press, *Survey of States with Boundary Review Agencies*, prepared for the Lane County Local Government Boundary Commission, Eugene, Ore.: 1978. See ACIR, *The State and Local Roles in the Federal System*.

14. See David E. Hunt, "The Constitutionality of the Exercise of Extraterritorial Powers by Muncipalities," *University of Chicago Law Review*, Vol. 45, No. 1 (Fall, 1977), pp. 154–56.

15. Melvin B. Hill, Jr., *State Laws Governing Local Government Structure and Administration* (Athens, Ga.: Institute of Government, University of Georgia, 1978), p. 43.

16. Ibid. For an account of home rule development, see William N. Casella, Jr., "A Century of Home Rule," *National Civic Review*, October, 1975, pp. 441–450.

17. Jefferson B. Fordham, *Model Constitutional Provisions for Municipal Home Rule* (Chicago: American Municipal Association, 1953).

18. *Constitution of Alaska*, Art. 1, Section 11. A borough is classed as a county.

19. ACIR, *Measuring Local Discretionary Authority*, p. 20.

20. Forwood v. The City of Taylor, 147 TEX. 161 at 165; 214 SW. 2nd 282 at 286 (1948).

21. The Oregon Constitution sets out a list of county powers with which the legislature cannot interfere. ACIR, *Measuring Local Discretionary Authority*, p. 2.

22. For example, see *Constitution of the Commonwealth of Massachusetts*, Art. LXXXIX of the Articles of Amendment.

23. ACIR, *The States and Distressed Communities: The 1981 Report*. A Report by the ACIR and the Staff of the National Academy of Public Administration (Washington, D.C.: Government Printing Office, 1982).

24. Major exceptions occur in Arizona, Illinois, Maine, and Texas where financial authority is relatively broad.

25. *Constitution of Oklahoma*, Art. XVII.

26. *Constitution of Maryland*, Art. XI.

27. U.S. Bureau of the Census, *Governmental Units in 1982, Preliminary Report No. 1, of the 1982 Census of Governments*, GC82 (P)-1, June, 1982.

28. Alan Klevit and ICMA Staff, "City Councils and Their Functions in Local Government," *Municipal Year Book, 1972* (Washington, D.C.: International City Management Association, 1972), p. 15 (1971 survey).

29. Ibid.

30. ACIR, *Profile of County Government*, Report M–72 (Washington, D.C.: 1971), p. 10.

31. Census of Governments, 1977.

32. Victor Jones, Jean Gansel, and George F. Howe, "County Government Organization and Services," *Municipal Year Book, 1972*, pp. 211–239.

33. ACIR, *State and Local Roles in the Federal System*, Chapter 6.

34. "Towns in New England states, and townships or towns in states that have adopted the general township organization system, partake of the nature of municipal corporations, being referred to sometimes as 'quasi corporations' or 'quasi-municipal corporations' possessing to a certain extent corporate capacity, and sometimes with the general control of matters of local concern. . . . Being merely quasi corporations or quasi-municipal corporations, towns or townships are not endowed with the full and plenary powers usually conferred by charter or general law on municipal corporations proper, and the mere conferment of additional and special powers on a town does not convert it into an actual municipal corporation." *Corpus Juris Secundum* 4.

35. State v. Williams, 35 A 24, 68 Conn. 131.

36. 1977 Census of Governments.

37. 1982 Census of Governments, Preliminary Report No. 1. There are also "dependent" school districts that are agencies of other governments.

38. ACIR, *Striking a Better Balance* (Washington, D.C.: 1973), p. 26.

39. ACIR, *Regional Decision Making: New Strategies for Substate Districts*. Vol. 1 of *Substate Regionalism and the Federal System* (Washington, D.C.: 1973), p. 222.

40. Daniel J. Elazar, "Fiscal Questions and Political Answers in Intergovernmental Finance," *Public Administration Review*, Vol. XXXII, No. 5 (September/October, 1972), p. 477.

41. See ACIR, *State Mandating of Local Expenditures*, Report A–67 (Washington, D.C.: July, 1978), p. 16.

42. Catherine H. Lovell, Robert Kneisel, Max Neiman, Adam Z. Rose, and Charles A. Tobin, *Federal and State Mandating on Local Governments: An Exploration of Issues and Impacts,* Final Report to the National Science Foundation, June 20, 1979 (Riverside, Cal.: Graduate School of Administration, University of California, Riverside, 1979), pp. 35–36.

43. ACIR, *State Mandating,* pp. 2–3.

44. Ibid., pp. 45–46.

45. Jane C. Roberts, "States Respond to Tough Fiscal Challenges," *Intergovernmental Perspective,* Spring, 1980, p. 24.

46. ACIR, *The States and Intergovernmental Aids,* Report A–59 (Washington, D.C.: February, 1977), p. 34.

47. General Accounting Office, *State and Local Government's Views on Technical Assistance,* Report GGD 78–58 (Washington, D.C.: July 12, 1978), pp. 38, 48.

48. *Constitution of the State of Wisconsin,* Art. VI, Sec. 4; *Constitution of the State of New York,* Art. III, Sec. 13.

49. See Martin Shefter, "New York City Fiscal Crisis: The Politics of Inflation and Retrenchment," *The Public Interest,* No. 47 (Summer, 1977), pp. 98–127.

50. Joseph F. Zimmerman, "State Agencies for Local Affairs: The Institutionalization of State Assistance to Local Governments," Mimeo. (Albany: State University of New York at Albany, Graduate School of Public Affairs, Local Government Center, 1968). See also George H. Klaus, Jr., "Role of the State Department of Community Affairs in Training and Development for Local Governments: Pennsylvania Experience," *State and Local Government Review,* Vol. 13, No. 2 (May, 1981), pp. 56–61.

51. ACIR, *State-Local Bodies: ACIRs and Other Approaches,* Report M–124 (Washington, D.C.: Government Printing Office, March, 1981), p. 3.

52. John N. Kolesar, "The States and Urban Planning and Development," in *The States and the Urban Crisis,* edited by Alan K. Campbell (Englewood Cliffs, N.J.: Prentice-Hall, Inc. for the American Assembly, 1970), p. 116.

53. Public Law 89–754, sec. 901.

54. A. Lee Fritschler, B. Douglas Harman, and Morley Segal, "Federal-State-Local Relationships," *Urban Data Service,* December, 1969. (Washington, D.C.: International City Management Association, 1969).

55. General Accounting Office, p. 63.

56. ACIR, *State Mandating,* p. 65.

57. ACIR, *State-Local Relations Bodies,* pp. 9–11.

58. Patricia S. Florestano and Vincent L. Marando, *The States and the Metropolis* (New York: Marcel Dekker, 1981), p. 140.

59. Patricia S. Florestano and Vincent L. Marando, "State Commissions on Local Government: A Mechanism for Reform," *State and Local Government Review,* Vol. 9, No. 2 (May, 1972), p. 50.

60. ACIR, *The States and Distressed Communities.*

61. Thomas R. Dye and Thomas L. Hurley, "The Responsiveness of Federal and State Governments to Urban Problems," *Journal of Politics,* Vol. 40, No. 1 (February, 1978), p. 204. For comments on the methodology used in this research and a response, see: Peter D. Ward, "The Measurement of Federal and State Responsiveness to Urban Problems," ibid., Vol. 43, No. 1 (February, 1981), pp.

83–101, and Dye and Hurley, "Measuring Responsiveness: A Brief Reply," ibid., pp. 102–103.

62. National Governors' Association Center for Policy Research, *Bypassing the States: Wrong Turn for Urban Aid* (Washington, D.C.: National Governors' Association, 1979), pp. 2, 12.

63. Robert M. Stein, "The Allocation of State Aid to Local Governments: An Examination of Interstate Variations," in ACIR, *The State and Local Roles*. See also his "The Allocation of Federal Aid Monies," *American Political Science Review,* Vol. 75, No. 2 (June, 1981), pp. 334–343.

64. ACIR, *The States and Distressed Communities.*

65. Graves, p. 724.

66. U.S. Senate Committee on Government Operations, Vol. 1, p. 121.

67. Stacy Jolna, "State is Sued by Boston over Tax Exempt Land," *Washington Post,* October 25, 1978.

68. 5 CAL. 3d. 584 (1971).

69. ACIR, *Pragmatic Federalism: The Reassignment of Functional Responsibility,* Report M–105 (Washington, D.C.: U.S. Government Printing Office, July, 1976), p. 37.

CHAPTER 5

NATIONAL-LOCAL RELATIONS: DYNAMIC FEDERALISM

N ATIONAL-LOCAL relations exemplify the dynamism of American government. Even a casual observer cannot miss their unprecedented growth, the shifting political forces they bring into play, and the concern they generate for the traditional place of the states in the federal system. The name of the game is CHANGE as the nation tries to solve the burgeoning problems created by a massive population explosion, urbanization, and tardy state action and aggravated by energy shortages, inflation, and unemployment.

FORCES OF CHANGE

In his book, *The Cities and the Federal System,* Roscoe C.Martin identified four major forces that conspired to modify the practice of American federalism from about 1930 onward:

First was the cash grant-in-aid which superseded the land-grant system after the substantial depletion of the public domain. . . . Second was the depression of the 1930s, which spurred the launching of urgent and massive recovery programs to whose success the cities held the key. Third was the emergence following World War II of a metro-urban society attended by problems without precedent in their magnitude and complexity. Fourth was the demonstrated incapacity of the states to play an effective role in the war on urban problems.[1]

To these must be added three other forces: (5) the growing assertiveness of local governments, fueled especially by general revenue sharing, in demanding a share of the national bounty; (6) an increased awareness on the part of local officials that it is often easier to look to Washington than to bear the brunt of popular opposition to increased local taxes or in some instances to work with the state; and (7) the growing sophistication of interest groups, particularly urban organizations, in recognizing population—and thus political—shifts and in mobilizing their resources to influence the channeling of funds and the development of programs. Conceivably at a later date the impact of the energy crisis, the resulting inflation, and the rising conservatism of the nation, and other factors that combined to usher into office the Reagan administration and the implementation of its version of the New Federalism can be assessed.

PATTERNS OF CHANGE

Early Developments

Because of the traditional dual nature of American federalism, any direct relations between the national government and local jurisdictions before the present century were minor. "Direct federalism," or national-local interaction not involving the state, was the exception to the normal pattern. The United States Constitution makes no mention of cities, towns, or counties. Their legal authority emanates from the states to which they are legally subordinate. Thus, since 1789, the state capitals have served as conduits between city halls and county courthouses on the one hand and the nation's capital on the other. Well into the twentieth century, Washington had no interactions with most local governments, and what there were resulted principally from federal installations such as post offices, courthouses, military bases, and other projects. Even in these instances, interaction was likely to be with municipalities and not with other general local governments such as counties or townships. As late as 1932, it was reported that the American delegation to the International Conference of Cities in London represented the only country of the more than 40 present with no direct administrative relationships between the central or national government and its cities.[2]

The current national-local relationship is bedded primarily in the fiscal assistance provided by the larger government to the smaller jurisdictions. It developed piecemeal as the central government, with its vast financial resources, responded to the local cries for help. Interest groups believing they were unable to coax rural oriented state legislatures into enacting programs to meet urban needs, converged on Washington for relief. Concurrently, others, both inside and outside the federal establishment, sought to modify the behavior of local officials through regulation of their activities. As a consequence, national-local relations are more frequent and overt than ever before in American history.

This intensified interaction provoked some students of American federalism to treat local governments, especially cities, as third partners in the federal system.[3] Such attitudes are relatively new. Until recently, local governments were ignored in discussions of the operations of federalism and the emphasis was placed on national-state relations with local jurisdictions treated as arms of the states.

The Depression and the War Years

According to Martin, the year 1932 constitutes a sort of "geologic fault line" in American federalism.[4] Since that time the local governments have become more vocal in its practice. This was the year when Congress first mentioned the word "municipalities" in a national statute authorizing the Reconstruction Finance Corporation to make loans to states and cities in economic distress.[5] In subsequent years of that decade, the New Deal produced a flood of federal assistance programs, a number of which circumvented the states and went directly to the cities because of the urgent need to distribute relief funds. Many of these programs were administered by agencies established for specific purposes (ad hoc agencies). For example, the Public Works Administration made grants to cities, states, and other governmental bodies for public works projects. The Works Progress Administration, directing a work relief program, supplied labor and administrative costs for the projects, with local governments furnishing most of the materials and equipment. The states were bypassed in the construction of most of the city streets, sewers, schools, and other public projects built under these programs.

Although much of the depression legislation was of a temporary, emergency nature, housing legislation adopted during the period had a more permanent impact on local affairs. The Housing Act of 1937 authorized the U.S. Housing Authority to make loans up to 90 percent of the cost of constructing public housing. Local housing authorities were responsible for administering the projects.

The flow of federal funds to the local level was even more significant than the increase in programs. Between 1932 and 1940, revenues that local governments received from the national government multiplied almost 28 times, growing from $10 million (most of which went to the District of Columbia) to $278 million. When World War II erupted, however, the emergency relief activities undertaken during the Depression were abandoned and national-city grants reduced to a trickle. By 1944 they amounted to only $28 million, barely a tenth of their previous level. According to Philip J. Gunigiello, President Franklin D. Roosevelt sought to restore the traditional federal relationship despite strong pressures from within his administration to promote greater federal involvement at the local level.[6] A number of defense-related grants-in-aid were developed during the war years, but they were terminated when the war was over.[7]

The Post World War II Period

The direct federal-local trends established during the Depression accelerated during the post-war years. The functional areas in which grants were made expanded as the national government began financing airports and urban renewal, and later air and water pollution control as well as a myriad of other programs. Particularly notable was the federal entrance into urban redevelopment with the enactment of the Housing Act of 1949. Under this legislation, urban redevelopment had a narrow meaning, referring to land acquisition, slum clearance, preparation of the land, and sale of the site to developers. Nevertheless, it was a "first" for federal urban development funds. The concept was broadened by the Housing Act of 1954 to include conservation, restoration, and rehabilitation of houses in accordance with a plan and rechristened "urban renewal." Subsequent legislation added other dimensions, eventually expanding the national presence through the provision of funds for all manner of community and economic development activities.

Different assistance mechanisms were emphasized as well. Noteworthy was the growing use of project grants as a favorite mechanism for federal financial assistance. Their number grew to the point that they outstripped formula grants in number, although not in dollar amounts, by almost two to one by the time President Eisenhower left office.[8] Their use afforded national authorities a closer control over local undertakings financed with federal funds.

The post-war period also produced a rise in the number and sophistication of conditions attached to federal assistance. More attention was paid to the establishment of standards for grant administration, and the federal administrative machinery developed a greater capacity to monitor and enforce national requirements. According to one authority, there emerged a "nonarticulated theory of grants administration that stressed the vertical, functional, bureaucratic linkages" among government levels. It deemphasized the administrative role of elected chief executives as well as the legislatures' prerogative to shape administration.[9]

The Johnson Years of the 1960s

The Lyndon B. Johnson administration sired a progeny of national grants-in-aid of all types, particularly those dealing with urban problems, bringing the number of federal assistance programs to a then all time high.

Between 1963 and 1966, a total of 219 national grants in 39 functional areas was added. If 1932 can be regarded as the geologic fault line in national-local relations, as Martin asserted, 1965 could well be considered a seismic avalanche of national grants. A total of 109 new grants-in-aid programs was adopted in that year alone. A number of these had to pass through the states to reach local treasuries. Nevertheless, by 1970, at least 72 could be identified as directly national-local.[10]

Urban Programs. Congress also recognized new frontiers for federal aid, adopting a wide range of programs to deal with urban problems. These encompassed additional areas of activity, such as manpower training, while increasing support for functions previously financed such as mass transit and sewer and water systems. Moreover, when Congress responded to the rioting and rising crime rates of the decade with the Omnibus Crime Control and Safe Streets Act of 1968, the national government undertook a major role in an almost sacred field of state and local activity—general law enforcement. This statute established the Law Enforcement Assistance Administration in the U.S. Department of Justice to administer a block grant providing massive funds for law enforcement. Local governments received their share of the monies from their respective states.

Another piece of major legislation, the Economic Opportunity Act of 1964, a major facet of the Johnson administration's "War on Poverty," provided relatively unrestricted funds to local community action agencies for use in a variety of ways to combat poverty. These included social programs, neighborhood organizations, and the establishment of neighborhood centers, to name a few. Funds were granted to community action agencies that often were private nonprofit organizations, out from under control of the general local governments. The program became the object of considerable venom from local officials because, in response to the congressional requirement for "maximum feasible participation of the poor," these organizations used federal funds to aggregate political power in competition with established local governments.[11] Subsequently, the Green Amendment of 1967,[12] permitted general local governments to assume control of the program, but not before bitter feuding erupted and "Community Action Agency" became a bad term to some officials.

In another move to break the poverty cycle, Congress established the model cities program by enacting the Demonstration Cities and Metropolitan Development Act of 1966. Depressed areas in selected central cities and urban counties were chosen for concentration of federal funds. The theory behind this legislation was that federal monies had been scattered too thinly in the past whereas targeting them on a small area might break the poverty cycles of poor neighborhoods. Consequently, under this program, once the neighborhood had been approved for funds, federal grants for both social services and physical redevelopment were concentrated there.

In tune with the urban orientation of the Democratic party, the Johnson years also saw the creation of a new cabinet department, Housing and Urban Development (HUD). Established by the Housing and Urban Development Act of 1965, HUD constituted a major national recognition of urban areas, particularly cities. Thereafter, HUD administered most of the direct federal-local programs.

Federal Aid for Schools (ESEA). Not necessarily urban in nature, but certainly landmark in its impact on local governments, was the Elementary and Secondary Education Act of 1965. Adopted after years of debate over federal aid to education, the legislation ignored general education funding. The programs it authorized were aimed at specific educational deficiencies —educationally deprived children, school library resources, supplemental education centers, education research, and the capacity of state education agencies. Its enactment raised the federal contribution to education to $3 billion in 1967–68, up from $1.1 billion four years earlier, and increased the federal share of expenditures for public education from 5 to 9 percent.[13] Because of the difficulties of reaching agreement in the legislative process, much of the determination of policy under the statute was left to the administrative process. The ultimate result was a growing national presence in the public school classroom.

New Emphasis and Increased National Supervision. The emphasis and administration of federal assistance to local governments also changed as Congress started to treat urban problems as national problems. This was done in response to urban interest groups that began to organize themselves on a national scale.[14] Traditional redevelopment project grants, for example, might now be awarded for planning redevelopment activities. These grants were distributed on a competitive basis, with case-by-case approval by federal agencies. Private and nonprofit organizations were allowed to compete with state and local governments for the funds. This last development meant that in some programs, such as the anti-poverty programs discussed above, the national government had a choice as to whether it would deal with the established agencies of local government, create wholly new bodies at the community level with loyalty to national agencies and policies, or even resort to the use of private organizations as the instrumentalities for the execution of federal programs.

At the same time, the national government increased its supervision over the spending of the federal monies. Federal agencies audited local accounts, prescribed hiring standards, and established accounting guidelines, among other practices. To extend the reach of its influence, the Congress replaced the old matching requirements for funds with 100 percent federal financing in some instances, and federal agencies set out to recruit participants by soliciting proposals. Instead of responding to state and local initiatives, federal agents became salespeople in some instances, creating a demand for federal aid.[15]

Developments under the New Federalism of Nixon, Ford, and Carter

Notwithstanding the Nixon administration's announced intention to devolve federal programs to state and local governments, the avalanche of federal financial assistance programs that almost inundated state and local governments during the Johnson administration continued unchecked during the "New Federalism" eras of Richard Nixon and Gerald Ford. Although some of this was the result of presidential prodding, the Congress took the initiative in adopting most of the programs.[16] To the more than 200 narrow-purpose categorical grants enacted during Johnson's Great Society era were added more than 90 programs during the Nixon-Ford years. Congress adopted 70 more during the Carter incumbency. Few categoricals (about 46) were eliminated during the drive for grant consolidation during the decade.[17]

General Revenue Sharing for Local Governments. Of particular importance to local governments was the adoption of general revenue sharing with its wide discretion for local governments. In enacting this facet of the Nixon administration's New Federalism, Congress was responding to state and local financial difficulties and to the administrative problems associated with the uncoordinated categorical grants-in-aid.

Although not an unmixed blessing, general revenue sharing provided relatively unfettered financial resources directly to general local governments (as well as to states at the outset) largely subject to their own control and independent of the states. At the same time it broadened and deepened federal influence in local affairs. Although unencumbered by the conditions normally accompanying categorical grants, general revenue sharing funds became subject to the crosscutting regulations incrementally attached to all federal financial assistance programs. This gave the national government an opportunity to broaden its influence over the behavior of local officials, especially as the advent of this program multiplied the number of local governments participating in federal grant programs. Nevertheless, national intrusion was not so deep as in activities financed under categorical grants. As the president of the National Association of Counties testified, "This program, as was promised, has allowed local officials and their citizens to consider, set and meet local priorities without the intrusion from above that is present in other federal assistance programs."[18]

At the same time, general revenue sharing placed the responsibility for ordering priorities squarely on the shoulders of local officials—a move not greeted with approbation in every quarter because of its impact on the distribution of political resources locally and its effect on access to the decisionmaking process. Thus, a dichotomy exists in nationally assisted programs with those financed by most grants increasingly oriented to national goals while those supported by general revenue sharing funds reflect local priorities.

New Block Grants: CDBG and CETA. Congress also expanded the discretion of local governments with the adoption of two block grants. The Housing and Urban Development Act of 1974 combined seven existing categorical grants-in-aid into a direct federal-local community development block grant (CDBG). (This program will be discussed later in this chapter.) CETA, the Comprehensive Employment and Training Act block grant, unlike CDBG, which was a pure federal-local program, was a hybrid grant providing monies for both local governments and states, although localities got the lion's share (about 85 percent). CETA consolidated 17 existing manpower programs under Title I, authorizing funds to state and local governments for training, employment, counseling, testing, and placement of the unemployed and for supportive services. Other titles authorized public service jobs for persons in substantial areas of unemployment, funds for assistance to special groups such as Indians, migrant workers, youths, and older workers, and an established emergency public service employment program.

CETA and CDBG together funneled more than $3 billion into local treasuries in 1978. These funds, as well as those required to be passed through to communities under an amendment to the Omnibus Crime Control and Safe Streets Act of 1968, a block for states, made block grants an important device for financing local governments.

Countercyclical Aid Programs. The CETA programs constituted only one facet of the congressional attempts to deal with a recession that set in early in the 1970s. Congress also enacted other countercyclical assistance legislation that poured money into local coffers to combat unemployment. Between 1973 and 1977, in addition to CETA, it adopted the Public Works Employment Act of 1976 establishing the Local Public Works program; passed the Anti-Recession Fiscal Assistance program as an addition to general revenue sharing legislation; and approved the Intergovernmental Anti-Recession Act of 1977 that expanded the Local Public Works program. Local governments enjoyed the salad days of federal aid.

Growth of Direct Aid. As a result of all these actions, direct federal-local aid also became more prevalent. It expanded by about 148 percent in constant dollars during the decade, reaching a peak of 28 percent of all federal assistance in 1978. With the reduction in countercyclical funds, such aid declined; however, it still amounted to more than a quarter of all national aid in 1980. The dollar amount continued to grow, although not as rapidly.

Cities benefitted the most from this development because direct aid programs were concentrated in the nontraditional areas of federal assistance such as manpower training, community development, local public works, and anti-recession fiscal assistance. Moreover, cities got more than 50 cents of every dollar of direct aid. This compares to 23 cents for counties, 3 cents for towns, and 6 cents for school districts.[19]

School districts, counties, and nonschool special districts, on the other hand, were the principal substate beneficiaries of the pass-through funds concentrated in the traditional areas of public welfare, education, health and hospitals, and highways. This type of aid grew also, rising from an estimated $7.3. billion in 1971–72 to more than $12 billion by 1977.[20]

Aid for More Functions. The functional areas touched by federal fiscal assistance continued to broaden as additional programs were enacted. Scarcely any activity was denied support. In addition to the broad program fields mentioned above, Congress designated narrower, more local activities as the focus of pigmy programs. Small sums were appropriated for local bicycle paths, urban parks, rat control, rural general fire protection, and other functions heretofore considered purely local.[21]

Wider Local Government Participation. More substate governments also participated in the national programs. Robert M. Stein's study of 810 cities with populations in excess of 25,000 illustrates the extraordinary expansion occurring between 1967 and 1977. Slightly more than half of these cities received federal aid in 1967. By 1972, the figure had climbed to almost two-thirds. Following enactment of general revenue sharing legislation, CETA, and CDBG, participation rose precipitously to 100 percent. Although it took general revenue sharing to push the figure over the top, participation in other grant programs increased by 23 percent in the years between 1972 and 1977. General revenue sharing accounted for less than one-third of the increased municipal use of federal assistance programs during this period.[22]

Increased Local Dependency. With the rise in federal funding and broadened participation came growing local reliance on national largesse. Almost all medium and large cities depended more heavily on federal monies. In several cities, notably in the Northeast and Great Lakes areas, direct federal aid equaled one-half or more of the funds these governments raised themselves. Such cities as Buffalo, Cleveland, Newark, Phildelphia, Detroit, and St. Louis got 50 cents or more from the federal treasury for every dollar they raised themselves. Cities, which had long been creatures of the states, had become in John Shannon's words, "financial wards of the federal government."[23]

The growing dependency was not limited to large cities, however. Federal aid as a portion of each dollar of all locally produced revenues grew from 3 cents in 1962 to 13 cents in 1975 and had climbed to 18 cents by 1978. These figures are reflected in the local government dependency index set out in Table 5–1. In terms of constant dollars, federal monies reached their peak in 1978 and began to decline before the end of the Carter presi-

TABLE 5-1
LOCAL GOVERNMENT DEPENDENCY INDEX,*
FISCAL YEARS 1962, 1975, 1978, AND 1980

Unit of government	1962	1975	1978	1980
Federal and state aid per $1 of own source general revenue				
All local governments	$0.44	$0.73	$0.76	$0.79
Counties	.60	.78	.80	.81
Municipalities	.26	.63	.62	.56
Townships	.28	.40	.41	.39
School districts	.65	.94	1.01	1.25
Nonschool special districts	.15	.42	.44	.42
Federal aid per $1 of own source general revenue				
All local governments	$0.03	$0.13	$0.18	$0.16
Counties	.01	.13	.19	.17
Municipalities	.05	.19	.26	.23
Townships	.01	.09	.13	.10
School districts	.02	.03	.04	.03
Nonschool special districts	.11	.28	.34	.33
State aid per $1 of own source general revenue				
All local governments	$0.41	$0.60	$0.58	$0.63
Counties	.59	.65	.61	.64
Municipalities	.21	.42	.37	.33
Townships	.27	.31	.28	.29
School districts	.63	.90	.97	1.22
Nonschool special districts	.04	.14	.10	.09

*Interpretation: A score of $.50 means that for each $1.00 of local own source revenue $.50 is received from the state or federal government.

Source: ACIR staff computations based on data from U.S. Department of Commerce, Bureau of the Census, *Census of Governments, Vol. IV, 1962,* and *Governmental Finances,* various years. U.S. Advisory Commission on Intergovernmental Relations, *Significant Features of Fiscal Federalism, 1980–81 Edition,* Report M–132 (Washington, D.C.: December, 1981), p. 62.

dency. By 1980, direct federal assistance as a portion of locally generated revenues had fallen to 16 cents.

Growing Regulations. Another important development during this period was the increasingly regulatory nature of national-local relations. The national government stepped up its control of the behavior of local officials to the point where some referred to this time as a period of "regulatory federalism." The sharp rise in the number of grants and their attached conditions was one factor in the tightening national grip. Other mechanisms that contained more elements of compulsion probably were more important, however. Direct orders, crosscutting regulations applied to all federal assistance, application of sanctions in one assistance program to influence actions of recipients in another, and partial preemption of local activities when local operations did not meet national standards—all of these were used to substitute national for local choices.

Carter's "New Partnership." Late in the decade, President Carter announced the nation's first comprehensive urban policy, termed the "New Partnership," designed to target federal assistance to the most needy areas, particularly central cities suffering economic decline. Its centerpiece was an innovative categorical assistance program, the Urban Development Action Grant (UDAG). Targeted specifically at distressed cities, the program provides funds to stimulate private development projects that cities deem desirable and that, in the absence of federal aid, would not be undertaken. According to John C. Bollens and Henry J. Schmandt, even though UDAG operates on a much smaller scale than the former urban renewal program, it has triggered such diverse projects as neighborhood revitalization in Baltimore, redevelopment of an historic hotel in Louisville, construction of a galleria in St. Paul, and renovation of a blighted area in Chicago. Since participating cities have wide choices in the projects to be undertaken, the action grants understandably are popular with local officials.[24]

Despite the success of many UDAG initiatives, the "New Partnership" in general amounted to little. Carter's short tenure in office after it was announced provided scant opportunity for implementation. Moreover it contained the seeds of its own ineffectiveness. It relied on the traditional approach—throwing categorical grants at every problem. In addition, the proposal for funding neighborhood organizations ran counter to the idea of targeting needy areas and spread funds even more thinly.

Another important factor undermining the policy was that congressional Democrats and others had begun to shift their thinking from an emphasis on *place* as the focus of national assistance to a concentration on needy *people* wherever they might live. This shift from place to people was reflected in the report of the President's Commission for a National Agenda for the Eighties, appointed by President Carter and reporting in 1980. The Commission wrote:

> It is time, then, despite all the difficulties entailed, to alter the pattern of place-oriented, spatially sensitive national urban policies, and to ask, instead, what more people-oriented, spatially neutral, national social and economic policies might accomplish. . . .[25]

The report hit the cities like a bombshell and ran into a torrent of criticism from the nation's mayors who feared the deterioration of their traditional assistance programs.

Carter's Rural Policy. The Carter administration also undertook to design a Rural Development Policy that would improve national programs for rural areas and small towns. Rather than create new programs for this purpose, the administration decided to direct existing programs toward the solution of long-standing problems in four areas—health, housing, transportation, and water and sewer facilities. The Rural Development Policy Act of 1980, enacted late in this period, required the design of a rural strategy. Its timing in the Carter tenure, however, meant that implementation fell on the shoulders of the Reagan administration, which established an Office of Rural Development Policy for the purpose.

Assessing the First New Federalism. In sum, the New Federalism of the 1970s turned out to be less "new" than its advocates had anticipated. Despite the efforts of the Nixon and Ford administrations, the avalanche of categorical grants continued to flow strongly, both in terms of number and dollar amounts. Funding, in constant dollars, peaked under the Carter administration in 1978 and began to decline, although in current dollars the rise continued through 1981. During the same period, Congress reduced its emphasis on state and local matching funds as a condition of federal assistance and markedly upgraded its reliance on direct national-local aid, bypassing state governments. The newer forms of assistance, namely general revenue sharing and direct national-local block grants, augmented local discretion as to the purposes for which federal funds could be spent and, along with the anti-recession programs, brought more local participants into federal grant programs. As a consequence of these developments, local dependence on national financial help increased dramatically.

For many (indeed the majority of local elected officials), this New Federalism period, with GRS and block grants, was a first encounter with federal aid. Some believe it changed the complexion of the national-local dialogue by expanding the range of participants. Rather than including only participants from large central cities and a few others that had strong grantsmanship, it brought in many cities, counties, towns, and townships whose officials had little experience with Washington and remarkably different views on national involvement in local affairs.

During this period, the focus of federal assistance shifted toward urban areas, especially cities, and was concentrated somewhat more on needy areas. Efforts were made by the Carter administration to put an urban policy into place; however, its impact was spotty. Carter's attempts to improve the management of grant programs met with somewhat more success. Nevertheless, the growing surge of regulations that spewed from the national bureaucracy counterbalanced what reductions there were in the paperwork burden. The penchant of those in Washington to pile on aid conditions, crosscutting sanctions, regulations, and other requirements resulted in less discretion than at the outset of the decade. To a substantial degree, cooperative federalism as it applied to national-local relations gave way to coercive federalism. By the time the Reagan administration arrived in Washington, the clamors for change were insistent.

Early Reagan Administration Moves

Ronald Reagan's avowed desire to reverse the direction of national policies did not leave federal-local relations untouched. At the outset, the Administration cut funding for local governments, promising at the same time to release revenue sources for subnational use. Since the squeeze in funding preceded the materialization of promised revenue sources, the weaning process was not popular with local officials. Moreover, the greater discretionary authority extended to subnational jurisdictions appeared to be vested in the states.

All nine of the new block grants created by the Omnibus Budget Reconciliation Act of 1981 gave funds to the states rather than to local jurisdictions, thus strengthening the hands of the larger jurisdictions at the expense of local officials. Forty-six of the replaced categoricals previously had gone to local governments and nonprofit organizations, either exclusively or in conjunction with the states. Local governments lost access to 27 education categoricals alone. These were consolidated into the Education Block Grant. In the State Community Development Block Grant, which allows state (rather than federal) distribution of national community development funds to jurisdictions under 50,000 population, a federal-state relation replaced a national-city relationship. This shifted the focus of local attention from Washington to the state capitals. States have to meet certain conditions, however, or the original national-local arrangement will prevail. Other blocks provide some protection for local governments as well.

Most affected by the shift to block grants were counties, especially sensitive to health and social services changes, school districts, which bear the brunt of education administration responsibilities, nonprofit organizations also concerned with health and social services, and small communities, affected by the changes in discretionary community development funding. The consolidations bore less heavily on large and medium-sized cities that still go directly to Washington for community development funds.[26]

The paring of the federal budget in the early 1980s affected the public interest groups representing local governments as well as the actual governmental programs and projects. Organizations such as the National League of Cities, the United State Conference of Mayors, and the national Association of Counties had to cut back on the staffs that had mushroomed during the salad days of the 1960s and 1970s as grant money from the national government, on which they relied heavily, began to dry up.

The central focus of early urban initiatives under the Reagan administration appeared to be centered on the urban enterprise zone concept. Under it, private businesses do not have to pay taxes (or pay at reduced rates) on earnings from enterprises established in designated economically depressed areas and are subject to fewer regulations. The idea is to stimulate investment and create jobs, especially in central cities.

The Administration and Congress made a number of other moves during the early months of the new regime. The Administration, particularly, promoted a reduction in federal regulation of state and local governments, as well as of private activities. It lightened the impact of environmental protection and civil rights rules on local governments, gave them more discretion in meeting requirements to permit the handicapped more access to mass transit, and withdrew Department of Education rules requiring the education of foreign-language students in their native tongue. Regulations in the latter two areas had caused consternation at the local level. New York's Mayor Koch claimed the city could provide private limousine service for every handicapped person cheaper than it could install elevators at all its subway stations. Arlington County, Virginia, school officials were appalled at the prospect of providing instruction in 41 different languages.

At the same time that the Reagan administration lightened some of the regulatory impact on local governments, it reduced the access of local officials to national regulatory decisionmaking.[27] They had difficulty retaining their positions in the bargaining process when the emphasis shifted to state allocation of funds under block grants and state determination of many of the rules of the game.

Other Reagan administration initiatives directly affected interlocal organizations. In promotion of its promise to reduce the national role in the federal system, the administration reversed the trend to promote regional organizations that had been prominent during the past two decades and eliminated most support for substate regional organizations. Gone, along with the financial underpinnings of the substate organizations, were the requirements of OMB Circular A-95 that notice of proposed federally aided projects be given to other governments who would have an opportunity to review and comment on them before federal funds were committed. The administration worked to design other information disseminating methods it hoped would be more effective.

THE CURRENT PATTERN

A complex network of national-local relations operates today. The national government interacts with cities, towns, counties, townships, school and nonschool special districts, and multijurisdictional agencies, such as economic development districts, in diverse ways. Its relations are not the same in terms of frequency, tenor, and impact with each of these categories of local government, or, indeed, with all jurisdictions within one group. It deals more with cities than it does with townships, for example, and more with large cities than with small ones. Most of the interactions revolve around federal fiscal assistance programs, although other activities such as technical and emergency assistance, regulation, or direct federal administration of national programs may be involved. For the most part, the interactions take place within the parameters of one functional area such as education or environmental protection. Not surprisingly, politics pervades them as each government struggles to advance its aims. The interaction between the two levels produces substantial ritual dancing and bargaining. Consequently, relations are fluctuating and uncertain, changing almost continuously.

Interactions and Influences

Federal-local contacts may occur by design as part of a national program, as with grants to local jurisdictions for the construction of low-income housing. Or they may result from a political action, such as a city obtaining a specific project under a vocational education program because of its influence over the allocation of funds rather than because the national government intended the program to be especially for cities. Or, within a specific geographic area, a Veterans' Administration hospital site is likely to be selected because of the political power of one community as opposed to all the others that would have desired the facility rather than because that site is the most logical location. It is no accident, for example, that so many military installations are located in Georgia; so many, in fact, that someone remarked that another would sink the state. For many years chairpersons of congressional committees dealing with military affairs and military appropriations represented that state and were in a position to steer installations to their home areas.

Other contacts occur in everyday operations as various governments attempt to solve problems or administer programs. In selecting a site for a new federal court building, the General Services Administration may have to deal with local planning officials as well as with city officials concerned with transportation, sewers, and the like. The larger role local governments now play in administering national programs also stimulated increased involvement between officials at the two levels.

The influence of the national government on local affairs exceeds that generated by direct federal-local interactions. Because of the involvement of the national government in almost every function of government as well as in many aspects of private life, hardly any aspect of local activity is shielded from the shadow of the "federal leviathan."[28]

Often the consequences of federal actions are accidental or unintended. They accompany policies begun to accomplish other purposes and are not aimed directly at influencing local governments. For example, it is difficult to think of any federal-local program that has the impact of national economic policy. Recession, inflation, and high interest rates affect governments as well as private individuals. A Department of Defense decision to open or close a military base may alter dramatically the local economy, traffic patterns, school and housing needs, welfare rolls, or other local interests. The influx of refugees in response to national policy has created severe demands on public services in communities where the newcomers concentrated.

Often national programs aimed at solving one problem generate difficulties in another area. Federal legislation providing tax exemptions for interest on home mortgages, provisions for FHA and Veterans' Administration loan guarantees, and national highway policies contributed to the problems of urban areas. Middle-income residents of central cities took advantage of the housing programs to construct homes in the suburbs and commute downtown to work, thus aggravating difficulties for both central city and suburban communities. The interstate highway programs encouraged the location of shopping centers on the outer fringes of cities, drawing business from downtown areas, diminishing central city tax bases, and aggravating disparaties between core cities and their suburbs. For the suburbs, demands for physical facilities, such as schools, water and sewerage lines, and streets, often preceded collection of tax revenues from the new enterprises.

Similarly, adoption of grant programs in one field may make adoption of other programs considerably less likely. For example, some freeways built under the interstate highway system choked cities and impeded construction of mass transit systems or the preservation of parkland and open spaces, aided by other national programs. Furthermore, the absence of any overall system of grants leaves each program to be legislated separately with no clear statement of its relationship to other programs or to any comprehensive national purpose. This makes possible the existence of several grants in the same policy area for essentially the same purpose. The "market basket" situation thus created enabled local applicants to shop around for the program best meeting their needs. Evidence of this exists in such program areas as parks and open spaces, planning, water supply, and sewage treatment.[29] A few years ago, a government official reported on a small community that applied to six different agencies for assistance in building a sewage treatment plant. If all six had responded favorably, which at first appeared probable, the town would have made a profit of $1½ million on the project.[30] Block grants, especially CDBG, alleviated this situation somewhat.

Political Relationships

National-local political relations pervade the entire system of American government. They range from the interplay of local interests with the members of Congress and the national administration through political party action to presidential selection. They are among the most important of national-local interactions.

The representation system in Congress gives local interests leverage in the national government. Because of their dependence upon local support for election, United States representatives (and frequently senators who are elected from the state at large) often respond more readily to local pressures than to national or party desires. This representation of local interests should be distinguished from representation of local governments on the national level. Local governments have no special voice in the selection of members of Congress or the Senate and the representative may not reside within their boundaries.

The national legislator and local government officials may have different party affiliations and thus may not be exposed to integrating party influences. This is not to say that local officials have no influence with national senators and representatives. Because local officials are elected leaders of their communities, because they have a public platform from which to speak, and because they may be important party leaders in the national legislator's party, they will have more access to that individual than most other people. A member of Congress needs the support of local governmental officials and their constituents because both are also constituents of the congressional representative. Furthermore, such a representative is anxious to advance the interests of communities in his district.

Congress members are likely to regard the mayor or county commissioner as better informed on local needs and problems than the governor who usually has fewer information sources in the area. Simply because of the geographic location of the city or county, the representative identifies the local official more closely with his own congressional district. Furthermore, the local official is a constituent of the Congress member while the governor may not be. In addition, the member during the course of service may develop into a de facto party leader in each county in the district as well as a districtwide representative. This accentuates representation of local viewpoints.

Local governments, as well as private citizens and groups, call upon members of Congress for assistance in dealing with national departments and agencies. This congressional-administrative interaction, coupled with the "oversight" of administration by congressional committees, provides another access point for local political influence on the national level. Party differences do not deter members of Congress in one state from joining forces to promote local interests.

The lack of centralization in the political party system enhances local political influence. Because the national Democratic and Republican parties are loose federations of the respective parties in the 50 states and the territories, and because state party committees and convention delegates are usually elected on a local basis, the local influence within the party is

strong. County committees are usually more powerful than state committees, for example. Local influence may be felt on certain issues, the location
of national facilities, the distribution of national patronage, or nomination
of candidates, to cite several instances of impact.

Large urban areas or combinations of smaller ones may be decisive in
the outcomes of presidential elections, although it is a mistake to regard
the citizens of any one area or type of area as homogeneous in their electoral
behavior. The local conduct of presidential elections, if closely contested or
if unfairly administered, as was claimed in both 1960 and 1968, may well
determine the victor on a national basis.

PIGS et al. The public interest groups (sometimes called PIGS because
of their acronym), mentioned above, enable local governments to enhance
their influence in Washington. Through them, local officials can join
together to exert collective pressure on national institutions.[31] Even small
communities, which initially ignored the federal munificence, have formed
associations to influence national actions. As the national bounty grew,
their leaders began to exhibit the same scorn for the states as their larger
colleagues and to organize and pressure for changes in grant-in-aid formulas
and for other advantages. They, too, wanted to be assured of a share of the
federal largesse.

Each category of local jurisdictions has its own association. Counties
are represented by the National Association of Counties (NACO), large
cities by the United States Conference of Mayors (USCM), medium and
small cities by the National League of Cities (NCL), and towns and townships by the National Association of Towns and Townships (NATT). Metropolitan councils of governments, often called regional councils, achieve
representation through the National Association of Regional Councils
(NARC). Professional managers, whether they administer city, county,
or town affairs, make their voices heard through the International City
Management Association (ICMA).

Other public and private groups representing local interests when they
are urban include the National Housing Conference, the Urban Coalition,
the National Association of Home Builders, and the National Association
of Housing and Redevelopment Officials. School districts, whether urban
or rural, gain access to federal decisionmakers through the multitude of
national education groups including the National Education Association,
the American Federation of Teachers, and the National Association of
Secondary School Principals. Other special districts also may belong to
national organizations that further their interests. The National Association
of Conservation Districts is an example.

Some larger local governments maintain individual Washington liaison
offices designed to gather information and represent their interests. Chicago, Detroit, Los Angeles City, Los Angeles County, New York, and San

Diego are examples. The New York City Board of Education supports a separate office of its own.

The collective influence of the local government lobbies can be substantial. Their bases in membership throughout the country and the political clout of such members as the mayors of Chicago, New York, Philadelphia, Los Angeles, San Francisco, Baltimore, Atlanta, and Houston ensure attention from national officials. This is particularly true when the "big-seven" PIGS (public interest groups)—USCM, NLC, NACO, NARC, ICMA plus the National Governors' Association and the National Conference of State Legislatures—unite in pushing a cause.

Limitations on Local Lobbying. Collective local influence in the national arena frequently is limited, however, because the basic interests of local jurisdictions are not necessarily the same. Cities and counties disagree on revenue-sharing allotments, for example, and as the nation moves into an era of more block grants, conflict among them is increasing. Large and small cities have diverse viewpoints on programs where city size is a factor. Geographic concerns may further aggravate the situation.

Local influence, whether collective or from a single jurisdiction, is also diluted because energy must be spread over a wide range of focal points at the national level. There is no one committee in each house of Congress that deals with all local affairs or even with all urban affairs. In the House of Representatives, for example, communities have to approach the Committee on Banking and Currency in regard to housing, the Committee on Education and Labor concerning education and manpower training, the Committee on Ways and Means to influence welfare programs, the Committee on Public Works for capital construction projects, and the Appropriation Committee for funds. A similar proliferation faces them in the Senate. Administratively, they deal with numerous executive departments and agencies, most frequently with the Department of Education, the Department of Housing and Urban Development, the Department of Agriculture, the Department of the Treasury, the Environmental Protection Administration, and the Department of Health and Human Services.

National Stimulation of Lobbying. Often national officials initiate local interest-group pressures—especially in the realm of urban affairs. Presidents, who often are amenable to pressure from big cities that make up their largest single constituency, use speeches and other actions to encourage local interests to arouse public opinion in support of presidential initiatives. President Reagan, with his polished communication skills, has been adept at stimulating local pressures on the Congress. Members of Congress and their staffs also engineer coalition building for favored projects and programs. They may assemble representatives of various groups to generate support for legislation, schedule hearings where they can appear, and take other actions to stimulate local interest group support for their positions.

The Functional Bias

Federal financial assistance promotes intergovernmental interactions as local governments seek to take advantage of the fiscal goodies the central government offers. The technical advice and assistance passed back and forth among Washington, the federal regional offices, and local governments in connection with federal programs is the life thread of program effectiveness. Professional workers of all jurisdictions interacting with each other generate a continuous flow of information among governments. More often than not, this exchange takes place within the confines of one functional area, albeit this tendency is not as strong today as it was in the 1960s.

The relations tend to be among those involved in the enactment or implementation of specific programs rather than between the general governments personified by the President on the one hand and the mayor, manager, or county executive on the other. Professionals involved in federal housing programs relate to local housing officials and national law enforcement personnel to local police departments or county sheriffs, for example. In program enactment, a congressional committee dealing with educational programs may invite local educational professionals to give testimony concerning educational problems. Or these committees or their staffs may visit local communities to gather information for new or improved national programs. All along the line, ideas and information are exchanged until the program that emerges is hallmarked by many smiths.

The professional identification with program may be stronger than with the unit of government in which the professional works. It may also be greater than the interdepartmental relationships among agencies within the city, town, or county. Administrators in the local health system may have more contact with their state and national counterparts than with administrators in the local police, park, fire, or housing agencies. They think of themselves as *health* rather than as *city, town,* or *county* officials.

This professional identification with program rather than governmental jurisdiction is in direct contrast to the attitude of policymaking officials who are more interested in records of accomplishment. For their part, mayors may be more concerned that it is a city project than that it is designed in the best possible manner.

To the extent that the vertical professional interactions interfere with the ability of local elected officials to coordinate and control local government departments, they contribute to less effective and less responsive government. The latter condition means that the election of a new set of officials may have little impact on the operation of the government. Major decisions may be made by appointed officials within the bureaucracy.

Although strong enough in the past to be labeled "picket-fence federalism" or "functional feudalism" the vertical lines among professionals on various levels have blurred in recent years so that neither of these meta-phors provides a completely accurate description. It is not that the ties no longer exist. Basically, they do. Rather, other forces have intervened to smudge the lines from Washington to city hall and make them indistinct. The multiplication of federal programs afforded more opportunities for access. Block grants and crosscutting regulations broadened the bases from which professionals operate and have permitted a wider span of interactions. The proliferation of interest groups concerned with a growing federal role as well as an intensified local dependency created a network of "issue interests" at each level.[32] Furthermore, the expanded capacity of the public interest groups focused attention on general government and, along with strengthened public policy analysis, advertised the problems that general local governments had with fractionated grant mechanisms.

The Financial Basis

Grants-in-Aid. Most of the relationships between the national govern-ment and local jurisdictions are based on a residue of mixed federal finan-cial assistance programs for local governments. The tripartite distribution of federal funding among categorical grants, block grants, and general revenue sharing is further diversified because some of the funds go directly to local governments, necessitating a direct federal-local encounter, while others are passed through the states and may require no interface or com-munication between Washington and local offices.

What is more, substantial variation occurs among types of local govern-ments as to the amount, type, and distribution method of federal aid. Urban Development Action Grants (UDAG), for example, go to cities for the most part, although some urban counties are involved. It is unlikely, however, that school districts would qualify for any of these funds. Neither would the latter be eligible for general revenue sharing dollars because these monies are awarded to general local governments. School districts, nonetheless, do receive federal assistance both directly and passed through the states.

Most federal financial assistance to local governments in 1980 was paid directly to the local jurisdictions. Municipalities received the lion's share of the $21 billion of direct federal-local aid, almost half. Counties were next, garnering approximately a quarter of the funds, while school districts ran a poor third with one in 20 of the dollars given. Other national funds, about $17 billion in 1980, came to local governments indirectly, having been channeled through the states. Here, counties, school districts, and other special districts, rather than cities, were the principal beneficiaries.

Other fiscal assistance. Loans, as well as grants-in-aid, are made by the national government to local units. While often necessary and valuable, they are not so popular with local governments as grants because they must be repaid. There is no general program of loans whereby a local unit in need of money may borrow from the national government. As a rule, local units borrow as the state and national governments do by selling bonds to the private sector. Under a few programs, nevertheless, the national government will loan money to localities for specific purposes. Usually the interest rate is low in these instances. Among the loans available are those for rebuilding public facilities destroyed by natural disasters; for the acquisition of sites for low-income housing in rural areas; for water and waste-disposal systems; for watershed protection and flood prevention; for access roads, port facilities, railroad sidings and spurs; and for health facilities construction. Excess property may also be loaned for local use.

Occasionally the rental of national property to local governments at an extremely low rate amounts to a loan. In a few cases the national government makes grants for subsidizing interest when public agencies (such as colleges and universities or housing authorities) borrow from private sources. National income tax laws that exempt interest from state and local governmental bonds from taxation are also a form of loan subsidy, and one subject to continued criticism. National loans may have major impacts in particular instances; overall their effect in intergovernmental relations is limited.

Although they do not involve any transfer of funds between treasuries, loan guarantees can offer substantial support to local jurisdictions. In these cases, the national government stands as surety for the repayment of the loan by the local government. The local jurisdiction borrows the money through the regular borrowing process and a federal agency guarantees its repayment permitting the community to secure the funds at a lower interest rate because there is less risk involved for the lender. Such guarantees are made for specific purposes rather than being generally available for local borrowing. A recent example is the loan guarantee to boost the financial standing of New York City in its financial crisis.

THE COMMUNITY DEVELOPMENT BLOCK GRANT PROGRAM (CDBG)

Because it is the only pure national-local block grant and is of major concern to local governments, a closer look at the Community Development Block Grant should increase understanding of relations between the two levels. Congress adopted CDBG in response to the difficulties associated with the plethora of categorical grants that had accumulated by the end of the 1960s. Its passage was stimulated by debates over President Nixon's unsuccessful proposal for special revenue sharing for community development.[33]

The Housing and Community Development Act of 1974 consolidated seven previous categorical grant programs administered by the U.S. Department of Housing and Urban Development into a $2.3 billion Community

Development Block Grant under which local officials determined how federal funds would be spent. Community development was not defined although some indication of its meaning can be gleaned from the categoricals subsumed under this heading. These were urban renewal, model cities, water and sewer facilities, open space, neighborhood facilities, rehabilitation loans, and public facilities loans.

Under this direct federal-local program, metropolitan cities (those with populations of 50,000 or more) and urban counties (with populations in excess of 200,000) were automatically *entitled* to an annual grant determined by a formula based on need, although they still had to submit an application. Population, overcrowded housing, and the extent of poverty were set out as factors in the formula. Any community that had received a higher amount of money under the replaced categoricals than it was entitled to under CDBG was "held harmless," that is, it would still receive the larger amount for three years. After that, the formula would be phased out gradually. Under the program, HUD also had *discretionary* funds that it could award to other jurisdictions.

CDBG was intended to do more than provide for a new strategy for achieving the same purposes as the seven previous categorical grants consolidated under it. It was supposed to provide the flexibility local governments needed to deal with the diverse community development problems they faced. Moreover, the processes involved were different since local government elected officials rather than HUD now would determine most of the projects to be undertaken.

As planned, the program concentrated on eliminating slums and blight, meeting the needs of low- and moderate-income families, and solving vital community development problems. Funds could be used for such physical redevelopment projects as rehabilitation of delapidated housing, construction of neighborhood facilities, removal of barriers to the handicapped, and housing code enforcement. In addition, a wide range of other capital improvement and social service projects were eligible—all in keeping with the program's principle of broad local discretion. Overall, in its first 18 years of operation, CDBG has funded activities ranging from drug abuse elimination to the installation of traffic lights.

To take advantage of the CDBG program, communities wanting money are required to: (1) submit annual applications and a three-year community development plan; (2) emphasize programs assisting low- and moderate-income families, preventing slums and blight, or dealing with urgent community development needs by giving them "maximum feasible priority;" (3) develop a housing assistance plan that outlines low- and moderate-income housing needs and indicates how the community intends to meet them; (4) provide for adequate citizen participation in developing the plan and hold two public hearings on it, and (5) certify that it will comply with the crosscutting requirements applying generally to grants-in-aid.

Consequences of CDBG

Donald F. Kettl's careful study of Community Development Block Grants in four Connecticut cities identified a number of consequences of the grants for the cities involved. He noted that the program "clearly shifted power over community development to the cities." Whereas under the old categoricals the ultimate decision as to how the money would be spent rested with HUD, under the block grant local communities could determine which projects should receive federal aid. The transfer of power was not total, nonetheless. HUD area officials often haggled over the eligibility of proposed projects and provided technical assistance that influenced them. Moreover, both the Congress and HUD ultimately rescinded some of the original authority granted to local governments.[34]

The block grants centralized power in city hall or the county building to a much greater extent than was the case with the categoricals. Programs under the latter often were administered by redevelopment or model cities agencies that were relatively independent of the general control of elected local officials. In contrast, CDBG gave the chief executive officer of each locality responsibility for the funds.

Such responsibility was not an unmixed blessing. Local officials were subjected to pressures from diverse groups as all areas of the city attempted to influence decisions on the spending of funds. According to Kettl, local officials were unable to resist these demands and the result was scattered, short-term, neighborhood projects in all parts of the cities he surveyed. Adding to the troubles of the officials was their inability to lay the blame for denial of funds at HUD's door. The decisions were theirs. In contrast to provisions of the urban renewal and model cities programs, they found that citizens had increased opportunities for citizen participation under national requirements. In Kettl's words, "local claimant organizations dominated the CDBG budget process."[35] Included were redevelopment agencies and public works departments from the city government itself, neighborhood-level organizations left over from the War on Poverty seeking jobs and continued political power, and private organizations such as the YMCA or Big Brothers–Big Sisters that wanted to maintain their "organizational health" by keeping, and building up if possible, the number of employees, functions, and funds available to them.

In the communities Kettl examined, CDBG spread money broadly because citizen participants throughout the city claimed a share of the funds. As far as distribution among economic groups was concerned, lower-income neighborhoods (those composed primarily of census tracts with median income of less than 80 percent of the city's median income) got 75 percent of the housing and rehabilitation funds and 84 percent of the social service monies. Upper income neighborhoods, on the other hand, received 58 percent of the funds earmarked for neighborhood parks and facilities and 70 percent of the funds for public works.[36] The allocation of benefits does not necessarily follow the expenditure of funds, it should be remembered.

Brookings researchers' findings supported the importance of citizen participation in the allocation of funds. Following the typical pattern, in Mt. Vernon, N.Y., it pitted citizens' groups favored under model cities programs against traditional citywide citizen and service organizations, including one ad hoc group pushing for funds to support a skating rink. As the years passed, the tide turned against the previously favored low-income groups, and city officials, bending to political pressure, funded a number of controversial citywide recreation projects. In the first years of CDBG in Minneapolis, a citizen advisory committee was created to determine the CDBG budget. Altogether, it received hundreds of submissions from interest groups and, in addition, consulted city staff members. Although the city council voted, in the end, it was the advisory committee that actually wielded the decisionmaking power.[37]

Important administrative changes developed from the switch to the block grant. The regulatory role of the national government grew. In the face of nearly automatic local entitlement to funds, HUD was unable to control the operation of the program at its outset. Consequently, its efforts were concentrated at the other end of the process, on making certain that local officials carried out national intent. In its efforts to ensure redistribution of federal funds to the poor, HUD, under the leadership of Secretary Patricia Roberts Harris and encouraged by the interest groups associated with the Democratic party, produced new regulations. These accrued incrementally; however, the result increasingly was to categorize the program. This brought more federal control and less local discretion although local governments still maintained substantial latitude.

Grant administration was also simplified. HUD regulations were reduced from the 2,600 pages in the *Federal Register* that applied to the previous seven programs to 25 pages.[38] Equally important, single applications replaced the multiple applications that the categoricals required. In large cities, the average number of applications fell from five annually during the 1968–72 period to one in 1975, the year the program was initiated. What is more, applications were both shorter and less expensive. Entitlement applications averaged 50 pages, and those for discretionary funds 40, both involving substantially fewer pages than the average 1,400 page applications filed each year for the categoricals. Costs were reduced, both in terms of dollars and in staff hours devoted to the application process. The average cost was $12,305 per application, or less than 1 percent of the grants, while staff hours averaged 1,025.[39] HUD review time was shortened, too, partially as the result of the legal requirement that entitlement applications were approved automatically unless HUD did not reject them in 75 days. Approval was limited to checking for basic compliance.

Recent Changes in CDBG

The 1977 reauthorization of CDBG expanded the eligible community development activities to include economic development and created the action grant program for distressed cities and urban counties (UDAG). Under a separate non-entitlement CDBG put forward by the Reagan administration, states were given the responsibility for allocation of discretionary awards to jurisdictions under 50,000 population. As part of the Reagan administration's regulatory relief drive, CDBG housing assistance plan, citizen participation, and targeting requirements that had increased under the Carter administration, were slated for reduction.

IMPACTS OF GRANTS-IN-AID ON LOCAL GOVERNMENTS

The impacts of federal financial assistance are too numerous to tabulate. Many of them have been discussed at other places in this book. Because of their importance, however, several aspects of grant effects on local governments are highlighted here—fiscal impacts, political consequences, functional assignment influences, structural modifications, and administrative effects.

Throughout the discussion it will be necessary to keep in mind that impacts are not necessarily the same for all types of local governments or even for all local jurisdictions within one class. Local diversity must be considered in all aspects of national-local relations.[40] Moreover, different grant mechanisms may produce divergent results. For instance, while categorical formula grants passed through the states may encourage state governments to add to the conditions of aid, funds provided by general revenue sharing shore up local political ability to bargain in the political arena.

Fiscal Effects

The financial impacts of federal fiscal assistance on local governments are in most ways similar to those on the states. Local financial capacity has been increased as hundreds of programs poured billions of dollars into local coffers. This assistance has been especially important to large cities that, as discussed previously in this chapter, have become increasingly dependent on the federal dollar. Small nonmetropolitan communities, on the other hand, received proportionately less of the federal largesse.[41] Nevertheless, as federal funds came in, new employees were added and expenditures rose in all types of local governments and, for awhile, local governments were the fastest growing segment of the economy.

National aid amounts varied throughout the country. The federal aid-local financing typology set out in Table 5-2 classifies states according to the relative importance of total national assistance (direct and pass-through) and local revenue sources in financing local governments. Not considered is state aid that, if minimal, may result in both a high federal and high local component, as in Hawaii. The states with low federal financing and high local financing are located in the upper left corner of the table and those with high federal and low local financing in the lower right-hand corner. Also shown (in parentheses) are per capital local taxes. There is no necessary relationship between high local financing and the amount of taxes collected for each individual in the state. These figures are included for information purposes.

Grants-in-aid cost local governments money, too. Or, at least the mandates attached to them do. These requirements impose ''substantial costs'' on local governments, according to an Urban Institute study of seven local jurisdictions. The $25 per capita cost in 1978 was roughly comparable to the general revenue sharing funds these localities received. Costs were not uniform for each mandate or for each jurisdiction, of course. Requirements for unemployment compensation imposed the lowest costs of the mandates studied while those stipulated by the Clean Water Act were the most expensive. The Education for All Handicapped Children Act was deemed the next most costly.[42]

Another survey, this one of seven counties differing widely in geographic location and size, indicated that county officials resented the ''heavy financial burdens'' federal mandates placed on them. They found ''excessive costs'' associated with requirements of Section 504 of the Rehabilitation Act of 1973 relating to the handicapped. Davis-Bacon provisions, requiring the payment of the prevailing wage in projects constructed with national funds, also significantly increased costs according to the respondents.[43]

The National League of Cities surveyed its nationwide membership in 1980. Respondents identified environmental impact statements, design requirements for federally assisted new bus purchases, water treatment facility stipulations, the education of special students, and the prevailing wage requirement as unreasonably costly. Other regulations were perceived as having low or reasonable costs in proportion to the benefits derived. Included in this category were citizen participation, flood protection, minimum wage requirements, historic preservation, and racial nondiscrimination.[44]

Political Impacts

The effects of federal grants are political as well as financial. For instance, direct national-local grants disturbed the balance of the federal system and promoted confrontations between mayors and governors over the form of grant programs. The mayor (or another local executive) and the governor may find themselves at cross purposes as the local leader

TABLE 5-2
A FEDERAL AID-LOCAL FINANCING TYPOLOGY
(1976-77)

	Low federal (Less than 12.2%)		Moderate federal (12.2% to 20.6%)		High federal (Greater than 20.6%)	
High local financing (Greater than 65.8%)	Nevada	($461)	New Jersey	($508)		
	Conn.	(416)	Mass.	(494)		
	Wyoming	(414)	Colorado	(413)		
	Nebraska	(382)	New Hamp.	(383)		
	Illinois	(294)	Montana	(355)		
	Texas	(263)	So. Dakota	(346)		
	Kansas	(257)	Vermont	(335)		
			Missouri	(276)	Hawaii	($209)
Moderate local financing (47.5% to 65.8%)	Alaska	(442)	New York	(652)		
	Iowa	(305)	California	(514)	Oregon	(384)
			Michigan	(348)	Maryland	(378)
			Rhode Is.	(323)		
			Arizona	(322)		
			Ohio	(307)		
			Penn.	(296)		
			Indiana	(283)		
			Virginia	(276)		
			Oklahoma	(256)		
			Washington	(247)		
			Florida	(241)	Georgia	(231)
			Utah	(233)		
			No. Dakota	(228)		
			Idaho	(210)		
			Tennessee	(208)	So. Carolina	(136)
			Alabama	(127)		
Low local financing (Less than 47.5%)			Wisconsin	(283)		
			Minnesota	(281)	Maine	(226)
			Louisiana	(205)	No. Carolina	(161)
			W. Virginia	(136)	Kentucky	(159)
			Mississippi	(122)	Delaware	(158)
			New Mexico	(122)	Arkansas	(120)

Note: Figures in parentheses are per capita local taxes. State-aid figures are not included.

Source: Computation by Maxwell School of Citizenship and Public Affairs, Syracuse University. Advisory Commission on Intergovernmental Relations, *Recent Trends in Federal and State Aid to Local Governments*, Report M-118 (Washington, D.C.: July, 1980), p. 24.

endorses national legislation providing grants directly to localities and the governor seeks to channel them through the states. As a consequence of state dissatisfaction, or to encourage state financial contributions, Congress occasionally allows states to "buy in" to direct national-local programs by contributing part of the funds. This is true of the new CDBG discretionary block grant, and most of the states have agreed to provide 10 percent of the funding to maintain administrative control. Pressure for direct grants developed relatively recently as cities grew in population and the larger ones rivaled states in size of operations. To some extent the struggle reflects the conflict of interests of those who operate in very large cities with those outside. In general, Congress would prefer to deal with the states, but city officials can exert strong pressure and often are supported by some interested national administrators.

Federal monies often have changed the distribution of political resources on the local level as well, enabling new groups to exert political power. Jeffrey Pressman has an interesting account of the development of new political arenas in Oakland, California, financed with funds from the antipoverty program. Because the national monies originally were allowed to go to a nongovernmental community action agency, the group involved there developed enough political strength to challenge the city government on some issues. At the same time, new politcal leaders were trained.[45] This happened in other communities as well

Federal aid conditions modify political processes and outcomes. The myriad of citizen participation requirements contained in grant-in-aid legislation, for example, had a modest impact on the number of types of citizens involved in trying to influence the way federal assistance funds were spent, according to an ACIR study. The impact of the citizens varies among programs, but in the case of general revenue sharing in particular, citizen participation influenced the selection of activities to be undertaken and the level of social service expenditures.[46]

The citizen participation requirements also affected the political process of stimulating the creation or growth of interest groups. In many cases, federal legislation stipulated representation of certain groups or interests on advisory boards or committees established for program implementation. Congress required, for example, the inclusion of farmers on certain agricultural advisory boards, and doctors or health personnel had to be named to boards of health systems agencies. Other legislation specified the representation of consumers, clientele, program beneficiaries, ethnic minorities, and parents, among others. Such participation added to the strength of the selected groups. The ability of federal programs to stimulate the organization of new political interest groups was apparent with the adoption of national programs for the aging. Constituency groups (that is, those who benefited from the programs) seemed to emerge almost overnight.

The more powerful the constituency groups, the more difficult it is for local officials to make changes in funding priorities. Organized and articulate, they can exert powerful pressures for program maintenance. What is more, administrators often use these groups to pressure for additional funding. According to George E. Hale and Marian Lief Palley, the tendency to enlist interest group support, at least by agencies on the state level, is enhanced by federal funding.[47]

Insofar as national money encourages the establishment of public interest groups made up of local *officials,* it might be stimulating actions contrary to the interests of local *residents* in some instances. Suzanne Farkas pointed up this possible divergence in the representation of metropolitan areas. The urban lobbies, such as the mayors, work to gain interest representation for local jurisdictions as *presently constituted,* a representation that makes the ignoring of boundaries difficult. The question arises as to whether this fragmented individual unit approach is consistent with the interests of the citizens of an entire metropolitan area. The vested concerns of the PIGs limits the national capacity to consider the interests of the region as a whole.[48]

Impacts on Functional Assignment

Congress intentionally encourages subnational governments to undertake new functions by holding out a carrot of federal aid. Stein's study points to "a growing, but narrow, influence of federal assistance on the assignment of municipal functional responsibility."[49] The functions added, however, were likely to be in areas, such as urban renewal, housing, and corrections, that give rise to diseconomics of scale.

The CDBG program provides a striking example. There, local governments became involved in some cases because they perceived the program as a source of ready funds for capital improvements—planned or ongoing. Later, as national officials began to pressure communities to use CDBG for housing-related activities in designated target areas, many municipalities found themselves in the business of housing rehabilitation, an activity foreign to their operations in the past. Sometimes the growth in local activities was a result of state requirements in response to national legislation. In one instance, the Maryland State Board of Health and Mental Hygiene drew up a comprehensive Mental Health Centers Program that emphasized the role of local governments. Shortly thereafter, the state required Maryland counties to provide less institutionalized forms of health care, thus expanding their work.[50]

Structural Impacts

Often more visible than other types of federal influence on local governments are those that affect local government structure. National programs have encouraged the establishment of new local agencies for a long time. There are two categories of nationally inspired local government organizations.[51] One class includes those special local organizations outside established local government institutions whose structure and responsibilities are set out by national law. They are created by the states to meet certain requirements for participation in national programs. Primary responsibility for their proliferation rests with the Department of Agriculture which was especially active in promoting them during the New Deal days of the 1930s. While enthusiasm for them has lessened since that time, they still blanket the country. There are nearly 3,000 soil conservation districts (many of them independent governments) in all states, Puerto Rico, and the Virgin Islands. There is also a host of other local agencies that are not separate governments. Included are Agricultural Stabilization and Conservation Service committees, Extension Service sponsoring groups, Grazing Service advisory boards, farm-loan advisory boards, and other agricultural organizations. The customary way of organizing these agencies is by local election of farmer committees.

Not all the nationally-inspired local organizations are creatures of the Department of Agriculture. The controversial community action agencies, which mobilize and funnel resources for the War on Poverty, emanated from the Office of Economic Opportunity (but have been under the Community Services Administration since 1974), and the Department of Commerce encouraged the establishment of rural economic development agencies. Further, Circular A–95 issued by the Office of Management and Budget in the Executive Office of the President required areawide planning reviews for almost all applications for national grants-in-aid. Many communities responded to these review requirements by creating new governmental agencies. The number of councils of government, for example, took an immediate spurt upward, rising from 18 to 81 in the three-year period between 1965 and 1968[52] and exceeding 660 by the late 1970s. Since about three-quarters of their funding came from the national government, the abolition of the A–95 review requirement in 1982 and the cutback in federal funds has already led to the withering away of some regional councils. During the same three-year period from 1965 to 1968, more than 40 new economic development districts were created. More recently, national laws have inspired the establishment of area agencies on the aging and agencies for health systems, water quality planning, and criminal justice planning.

Critics of the nationally inspired local governments and agencies point up their effect on established general local governments. Speaking of the Department of Agriculture, the late Morton Grodzins said:

The Department has contributed to the low state of rural (especially county) government. First ASC offices in every rural county compete with the county government in attracting leaders, skilled personnel, electorate attention, and in other ways. In many areas, county operations are dwarfed by ASC programs, as measured by dollar expenditures or impact on the resident, or both. This competition has without doubt been deleterious to county government. More important, by not working collaboratively with local governments (or states) the Department of Agriculture has deprived these governments of significant advantages. Grant programs in other fields have been used to raise standards of personnel, organization, and performance. They have increased the scope of activity of states and cities, and they have added to the stature of those institutions.[53]

The second category of local organizations inspired by national statutes are more immediately under the supervision of the state or regularly constituted local governments. The former selective service system and the civil defense agencies are examples. So are the 140 local government consortiums established under CETA. Local jurisdictions too small to qualify as prime sponsors on their own joined to aggregate sufficient population to meet the requirement.

Administrative Problems

Many administrative problems generated for local governments by federal assistance programs also plague the states. The time and effort required for grant applications, conflicting and confusing grant requirements, the uncertainty of federal funding, the fractionalization of control by elected officials because of the ties developed by bureaucrats in one functional area all affect both levels. Impacts at the local level are likely to be more acute, however, because of the very nature of local governments themselves. In the first place, local governments are the major deliverers of public services, both those that are locally generated and those associated with national or state activities. They deal directly with the public to a greater extent than any other level of government. They are the most labor intensive. The scale of their operations is usually, although not always, smaller than that of the other levels. They operate under constraints emanating from state or national requirements and must rely on their parent states for authority to act.

An additional problem for local administrators is that federal grant requirements often treat local governments as though they were all alike or as though state-local relations were all the same. The *New York Times* recently published an account of the perplexity of Putnam County, N.Y. officials who were trying to widen a bridge on a county road to 21 feet. The project would cost $240,000, all of which would have to be paid by local citizens. They could receive federal assistance for the construction, however, if they met national requirements to make the bridge 44 feet wide. The toal cost then would be $640,000, but the county would have to pay only $31,200, making it cheaper for local taxpayers if the more expensive bridge were built.[54] American local governments are not all alike, and attempts to deal with them all in the same way create problems for all concerned. This is one reason for the move to more discretion by recipients of federal aid.

Other local administrative difficulties are created by the position of local jurisdictions at the bottom of the governmental system. They often must respond to requirements and directions of two levels above them— experiences that can stultify administrative innovation. Their options may be circumscribed by superior actors in the political hierarchy. Just the difficulty of getting information about federal programs and decisions may present formidable obstacles and result in delays. Federal statutes may require cooperation with other local governments, mandate certain administrative procedures, and require approval of plans, auditing of accounts, and compliance with regulations.

THE JUDICIAL FACTOR

Since functions undertaken by the myriad of local governments encompass such a wide variety of activities, actions by all branches of the national government have an impact at the local level. Increasingly, Supreme Court decisions adjudicating individual rights have consequences for substate jurisdictions. The effect of major court decisions, such as *Brown* v. *Board of Education of Topeka* (1954),[55] which outlawed segregation in the public schools, or the reapportionment cases of the 1960s, are important examples. A more recent decision extended the protection of the Fourteenth Amendment's due process clause to illegal aliens when the Court held that Texas must provide free public education to illegal alien children.[56] This decision affects many school districts all across the nation.

Lesser known decisions have affected personnel practices, immunity from suit of local officials, police procedures and practices, regulation of morals, zoning, and municipal tort liability (torts are civil, as opposed to criminal, wrongs).[57] In recent years, Supreme Court decisions have circumscribed local government actions to a marked degree. One notable example is the decision in *Elrod, Sheriff* v. *Burns* (1976)[58] in which the Court invalidated dismissal of patronage employees in Cook County, Illinois. Involved were several non-civil service, nonpolicymaking Republican employees of the sheriff's office who challenged their dismissal by the newly-elected Democratic sheriff. The Court cited the First Amendment's protection of freedom of association in ruling that such employees could not be discharged because they were members of the opposition political party. The decision struck at a practice widely employed on the local level.

Several cases affected the immunity from suit that local jurisdictions, in the exercise of their governmental functions, share with the states. Under the Eleventh Amendment to the U.S. Constitution, cases against states by citizens of another state are removed from federal court jurisdiction. Suits may be brought against a state only with its permission and in its own courts. Recently, several cases arising over individual rights have whittled away at immunity for both state and local governments, although the issue has not been completely resolved. The consequences of immunity loss can be major as local governments defend suits for improper actions by their officials and employees or for their failure to act. They face the likelihood of paying substantial damage claims. Perhaps more important, they may react to the prospect of being held liable for improper actions by hesitating to undertake new initiatives or adopt innovations.

Local governments do not always lose in court or have their powers restricted. In *National League of Cities* v. *Usery* (1976),[59] the organization of cities brought a successful suit against the Secretary of Labor to have declared unconstitutional a national requirement that state and local governments pay minimum wages and set maximum hours for their employees. Local governments won, too, in *Holt Civic Club* v. *City of Tuscaloosa* (1978),[60] in which the Court upheld a state law granting extraterritorial jurisdiction to Alabama cities. Citizens outside the city boundary but within three miles of it were made subject to a city's exercise of its police (regulatory) powers, criminal court jurisdiction, and business licensing, although they were not permitted to vote in municipal elections. Local authority to require employees to reside within their boundaries, to be citizens, and to meet other reasonable requirements have been upheld as well.

In addition to their function of making decisions affecting local governments, the courts have taken on a strong management role in activities once considered solely within the domain of local governments. Faced with the unwillingness or inability of local jurisdictions to comply with their orders, the federal courts began to operate school districts to ensure compliance with desegregation requirements, draw lines for school attendance zones, establish districts for council elections, and supervise the operation of local jails.

PARTNERS, ADVERSARIES, OR BARGAINERS?

The amount of conflict or cooperation engendered by national-local interactions varies according to the specific issue at hand and the individuals involved in the relationships. A substantial amount of cooperation exists along the frontiers of national-local relations, but there is friction at many points, too. In fact, the predominant theme may be abrasion rather than harmony. Because national and local officials approach public policy from different directions and with different objectives, tensions result from many interactions. The thrust of national agencies is to spend the money and carry out national policies. The local actors are inclined to be more conservative in their actions because they must bear the brunt of any unfortunate consequences. They try to avoid changes that might produce criticism. The perceptions those on each level have of the other also produce tension, as officials on one tend to fit actions of participants on the other into preconceived images of how they are likely to act.[61]

Benefits of Relationships Vary

Some relationships are beneficial to one level of government, others to both. A few may be competitive, a number one-way coercive. Arranged on a continuum, they might look like Figure 5–1.

The United States Coast and Geodetic Survey provides a service to local units that is not reciprocated. It is one-way beneficial. On the other hand, national, state, and local governments participate in the support of the Agricultural Extension Service, which maintains county extension

FIGURE 5-1 A CONTINUUM OF NATIONAL-LOCAL RELATIONSHIP

One-way beneficial	Mutually cooperative	Competitive	One-way coercive
U.S. Coast & Geodetic Survey provides geodetic controls for land surveys and mapping	Agricultural Extension Service gathers and disseminates agricultural information	FBI versus local police or sheriff	Department of Justice enforces Voting Rights Act
County provides space for U.S. agency meeting	U.S. Public Health Service cooperates with county health department to contain spread of contagious disease	Nuclear Regulatory Commission site approval versus local zoning opposition	U.S. Department of Education enforces school desegregation
U.S. Department of Labor arbitrates dispute between a city and its garbage collectors	U.S. Fire Administration and local fire departments exchange data on fires.	U.S. Department of Transportation versus local departments of and zoning over route of interstate highway	Environmental Protection Agency forces local adherence to air quality standards

agents in counties throughout the nation to gather and disseminate agricultural and homemaking information. All three levels of government profit from this arrangement. Although the Federal Bureau of Investigation and local law enforcement agencies cooperate, the relationship is more likely to be competitive. Local officials are reluctant to call in national agents and, when they do, friction often develops over credit for crime solving.

The national government may occasionally force local officials to do things they do not want to do or to refrain from a contemplated activity. The Attorney General's move to force some counties to register black voters by sending in national registrars and by instituting suits against local officials is an example. The action of the Department of Education in withholding federal funds for public schools until some semblance of racial balance in the schools was achieved is another.

Local governments have little opportunity to take a coercive stance against the national government because they can neither withhold money nor exert force. Nevertheless, they may sometimes bring suit to force the release of funds appropriated for local use or to contest national mandates. A recent example of the latter is *National League of Cities* v. *Usery*, discussed earlier in this chapter.

Relationships Modified

Federal assistance programs have shifted from an emphasis on helping local government solve their problems and, to some extent, equalizing finances among them to the promotion of national goals brought a modification in the relationship. Although the basic goals of providing a better service may coincide,[62] the aims of the donor and the recipient in the process vary. Pressman points out that donors seek to move money, obtain information about the recipient's performance, control the outcome of the project, justify the expenditure of funds, and insure local stability and support. The recipient, on the other hand, seeks to attract money, achieve a steady flow of funds, retain autonomy from donor control, and establish stable and supportive relationships with donor agencies. These conflicting objectives produce tensions among those involved, especially in program implementation. The donor prefers long-term planning, short-term financing, and a number of guidelines as to how the money is to be spent. The recipient favors short-term plans, long-term funding, and relatively few guidelines.[63] As grants became more regulatory, each side undertook to bargain in order to achieve its goals.

Unequal Negotiators

At the bargaining table, there is an imbalance of power between the national and local governments. Since federal laws dominate the legal framework in which interactions occur and since most of the national-local interactions are based on federal programs for which the national treasury supplies most of the funds, the national government is in a position to prescribe guidelines and controls to accompany the money. It may rely on such strategies or "ploys," to use Donald Rosenthal's term,[64] to dominate the bargaining as the threat to withhold funds, delays in approval of plans and projects, resort to legal means, and the like. Local governments, desperately in need of additional funds, are in a poor position to argue about the conditions of a grant. As Pressman commented, "Cooperative federalism between relatively wealthy and powerful federal agencies and relatively poor and powerless local agencies is an illusion."[65]

At the same time, as Pressman recognized, the national government's dependence on local implementation of its programs provides bargaining counters for the localities. Local officials may mitigate the impact of federal conditions and guidelines by threatening to opt out of the program or to create a controversy costly to both levels. Or, alternatively, they can demonstrate such need that national officials may find it necessary to provide emergency aid rather than refuse assistance.[66] What is more, they may call for congressional backing, mobilize other support, and give evasive responses.[67]

Upon participating in a program local officials have many options as to the speed and vigor with which they perform their part of its implementation. The latter recourse often has operated to impede federal regulation. Note here the long drawn out battles over school integration, busing to achieve racial balance, and compliance with equal apportionment formulas for the drawing of district lines for local elections. Rosenthal notes that "Intergovernmental relations in the United States is carried on with the knowledge that the Federal bark is worse than its bite."[68]

Some doubt that the national government could ever monitor all of its intergovernmental regulations. Just think of the task of keeping track of what more than 82,000 sets of public officials were up to! As a case in point, an official of a midwestern county reported that in all the years of the CDBG program his county had never prepared a housing assistance plan. Each time HUD officials queried whether programs were in conflict with it, the county reported they were not, "After all," this official remarked, "we never had one, so how could anything conflict with it?"

The power imbalance between the national and local governments does not ensure the former's dominance, although the larger government more often prevails. The mutual dependence of the two levels allows them to negotiate over the implementation of federal programs. Richard P. Nathan and Paul R. Dommel's study of federal-local relations under block grants suggests that on procedural issues the national agency (in this instance, HUD) is likely to prevail while on substantive issues the local governments tend to win.[69]

Sticking Points for Negotiators

"Sticking points" in national-local bargaining may be the result of factors external to intergovernmental relations—that is, citizens, interest groups, or private institutions. All of these may act in such a way as to make cooperation among governments difficult. In addition, there may be disagreements among those on one side of the bargaining process. It is difficult to develop a "local position." As noted earlier, large cities and small towns often have opposing positions as do cities and counties. Even within one community, agreement is uncertain as the mayor, the council, the chamber of commerce, and other groups take different positions.[70]

The question raised in the heading of this section—Partners, Adversaries, or Bargainers?—cannot be answered with definitiveness. It appears that relations are sometimes cooperative, sustaining the partnership image of American intergovernmental relations. At other times, they are downright conflictual and may even involve the use of force. Throughout, people at the two levels tend to bargain, producing tradeoffs that allow the system to work. Officials select whatever role is appropriate at the moment, making pragmatic adjustments to meet the need.

SHIFTING RELATIONSHIPS

This chapter has attempted to explain the dynamism of national-local relationships—their shifting patterns as needs have changed. In the recent past, the proclivity of the Congress to consider local problems as national problems, even in instances where they may have been only an aggregation of local difficulties occurring throughout the nation, led to expansion of interactions between the two levels. This expansion is likely to continue in instances where groups have the political power to convince federal officials that this perception is accurate or where national figures consider it advantageous to act as entrepreneurs in advancing local causes. Currently, the financial retrenchment being undertaken at the national level is limiting moves in this direction. Programs and funds are being cut. Moreover, the designation of states as administrators of block grants impedes direct national-local interactions. These recent shifts stand as evidence of the continual adjustments that are being made, but the relationships they engender are not necessarily permanent. There can be little expectation that local governments, like good children, will go back to being seen and not heard.

The national-local relationship that has been established over the years is elastic enough to allow room for the ebb and flow of local participation as a "partner" in the federal system. Its very flexibility means that it is likely to withstand the gales of attack on the growing local role by imitating the wise bamboo of Japanese folklore and bending with the wind.

NOTES

1. Roscoe C. Martin, *The Cities and the Federal System* (New York: Atherton Press, 1965), p. 111.

2. W. Brooke Graves, *American Intergovernmental Relations* (New York: Charles Scribner's Sons, 1964), p. 655.

3. See Martin, *The Cities and the Federal System*.

4. Ibid., p. 111.

5. Daniel R. Grant and H.C. Nixon, *State and Local Government in America*, 3rd. ed. (Boston: Allyn and Bacon, Inc., 1975), p. 2

6. Philip J. Funigiello, *The Challenge of Urban Liberalism: Federal City Relations During World War II* (Knoxville: University of Tennessee Press, 1978). For another look at this period see Mark I. Gelfand, *A Nation of Cities: The Federal Government and Urban America, 1933-1965* (New York: Oxford University Press, 1975).

7. Advisory Commission on Intergovernmental Relations, *Categorical Grants: Their Role and Design* Report A–52 (Washington, D.C.: Government Printing Office, 1978), p. 23. Future references in this chapter to this Commission will be ACIR.

8. ACIR, *Fiscal Balance in the American Federal System*, Report A–31 (Washington, D.C.: The Commission, October, 1967), Vol. 1, p. 151.

9. David B. Walker, *Toward A Functioning Federalism* (Cambridge, Mass.: Winthrop Publishers, 1981), p. 84.

10. ACIR, *Categorical Grants*, p. 27.

11. See Jeffrey L. Pressman, *Federal Programs and City Politics* (Berkeley: University of California Press, 1975), chap. 3.

12. U.S. Congress, *Equal Opportunity Act Amendments of 1967*, 90th Congress, 1st Session, Sec. 210 ff.

13. ACIR, *Intergovernmentalizing the Classroom: The Federal Role in Elementary and Secondary Education*, Report A–81 (Washington, D.C.: The Commission, March, 1981), p. 4.

14. See Frederic N. Cleaveland, ed., *Congress and Urban Problems: A Casebook on the Legislative Process* (Washington, D.C.: The Brookings Institution, 1969), p. 4.

15. Daniel J. Elazar, "The Evolving Federal Grant System," in *The Power to Govern: Assessing Reform in the United States*, Proceedings of the Academy of Political Science, edited by Richard M. Pious, Vol. 34, No. 2 (New York: 1981), p. 8.

16. Cynthia Cates Colella, "The Care and Feeding of Leviathan: Who and What Makes Government Grow," *Intergovernmental Perspective*, Vol. 5, No. 4 (Fall, 1979), p. 7. See, also, David R. Beam, "The Accidental Leviathan: Was the Growth of Government a Mistake?", ibid, pp. 12–19. *Intergovernmental Perspective* is published by ACIR.

17. See ACIR, *Categorical Grants* for an account of grant development and program consolidation.

18. *County News*, October 26, 1973 (Washington, D.C.: National Association of Counties), p. 1.

19. ACIR, *Significant Features of Fiscal Federalism, 1980-81 Edition*, Report M-132 (Washington, D.C.: The Commission, December, 1981), p. 59.

20. ACIR, *Recent Trends in Federal and State Aid to Local Governments*, Report M-118 (Washington, D.C.: July, 1980), p. 9.

21. See footnote 19, Chap 3 of this book for a list of the studies in ACIR's *The Federal Role in the Federal System: The Dynamics of Growth*.

22. See "The Impact of Federal Grant Programs on Municipal Functions: Empirical Analysis" in ACIR, *The Federal Influence on State and Local Roles in the Federal System*, Report A-89 (Washington, D.C.: The Commission, November, 1981).

23. John Shannon, "The Slowdown in the Growth of State-Local Spending," in *Financing State and Local Governments in the 1980s: Issues and Trends*, ed. by Norman Walzer and David L. Chicoine (Cambridge, Mass.: Oelgeschlager, Gunn and Hain, Publishers, Inc., 1981), p. 239.

24. John C. Bollens and Henry J. Schmandt, *The Metropolis*, 4th ed. (New York: Harper and Row Publishers, 1982), p. 154.

25. *A National Agenda for the Eighties: Report of the President's Commission on a National Agenda for the Eighties* (Washington, D.C.: Government Printing Office, 1980), p. 70.

26. David B. Walker, Albert J. Richter, and Cynthia Cates Colella, "The First Ten Months: Grant-in-Aid, Regulatory, and Other Changes," *Intergovernmental Perspective*, Vol. 9, No. 1 (Winter, 1982), pp. 12–13.

27. We are indebted to Margaret Wrightson, Georgetown University, for alerting us to this development.

28. Beam; Colella; and ACIR, *The Federal Influence*.

29. Norman Beckman, "Changing Governmental Roles in Urban Development," in *Shaping an Urban Future: Essays in Memory of Catherine Bauer Wurster*, ed. by Bernard J. Frieden and William W. Nash, Jr. (Cambridge, Mass.: MIT Press, 1969), p. 151.

30. Ralph M. Widner, then executive director of the Appalachian Regional Commission, in *Creative Federalism: William A. Jump—I. Thomas McKillop Memorial Lectures in Public Administration, 1966*, ed. by Donald E. Nicoll (Washington, D.C.: Graduate School Press, U.S. Department of Agriculture, 1967), p. 93.

31. Catherine H. Lovell, Robert Kneisel, Max Neiman, Adam Z. Rose, and Charles A. Tobin, *Federal and State Mandating on Local Governments: An Exploration of Issues and Impacts*, Final Report to the National Science Foundation, June 20, 1979 (Riverside, Cal.: Graduate School of Administration, University of California, Riverside, 1979), p. 71.

32. For a discussion of issue networks, see Hugh Heclo, "Issue Networks and the Executive Establishment," in *The New American Political System*, ed. by Anthony King (Washington, D.C.: The American Enterprise Institute for Public Policy Research, 1978).

33. The proposal would have consolidated four categorical programs (urban renewal, model cities, neighborhood facilities, and rehabilitation loan) into a single grant financed by special revenue sharing. It was introduced on April 21, 1971 as the Urban Community Development Revenue Sharing Act of 1971 (H.R. 8853, 92nd Congress, 1st Session (1971); S. 1618, 92nd Congress, 1st Session). For an analysis of the politics of this legislation and other special revenue sharing proposals,

see Timothy J. Conlan, "Congressional Response to the New Federalism: The Politics of Special Revenue Sharing and Its Implications for Public Policy Making," Ph.D. dissertation, Harvard University, 1981.

34. Donald F. Kettl, *Managing Community Development in the New Federalism* (New York: Praeger Publishers, 1980), pp. 85–86. See also ACIR, *Community Development: The Workings of a Federal-Local Block Grant*, Report A–57 (Washington, D.C.: The Commission, March, 1977).

35. Kettl, p. 102.

36. See one of the four monitoring studies of the CDBG. Paul Dommel, Richard Nathan, Sarah Liebschutz, and Margaret Wrighton, *Decentralizing Community Development* (Washington, D.C.: Department of Housing and Urban Development, Government Printing Office, 1978).

37. Kettl, p. 98.

38. ACIR, *Community Development*, p. 44.

39. U.S. Department of Housing and Urban Development, *Community Development Block Grant Program: First Annual Report*, December, 1975, p. 44.

40. For a discussion on this point, see Robert D. Reischauer, "Governmental Diversity: Bane of the Grants Strategy in the United States," in *The Political Economy of Fiscal Federalism*, ed. by Wallace E. Oates (Lexington, Mass.: Lexington Books, 1977), pp. 115–127.

41. Mark W. Huddleston and Marian Lief Palley, "Short-Changing Nonmetropolitan America," *Public Budgeting and Finance*, Vol. 1, No. 3 (August, 1981), pp. 36–45.

42. See Thomas Muller and Michael Fix, "The Impact of Selected Federal Actions on Municipal Outlays," in *Government Regulation: Achieving Social and Economic Balance*, Vol. 5 of *Special Study on Economic Change*, U.S. Congress, Joint Economic Committee (Washington, D.C.: Government Printing Office, 1980), pp. 326–77.

43. National Association of Counties, "The Effects of Crosscutting Requirements on County Governments," memorandum (Washington, D.C.: National Association of Counties, February 19, 1981), pp. 3, 12, 13.

44. See William Davis, "Results of NLC Poll of City Officials. Many Mandates Impose Burdens on Local Budgets," *Nation's Cities Weekly*, June 22, 1981, pp. 3, 4. See also National League of Cities, "Municipal Policy and Program Survey," memorandum (Washington, D.C.: National League of Cities, 1981), pp. 6–8.

45. Pressman, Chap. 3.

46. As of December, 1978, citizen participation requirements were attached to 155 separate federal grant programs, involving 80 percent of the grant funds. Most were affixed to educational programs. ACIR, *Citizen Participation in the American Federal System*, Report A–78 (Washington, D.C.: The Commission, 1980), and ACIR, *The Federal Influence*, pp. 138–39.

47. For the operation of this process on the state level, see George E. Hale and Marian Lief Palley, "Federal Grants to the States: Who Governs?" *Administration and Society*, Vol. 11, No. 1 (May, 1979), p. 7. See also the same authors' *The Politics of Federal Grants* (Washington, D.C.: Congressional Quarterly, Inc., 1981).

48. Suzanne Farkas, *Urban Lobbying: Mayors in the Federal Arena* (New York: New York University Press, 1981), p. 22.

49. See ACIR, *The Federal Influence*, p. 115.

50. Taru Spiegel, "Successful Policy Implementation and the Disposition of Implementors," Unpublished Ph.D. Dissertation, University of Maryland, 1982, p. 54.

51. Morton Grodzins called these "federally engineered local governments." For elaboration, see his *The American System: A New View of Government in the United States,* ed. by Daniel J. Elazar (Chicago: Rand-McNally and Co., 1966), pp. 191–3. Also see John C. Bollens, *Special District Governments in the United States* (Berkeley: University of California Press, 1957).

52. Parris N. Glendening, "The Federal Role in Regional Planning Councils: Trends and Implications," *The Review of Regional Studies,* Vol. 1, No. 3 (Spring, 1971–72), pp. 93–111.

53. As quoted in ACIR, *Intergovernmental Relations in the Poverty Program* (Washington, D.C.: The Commission, 1966), p. 34.

54. *New York Times,* June 1, 1982.

55. Brown v. Board of Education of Topeka, 347 U.S. 483 (1954)

56. Plyer v. Doe and Texas v. Certain Undocumented Alien Children. 50 LW 4650 (1982).

57. A year-by-year analysis of national actions affecting local governments by Reeves and Glendening appears in the *Municipal Year Books* from 1977 through 1980.

58. Elrod v. Burns, 427 U.S. 347 (1976).

59. National League of Cities v. Usery, 426 U.S. 833 (1976).

60. Holt v. City of Tuscaloosa, 439 U.S. 60 (1978)

61. See Pressman, Chaps. 4 and 5.

62. Brian Gardner, "Intergovernmental Fiscal Relations and Local Government Policy: A Study of Federal Wastewater Treatment Grants in Maryland." Unpublished Ph.D. Dissertation, University of Maryland, 1982.

63. Pressman, pp. 107–8.

64. Donald B. Rosenthal, *Sticking Points and Ploys in Federal-Local Relations* (Philadelphia: Center for the Study of Federalism, 1980).

65. Pressman, p. 12

66. Ibid., p. 14.

67. Rosenthal.

68. Ibid.

69. Richard P. Nathan and Paul R. Dommel, "Federal-Local Relations under Block Grants," *Political Science Quarterly,* Vol. 93 (Fall, 1978), pp. 421–22.

70. Rosenthal.

CHAPTER 6

FINANCING THE
FEDERAL SYSTEM

F_{ISCAL} relations among governments in the United States are complex and confusing. Although each government has its own revenue and spending system—different from those on other levels and from those of similar neighboring jurisdictions—the interrelationships are strong. Moreover, the systems are often duplicative and overlapping. This may mean another government may have a determining voice in what taxes a given jurisdiction can levy and spend. Citizens may pay duplicate taxes and suffer the inequities of disparate spending patterns. For public officials, it often leads to frustration because a multiplicity of fiscal systems constricts options, increases costs, and undermines control.

Yet, within this dark picture, general positive images clearly stand out. Most important is that the system works, albeit with occasionally significant problems. Revenues are collected and expenditures are made while most state and local governments stay far from the abyss of total financial collapse predicted by the strongest critics of American fiscal federalism. Some would argue that the lack of a more centralized, ordered—perhaps, even rational—system of fiscal relations promotes certain values crucial to American federalism, for example, diversity and decentralization. As a leading student of American public finance, L. L. Ecker-Racz, observed,

> Federal democracies aspire to decentralized decision-making in both taxing and spending. They want to leave maximum responsibility for domestic government in the hands of those close to the people—at the local level, if possible; at the state level, if necessary; but rarely at the

federal level. With this goes a preference for each level of government to raise its own revenues so that the responsibility for taxing can go hand in hand with that for spending. We are reassured when those who have the pleasure of spending have to suffer the pain of imposing taxes[1]

Finally, the present fiscal system, all its shortcomings notwithstanding, finds a defense in its acceptance by the American people. It is a reluctant and begrudging acceptance to be sure, but one that stands firm in the face of proposals for a sweeping reordering of responsibilities. Perhaps the public in some vague way recognizes that a major remodeling of the financial system poses a potential threat to inherited values and traditions. Perhaps their defense of the current fiscal arrangements comes more from a visceral conservatism of the American electorate than from implicit or explicit consideration of the United States' political theory heritage.[2]

Whatever the cause, it seems clear that a major restructuring of the financial system will not take place in the near future. Change will come, as it has in the past, in incremental and limited steps rather than in an immediate, major overhaul. Even the much heralded national revenue-sharing program enacted in 1972 or the "Taxpayers Revolt" of the 1970s must be viewed as relatively minor changes when considered in the context of the total American fiscal system.

THE CONSTITUTIONAL BASIS OF REVENUE RAISING

The current array of revenue-raising efforts and fiscal interactions among governments has its genesis in the broad grants of taxation powers found in the national and state basic laws. The power to tax is defined as the ability to extract compulsory contributions to be used for public purposes by a government. In the American system both the national and state governments have indigenous taxing powers. These powers are subject to both formal legal and informal political limitations.

National Taxing Powers and Limitations

The United States Congress has almost unlimited taxing power. In large part this constitutional grant of power grew out of the difficult financial situation facing the central government under the Articles of Confederation. Under that document the national government lacked the power to levy taxes. Instead, the states were to supply revenues to the United States treasury in proportion to the land occupied in each state. Not surprisingly, states soon fell far behind in their contributions to the national government, leaving it financially impotent. In this environment, the members of the Constitutional Convention stood nearly unanimous in their demand that the new national legislature be given broad powers to raise its own revenues.

Accordingly, the first part of Section 8 of Article I of the Constitution states that "the Congress shall have power to lay and collect taxes, duties, imposts and excises, to pay the debts and provide for the common defense and general welfare of the United States. . . ." This is, indeed, a broad open-ended grant of taxing power. The Supreme Court has strengthened and broadened this authority even further by consistently asserting that the Congress itself is the sole interpreter of what is "necessary and proper" in providing "for the common defense and general welfare of the United States." According to the Court,

> The discretion, however, is not confided to the Courts. The discretion belongs to Congress, unless the choice is clearly wrong, a display of arbitrary power, not an exercise of judgment. This is now familiar law. "When such a contention comes here we naturally require a showing that by no reasonable possibility can the challenged legislation fall within the wide range of discretion permitted to Congress." Nor is the concept of the general welfare static. Needs that were narrow or parochial a century ago may be interwoven in our day with the well-being of the Nation. What is critical or urgent changes with the times.[3]

Most authorities today agree that the wording of Article I, Section 8, in tandem with Court interpretations, gives Congress practically unlimited taxing powers.

Is there any limitation to the national taxing power? The Constitution explicitly specifies a few limitations. Article I, Section 8, provides that all duties, imposts, and excises shall be uniform, meaning geographic uniformity, throughout the United States. Section 9 of the same Article prohibits preference to one state's ports over those of another and forbids the levying of an export tax. That Article's provision stating that "No capitation, or other direct, tax shall be laid, unless in proportion to the census" was originally interpreted by the Court to negate a progressive income tax law (1895). This interpretation was reversed when the Sixteenth Amendment was adopted. Also, taxation methods that fail to conform to the due process standard would obviously be in violation of the Fifth Amendment. These few restrictions have placed no real obstacle on congressional taxing ability.

The judicial branch of government has looked carefully at national taxing power and, with the exceptions of restrictions on taxation of state and local governments, has not found the occasion to add substantially to limitations on this authority. Demonstrating the extent of the acceptance of nearly open-ended interpretation of national taxing powers, the Court has ruled that a national taxpayer, because he pays taxes to support a particular program, does not automatically gain standing to sue (that is, a direct personal interest necessary to enter the courts) to stop a national government expenditure.[4] Further, Congress can use its taxing powers to regulate in social and economic areas traditionally viewed as state prerogatives. The unlimited power of Congress to regulate in these areas (e.g., narcotic, marijuana, and gambling controls) and to intervene in accepted areas of state police powers has been with a few notable exceptions⁵ repeatedly affirmed by the Court.

An area in which the national government's taxing ability has been restrained by the judicial branch concerns its powers to tax other governments. *McCulloch* v. *Maryland* provided the headwater for a stream of judicial decisions addressed to the question of intergovernmental immunity from taxation.⁶ Growing out of an attempt by the 1818 Maryland state legislature to tax the Baltimore branch of the Bank of the United States, this decision set the tone for future consideration of attempts by one government to tax another government. It declared "that the power to tax involves the power to destroy, that the power to destroy may defeat and render useless the power to create, that there is a plain repugnancy in conferring on one government a power to control the constitutional measures of another. . . ."⁷ Chief Justice Marshall's opinion was based largely on his strongly-voiced view of the supremacy of the national government:

> The American people have declared their constitution and the laws made in pursuance thereof, to be supreme; but this principle [of state taxation of national activities] would transfer the supremacy, in fact, to the states. If the states may tax one instrument, employed by the government in the execution of its powers, they may tax any and every other instrument. They may tax the mail; they may tax the mint; they may tax patent rights; they may tax the papers of the custom-house; they may tax judicial process; they may tax all the means employed by the government, to an excess which would defeat all the ends of government. This was not intended by the American people. They did not design to make their government dependent on the states.⁸

In a dictum contained within the decision, Marshall, demonstrating his concern for national supremacy, argued that while the national government was immune from state taxes, state activity may in turn be taxed by the central government. This view was rejected by later courts that moved to a position of reciprocal immunity, thus offering both the national government and the states immunity from intergovernmental taxation.⁹ The principle of reciprocal immunity—attempting to assure the equality and integrity of both levels of government—did more than exempt from taxation property and activities of both the national and state governments. It also exempted the salaries of national, state, and local employees, private businesses for that part of their activity dealing with a government, and the interest on national, state, and local bonds.

Starting in the late 1930s the Court released a series of opinions that gradually eroded the principle of reciprocal immunity. The rule today is that intergovernmental taxes are generally prohibited if they are seen as providing an obstacle to the performance of another government's activities. At present, reciprocal immunity has been reduced to the point that it serves as a rather weak limitation on national taxing power, or for that matter on state taxing power. The physical facilities of one government are still exempt from taxation by another government. Nevertheless, taxes may be levied on other governmental concerns provided they do not harm the taxed government's ability to perform its functions. For example, a national judge living in New York City is subject to state and city income taxes on his public wages, just as a New York state legislator pays an income tax to the national government. In neither case does the tax interfere with the official's ability to perform his job. Congress exempted its members, however, from paying income tax to the state of Maryland on the premise that even though more than 125 members lived in that state, their legal residence was in their home district, not in Maryland (or the District of Columbia or Virginia). The Court upheld the exemption, thus costing Maryland approximately $225,000 in potential income taxes.[10]

A major controversial exception to the end of tax immunities is the continued exemption of the interest on municipal bonds from the national government's income tax. (The controversy, however, is centered on questions of equity, rather than a concern about intergovernmental taxing relations.) A last "gray area," which still has not been entirely cleared by the courts, concerns taxing state or local activities that are not exclusively governmental in character. In 1905, for example, the Court upheld a tax on South Carolina's liquor-dispensing business.[11] What of other services that are *sold* to the public, rather than supported by general taxes, such as water or mass transit? Are such sales taxable? The Court has not yet given a definite response.

Thus, a long history of judicial review of these concerns—the standing of a taxpayer to sue, the propriety of regulation through use of the taxing power, and intergovernmental taxing immunity—has produced only a few limited restrictions on national taxing authority. Effective limitations on congressional revenue-raising activities come as will be shown later in this chapter, from the political arena rather than from the Constitution or the courts.

State Taxing Powers and Limitations

In theory, the state taxing power is even greater than that of the national government. The authority of the central government to raise revenues, as great as it is, is still a specific enumerated grant of power. However, the states possess residual powers, that is, those "powers not delegated to the United States by the Constitution, nor prohibited by it to the States."

The broad grant of taxing authority specifically delegated to the national government is not exclusive and is shared with the states. Nor does the national Constitution prohibit the states from taxing. They possess an open-ended power to tax. Because of these characteristics, state taxing authority is best understood by examining the limitations placed on it. What is left, free of those limitations, provides a fairly strong reservoir of power.

The limitations on a state's revenue-raising authority come from three sources—the United States Constitution, the state's own basic law, and political realities. The national Constitution contains several restrictive measures against state activity in the tax area. Article I, Section 10, provides that "No state shall, without the consent of the Congress, lay any imposts or duties on imports or exports, except what may be absolutely necessary for executing its inspection laws: and the net product of all duties and imposts, laid by any state on imports or exports, shall be for the use of the treasury of the United States and all such laws shall be subject to the revision and control of the Congress." Further, "No state shall, without the consent of Congress, lay any duty on tonnage. . . ."

Other limitations come from that same section's prohibition against state "law impairing the obligation of contracts," Article IV's "privileges and immunities" clause prohibiting discrimination against nonresidents of a state, Article I, Section 8's "commerce clause," and the Fourteenth Amendment's "equal protection" and "due process" standards. All these provisions have limited the states' ability to tax. A voluminous number of Supreme Court decisions have attempted to define the extent of these restrictions.

The sum of almost 200 years' interpretation of these vague, but crucial limitations on state taxing power is that a state tax may not (1) impair interstate commerce, (2) discriminate against citizens of other states, (3) deny equal protection and due process to its own citizens nor those of other states, or (4) conflict with national legislation. While the acceptable limits of the state taxing authority are still not clearly defined, Congress and the courts have shown a liberal and flexible attitude toward state powers of taxation.

Confrontations among the states over taxation regularly occur. The energy crisis of recent years illustrates the flexible but fine line the Supreme Court walks in determining the limits of state taxing power. The Court rejected a Louisiana special tax on offshore natural gas passing through that state. Eight other states had brought suit claiming the tax, which cost consumers between $200 and $300 million a year, was unconstitutional because it was the equivalent of a duty charged by a foreign nation. The Court agreed, noting that Louisiana unconstitutionally obstructed free commerce between the states with a discriminatory tax and "usurped" federal authority to oversee natural gas costs.[12] A few months later the Court ruled constitutional a Montana severance tax of 30 percent on the sale of coal. The justices based their conclusion on two points: (1) the tax is the same for in-state and out-of-state consumers and therefore not discriminatory; and (2) while the national government alone has the jurisdiction to regulate natural gas prices, no similar regulations exist for coal.[13] As energy shortages continue and "frostbelt-sunbelt" regional competition increases, the Court can be expected to settle a growing number of similar conflicts.

State Constitutional Limitations

State constitutions are not nearly so liberal and flexible as the federal document about the power of the states to tax. Nor are their provisions as complex and nebulous as those limitations imposed by the United States Constitution and the Supreme Court's interpretation of it.

State constitutions adopted soon after independence placed relatively few restraints on the taxing powers of the legislatures. Later, however, as a result of excessive spending and taxing, incurrence of debts, and repeated scandals and corruption, particularly during the last half of the nineteenth century, state constitutions were rewritten to restrict substantially the legislatures' taxing abilities.

Some of these curbs are in the form of exclusions from taxation. All states' basic laws provide for certain outright exemptions for particular types of property. Land and facilities owned by public agencies, for example, uniformly go untaxed throughout the United States. In addition, most states exempt property used for educational, religious, and charitable purposes. Approximately 40 percent of all land in the United States falls into one of these excluded categories, including the publicly owned land. Many states grant a "homestead" exemption (e.g., the first $5,000 assessed valuation of a private home) to their residents. Others have established "circuit breaker" arrangements that shield low-income individuals from high property taxes on their homes. In some cases, both the homestead exemption and the circuit breaker apply to certain groups of properties, such as those owned by the elderly. Some state constitutions place an absolute ban on taxation of income, either personal or corporate, or both.

In addition to these exemptions, some state constitutions specify certain types of limitations on the rate of taxation. Industrial and agricultural property is often required to be taxed at a lower rate than other properties in a state. This mandated tax differential is designed to promote industry and jobs. In the case of the agricultural limitations—the so-called "greenbelt" laws—the promotion is aimed not only at agricultural, ranching, and forestry interests, but also increasingly at preserving open-space and reducing land speculation in urbanizing areas. The limitations and exemptions found in state basic law, when combined with those imposed by the national charter and with political restrictions, greatly reduce the taxing power of the states.

Local Taxing Powers and Limitations

Of the three levels of government, the local level has the least taxing power. Being creatures of the states, municipalities, counties, townships, and special districts do not possess indigenous authority in this area. Instead, they must rely on grants of particular taxing powers from the states. The grant of revenue-raising powers to localities is a restrictive and very controlled process throughout the Republic. Even those local governments enjoying home rule, whether statutory or constitutional, find that their discretionary power in the area of taxation is carefully circumscribed.

This very minimal taxing authority is further limited by the same national and state constitutional strictures that affect state power of taxation. Further, many states place by constitution or statute maximum tax rates (mills) on local government property taxes, which is their major source of revenue. The maximum millage may be set according to function, e.g., 10 mills for roads, 25 mills for education, and so on, or there may be a stated total millage for all functions combined. To their dismay, local officials find that variations of this approach are becoming increasingly popular as state legislatures seek to subdue the "taxpayers' revolt" generally focused on local property taxes.

As with the national and state governments, local units find that major obstacles to their revenue-raising capabilities come from the political arena. This may be even more true at the local level because of the proximity of the voters' wrath and because of the great unpopularity of the property tax.

EXTRA-CONSTITUTIONAL CONSTRAINTS ON TAXING POWERS

All three levels of government are subject to major restraints on their ability to tax beyond the formal constitutional strictures. In many ways, informal, extra-constitutional constraints may be more determinative of the amount and source of revenues that are available to the fiscal federal system than all the constitutional-legal restrictions combined.

The "Taxpayers' Revolt"

The most important and most powerful of these informal limitations is that imposed by the growing opposition of the American public to new

and higher taxes. While the dissatisfaction has not yet reached the proportion of the Whiskey Rebellion's protest (1791–1794) over excise taxation,
during which President Washington had to use national troops to restore
order, public officeholders are aware that politically the results can be
just as deadly.

How real is the public dissatisfaction? The Harris survey reported in
1971 that almost 70 percent of those interviewed in a nationwide sample
said they would sympathize with a "taxpayers' revolt." This is 26 percent
more than felt the same way only two years before.[14] This observation is
reinforced by survey data which indicate that for the decade before the
1978 emergence of the "Taxpayers' Revolt," approximately two-thirds of
the public believed that the tax burden had "reached the breaking point"
and four-fifths believed "taxes in this country are unreasonable."[15]

Public opinion polls, referenda, and election results showed a growing
dissatisfaction during the late 1960s and early 1970s with both the tax
structure and the level of taxes in the United States. Although state legislatures and popular initiatives had imposed many strict limitations on local
government property taxing capacity, the June, 1978, adoption by the
California voters of one more such limitation, called Proposition 13, became
a highly publicized symbolic event. It was quickly hailed by many as the
start of a modern "Taxpayers' Revolt." Proposition 13 was a constitutional
amendment, petitioned to the ballot. It cut property taxes in half, limited
taxes to one percent of market value (based on 1975 values), allowed only
a 2 percent annual increase for inflation, and required that any new taxes
or increases in existing ones must receive a two-thirds vote of the state
legislature or local electorate.

The approval of Proposition 13 by the California voters, which economist Paul Samuelson called "The most important U.S. political-economic event
of 1978, perhaps even the 1970s,"[16] and which an Advisory Commission
on Intergovernmental Relations' poll ranked as the fourth most important
intergovernmental event of the past 20 years,[17] opened a floodgate of
taxing and spending limitation efforts in other states and in hundreds of
local communities. Future developments may well show November 5,
1980, when the voters elected a President and Congress committed to
substantial tax reductions at the national level, as a similar break point for
the national government. The combination of these events will have a
major impact on financing the federal system.

The Proposition 13 vote turned a general unfocused discontent into a
targeted, achievable protest action. As one study notes, prior to that referendum protests against taxes seemed futile. The complexity of our state and
local finance systems coupled with widespread determinism toward taxes—
only death was said to be equally certain—served as major factors insulating
governments' budgets. State and local intergovernmental finance may

remain baffling to many citizens, but the November 1978 elections in 12 states and subsequent public opinion data suggest that many are no longer afraid to impose formal tax and expenditure limitations on their state and local governments.[18]

Results. The early focus of the "Taxpayers' Revolt" was on property taxes. From that limited perspective, this revolt was successful. In 1979, for example, property tax revenue collections showed their first decline since World War II, dropping from $66.4 billion to $64.9 billion.

An unanticipated outcome has been to add substantially to national and state control over local affairs and to centralize government. As Lyle C. Finch, president of the Institute of Public Administration, stated in recent testimony before Congress, "The most significant single effect of Proposition 13 has been the shift in financial and other powers to the state government in what traditionally has been a strong home-rule state."[19]

Ironically, a decade from now the whole anti-government, anti-tax movement may be viewed as a major stimulus for growing centralization. Charles Levine and Paul L. Posner discussed some of the dilemmas coming from current public opinion and resultant adjustments in the federal system.

> By trying to reduce local government expenditures, voters supporting tax limitation initiatives may have inadvertently helped to increase the cost of government by pushing decision making to higher levels of government. At higher levels of government, feedback on local problems is weak, inaccurate, and sluggish, making control and implementation more difficult and cumbersome. Furthermore, by forcing policy making upward, we run the danger of overloading state and national policy making bodies with problems that used to be the exclusive concern of governors, mayors, state legislators, and city councilmen. This leaves us with the central question of intergovernmental administration: Is it possible to transfer responsibility for funding services upward in the political system—and thus remove the link between revenue raising levels of government and levels which expend and implement—without eroding traditional constraints on spending and the traditional responsiveness of local government?[20]

The elected officials' reactions to the "Taxpayers' Revolt" have been mixed. Some have moved to hold taxes constant or reduce them—often, however, at the expense of another level of government. Thus, the state legislator introduces a bill to freeze the millage or the assessment levels for local governments. Others seek relief through the transfer of expensive functions to different levels of government. Witness in this respect state and local efforts to make welfare assistance a national responsibility or local attempts to make capital construction for schools a state responsibility, or the Reagan administration's efforts to return many functions to state governments. Still others seek assistance from higher levels of government, as in the state and local quest for revenue sharing funds or local demands for larger state grants-in-aid. Intergovernmental aid, however, is generally an easy place to cut cost for the donor government. Not surprisingly, federal aid to the states and localities has begun to decline, as has state assistance to localities in some jurisdictions.

Other Limitations on Taxing Powers

Another limitation of governmental taxing power is found in established patterns that make changes in some revenue collection efforts very difficult politically. Long traditions of tax exemptions, such as those given to religious or charitable groups, for example, are hard to overcome. Many states have established patterns of high or low tax efforts or long-existing limitations on certain kinds of taxes, e.g., avoidance of personal income taxes or of a sales tax on food and medicine. In some instances these "traditions" are carefully cultivated by vested interests who benefit from them; other times the traditional patterns are just recognized by the people as "the way things are done."

In line with this restraint by tradition, governments often find themselves limited by the deference they show to the tax needs of other partners in the federal system. The national government, for instance, has for a variety of reasons, including deference for state revenue needs, avoided major reliance on direct national sales taxes. In a similar manner, the states have strengthened the fiscal capacity of local governments by minimizing reliance on state property taxes. Accordingly, although the states received more than 50 percent of their tax revenue from that source at the turn of the present century, by 1980 state property taxes accounted for only 2 percent of state-collected taxes.

The same attitude is shown by local governments when they avoid, for the most part, attempts to tax residents of neighboring jurisdictions through devices such as the commuter tax or the nonresident income tax. This avoidance in part comes from legal and political restrictions, including the likelihood of retaliatory action by nearby jurisdictions, but also comes from a deference to the sovereignty and needs of other governments.

Both states and localities often find their revenue-raising abilities muted by perceptions of government competition with nearby governments. These perceptions see large cities within a state in competition with each other for industry, business, and the "right kind" of citizens, generally meaning the upper-middle and upper-income strata of society. Similar rivalries exist between central cities and suburbs and among states within a region. The competition is often given as the reason for avoiding higher taxes or certain kinds of taxes. While it is questionable what weight individuals or businesses give to lower taxes compared to adequate government services and amenities of public life, the perception of this type of competition has often influenced public finance decisions. As one expert on business and industrial development remarks:

> Tax abatement is not an incentive to prevent a relocation from Ohio to Alabama or Texas. If a major manufacturer is considering a location in the South or West versus the North, the cost considerations would be wages and the distance to suppliers and customers. Taxes probably would not play a major role.[21]

This generally accepted conclusion notwithstanding, "fiscal capacity is," as Michael D. Reagan and John G. Sanzone note, "a political as well as an economic concept. Interstate and intercommunity rivalries for business location severely dampen tax-raising proclivities—where such exist at all."[22]

Another explanation of limitations on revenue-raising capabilities of the state and local portion of the federal system comes from recent policy analysis research indicating that legal and political considerations may be of secondary importance in determining state and local governments' abilities in this area. Socio-economic variables, geographic region, past taxing and spending patterns, and intergovernmental aid are increasingly offered as inputs that are more likely to affect taxing and spending activities than are constitutional, structural, or political variables. While the full extent of the import of these variables and the way they affect the public finance system is still not completely understood, it has been demonstrated that certain arrangements of these variables are correlated with particular taxing and spending patterns.[23]

TAX OVERLAPPING IN THE FEDERAL SYSTEM

Although each level relies heavily on one type of tax, the American federal system is characterized by tax duplication and overlapping to an extent not found elsewhere in the world. Despite the deference shown by one level of government to another, with very few exceptions all levels of government utilize the same taxes. There is a national tax on liquor and tobacco, a state tax and, depending on the municipality or county, a local sales tax on those products. Likewise, it is possible to pay taxes on one's wages to the national, state and local governments. This duplication exists for all the major taxes and most of the minor ones. The one real exception is the customs tax which is reserved for the national government, and that, in today's world, is an increasingly insignificant portion of national revenues.

In addition to the vertical duplication within the federal system, there is great overlapping of taxes on the horizontal plane, especially within the more urbanized areas. It is possible to have property taxed by the municipal government, the county, the school district and perhaps three or four special districts. The overlapping may not be immediately obvious to the taxpayer because of the practice of letting one government, generally the county, assess, bill, and collect taxes for all property in the area with subsequent distribution to the taxing bodies, but the impact is just the same.

A serial tax duplication also will add many taxes to one item. A home appliance, for example, may have its base metals taxed at the mines, be the subject of a levy at the manufacturing level, be taxed indirectly through motor fuel levies as it is transported during the manufacturing process and to the point of sale, be subjected to an inventory tax as it waits in the warehouse, be the subject of sales taxes for the state and municipality, and, finally, in a last ignoble act, in many jurisdictions provide the occasion for annual impositions of a personal property tax.

EXPENDITURES

Untangling the web of expenditure patterns is an extremely complex task. It is not sufficient to state that one level of governments performs a particular function or pays for a certain percentage of that expenditure. The expenditure system is far more mixed intergovernmentally. Since almost all functions in the United States are shared, many are supported not just by one or two levels of government but by a host of governmental jurisdictions. For example, law enforcement in a particular geographic area may be dependent on expenditures by national, state, county, township, and interlocal authorities.

Intergovernmental Transfers Complicate Understanding

The picture is further clouded by a constantly shifting mass of intergovernmental financial transfers designed to help other governments pay for a public function. The complexity is illustrated if we follow a million dollar grant from the National Endowment for the Arts to a New York state government art program. The grant is an expenditure for the arts by the national government but a revenue for New York State. If the state then adds $500,000 of its own money (often required by federal law as a grant condition) and then awards $1.5 million to New York City for its arts and museum program, it would record an arts expenditure of $1.5 million and the City would receive that amount in additional aid. New York City, then, may raise another $250,000 in local revenues and, perhaps, $250,000 in private contributions, and announces a $2 million acquisition program for the New York Metropolitan Museum of Art. While only $2 million were actually expended on the purchase of goods and services for the museum, the combined intergovernmental budgetary system will record $4.5 million, that is, $1 million by the national government, $1.5 million by New York State, and $2 million by New York City.

The process of one level of government's expenditures being recorded as a revenue by another level of government and then re-recorded as a new expenditure is complicated by two other features of the fiscal system. First, the matching requirements among levels of government and among programs vary greatly. An arts grant may require an equal contribution by the receiving jurisdiction, while an interstate highway construction grant may be on a 90–10 matching formula, and other grants may require no match at all. Second, expenditure patterns differ among states. One state will, for example, pay 100 percent of local school construction costs while another will contribute only 10 percent. Nationwide aggregate school construction costs data are, therefore, often misleading about cost sharing in one region, state, or locality.

Growth and Shifts in Public Expenditures

Total public expenditures, as shown in Table 6–1, increased from approximately $10 billion just before the Depression (1929) to $1,085 billion in 1982. It is important to note the way the proportion of expenditures has shifted among the levels of government over the intervening years. In 1929 the federal and state governments together spent far less than the local governments. With the impact of the Depression, World War II and the subsequent arms race, the national government began spending more than the combined state-local sector. Reflecting the change in its role, the national government by 1949 was spending approximately the same amount on its domestic programs ($17.2 billion) as state ($7.7 billion) and local ($12.5 billion) governments combined. Recent years witnessed a furtherance of this trend with the central government spending more ($427 billion in 1982) for domestic programs than the combined state-local expenditures ($405 billion). These figures are in current dollars, not adjusted for inflation, and are after intergovernmental transfers.

Examining the growth in governmental expenditures from a different perspective, Table 6–1 also shows the relation of public sector purchase of goods and services to the gross national product (GNP). In 1929, all governments' costs were less than 10 percent of the GNP. By 1982, this had increased to over one-third. While a decrease is projected as a result of recent changes in national spending policies, the change from the 1920s to the 1980s is dramatic and not expected to be reversed significantly.

Finally, Table 6–1 places the total government expenditures in a perspective more meaningful to the average citizen—per capita expenditures. In 1929 the cost in constant, or 1972 dollars, of running all governments was $258 for each man, woman, and child in the United States. That figure was dominated by $151 for local government costs. By 1982, it cost $2,257 for each individual to run government in America, now dominated by $1,413 for federal expenditures.

Reasons for Expenditure Growth

What accounts for the massive growth in national expenditures in recent years? Table 6–2 reveals two major determinants. The first is the cost of social security payments. Accounting for 3.6 percent of federal domestic expenditures in 1949, these payments increased to 41.3 percent in 1982. That is, more than 41 cents of every nondefense dollar the national government spent went for social security. Further, and most important for the focus of this book, federal aid to state and local governments increased from less than $1 billion in 1929 to $83.5 billion in 1982. As a percentage of domestic expenditures, this is an extraordinary increase from 6.7 percent to 16.4 percent. Note also that the federal aid percentage actually declined from the 1978 high of 24 percent for intergovernmental aid. The dominance of these two expenditures (social security payments and federal aid) which together account for almost 58 percent of national domestic expenditures, is emphasized by the table's depiction that *all other* federal domestic program expenditures *declined* from 93 percent of the budget in 1929 to 42 percent in 1982. Clearly, social security and federal aid emerge as the fastest growing components of steadily expanding federal domestic expenditures.

Expenditures in the United States are, then, extraordinarily intergovernmental. The patterns of support for a service are dynamic with constant adjustments and shifting responsibilities. Indeed, the question of which government should pay for which function or service, is at the heart of much of the debate about the future of the federal system.

Which Level Spends the Most Wisely?

Table 6–3 analyzes public perceptions as to which level of government spends money the most wisely. For the past several years, the ACIR has asked the public "From which level of government do you feel you get the most for your money—Federal, state, or local?" For nine of the eleven years of the poll the national government was perceived as giving "the most for your money." Only in 1979 and 1981 did it fail to gain that honor, slipping behind the local governments by 3 to 4 percent. States consistently remained in third place although their percentage has varied.

TABLE 6-1
GOVERNMENT EXPENDITURE, *AFTER INTERGOVERNMENTAL TRANSFERS,*[1] SELECTED YEARS 1929–1982

Calendar year	Total public sector	National			State and Local		
		Total	Defense[2]	Domestic[3]	Total	State	Local
Amount (Billions of current dollars)							
1929	$10.3	$2.5	$1.1	$1.4	$7.8	$1.7	$6.1
1939	17.6	7.9	1.5	6.4	9.6	3.0	6.6
1949	59.3	39.1	21.9	17.2	20.2	7.7	12.5
1959	131.0	84.1	53.2	30.9	46.9	17.5	29.4
1969	286.8	168.1	94.6	73.5	118.7	44.9	73.8
1974	459.9	256.3	104.0	152.3	203.6	79.4	124.2
1979	753.2	430.4	155.7	274.7	322.8	127.8	195.0
1981	985.5	602.5	219.7	382.8	383.0	157.0	226.0
1982 est.	1,084.5	679.2	252.0	427.2	405.3	166.2	239.1
As a percent of GNP							
1929	10.0	2.4	1.1	1.4	7.5	1.6	5.9
1939	19.4	8.7	1.7	7.0	10.6	3.3	7.3
1949	23.0	15.1	8.5	6.7	7.8	3.0	4.8
1959	26.8	17.2	10.9	6.3	9.6	3.6	6.0
1969	30.4	17.8	10.0	7.8	12.6	4.8	7.8
1974	32.1	17.9	7.3	10.6	14.2	5.5	8.7
1979	31.2	17.8	6.5	11.4	13.4	5.3	8.1
1981	33.5	20.5	7.5	13.0	13.0	5.3	7.7
1982 est.	35.5	22.2	8.2	14.0	13.3	5.4	7.8

Per capita in constant dollars (1972 dollars)

1929	$258	$62	$28	$34	$193	$42	$151
1939	472	212	41	172	257	80	177
1949	756	498	280	219	257	98	159
1959	1090	700	443	257	390	146	244
1969	1631	955	538	417	676	256	420
1974	1869	1041	422	619	826	322	504
1979	2047	1171	423	746	878	347	531
1981	2193	1340	489	853	853	350	503
1982 est.	2257	1413	524	890	843	346	498

[1] National Income and Product Accounts. See U.S. Department of Commerce, Bureau of Economic Analysis, *Survey of Current Business* [monthly].

[2] National defense, international affairs and finance and space research and technology. Also includes the estimated portion of net interest attributable to these functions. See *Survey of Current Business*.

[3] Includes Social Security (OASDHI). All federal aid to state and local governments, including general revenue sharing payments included as state and local expenditure.

Source: Adapted from Advisory Commission on Intergovernmental Relations, *Significant Features of Fiscal Federalism. 1981-82 Edition*. Report M-135. Washington, D.C.: The Commission, April, 1983, pp. 14-15.

TABLE 6-2
FEDERAL DOMESTIC EXPENDITURE,[1]
SELECTED YEARS 1929-1982

Calendar Year	Federal Domestic Expenditure		
	Social Security (OASDHI)[2]	Federal Aid[3]	All Other[4]
Amount (in billions of current dollars)			
1929	$ —	$0.1	$ 1.4
1939	*	1.0	6.4
1949	0.7	2.2	16.4
1954	3.7	2.9	16.2
1959	10.4	6.8	20.4
1964	16.5	10.4	27.6
1969	34.0	20.3	39.1
1974	72.1	43.9	78.8
1975	83.5	54.6	105.2
1976	95.2	61.1	110.2
1977	107.4	67.5	118.7
1978	119.0	77.3	125.2
1979	134.7	80.4	137.5
1980	157.3	88.7	171.0
1981	185.4	87.7	194.1
1982 est.	210.0	83.5	215.5
Percentage distribution			
1929	—	6.7	93.3
1939	**	13.5	86.5
1949	3.6	11.4	85.0
1954	16.2	12.7	71.1
1959	27.2	18.1	54.3
1964	30.3	19.1	50.6
1969	36.4	21.7	41.9
1974	37.0	22.5	40.5
1975	34.3	22.4	43.2
1976	35.7	22.9	41.4
1977	36.6	23.0	40.4
1978	37.0	24.0	38.9
1979	38.2	22.8	39.0
1980	37.7	21.3	41.0
1981	39.7	18.8	41.5
1982 est.	41.3	16.4	42.3

*Less than $50 million.
**Less than 0.05 percent.
[1]National Income and Product Accounts.
[2]Old-Age and Survivors Insurance, Disability Insurance and Medicare.
[3]Federal Aid under this series "National Income Account," differs slightly from the federal payments (Census) series. The major difference is the inclusion of federal payments for low-rent public housing (est. at $3.5 billion in 1980) in the Census series but excluded by definition from this series. Includes federal general revenue sharing.
[4]Includes direct federal expenditure for (listed in descending order of magnitude for 1982): interest on the public debt, income maintenance (other than Social Security), health, education, veterans benefits and services, and transportation.

Source: Advisory Commission on Intergovernmental Relations, Significant Features of Fiscal Federalism, 1981-82 Edition. Washington, D.C.: The Commission, April, 1983. Report M-135. p. 16.

TABLE 6-3
PERCEPTIONS OF "MOST FOR YOUR MONEY,"
BY LEVEL OF GOVERNMENT

Question: From Which Level of Government Do You Feel You Get the Most For Your Money—Federal, State, or Local?

Percent of U.S. Public

	May 1982	Sept. 1981	May 1980	May 1979	May 1978	May 1977	March 1976	May 1975	April 1974	May 1973	March 1972
Federal	35	30	33	29	35	36	36	38	29	35	39
Local	28	33	26	33	26	26	25	25	28	25	26
State	20	25	22	22	20	20	20	20	24	18	18
Don't know	17	14	19	16	19	18	19	17	19	22	17

Source: Advisory Commission on Intergovernmental Relations, Changing Public Attitudes on Government and Taxes, 1982. Report S-11 (Washington, D.C.: The Commission, 1982), p. 2.

DEALING WITH FISCAL DISPARITIES

An area of vital concern in the operation of the federal system is the fiscal disparities and inequities among the several states. Simply stated, there are very rich states and very poor states. The 1981 per capita income for Alaska of $13,763 or for Connecticut of $12,816 is almost twice Mississippi's $7,408. Given the importance of the impact of many state and local functions on an individual's future (e.g., health care, and education), can the United States long tolerate a type of federal lottery system in which one person receives more and better basic services because, by accident of birth, he or she was lucky enough to live in a relatively affluent state-local system? Should state boundaries artificially segregate resources and perpetuate inequities?

These questions, probably in a more extreme form, are also applicable to another area of concern, that of interlocal resource disparities. The imbalance of resources among the states is relatively minor compared to that among local governments. Wealthy communities with an abundance of human and financial resources are separated from less affluent neighbors by the legal stricture of municipal and county boundary lines. By every major index, e.g., tax base, functional expenditure, socio-economic characteristics, the disparity between central cities and their suburbs is steadily increasing.

With the political system taking only limited actions to alleviate these conditions, the courts have begun to intervene to relieve the grossest of inequities. In the area of school financing, courts in California, Michigan, Minnesota, New Jersey, and Texas have ordered the states to take necessary steps to reduce fiscal disparities among school districts resulting from local reliance on property taxes for school financing. In the precedent-making case of *Serrano* v. *Priest* (1971),[24] the California Supreme Court ruled that state and local governments could not allocate funds solely on the basis of a school district's wealth. In Los Angeles County, for example, the Beverly Hills School District had a per pupil assessed property base of $50,885 and a per student expenditure of $1,232; in the Baldwin Park District the assessed value was only $3,706 per student and the expenditure was $577, less than half of that of Beverly Hills. This disparity existed despite the fact that the Baldwin District had a much higher tax rate. The Court turned down the state's defense of the existing arrangement in the following words:

> More basically, however, we reject the defendants' underlying thesis that classification by wealth is constitutional so long as the wealth is that of the district, not the individual. We think that discrimination on the basis of district wealth is equally invalid. The commercial and industrial property which augments a district's tax base is distributed unevenly throughout the state. To allot more educational dollars to the children

of one district than to those of another merely because of the fortuitous presence of such property is to make the equality of a child's education dependent upon location of private commercial and industrial establishments. Surely, this is to rely on the most irrelevant of factors as the basis for educational funding.[25]

Even though the United States Supreme Court has refused to follow the lead of the state courts and even though some state courts, such as New York's, have rejected Serrano-type arguments, continued judicial intervention to reduce these inequities appears inevitable for two reasons. First, many cases have been successfully argued on the basis of the Fourteenth Amendment's comprehensive and far-reaching equal protection provisions. Second, the courts are viewing the extreme disparities of some basic services such as education with care because of what the Minnesota Federal District Court called the "fundamental interest" of essential state and local services. For example, that Court ruled in *Van Dusartz* v. *Hatfield* that education "has a unique impact on the mind, personality and future role of the individual child. It is basic to the functioning of a free society and thereby evokes special judicial solicitude."[26]

A variety of devices has been proposed or implemented in an attempt to reduce these three types of inequities and disparities within the federal system. One of the more imaginative state actions designed to reduce metropolitan fiscal disparities is the Minnesota Metropolitan Revenue Act of 1971 that provides for local government sharing of the growth in the commercial-industrial tax base in the seven-county Twin Cities area. Most approaches, however, center on shifting resources within the federal system to assist the lower-level governments. Among the more famous proposals are (1) reduced national taxes; (2) direct national assumption of functions; (3) tax credits; (4) grant-in-aid reform; and (5) revenue sharing.

Reduced National Taxes

One of the least complicated proposals for fiscal adjustment is the often repeated suggestion that the national government reduce its taxes. The intention is that the state and local governments will take up the "tax slack" through their own tax increases. After all, it is argued, the primary obstacle to higher taxes at the state-local level is political, not economic, since most industrial nations of the world have taxes far higher than those of the United States. The political difficulties, it is believed, would be lessened if at the time of a national tax decrease, the Congress and the President announce that it is hoped and intended that the state-local sector will pick up all or the greater portion of that decrease. President Reagan emphasized this approach when he told officials of the National Association of Counties:

> I have a dream of my own; I think block grants are only the intermediate steps. I dream of a day when the federal government can substitute for those, the turning back to local and state governments of the tax sources that we ourselves have pre-empted here at the federal level, so that you would have the resources.[27]

This method of fiscal adjustment—often popularly called the "turn back" approach—would give the maximum flexibility to the state and local officials to determine how they wish to secure the new tax revenues, if indeed they do seek a tax increase, and how they will spend the new funds.

The past utilization of this approach has had mixed success. The elimination of national excise taxes has not automatically meant a state expansion in those areas. The reduction of national government taxes on amusement admissions, utilities, and telephone services was not greatly absorbed by other levels, perhaps because "an industry with enough political influence to persuade Congress to give it tax relief is likely to have the capability to restrain states or cities from increasing their taxes on it."[28]

Success with income tax reduction has been more notable. Not only may states pick up the "slack" through tax increases but also when states permit deduction of national tax payments in the computation of state income taxes, less national taxes mean a smaller deduction and, therefore, more state tax yield. Assessing an earlier effort at this approach, Senator Jacob Javits (R–N.Y.) estimated that as much as one-third of the $6.5 billion 1964 national tax reduction ended up in state coffers.[29]

Critics of this idea argue that there is no guarantee that other governments will pick up national tax reductions. Such action therefore is sometimes seen as a "gimmick" designed by conservatives to reduce public expenditures rather than to transfer revenues within the federal system.

Second, it is asked, from where will the national monies come? In these days of continuous national deficit a significant tax reduction must mean a decrease in national programs, probably those designed to aid state and local governments since they are the cause of the national tax reductions. John Gunther, executive director of the U.S. Conference of Mayors, after meeting with the President to discuss the 1981 "turn back" program, noted, "I think the President's made it very clear that it's his goal to get rid of federal aid to state and local government."[30] Subsequent budgets did, indeed, show a decline in federal aid. The net effect may be to cancel out any advantage to the state and local governments. Lastly, it is strongly and justifiably pointed out that even if such a transfer of revenues does take place, it will not alleviate the disparities within the horizontal levels of the system. The wealthy jurisdictions will get more; the poorer ones will get less.

Direct National Expenditure

The financial problems of the state and local governments and the disparities among governments can be lessened by direct national expenditure, that is, the transfer of certain functions to the national government. Direct expenditures have been expanding markedly in recent years. As national expenditures for the traditional areas of retirement and disability (social security) continue to expand dramatically they are joined by newer and costly direct expenditures such as medicare, food stamps, and family assistance. Combined, these programs account for an ever increasing portion of recent national budgets. President Reagan sought a "swap" to have the states participate in the funding of some of these programs. The proposal met with stiff resistance by the states' governors. In general it appears likely that these functional areas will become increasingly dependent on direct national expenditures. Similar transfers are underway at other levels of government.

Tax Credits

This third adaptive device regularizes the stimulus that would be available under the national tax reduction approach and encourages state and local officials to increase taxes. In simplest terms, the tax credit permits a taxpayer to subtract, that is, credit, from his or her national income tax responsibility a set percentage of his total state and local taxes. For example, if a citizen has paid $800 in local property taxes and $700 in assorted state taxes, and he owes $2,500 to the national treasury, assuming a 50 percent tax credit, he would subtract $750 from the amount owed the national government. This serves as a stimulus for greater state-local tax effort. If in this hypothetical case a 50 percent credit were given, it would be politically more acceptable to raise taxes since 50 percent of the increase would come off national taxes. The computation for the above example before and after a tax increase is as shown:

Before tax increase	After state and local tax increase ($100 each)
$ 800 local taxes	$ 900 local taxes
+ 700 state taxes	+ 800 state taxes
1,500 total state and local	1,700 total state and local
x 50% assumed tax credit rate	x 50% assumed tax credit rate
$ 750 national tax credit	$ 850 national tax credit
$ 2,500 national taxes due	$ 2,500 national taxes due
− 750 tax credit	− 850 tax credit
$ 1,750 owed national government	$ 1,650 owed national government

This method, strongly preferred by many economists, has two major disadvantages. It does not reduce interjurisdictional disparities; and, second, a large enough credit, without an upper limit, will soon substantially reduce national revenues. If the credit is set too low, for example, at 10 or 20 percent, or if there is a maximum deduction, its effectiveness will rapidly dissipate.

The tax credit approach has been successfully utilized in a few select national areas, e.g., inheritance tax credits and unemployment insurance tax deductions, as well as by many states. In the latter case, credits are normally given for select excise taxes paid at the local level such as a local tax on cigarettes.

Grant-in-Aid Reform

Because grants are at the heart of the intergovernmental fiscal system, it is best to understand exactly what they are, how they are awarded, and the purposes and functions for which they are used, before discussing reform. Other aspects of their use will also be noted.

Characteristics of Grants-in-Aid. As gifts from one government to another, grants originate as authorizing legislation, enacted by Congress or a state legislature, either for a specific number of years or on a continuing basis. Concerning federal grants the recipient state or local government ordinarily must submit an application, designate an agency or department to receive the funds, agree to abide by national conditions for their expenditure, permit federal agency inspection of the results, and often provide matching funds. The conditions and matching requirements vary from grant to grant, although some apply to most of them (e.g., nondiscrimination requirements).

Money to fund federal grant programs or projects is appropriated by the Congress each year. Although it is often less than the authorized amount, it cannot exceed it. It is distributed by federal agencies, usually in accordance with a formula written into the authorizing legislation. The federal agencies ordinarily prepare "guidelines" or regulations that govern the grant process. As far as recipient governments are concerned, these have the effect of law.

A typology of grants is set out in Table 6–4. It distinguishes the various types and provides illustrations of each.

Categorical grants are the most numerous of the grants. What is more, they are used to distribute about 80 percent of federal grant funds.

On the other hand, they afford the least discretion to the receiving government of any of the types of fiscal assistance. Administering agencies are provided more control when they are used, however. The relative discretion and control for each type of intergovernmental transfer is shown on the

TABLE 6-4
A GRANT-IN-AID TYPOLOGY

I. CATEGORICALS. These specific, narrowly focused grants are made for specific purposes or projects. Categoricals may be:
A. *Formula based* grants distributing funds on the basis of factors in a formula unique to each program. Formula grants may be:
1. *Open-end Reimbursement* grants that specifiy no total authorization or appropriation but make the amount received dependent on the cost of the program. Examples include the two most costly grants:
   Medical Assistance Program (Medicaid)
   Aid to Families with Dependent Children (AFDC)
2. *Closed-end* formula grants specifying a total amount available and providing that each recipient will receive a proportionate share of the specified total depending on conformance to the formula. Examples include:
   Federal Aid to Highways: Hazard Elimination
   Older Americans Program: Social Services
   Public Library Service
B. *Project* grants are nonformula grants. Each applicant must submit an application for an individually designed project as specified by the administering agency. Often applicants compete for shares of the money. Examples are:
   Urban Development Action Grants (UDAG)
   Low-Income Housing Projects
   Indian Education: Special Programs and Projects
C. *Mixed Project-Formula.* These are categoricals for which each state receives a portion of the available money under a formula specified in the statute or regulations. The state then awards funds to local governments on the basis of project applications and at its own discretion, subject to applicable federal requirements. Examples include:
   Water and Waste Disposal Systems for Rural Communities
   Industrial Development

II. BLOCKS. These are formula grants for recipient-selected activities in a broad functional area—such as manpower training. They generally go to states or general purpose local governments (cities, counties, towns, and townships). The conditions attached to them are fewer and national supervision is less. Examples include:
   Community Development Block Grant (CDBG)
   Social Services Block Grant
   Primary Health Care Block Grant
   Alcohol, Drug Abuse, and Mental Health Block Grant

This typology draws heavily on Advisory Commission on Intergovernmental Relations, *Summary and Concluding Observations—The Intergovernmental Grant System: An Assessment and Proposed Policies,* Report A-62 (Washington, D.C.: The Commission, 1978).

continuum below. Naturally, government officials receiving assistance prefer general revenue sharing (GRS) because it allows them more discretion.

Least recipient discretion/ Most donor control	Project	Mixed– Project formula	Formula	Block	GRS	Most recipient discretion/ Least donor control

Purposes of Grants. Fiscal assistance is given for a variety of purposes. Some of these are perceived as benefitting the donor government, others the recipient. Advantages for the two are so closely intertwined, however, that the distinction is blurred. Some grants are offered in a spirit of helpfulness to alleviate problems caused by natural disasters or other emergencies, or the donor may be trying to stimulate economic development or upgrade conditions for the poor. In other instances, the purpose may be to equalize resources among jurisdictions.

Grants are a means of changing the behavior of officials of the governments receiving the money. The donor government may offer grants to stimulate these officials to undertake new programs, spend more money and offer more services in existing functions, and upgrade the quality of program administration. Sometimes the aim is to encourage planning or experimentation by the recipient government.

Grant Impacts on Recipient's Expenditures. Although much research remains to be done on the effects of grants-in-aid, their impacts can be said to be of three major types—*additive, stimulative,* or *substitutive.* In the aggregate, grants are additive; that is, they increase spending by the government receiving them. Since public officials normally spend all the money available to them, larger sums increase outlays. A grant is stimulative when the jurisdiction receiving the money increases its spending for the aided-program by more than it has to contribute to match the grant. Grants are said to be substitutive when recipient money can be shifted away from the assisted program and used for other purposes. This interchangeable nature of grant money is sometimes called "fungibility." It should be kept in mind that grants vary in their impact.

Need for Reform. As discussed in Chapter 3, from a modest start grants evolved of approximately $90 billion with more than 500 grant alternatives at one period of time. The offering was so massive that the annual *Catalog of Federal Domestic Assistance* ran as high as 800 pages (although some of its contents related to nonmonetary aid) and grant data subsequently were computerized for more convenient information retrieval. As a result of this growth, many criticisms and fears have been voiced about the operation and impact of the grant-in-aid system. These concerns can be classified as administrative or systemic.[31]

Administrative concerns center on the proliferation of grant programs. The sheer number of programs can awe and overwhelm state and local officials to the point that they overlook assistance for which they are eligible. This is especially true of small jurisdictions that lack specialized staffs to play the "grantsmanship" game. Further, technical and administrative requirements often produce irritation.[32] From the first application—many times running to several hundred pages—to required periodic statements of use, to final audit, a massive amount of expertise and paperwork is required. To illustrate, until recently the Department of Health, Education and Welfare (now Health and Human Resources) required over 7,000 pages of documentation from the states about the use of that department's grants.

The complex requirements led to the emergence of specialists who play the "game of grantsmanship." Most states and large cities and counties have special offices of intergovernmental aid exclusively assigned to procurement and coordination of national grants. Increasingly, these governments are establishing special Washington offices to facilitate the awarding of national money. The smaller and poorer jurisdictions complain that they, who most need the assistance, cannot afford such expertise although some smaller jurisdictions have pooled their resources to produce a regional source of grantsmanship skills.

The systemic concerns center on the long-range impact on American federalism of the national government's grant-in-aid programs. For example, the current grant system has had, according to most observers, a major impact on state and local policymaking. This is most obviously true with reference to the state and local budgetary processes. Budgets have been influenced both with regard to level of expenditures and allocation of funds.[33]

As far as total state and local expenditures are concerned, the national assistance policy obviously stimulated new demands whose political implications are evident. Less evident, but perhaps more important, is the pressure to pick and choose among areas of expenditure according to the availability of national aid funds rather than according to an established criteria of need. One million dollars spent for a non-aided function will give the public one million dollars of services (assuming a pure input-output ratio). One million dollars spent on an aided function may produce anywhere from 2 to 10 million dollars in services, depending on the matching formula. Recipient governments are under pressure to change their priorities and opt for financing the assisted activity.

The policy consequences of the grant system have been well summarized by Deil Wright:

> The lesser financial sacrifice required to undertake aided rather than non-aided programs alters the agenda of state and local policy issues.

FIGURE 6-1 STAGES OF A GRANT-IN-AID PROJECT AS IT ADVANCES THROUGH THE APPROVAL PROCESS

As proposed by the project sponsor   As specified in the project request.

 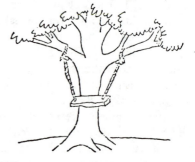

As designed by the senior analyst.   As produced by the programmers.

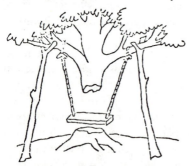 

As installed at the user's site.   What the user wanted.

Adapted from *Front Lines*, a publication of the U.S. Agency for International Development.

The priorities of state and local units are revised or made less clear. Moreover, decisions about the number of programs to pursue and the service levels to maintain for the various programs become more complex.

. . . grants set conditions in which federal administrative officials may substantially restrict the policy action and discretion of elected state and local officials. Given the financial inducements and conditions attached to grants, the states and their local units are all but required to adjust their behavior to fit specified nationally-prescribed constraints.

Federal grants bring about a direct confrontation between conflicting national and state (or local) policy preferences.[34]

Further, the detailed prerequisites for national funds have created a situation of close rapport and professional interaction among grant administrators at all levels that tends to weaken the power of elected executives.

People concerned about the systemic impact of massive amounts of intergovernmental transfers through the grant-in-aid device are particularly suspect of the continued ability of the state-local sector to maintain its relative autonomy and viability as increasingly large portions of its budget come from the central government. For example, K. C. Wheare's authoritative work on federalism notes that to be effective and viable on a continuing basis all the component units of a federal system must

possess sufficient economic resources to support both an independent general government and independent regional governments. It is not enough that the general government should be able to finance itself; it is essential also that the regional governments should be able to do likewise.[35]

Commenting on this observation, Michael D. Reagan and John G. Sanzone, after reviewing the growing dependence of the state and local governments in the American federal system, write that

the state-local governments are by no means financially independent. Furthermore, it seems beyond cavil that this financial dependence will increase further over time. . . . If Wheare's requirements are accurate, then the fiscal facts . . . suggest that federalism in the United States is dead.[36]

Reagan and Sanzone go on to distinguish between *financial dependence* and *programmatic dependence.* The loss of the latter would surely mean the end of viable federalism, but it is not clear that programmatic dependence always follows the loss of financial independence. Unfortunately, our understanding of the probable impact of the recent changes is very meager. The outlook for continued independence, however, is occasionally bleak. Witness the success of the national government's efforts to enforce ''busing'' school children for the purposes of racial balance, a success that was not

based as in earlier years on the use of national marshals and national guards-
men, but rather a success based on the *threat* to end national school assistance funds.

Recent massive increases in federal assistance have augmented potential
control significantly. In many ways the pre-1960 federal aid was a sharing
of the costs of *state and local priorities*, while more recent programs increasingly have funded *national* priorities with a concomitant rise in conflict.

Finally, state officials opposed the growing number of national grants
bypassing the states and going directly to local governments and, in some
instances, even to private groups or individuals. This rise of "direct federalism" and "private federalism" is seen as substantially weakening the ability
of the states to maintain long-established patterns of relations with their
political subdivisions.

Some of the federal aid programs have had unintended impact of
major significance. Massive national support for interstate highways, other
roads, and mass transit programs, for example, helped fuel the suburbanization of America. The outflow of middle income residents, industry,
and trade to the suburbs with a greater concentration of the poor, elderly,
and minorities in the central cities helped create another whole set of
problems. Many, ironically, resulted in massive new federal aid programs
designed to help solve them (e.g., urban renewal, War on Poverty). Likewise, the general revenue sharing program gave greater fiscal viability to
smaller independent suburban jurisdictions that otherwise might have
sought a more rational association with the central city through consolidation or, more likely, some other type of local cooperative organization.
Ironically, too, this occurred during the 1970s when the national government made its greatest effort to encourage local government reorganization
and integration through the A-95 and other review requirements, and by
supporting local councils of governments.

All these concerns, administrative and systemic, have prompted many
proposals for change and reform in the grant-in-aid system. Numerically,
most of them focus on procedural and technical administrative changes to
reduce the need for lengthy grant applications and the many paperwork
and red-tape requirements. Some of these proposals have met with success.
For example, the national government no longer routinely requires a
separate audit for the use of national funds nor does it require as many
periodic reports on the expenditure of grant money. Further, much of the
post-grant review and evaluation is now left up to the discretion of the
recipient unit. Many of these administrative proposals were incorporated
into the Intergovernmental Cooperation Act of 1968[37] and its subsequent
amendments.

Since the 1968 legislation most national administrations have made
concerted efforts to simplify further the grant-in-aid process. Significant

improvements were made under the Nixon, Carter, and Reagan administrations. Reagan, for example, issued Executive Order 12291, that established for the first time a centralized mechanism for executive management of agency aid regulations. Further, OMB Circular A-102, "Uniform Administrative Requirements for Grants to State and Local Governments," included streamlined procurement standards that placed greater reliance on state and local purchasing systems.[38] In addition, mandates, requirements, and other "strings" attached to grants have been reduced dramatically. The Reagan administration identified an average of 500 mandates for six major program areas and terminated many of these, reducing by 65 percent the mandates for transportation grants, 75 percent for Environmental Protection Agency awards, and a staggering 85 percent for education programs,[39] at an estimated savings of billions of dollars.[40]

Other proposals for change have centered on the structure of the grant system itself. There is currently very strong support for the use of block grants. The popularity of this mechanism under the Omnibus Crime Control and Safe Street Act and the Community Development Block Grant gave momentum to the movement away from categoricals and toward the use of block grants.

Before 1972 there were few block or general purpose grants. Ten years later they accounted for approximately a fifth of total federal intergovernmental aid. The increased reliance on them is reflected in Table 6–5.

The likelihood of further block grant replacement of categorical programs is enhanced by the fact that 80 percent of all federal assistance money was concentrated in the 20 largest programs in 1980 (Table 6–6). The remaining 20 percent was divided among more than 400 separate programs. By 1983, as a result of the creation of several more block grants, the elimination of some programs and other changes, the top 20 programs accounted for 87 percent of the assistance funds. The remaining 170 programs were spread out over 13 percent of the grant budget and were being described by the Office of Management and Budget as "categorical grants with different matching requirements, timing difficulties, complex application procedures, program duplication, and other administrative problems."[41] These are obvious candidates for further consolidation under future block grant efforts.

The dramatic emergence of block grants and the decline in categoricals is based on two major premises: (1) there should be more discretion and true decisionmaking at the state and local levels with less national interference; and (2) it is more efficient to administer these programs through a wide-discretion, limited-"strings" approach.

The Reagan administration repeatedly stressed the first point during the crucial 1981–1983 period. The 1981 budget message set the theme by noting that "the federal government in Washington has no special wisdom

TABLE 6-5
FEDERAL OUTLAYS FOR GENERAL-PURPOSE, BROAD-BASED (BLOCK) AND CATEGORICAL GRANTS, BY SELECTED FISCAL YEARS

(Dollar amounts in millions)

	Actual					Estimate		
	1972	1976	1980	1982	1983	1984	1985	1986
General-purpose grants:								
General revenue sharing		$6,243	$6,829	$4,569	$4,567	$4,567	$4,567	$4,567
Other general purpose fiscal assistance and TVA[1]	$516	907	1,765	1,941	1,878	2,501	2,475	2,708
Subtotal, general-purpose grants	516	7,150	8,594	6,510	6,445	7,068	7,042	7,275
Broad-based (Block):								
Community development		983	3,902	3,792	3,525	3,526	3,474	3,497
Health	90	128	83	661	1,115	1,299	1,357	1,357
State education block grants				48	35	440	451	451
School aid in federally affected areas	602	558	622	546	572	499	478	468
Employment and training		1,698	2,144	1,793	1,639	1,415	1,886	1,886
Social services	1,930	2,251	2,763	2,567	2,571	2,500	2,600	2,700

Low-income home energy assistance				1,685	1,961	1,396	1,349	1,298
Other	233	554	818	390	414	476	689	972
Subtotal, broad-based grants	2,855	6,172	10,332	11,482	11,832	11,551	12,284	12,629
Categorical grants	31,001	45,771	72,546	70,202	75,260	77,307	79,836	82,564
Total	34,372	59,093	91,472	88,194	93,537	95,926	99,162	102,468
ADDENDUM: PERCENT OF TOTAL								
General-purpose grants	1.5%	12.1%	9.4%	7.4%	6.9%	7.4%	7.1%	7.1%
Broad-based grants	8.3%	10.4%	11.3%	13.0%	12.6%	12.0%	12.4%	12.3%
Categorical grants	90.2%	77.5%	79.3%	79.6%	80.5%	80.6%	80.5%	80.6%
Total	100.0%	100.0%	100.0%	100.0%	100.0%	100.0%	100.0%	100.0%

Source: Adapted from Office of Management and Budget, Special Analyses: Budget of the United States Government, 1984, "Special Analysis H: Federal Aid to State and Local Governments," p. H–20.

TABLE 6-6
FEDERAL GRANT PROGRAMS, ESTIMATED OBLIGATIONS, RANKED IN DESCENDING ORDER OF DOLLAR MAGNITUDE, FY 1980 (in thousands of dollars)

Rank	Program number	Title		FY 1980 Estimated obligations (descending order)
1	14.156	Lower Income Housing Assistance—dp		$20,045,328
2	13.714	Medical Assistance (Medicaid)—fg		12,616,799
3	20.205	Highway Research, Planning, and Construction—pg, fg		8,400,000
4	17.232	Comprehensive Employment and Training—pg, fg		8,201,207
5	13.808	Public Assistance (Aid to Families with Dependent Children and Aid to Disabled)—fg		7,056,710
6	— —	General Revenue Sharing		6,863,000
7	10.551	Food Stamps—dp		6,401,000
8	66.418	Construction Grants, Wastewater Treatment—pg, coop agreements		3,600,000
9	14.218	Community Development Block Grant (CDBG) Entitlement Grants—fg		2,753,838
10	13.428	Grants for Educationally Deprived Children—fg		2,625,594
11	13.642	Social Services (Title XX)—fg		2,475,000
12	10.555	School Lunch—sales, exchange		2,123,100
13	14.146	Public Housing—pg, direct loans		2,082,500
14	17.225	Unemployment Insurance—pg, dp		2,034,600
15	20.500	Urban Mass Transportation, Capital		1,400,000
16	10.418	Rural Water and Waste Disposal—pg, guaranteed loans		965,000
17	14.219	CDBG, Small Cities—pg		939,626
18	20.507	Urban Mass Transportation, Operations		850,000
19	10.550	Surplus Food Distribution—sale, exchange	80% +	813,535
20	13.449	Education of Handicapped Children—fg	Level	804,000
		Total		98,050,837

(pg = project grant, fg = formula grant, dp = direct payment.)

Source: Adapted from U.S. Advisory Commission on Intergovernmental Relations, *The Federal Role in the Federal System: The Dynamics of Growth. An Agenda for American Federalism: Restoring Confidence and Competence.* Report A–86 (Washington, D.C.: The Commission, June, 1981), p. 158.

in dealing with many of the special and educational issues faced at the state and local levels." OMB Director David Stockman, testifying before the House Manpower and Housing Subcommittee, responded to criticism that block grants merely transfer resource allocation battles to the state level by remarking: "Yes, and that's good. We are overloaded at the national level. We simply can't make wise decisions on the thousands of issues that come before us. There has to be a better division of labor and redelegation of decisionmaking to lower levels of government."[42]

The second thrust for block grants is based on efficiency and cost savings. Study after study notes the high costs of the categorical programs. For example, the Administration pointed out that the 84 health, education, and social services programs proposed for consolidation into six block grants "encompass 616 pages of laws, 1,400 pages of regulations, more than 10,000 separate grants and about 88,000 grant sites. Administering the grants requires more than seven million hours of paperwork and several thousand federal employees."[43]

The block grant approach generates considerable enthusiasm and optimism from its supporters, but it is not without strong critics. Urban interests are very suspicious of the tie-in between state control and the block grants as initiated by President Reagan. Fred Jordan, a spokesman for the National League of Cities, for instance, pointed out that there are only three major broad-based federal aid programs cities consider "truly flexible"—general revenue sharing, Urban Development Action Grants (UDAG) and Community Development Block Grants.[44] Most other block grants are much more oriented toward state control and, as Jordan notes, the League of Cities "is strongly opposed to wholesale handing of responsibilities and programs back to the states."[45]

Another criticism focuses on the misconception that block grants are automatically less costly and less administratively complex than the categoricals they replace. For example, in the CETA *block grant* program the Federal Paperwork Commission found "one set of instructions 106 pages long among more than 150 transmittals to local governments in one region over a 27 month period—three transmittals every two weeks."[46]

Finally, a number of critics argue that the block grants are destroying the liberal people-oriented programs of the Kennedy-Johnson era that found birth in the explosion of categorical grants in the 1960s and early 1970s. Vernon E. Jordan, Jr., the president of the National Urban League, illustrated this concern in an essay called "Block Grants Are a Dead-End Street." Jordan contended that the blocks are "against the best interest of disadvantaged citizens and of the nation," and that they are a tool for "dismantling virtually all federal social programs and turning them over to the states."[47]

As one study notes, the Reagan administration's shift to the states-oriented block grant emphasis has had the net impact of:

a greatly enhanced role for state governments;

major reduction in the direct ties between local governments and the federal government;

an uncertain and hazardous future for the community-action and non-profit organizations, which have served as quasi-public entities at the local level, dispensing social services largely with federal dollars; and

a fifty-state ''free-for-all'' competition for block-grant funds among interest groups currently served by the social services, education, and health categorical grants.[48]

Further, as the *Congressional Quarterly* observes, the philosophical positioning and debate notwithstanding, the impact of the block grant thrust to date is that ''in the real world, states and localities have been given a lot more responsibility, slightly more authority and much less money.''[49]

Another approach for dealing with the multiplicity of categorical grants without moving to substitute blocks is the proposal for joint funding simplification (JFS). Under this plan a state or local government undertaking a project that involves many categorical grants could designate one national agency to process all the grant applications and to secure a simultaneous single management and review organization. This would eliminate the need for duplicate paperwork to many agencies. This could also preserve the advantages of categoricals for accomplishing specific congressional purposes—such as stimulating greater activity in a particular area—at the same time as it allows increased policy choices for state and local governments.

Revenue Sharing

In 1972 revenue sharing was added as a major device to reduce fiscal disparities within the federal system. Basically, this approach provides for the distribution of a sum of national money to local governments, with the distributed funds having no national requirements as to expenditure other than those required by the Constitution and law (e.g., cannot be used to promote discrimination). Revenue sharing is used by most federal systems in the world.[50] It occasionally has been used in the United States to dispose of early national budget surpluses and more recently to share certain limited funds (generally in the natural resource area and amounting to less than $500 million per year). Nevertheless, revenue sharing had its modern beginning in the United States in 1958 when then Representative Melvin Laird introduced a tax-sharing bill in the House of Representatives.[51] Even though tax sharing had been long used by the states as the major method of assisting the localities, Laird's proposal became controversial enough to take 13 years to be enacted.

The plan received a major boost in 1964 when it was endorsed by famed economist, and then chairman of the President's Council of Economic Advisors, Walter Heller. In early debates on revenue sharing, as a result of the strong endorsement, the approach was often referred to as "the Heller Plan." Debate over this program became intense in 1967, perhaps as a result of the upcoming election, and resulted in many variations of the tax-sharing plan being introduced into Congress. Finally, in 1972 the State and Local Fiscal Assistance Act was passed. The legislation provided for a total of $30.2 billion to be distributed to the states and localities over a five-year period with appropriations growing from $5.3 billion in 1972 (including 1971 retroactive payments) to $6.5 billion in 1976. The act subsequently was extended; however, the Reagan administration dropped the states from the program, thereby reducing the cost to the federal treasury from $6.5 billion a year to the current $4.567 billion to be shared solely with general purpose local governments.

There have been a number of criticisms of general revenue sharing, many of which are still heard. Among them are five complaints:

1. It is believed that revenue-sharing money is coming from prior grant-in-aid funds and that there is not a major increase in total revenues going to the states and localities as was promised.

2. If in fact money is coming or will come from the grant-in-aid programs, it is likely to hurt the poor and minorities who have received continued special assistance under the grant approach.

3. Revenue sharing supports the continuation of the fragmented governmental structure in the metropolis by giving financial support to smaller governments that might otherwise seek unification because of financial pressures.

4. The demand for revenue-sharing funds is certain to increase, thereby creating a drain on the national treasury and a further dependency for state and local governments. As a recognized authority on fiscal federalism, William Anderson, observes, revenue sharing may be

a pork barrel to out-pork-barrel anything ever proposed. And of course the barrel will never be large enough to satisfy the appetites of the state spenders. It looks like "easy money" but easy come can also be easy go —or else Uncle Sam will have to control the states' expenditures as never before.

This "tax-sharing" . . . is not just a fiscal matter. Its ramifications are beyond calculation and prediction. I think [it] is as bad for the states as it is for the income taxpayers.[52]

5. Many critics complain that revenue sharing was first debated when the national coffers were relatively affluent and the states and localities were in desperate financial straits. Now it can be argued that the situation is reversed, with many state and local governments being in a fairly healthy fiscal position while the national government suffers continued massive deficits. Therefore, revenue sharing should be declared a success and terminated.

Public support for revenue sharing has fluctuated. From a post-enactment high of 65 percent in favor in 1974, it declined to a post-enactment low of 51 percent in 1979 (the most recent year this question was surveyed). The strongest support steadily came from the Northeast region of the nation, where states and local governments face the most difficult financial problems.[53]

An interesting study by David M. Hedge focused on the type of intergovernmental assistance mechanism used. Hedge found that the distribution of all forms of aid—general revenue sharing, block grants, and varied categoricals—is largely unrelated to service and fiscal need. Further, a greater reliance on formula funding, revenue sharing, or block grants is not likely to produce a more need-based allocation pattern. It will, however, reduce the ability of cities to influence federal aid allocation decisions.[54]

WHO FARES BEST?

Throughout all the attempts at cooperation and efforts to devise formulas for grants-in-aid and revenue sharing that will be "equitable," obviously some states are likely to benefit more than others in the federal system. Some will find national policies more acceptable to them than others will. Some will subsidize others because they pay relatively more money into the national treasury in proportion to what they receive in national assistance or direct expenditures within their boundaries. What are the factors that determine which states will be most satisfied with the policy and fiscal outcomes at the national level?

Numerous suggestions have been made as to the determinants of state success with national fiscal and policy matters. Some of them are size and wealth of the state, party competition, civil service arrangements, personality of state leaders, state representation in the national leadership structure, political culture, and policy preferences in an individual state. Additional determinants proposed have included national administrative factors and modernized state governmental machinery.

Richard Lehne, in an interesting study of policy and fiscal success in which he analyzed the amounts paid to and received from various states and compared the states' congressional vote on key issues, found some intriguing correlations.[55] States profiting financially were those with low incomes and traditional political cultures, frequently agrarian, and those whose representatives in Congress possess high seniority. Wealthy states with innovative bureaucracies, strong governors, professionally-staffed legislatures, and substantial representation in the national executive and judicial cadre tend to lose and to subsidize the remaining states. This is not to say that they lose because they have these characteristics, but there is a positive correlation between states with these characteristics and financial loss. These traits are often associated with relatively affluent and rapid growth states. It is probable that wealth and growth are the more important determinants.

Each year the Tax Foundation estimates how much a state pays into the federal treasury for support of federal assistance and how much that state receives in return. There are clear benefit states (winners) and deficit states (losers). Texas in 1980 headed the latter list, paying $1.46 in taxes for each dollar of aid. Next came Connecticut ($1.41), Florida ($1.33), Kansas ($1.28), and New Jersey ($1.27). The benefit states, or winners, were led by Vermont which only paid 56 cents for each dollar in federal aid received. Next came Alaska (57 cents), Mississippi (60 cents), South Dakota (60 cents), and Maine (66 cents).[56]

Federal aid on a per capita basis varies widely among regions. Lightly populated states in the West traditionally receive more aid per capita because of highway construction grants, which include mileage as part of the formula, and shared revenues for federal lands. This bias to the western states declined in recent years as human resource assistance has grown relative to physical construction programs. General revenue sharing also has had some equalizing effect.

Just as states fare differently in the amount of national aid received, so do local governments. A 1969 survey by Morley Segal and A. Lee Fritschler showed great disparities among cities. Population size was a major factor in the unequal treatment with smaller cities (under 50,000 population) faring best and medium cities (250,000–500,000) doing the least well. The largest cities (over 500,000) fared slightly better than the average. Additional factors identified were location and region. Cities outside metropolitan areas received far more per capita than central cities or suburbs. As far as regional advantages were concerned, northeastern cities got more, followed by those of the Middle Atlantic region. Cities in the West South Central area (Arkansas, Louisiana, Oklahoma, and Texas) did the poorest of all.[57] Other determinants that Segal and Fritschler and other researchers determined to be significant in aid distribution are the existence of a municipal national liaison office or grant coordination office, the attitude of local officials toward grants, and the knowledge of local administrators, especially city managers, of the grant process and grant availability.[58]

TRENDS IN THE FISCAL FEDERAL SYSTEM

The fiscal arrangements of the federal system were not always so complex. In the early years of the Republic the public sector did far less than is expected of it today. At the national level, for instance, most functions now associated with the Departments of Education, Health and Human Resources, Housing and Urban Development, Labor, and Transportation, were then firmly rooted in the private sector. Similarly, many services now routinely expected from the state and local governments, e.g., water and sewage disposal or transportation, were rarely performed by public bodies in the early period. Equally important, at that time the governments of the federal system were somewhat isolated from one another in terms of the functions performed and financial interactions. The relatively limited demands on government in general and the governments' fiscal isolation insured fairly small budgets and a great deal of tax concentration. The national government's budget in 1789, for example, was only $4.4 million, of which 99.6 percent came from customs collections. As late as 1862, the national government received 94.4 percent of its $51.9 million receipts from import duties.

Beginning with the Civil War dramatic changes started to take place in the size of governmental budgets and sources of income. The national treasury, for instance, went into that conflict with $41.5 million total receipts; by 1866 this skyrocketed to $558 million. More important, only 32 percent of the 1866 income came from the previously dominant customs tax, the other 68 percent coming from a multitude of new national taxes. While the central income declined somewhat after the fratricidal conflict, a gradual increase in the national budget began after the turn of the twentieth century, accelerated under the demands of World War I, leveled off again after that struggle, and then realized extraordinary increases during and after World War II.[59]

As a result of new international responsibilities assumed by the United States at the end of World War II and as a consequence of the emergence of "a more positive" view of the role of government following the Depression of the 1930s, the national budget began an inexorable pattern of growth. By the Bicentennial the budget was over $400 billion and pushed on toward a trillion dollars in the early 1980s. A similar outline of growth, decline, spurts forward and then unrelenting expansion could be traced for state and local revenues. The main point is that the old system of limited governments operating in relatively autonomous tax-raising spheres has been replaced by a public sector requiring ever-increasing income. That, as a result, constantly adds to the complexity of the system through new taxes and expanding patterns of intergovernmental fiscal relations. A brief examination of a few clear trends will help to explain where the fiscal federal system is and where it is headed.

The Trend of Increased Taxes

A trend obvious to the taxpayer, the elected official, and the student of government finances is that recent years have seen a phenomenal demand for new revenues. Whether measured by per capita tax rates or by public revenues as a percent of the gross national product, the upward trend is unmistakable. Only in very recent years has this upward spiral leveled off as the pressure of the "Taxpayers' Revolt" began to be felt.

The combined per capita tax receipts for all governments in the federal system were only $18 at the turn of the present century ($7 national, $2 state, and $9 local). At that time 51 percent of the taxes went to local governments. As table 6–7 shows, by the beginning of World War II, the per capita tax amount had multiplied almost tenfold to $172, and by 1982 it had increased more than twentyfold again to $3,789. Also of importance to note from the same table is that the national share of these taxes increased to 67 percent, while the local portion declined from more than one-half at the start of the twentieth century to a current 12 percent.

Recent years have seen a slight stabilizing of this trend. The widespread adoption of state and local tax and revenue limitations, the 1981 federal tax reductions, and continuing political hostility to the current level of taxation may move these figures downward incrementally in the near future. A projected growth in defense spending and changes in the demographic makeup of American society, resulting in more elderly citizens whose medical care and income support the national government has assumed major responsibility, however, may counterbalance the fiscal retreat. Moreover, many states have had to face up to the reality of new revenue needs in view of inflation, federal aid cutbacks, growing populations, and revenue shortfalls resulting from economic recession.[60]

The Trend of Specialization of Taxation

This chapter began by discussing the myriad of overlapping, duplicating taxes that exist in the fiscal federal system. While that perception is true, there is, however, much tax specialization in the American intergovernmental system. As Ecker-Racz noted, "governments at each level have one workhorse, one type of tax on which they generally rely for most of their tax revenue."[61]

The shift by the national government from near total reliance on custom collections (99.6 percent) to a similar reliance on income tax revenues (90 percent) demonstrates that the "workhorse" to which Ecker-Racz refers has been part of the fiscal federal system for some time although new horses are occasionally lassoed. The states abandoned the property tax for an increasing dependence on consumption taxes and now get approximately one-half of their tax revenues from general sales and special excise taxes.

TABLE 6-7
FEDERAL, STATE, AND LOCAL TAX RECEIPTS: PER CAPITA AND PERCENTAGE DISTRIBUTION SELECTED FISCAL YEARS 1902–1982

Year	Per capita				Percentage distribution			
	Total	Federal	State	Local	Total	Federal	State	Local
1902	$18	$7	$2	$9	100.0	37.4	11.4	51.3
1913	24	7	3	14	100.0	29.2	13.3	57.6
1922	68	31	9	26	100.0	45.6	12.8	41.5
1927	80	28	14	28	100.0	25.6	17.0	47.4
1932	64	15	15	34	100.0	22.7	23.7	53.6
1934	70	23	16	31	100.0	33.2	22.4	44.4
1936	83	30	21	32	100.0	36.6	24.9	28.5
1938	110	45	30	35	100.0	41.4	27.0	31.6
1940	108	42	32	34	100.0	39.2	29.2	31.6
1942	172	100	37	35	100.0	58.1	21.7	20.2
1944	359	313	40	25	100.0	80.6	10.4	9.0
1946	357	276	44	28	100.0	77.3	12.2	10.5
1948	377	277	54	46	100.0	73.6	14.3	12.1
1950	365	252	60	53	100.0	69.1	16.3	14.6
1952	548	414	73	61	100.0	75.5	13.3	11.2
1953	571	429	76	66	100.0	75.2	13.3	11.5
1954	569	423	77	69	100.0	74.3	13.6	12.1
1955	539	388	78	73	100.0	72.0	14.5	13.5
1956	602	436	88	78	100.0	72.3	14.7	13.0

1957	637	457	95	85	100.0	71.8	14.9	13.3
1958	631	446	95	90	100.0	70.6	15.1	14.2
1959	630	435	100	94	100.0	69.1	15.9	15.0
1960	709	495	113	101	100.0	69.8	15.9	14.3
1961	724	497	118	109	100.0	68.7	16.3	15.1
1962	756	516	126	114	100.0	68.3	16.6	15.1
1963	794	543	134	117	100.0	68.4	16.9	14.7
1964	834	567	144	124	100.0	67.9	17.2	14.9
1965	859	578	151	130	100.0	67.2	17.6	15.2
1966	949	642	167	141	100.0	67.6	17.5	14.8
1967	1,056	731	177	148	100.0	69.2	16.8	14.0
1968	1,096	743	196	157	100.0	67.8	17.9	14.3
1969	1,297	901	222	174	100.0	69.5	17.1	13.4
1970	1,257	916	249	192	100.0	67.5	18.4	14.1
1971	1,354	879	263	212	100.0	64.9	19.4	15.6
1972	1,519	975	304	240	100.0	64.2	20.0	15.8
1973	1,657	1,065	347	254	100.0	64.0	20.8	15.2
1974	1,640	1,195	377	268	100.0	65.0	20.5	14.6
1975	1,943	1,255	400	288	100.0	64.6	20.6	14.8
1976	2,068	1,326	446	316	100.0	63.5	21.4	15.1
1977	2,424	1,569	508	347	100.0	64.7	21.0	14.3
1978	2,690	1,754	524	370	100.0	65.2	21.1	13.8
1979	3,008	2,017	624	368	100.0	67.0	20.7	12.2
1980	3,220	2,176	661	382	100.0	67.6	20.5	11.9
1981	3,655	2,507	782	416	100.0	68.6	20.0	11.4
1982	3,789	2,556	773	460	100.0	67.5	20.4	12.1

Source: 1902–1977: Tax Foundation Inc., *Facts and Figures on Government Finance.* 20th ed. (New York: The Foundation, 1979), p. 21; 1978–1980: Tax Foundation, Inc., staff reports; 1980–1982 data obtained directly from the Foundation.

They have diversified their revenue systems in the last decade, with all but 10 states now using broad-based income taxes. Revenue from that source accounts for about one-third of state taxes. The local jurisdictions have been more constant in their reliance on property taxes; over the years they have consistently drawn about four-fifths of their locally-raised tax revenues from ad valorem taxes. Viewed from a different perspective, approximately 84 percent of all income taxes collected in the United States goes to the national government while local governments levy 96 percent of all property taxes and states take in more than half of all sales taxes.

It is clear that the jungle of tangled, duplicated taxes accounts for only 20 percent of the system's tax intake. The reduction or reassignment of this one-fifth could assure a specialized, orderly, and non-overlapping tax structure. Nevertheless, it is not clear that such a restructuring is, from the viewpoint of either economics or politics, feasible or desirable.

The Trend of Increased Intergovernmental Aid

One of the most important trends—and many observers would argue *the* most important trend—within the fiscal federal system has been the great growth of intergovernmental financial assistance, both from the national government to states and localities and from states to their local jurisdictions.

Growth of Federal Grants-in-Aid. In 1950, the transfer of monies from the national government to other governments was $16 per capita. A decade later, this figure had more than doubled to $39. That figure doubled again by 1967, and by 1981 the national government was contributing $408 for every man, women, and child in the United States. The increase is depicted graphically in Figure 6–2. Note particularly the downturn in national assistance (in terms of constant or deflated dollars) that began in 1978 and accelerated sharply in 1981.

Other Federal Financial Assistance. The national government gives financial support to state and local governments through approaches other than direct grants and revenue sharing. It loans small amounts of money to states and localities for such purposes as community development, transportation, construction of college and university facilities, and reconstruction projects after national disasters. It also guarantees loans—currently about $10 billion a year—that aid states and localities in obtaining low interest credit. The best known example of this was the $1.65 billion guarantee of principal and interest for New York City.

Federal assistance is also provided through the deductibility of many state and local taxes and the exclusion of interest from state and local bonds from federal taxation. This permits lower level governments to raise a dollar in revenue with less than a dollar net cost to their citizens. The "lost

FIGURE 6-2 FEDERAL GRANTS TO STATE AND
LOCAL GOVERNMENTS, 1972-1982

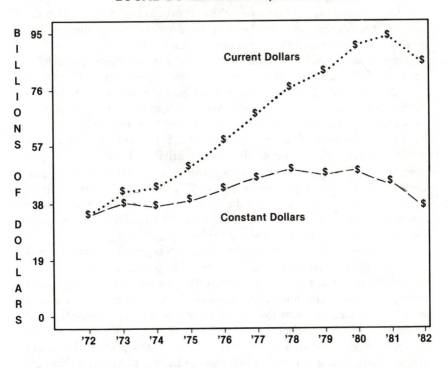

Source: John Shannon, "The Great Slowdown in State and Local Government Spending in the United States: 1976–1984," (Washington, D.C.: Advisory Commission on Intergovernmental Relations, July 30, 1981), Appendix 6.

revenue" for the national coffers becomes a subsidy for state and local treasuries. Lost federal revenue from property tax deductions on owner-occupied homes in 1981 was estimated at $9 billion and for other nonbusiness state and local taxes—primarily income and sales taxes—approximately $17 billion.[62]

Interest on almost all state and local securities (called state and municipal bonds) is exempt from federal taxes. This subsidy cost the national government $6.5 billion in 1981. Interest on state and local industrial development bonds (IRBs), which finance industrial development, transportation projects, pollution control projects, and public and private housing construction, is also exempt from federal taxes. The tax loss for industrial development bonds for 1981 was $695 million, with another $1.6 billion lost to housing bond subsidies. The great expansion of the use of industrial development bonds in recent years, especially for housing, has produced major controversy. Some see it as a legitimate means for national support of state and local goals and as an aid for business and homeowners coping with high interest rates. Others view these devices as backdoor raids on the national treasury that must be closed in the interest of fiscal solvency. The battle for resolution of this debate continues to be intense.

State Financial Aid to Local Governments. The states give considerable amounts of their own resources as intergovernmental assistance. Accounting for only 6 percent of the revenues of local governments at the beginning of the present century, state aid equaled 62.7 percent of the general revenues local governments raised themselves by 1981, an extraordinary figure considering the public fixation with national aid. (Table 6–8). It should be noted, however, that some of this money originated with the national government. That government makes grants to states which in turn "pass through" to their local governments about 27 percent of the national funds they receive. States provide from their own funds more than one-third of the money local governments spend, however, still a significant amount and more than the national government provides.

State financial assistance to local governments is generally of two types— grants-in-aid and shared taxes and receipts. The former are appropriations specifically authorized by the state legislature or national funds being passed through the state to its political subdivisions. Categorical grants, distributed on a formula basis, account for most of these monies. The shared taxes and receipts are revenues collected by the state, such as an extra penny in sales tax for local government or a portion of state liquor store profits. The money is shared with local governments either on the basis of an allocation formula or according to the place where the revenue originated (e.g., the location of a state liquor store), neither of which is redistributive in terms of equalizing revenues throughout the state. More recently, certain allocations have been redistributive because funds were sent to local governments on some other basis, ranging from payments per capita to a complex need formula. The latter might include such items as revenue-raising ability, physical decay, and economic development.

Alternative Forms of Financial Assistance. States pursue other general approaches to providing local fiscal assistance. These include: (1) payments in lieu of taxes for state land or buildings located in a local jurisdiction; (2) use of shared facilities; (3) gifts of real or personal property; and (4) the assumption of certain costs of local government.

When the state assumes direct financial responsibility for a previously local function, the locality is relieved of the burden of financing it and may spend its funds for something else. A 1976 ACIR survey of municipalities over 2,500 in population found that between 1965 and 1975 there were 1,708 transfers of functions or components of functions. The states took on 14 percent of these, largely as a result of state law. Most often shifted activities were public health, public welfare, municipal courts, pollution

TABLE 6-8
STATE AID TO LOCAL GOVERNMENT
(INCLUDING FEDERAL "PASS THROUGH" FUNDS),
1902-1981, BY SELECTED YEARS

	Total state intergovernmental aid (in millions)	State intergovernmental aid as a percent of total locally-raised general revenue
1902	$ 52	6.1%
1927	596	10.1
1934	1,318	22.7
1948	3,283	28.9
1954	5,679	41.7
1964	12,968	42.9
1967	19,056	32.4
1969	24,779	54.0
1970	28,892	56.2
1971	32,640	57.3
1972	36,759	57.0
1973	40,822	57.9
1974	45,600	59.4
1975	51,004	60.5
1976	56,678	60.8
1977	61,084	59.9
1978	65,815	59.4
1979	74,461	63.5
1980	82,758	63.6
1981	91,307	62.7

Source: Adapted from U.S. Bureau of Census, *1967 Census of Governments,* Vol. 6 *State Payments to Local Governments.* Updated from data in Advisory Commission on Intergovernmental Relations, *Significant Features of Fiscal Federalism, 1981–82 Edition* (Washington, D.C.: April, 1983), p. 69.

abatement, property tax assessment standards, building codes, land use regulations (including coastal zone wetlands), and the regulation of surface mining.[63] The largest single transfer of functions occurred when Connecticut abolished its counties in 1960 and the state assumed their functions. The variations in state financing for several functions appear in Table 6–9.

Notice that some states pay all or almost all the costs of one or more functions while others rely more heavily on local financing (or provide substitute amounts of aid). As can be seen, Rhode Island pays 100 percent of the state-local health and hospital costs, but only 40.2 percent of highway expenditures. South Carolina, on the other hand, pays 97 percent of state-local highway costs but only 48.7 percent of the outlays for health and hospitals.

TABLE 6-9
STATE PERCENTAGE OF STATE-LOCAL GENERAL EXPENDITURE, *FROM OWN REVENUE SOURCE,* TOTAL AND FOR SELECTED FUNCTIONS, BY STATE, 1978–79

Total General Expenditure		Local Education		Public Welfare[1] (including Medicaid)		Health & Hospitals[1]		Highways	
Hawaii	84.5	Hawaii	95.5	Illinois	100.0	Rhode Island	100.0	South Carolina	97.0
Delaware	79.6	Kentucky	79.7	Missouri	100.0	North Dakota	99.7	Maryland	94.0
New Mexico	76.4	Alaska	78.6	Washington	100.0	Delaware	98.6	West Virginia	93.3
West Virginia	76.2	New Mexico	77.4	Alaska	99.0	Hawaii	97.9	Arkansas	90.1
Kentucky	75.6	Alabama	76.6	Vermont	98.7	Vermont	96.4	Kentucky	87.7
Alaska	70.5	North Carolina	74.5	Hawaii	98.6	New Hampshire	91.5	North Carolina	84.8
Vermont	68.7	Delaware	73.9	Delaware	98.2	Connecticut	89.5	Indiana	83.9
Arkansas	68.3	California	73.1	Maryland	98.1	Alaska	82.9	Virginia	83.6
North Carolina	68.3	Mississippi	69.5	West Virginia	98.0	Virginia	77.9	Idaho	82.1
Louisiana	66.3	West Virginia	67.9	California	97.3	Pennsylvania	77.6	Oregon	79.3
South Carolina	66.0	Washington	67.7	Utah	97.3	Maryland	76.6	Tennessee	78.0
Mississippi	65.7	Louisiana	66.7	Rhode Island	97.1	Maine	75.8	New Mexico	76.5
North Dakota	65.2	South Carolina	64.0	Oklahoma	96.8	Utah	75.6	Ohio	76.4
Maine	64.9	Oklahoma	62.6	Massachusetts	96.7	Oregon	69.7	Delaware	75.7
Rhode Island	64.8	Florida	61.9	Arkansas	96.6	Kentucky	68.3	Michigan	75.4
Alabama	64.5	Arkansas	60.8	Kentucky	96.6	South Dakota	68.3	Oklahoma	75.4
Minnesota	64.2	Georgia	60.0	Louisiana	96.6	New Mexico	67.3[1]	Wyoming	75.4
Oklahoma	63.6	Minnesota	59.7	Kansas	94.8	Massachusetts	62.9	Utah	73.6
California	63.2	Utah	57.5	Michigan	94.7	New Jersey	62.1	Georgia	72.3
Utah	63.2	Indiana	56.7	Alabama	93.7	North Carolina	58.6[1]	Florida	71.6
Idaho	63.1	Montana	56.2	South Carolina	93.7	Kansas	57.4	Washington	71.5
Wisconsin	60.7	Texas	53.9	Connecticut	92.3	Louisiana	56.9	Pennsylvania	70.2
Indiana	60.6	Idaho	53.7	Idaho	92.2	West Virginia	56.5	Mississippi	69.5
Washington	60.5	Tennessee	53.5	Texas	91.7	Illinois	56.4	Louisiana	68.0
Maryland	60.0	Maine	53.3	South Dakota	90.0	Ohio	54.6	Arizona	67.9

State	Value		State	Value		State	Value		State	Value		State	Value
Iowa	59.7		North Dakota	50.3		Oregon	89.4		New York	53.3		Alabama	66.9
Virginia	59.2		Pennsylvania	49.8		Maine	89.2		Oklahoma	51.2		Iowa	66.4
Georgia	57.3		Arizona	48.2		Tennessee	88.5		Michigan	50.7		Missouri	65.9
Michigan	57.3		Virginia	46.8		Mississippi	87.5		Montana	50.1		Illinois	64.1
Pennsylvania	55.5		Illinois	46.4		Pennsylvania	87.3		Minnesota	48.9		Texas	62.7
Arizona	55.0		Kansas	46.3		Wisconsin	83.5		South Carolina	48.7		Nebraska	62.4
Wyoming	54.9		Ohio	46.0		Florida	82.2		Missouri	48.5		Alaska	62.2
Connecticut	54.8		Maryland	43.6		Iowa	81.5		Wisconsin	48.5		Vermont	58.5
Tennessee	54.7		Michigan	43.3		Wyoming	81.0		Colorado	47.0		Connecticut	58.0
Illinois	54.4		Iowa	42.7		North Dakota	78.4		Alabama	46.6		Colorado	58.0
Massachusetts	54.3		Rhode Island	42.6		Nebraska	78.3		Washington	45.7		North Dakota	57.9
South Dakota	54.3		New Jersey	42.2		New Jersey	77.3		Nebraska	44.6		Nevada	56.4
Ohio	52.9		New York	41.6		Colorado	75.7		Texas	44.1		New Hampshire	56.3
Oregon	52.8		Colorado	41.5		Virginia	75.3		Indiana	43.4		Hawaii	55.5
Kansas	52.6		Missouri	39.4		Ohio	75.2		Iowa	42.2		Massachusetts	55.1
Montana	52.5		Wisconsin	38.2		Arizona	71.1		Arkansas	41.4		Maine	55.0
Missouri	52.0		Massachusetts	37.7		Indiana	61.6		Georgia	41.4¹		California	51.7
Florida	51.7		Nevada	35.7		Minnesota	58.3		Arizona	40.1		Minnesota	50.7
New Jersey	51.4		Wyoming	32.5		New Hampshire	53.4		California	39.3		Kansas	50.6
Colorado	50.5		Connecticut	31.8		Nevada	50.3		Mississippi	36.1		New Jersey	48.9
New Hampshire	50.5		Oregon	30.7		New York	43.4		Tennessee	35.3		South Dakota	48.1
Texas	49.8		Vermont	29.0		Montana	40.7		Idaho	34.2		Montana	46.3
Nebraska	48.6		South Dakota	18.7		U.S.²	83.9¹		Florida	32.1		Rhode Island	40.2
Nevada	45.9		Nebraska	17.7					Wyoming	29.0		Wisconsin	39.8
New York	45.1		New Hampshire	9.9					Nevada	22.4		New York	37.9
U.S.²	57.0		U.S.²	51.9					U.S.²	51.4¹		U.S.²	65.6

¹Public welfare expenditures for Georgia, New Mexico, and North Carolina are included with health and hospital expenditures. Data necessary for separation by function, by source of financing, are not available for FY 1979.

²Excluding the District of Columbia.

Source: Compiled by ACIR staff from various reports of the Governments Division, U.S. Bureau of the Census; and National Education Association, Estimates of School Statistics, 1979–80 (copyright 1980 by the National Education Association, all rights reserved). Contained in Advisory Commission on Intergovernmental Relations, Significant Features of Fiscal Federalism, 1980–81 Edition (Washington, D.C.: 1981), p. 24. Reprinted with permission.

States can select another form of fiscal assistance by authorizing localities to diversify their revenue sources. State action to allow localities to impose a variety of taxes, fees, and charges to supplement property tax revenues ensures both more funds and a more balanced and flexible local tax system. Two-thirds of the states now permit all or some of their cities or counties or both to use either local sales or income taxes.

States can, and do, select and combine these alternatives with direct grants-in-aid, tailoring an assistance package to meet their particular needs. Currently, they use multiple forms of fiscal assistance simultaneously. Employment of one technique does not necessarily substitute for another.

Other Trends

Other trends in the fiscal federal arrangement should be noted. Major ones include increased reliance on deficit financing by all levels of government, shifts in functional allocations in intergovernmental aid, increased direct national fiscal involvement in domestic programs, and changes in the relative tax effort and fiscal capability of various governments, to name several significant but somewhat less visible areas of change. Nevertheless, they are not as important from an intergovernmental viewpoint, as those previously discussed.

A few conclusions are evident from the financial trends reviewed. (1) The system is in a dynamic state of fluctuation and change. (2) While patterns are evident, their lasting impact on the continued viability of all participants in the federal agreement is not so readily understood. (3) For all its strengths, the fiscal federal system still has some major inequities, stress points that appear to be weakening, and potential pitfalls. (4) The system appears to be in a period of increased intergovernmental conflict.

A SHARED, ADJUSTING FINANCIAL SYSTEM

Nothing reveals better the shared nature of the American federal system than an examination of its fiscal operations. American governments at all levels not only share in the provision of services, but they also help with their financing. The patterns vary from place to place and from time to time, but almost every government is involved in each activity.

Americans continuously change their minds about how they are going to provide and finance public services. At one time, for example, they want certain services totally under local control. At another, the function and its financing shift to the state. The taxes used to support it are periodically modified with property and tariffs favored at one stage of development and sales and income at another. All of this has necessitated the design of new revenue sources, shifts in expenditures, and experimentation with new mechanisms for transferring intergovernmental aid. The consequence is a constantly changing fiscal system.

These changes are not the result of careful, comprehensive planning. Rather, they are the outcome of literally thousands of relatively minor pragmatic decisions—officials doing whatever seems to solve the problem at the moment.

NOTES

1. L. L. Ecker-Racz, *The Politics and Economics of State-Local Finance* (Englewood Cliffs, N.J.: Prentice-Hall, Inc., 1970), p. 152.

2. Acceptance of the current fiscal federal arrangements should not be equated with acceptance of current tax laws or tax levels. The former can be accepted while at the same time calling for comprehensive tax reform.

3. Helvering v. Davis, 301 U.S. 619 (1937), at 641–642. See also Steward Machine Company v. Davis, 301 U.S. 548 (1937).

4. Frothingham v. Mellon, 262 U.S. 447 (1923). For a major exception to this position, see Flast v. Cohen, 392 U.S. 83 (1942), in which the Court ruled that because of the overriding importance of the First Amendment's establishment of religion clause, a taxpayer can urge more than his general interest in the expenditure of funds.

5. These exceptions were largely the product of a conservative court in the 1920s and the 1930s and do not serve as a basis for judicial approach today. See, for example, Bailey v. Drexel Furniture Company, 259 U.S. 20 (1922); and United States v. Butler, 297 U.S. 1 (1936). Justice Frankfurter wrote a scathing dissent to the prevailing view of unlimited congressional taxing authority in United States v. Kahriger, 345 U.S. 22 (1953).

6. 4 Wheaton 315 (1819).

7. Ibid.

8. Ibid.

9. See Collector v. Day, 11 Wall. 113 (1871).

10. Maryland et al. v. U.S., 451 (1981). Docket No. 80–1536.

11. South Carolina v. U.S., 199 U.S. 437.

12. Maryland v. Louisiana, 451 U.S. (1981). Docket No. 83.

13. Commonwealth Edison v. Montana, 453 U.S. (1981). Docket No. 80–581.

14. "The Harris Survey," *The Washington Post,* April 18, 1971, p. G–4.

15. Poll by Louis Harris and Associates. Everett Carll Ladd, Jr., et al., The Polls: Taxing and Spending," *Public Opinion Quarterly,* Vol. 43, No. 1 (Spring, 1979), pp. 127–128.

16. Quoted in Mervin Field, "Sending a Message: California Strikes Back," *Public Opinion,* Vol. 1, No. 3 (July/August, 1978), p. 3.

17. "ACIR's Poll of Major Intergovernmental Events of the Past 20 Years," *Intergovernmental Perspective,* Vol. 6, (Winter, 1980), p. 5.

18. Richard A. Eribes and John S. Hall, "Revolt of the Affluent: Fiscal Controls in Three States," *Public Administration Review,* Vol. 41 (Jan, 1981), p. 107.

19. Quoted in *Local Distress, State Surpluses, Proposition 13: Prelude to Fiscal Crisis or New Opportunities?* Hearing before the Subcommittee on the City of the Committee on Banking, Finance and Urban Affairs, U.S. House of Representatives, 95th Cong., 2nd Sess., July 2 and 26, 1978, p. 212. For a more detailed discussion of this theme, see Parris N. Glendening, "Public Opinion and Taxes and Expenditures: Implications for Public Administration," in Charlie B. Tyer and Marcia W. Taylor, eds., *Perspectives on the Limitation of Taxing and Spending in the Public Sector in the United States* (Columbia, S.C.: University of South Carolina, Bureau of Governmental Research and Service, 1981), pp. 35–57.

20. Charles H. Levine and Paul L. Posner, "The Centralizing Effects of Austerity on the Intergovernmental System," *Political Science Quarterly,* Vol. 96, No. 1 (Spring, 1981), p. 85.

21. Gerard Sheehan, quoted in Advisory Commission on Intergovernmental Relations, *Regional Growth: Interstate Tax Competition.* Report A–76. (Washington, D.C.: The Commission, March, 1981), pp. 32 and 34. See also Advisory Commission on Intergovernmental Relations, *Regional Growth: Historic Perspective.* Report A–74. (Washington, D.C.: The Commission, June, 1980).

22. Michael D. Reagan and John G. Sanzone, *The New Federalism.* 2d ed. (New York: Oxford University Press, 1981), p. 45.

23. One of the best and most readable works on this subject is Ira Sharkansky's *Spending in the American States* (Chicago: Rand McNally and Co., 1968).

24. 5 Cal. 3d 584 (1971). See also the very important Rodriguez v. San Antonio Independent School District, 93 S. Ct. 1278; 36 L Ed. 2, 16 (1973).

25. Serrano v. Priest.

26. U.S.D.C. (Minn. Third District) Federal No. 3–71 Civ. 23a (1971).

27. March 10, 1981.

28. Ecker-Racz., p. 166.

29. *Congressional Record,* October 11, 1965. Nationally known economist Walter W. Heller supports this estimate. See Heller's *New Dimensions of Political Economy* (Cambridge: Harvard University Press, 1966), p. 140.

30. *Congressional Quarterly Weekly Report,* Oct. 24, 1981, p. 2047.

31. A summary of some views about grants-in-aid is contained in Deil S. Wright, *Federal Grants-in-Aid: Perspectives and Alternatives* (Washington, D.C.: American Enterprise Institute for Public Policy Research, 1968), esp. pp. 35–111.

32. For an interesting account of one city's dealings with the grant process, see Jeffrey L. Pressman, *Federal Programs and City Politics: The Dynamics of the Aid Process in Oakland* (Berkeley: University of California Press, 1975); and Jeffrey L. Pressman and Aaron B. Wildavsky, *Implementation: How Great Expectations in Washington Are Dashed in Oakland: or, Why It's Amazing that Federal Programs Work at All, This Being A Saga of the Economic Development Administration as Told by Two Sympathetic Observers Who Seek to Build Morals on a Foundation of Ruined Hopes* (Berkeley: University of California Press, 1973).

33. For a review of the literature on this topic, see Edward M. Gramlich, "Intergovernmental Grants: A Review of the Empirical Literature," in Wallace Oates, *The Political Economy of Fiscal Federalism* (Lexington, Mass.: D.C. Heath and Company, Lexington Books, 1977), pp. 219–239.

34. Wright, pp. 48–49.

35. K. C. Wheare, *Federalism*, 3rd ed. (New York: Oxford University Press, 1953), p. 6.

36. Reagan and Sanzone, p. 49.

37. P.L. 90–577.

38. For a review of these changes, see Office of Management and Budget, "Special Analysis H: Federal Aid to State and Local Governments," *Special Analyses: Budget of the United States Government, 1983*, esp. pp. 19–26.

39. Ibid., pp. 22–23.

40. U. S. Office of Management and Budget, "Special Analysis H: Federal Aid to State and Local Governments," *Special Analyses: Budget of the United States Government*, 1984, p. H–21.

41. Ibid., p. H–19.

42. Testimony before the House Subcommittee on Manpower and Housing, April 28, 1981.

43. *Congressional Quarterly Weekly Report*, March 14, 1981, p. 449.

44. Ibid., October 24, 1981, p. 2051.

45. *Washington Post*, May 24, 1981, p. A–4.

46. Donald F. Kettl, "Regulating the Cities," *Publius*, Vol. 11 (Spring, 1981), p. 122.

47. *Washington Star*, March 6, 1981, p. A–13.

48. Claude E. Barfield, *Rethinking Federalism: Block Grants and Federal, State, and Local Responsibilities* (Washington, D.C.: American Enterprise Institute for Public Policy Research, 1981), p. 47.

49. *Congressional Quarterly Weekly Report*, October 24, 1981, p. 2047.

50. See R. J. May, *Federalism and Fiscal Adjustment* (London: Oxford University Press, 1969).

51. H.R. 748. See also his 1967 proposal, H.R. 5450.

52. Quoted in Mavis Mann Reeves and Parris N. Glendening, *Controversies of State and Local Political Systems* (Boston: Allyn and Bacon, 1972), p. 475. For a discussion of many of these and other adverse conclusions about revenue sharing, including pre-adoption arguments, see Edward C. Banfield, "Revenue Sharing in Theory and Practice," *The Public Interest*, No. 23 (Spring, 1971), pp 33–45.

53. Advisory Commission on Intergovernmental Relations, *Changing Public Attitudes on Governments and Taxes: 1982*, Report S–11 (Washington, D.C.: The Commission, 1982), pp. 34–35.

54. David M. Hedge, "The Effects of Alternative Grant Mechanisms on the Distribution of Federal Aid to the Cities," A Paper presented at the 1980 meeting of the Midwest Political Science Association, April, 1980.

55. Richard Lehne, "Benefits in State-National Relations," *Publius*, Vol. 2, No. 2 (Fall, 1972), pp. 75–93.

56. Tax Foundation, *Monthly Tax Features*, May, 1982, p. 1.

57. Morley Segal and A. Lee Fritschler, "Emerging Patterns of Intergovernmental Relations," *The Municipal Year Book, 1970* (Washington, D.C.: International City Management Association, 1970), pp. 13–38.

58. Ibid.; see also F. Ted Herbert and Richard D. Bingham, "The City Manager's Knowledge of Grants-in-Aid: Some Personal and Environmental Influences," *Urban Affairs Quarterly*, Vol. 8 (March, 1972), pp. 303–306.

59. Statistics for this section are drawn from data in Bureau of the Census, *Historical Statistics of the United States, 1889-1945* (Washington, D.C.: Government Printing Office, 1949).

60. There are substantial variations in state tax bases and consequently in their tax yields.

61. Ecker-Racz, p. 32.

62. Much of the data for the discussion of intergovernmental aid is derived from the Office of Management and Budget, *Special Analysis: Budget of the United States Government, Fiscal Year 1981,* especially, "Special Analysis H: Federal Aid to State and Local Governments," (Washington, D.C.: Government Printing Office, 1980).

63. Advisory Commission on Intergovernmental Relations, *Pragmatic Federalism: The Reassignement of Functional Responsibility,* Report M-105 (Washington, D.C.: July, 1976, p. 37.

CHAPTER 7

INTERSTATE RELATIONS: INTERACTIONS AMONG EQUALS

RELATIONSHIPS among the states demonstrate all the diversity that contributed to making this nation both vigorous and complex. These relations are quite a different matter than those between the national government and the states or between a state and its local jurisdictions. First, interactions are among equals on a horizontal rather than on the hierarchical basis that marks the other instances. Consequently, the element of compulsion is absent. A higher degree of persuasion is necessary for joint interstate action or agreement. Second, the political rewards of dealing with interstate issues may be negligible, leading state officials to ignore them or to devote as little energy as possible to their solution. Furthermore, actions that damage citizens of other states, such as diverting waters of streams flowing through several of them, may enhance the position of the governor or another official within his or her own state. This makes it advantageous for that official to act selfishly in the pursuit of home-state interests.

OPPORTUNITIES AND PROBLEMS

The diversity of 50 political entities, each with its own unique political culture, stands in refreshing contrast to the uniformity that could prevail were the American system to operate on a unitary basis. There are opportunities for experiment on a state rather than on a nationwide scale; and, in fact, past commentators have referred to this type of uncentralized system as a "laboratory for democracy." Citizens are offered choices as to the kind of place where they would like to live. Differing standards can be established in matters dividing society such as the sale of alcoholic beverages, legalized abortions, obscenity, or the quality of public services.

At the same time the diversity among the states can cause confusion and increase the problems that occur near interstate boundaries, in the flow of interstate commerce, or in the lives of citizens who move from one state to another. Some sticky, fundamental matters are involved, such as State A diverting the water or polluting the streams of State B, or State C limiting the fishing rights, and thus the livelihood, of residents of State D. In the past it has meant that persons who thought they were lawfully married for the second time discovered that their out-of-state divorces were not legal and that they were therefore bigamists.

Women have found that their share of the family property differs as they move from state to state. Commerce and other interstate activity have been impeded. Multiple traffic regulations have slowed movement of goods and increased highway hazards. Persons old enough to buy alcoholic beverages in one state have been denied that privilege in a neighboring jurisdiction. Until the enactment of the Twenty-sixth Amendment in 1971 lowering the voting age to 18, a citizen might vote at that age in Georgia or Kentucky, but be unable to vote for one more year if he moved to Alaska, two more if it were to Hawaii, or three more if he went to one of the other states. The tremendous variety among the states produces both creative and confusing situations requiring accommodation by all participants.

Interactions among the states are increasing. This demonstrates the growth of intergovernmental relations among all jurisdictions. An interesting aspect of this expanding intergovernmental contact is the ebb and flow of conflict and cooperation among the states. Just as the trend seems to be toward greater cooperation, other elements enter the picture and produce controversy. Similarly, the penchant for establishing regional interstate organizations fluctuates over time.

FRICTION AMONG THE STATES

Dissonance existed among the colonies and under the Articles of Confederation; in fact, 10 serious boundary disputes raged at the time of the Philadelphia Convention. Despite the general growth of interstate cooperation since then, all interstate relations are not harmonious. It is not always possible to avoid friction with one's neighbors, especially if their activities affect the welfare of one's family. States continue to disagree, sometimes loudly.

Matters in Dispute

Many arguments have been over boundary lines and riparian rights, an outgrowth of conflicting charter grants and interpretations. The Mason-Dixon line grew out of a dispute between Maryland and Pennsylvania; and boundary conflicts have raged between Colorado and New Mexico, Delaware and New Jersey, and Indiana and Kentucky, to name a few.

Since rivers form many interstate boundaries, they are the bones of contention in many controversies. Disputes have risen as to which state owns the rivers and can regulate their navigation and fishing rights, how the water will be allocated, and how pollution will be controlled. The allocation of water is particularly important in the western states where water is scarce. Arguments over the diversion of streams have not been limited to the western section of the country. New Jersey and New York went to court over New York's diversion of the Delaware River, and Minnesota and North Dakota were also involved in a contest over the straightening of rivers and the flooding of land. South Dakota's decision to sell water from the Missouri River for use in the coal slurry pipeline provoked outrage and generated court suits from downstream states recently. Fishing and the use of boats cause much interstate irritation. Virginia and Maryland engaged in an "oyster war" for more than two hundred years, contesting the right to harvest oysters in the Chesapeake Bay, and many states have been involved in controversies over the licensing and regulation of boating.

In the commercial field, states compete for the location of industries by reducing business taxes, and they are rivals for chartering corporations. The Depression of the 1930s encouraged economic competition among the states and the erection of trade barriers to protect home industries. States used their police, taxing, and licensing powers to impose rigid rules of inspection, regulate the sale of selected products (for example, sausage), and restrict the importation of certain agricultural products. (They ostensibly limited importation for protection from disease but actually did so to prevent sales in competition with the state's own products.) In addition, they regulated trucks as to length, width, weight, and number of lights. They further imposed chain store taxes, discriminatory taxes on nonresidential commercial vehicles, special license fees for out-of-state corporations, vendors license fees on nonresident sellers, and discriminatory premium taxes on foreign insurance companies. Other states retaliated in kind, bringing forth impediments to commerce, overlapping taxes, and increased intergovernmental friction. Interpretation of the power of Congerss "to regulate commerce with foreign nations, and among the several states," means that the states cannot levy these types of taxes and fees to the point of interfering with interstate commerce. The special levies, however, are often designed to give a slight competitive advantage to a state's own commerce.

More recently, states have changed their banking laws to encourage the growth of such financial establishments within their boundaries. As a consequence of two such actions, a New York City bank announced a move to Delaware, and Citicorp, a credit card operation that previously had been quartered in New York, moved its collection center to South Dakota so it could collect higher interest rates on outstanding accounts.

Environmental pollution surged to the fore as a source of interstate controversy at the middle of the present century as states sought to clear the air, oceans, lakes, and rivers of waste. Whenever the source of pollution was over the state boundary in another state, the difficulties of solving the problems were increased, particularly when the polluter was a governmental jurisdiction.

Solid waste disposal became an intense point of friction as large urban communities looked across the border at rural areas as potential waste disposal sites. And hazardous wastes magnified the decibel of the screams of protest. Understandably, no state wants to be the dumping ground for nuclear or toxic wastes or even the transmission route for their disposal elsewhere.

Irritation surfaces in the apportionment of responsibility for the solution of urban-suburban problems—such as those of transportation and housing—in interstate metropolitan areas. The overflow of troubles from a large city located on one state boundary to the small city bordering the large center but situated on the other side of the boundary also creates friction. Some difficulties of Whiting or East Chicago in Indiana, for example, are interstate in nature because of the proximity of these cities to Chicago.

Energy and taxation emerged in the late 1970s as major friction points. The energy poor states of the Northeast sought to require energy rich states to share oil and gas and went to court to restrain the latter from collecting severance taxes on fuel. Moreover, the "have not" states organized to pressure the national government to take actions that would ensure an adequate energy supply and thus reduce the industrial and residential attractiveness of the warmer states. The Northeast-Midwest Congressional Caucus is one example of such an association.

A major conflict, sometimes called the "Second War between the States," developed between the states in the Frostbelt and those in the Sunbelt during the decade of the 1970s. This controversy, centering on economic development and aggravated by fuel shortages, is discussed later in this chapter.

Factors Contributing to Interstate Conflict

The factors contributing to interstate conflict are many and varied. Some rise from historic causes and their beginnings are long buried. Nevertheless, the contentious attitudes remain, allowing controversies to flair up for little cause. Interstate rivalries for industrial development contribute to the strain. In some instances, disputes continue because of state laws that prevent amelioration, or because of beliefs of the citizens of each jurisdiction that they bear a disproportionate share of the costs of any cooperation.[1]

A substantial proportion of any blame for interstate conflicts can be laid at the door of a political leadership that uses the dispute as an occasion for political gain by demonstrating concern for the "home folks." In other instances, leaders may be uncertain about the political costs of cooperation or be too timid to take a chance. Anti-cooperation attitudes may be reflected in the refusal to participate in interstate planning aimed at avoiding or solving problems flowing across state boundaries. A few years ago, a representative of the then-governor of Indiana arrived at a conference on "Intergovernmental Cooperation in Energy and the Environment in the Ohio River Valley" and announced that he was not interested in regional cooperation of any kind—an announcement that put a damper on the enthusiasm of the participants.

A pervasive factor in aggravating the difficulties that arise is the absence of effective mechanisms for communication. It is not enough to be able to write a letter or use the telephone. Officials in state A must know whom to contact in state B when a problem arises. Moreover, they need to be aware of the problem before it creates friction. This is often impossible because officials cannot know everything going on within their boundaries, even when it is a state activity. Consequently, disputes may erupt that might have been avoided with a better information flow. The regional organizations that have developed have not improved communications sufficiently to prevent the rise of unnecessary conflict.

Settlement of Disputes

Many minor disputes are settled by negotiation among the respective state officials. These individuals often are acquainted with their counterparts in the other jurisdictions because they are members of interstate professional or public interest group organizations, or because other activities have thrown them together. A governor can pick up the telephone and talk to the governor of a neighboring state, or a state highway engineer to his counterpart across the river. Sometimes national agencies stimulate the interface of state officials.

Disagreements involving more complicated matters, such as the conservation and use of water resources, may be resolved by formal agreement involving interstate compacts or other contracts. (They will be discussed later in this chapter.) In the past, Congress occasionally has been able to placate both parties as in the boundary dispute between Ohio and Michigan. When Ohio was admitted to the Union in 1803, its exact northern boundary was not determined because of conflicting language in two acts of Congress. Michigan, which was still a territory, objected to the boundary described by the Act of 1802; she claimed her territory existed by authority of the Northwest Ordinance of 1787 to a line drawn east from the southern tip of Lake Michigan. Responding to pressure from the Ohio legislature, Congress authorized a survey of the disputed territory, but Michigan refused to agree to its findings. Congress eventually satisfied both parties in 1836 by granting to Ohio the disputed territory and compensating Michigan with the upper peninsula, located north of Lake Michigan, an area about nine times the size of the land that was lost.[2]

Court Settlement. If matters reach an impasse, states occasionally go to court. When one state sues another, it is a civil suit originally brought in the United States Supreme Court. According to one student of the judiciary, the Court treats cases between states as matters of arbitration rather than as questions of law and encourages states to settle the dispute themselves if possible. It attempts to avoid having to force states to comply.[3] Under the Articles of Confederation, Congress was made the arbiter of disputes between states and actually settled at least six during the Confederation period. The most important was a conflict between Pennsylvania and Connecticut over what is now western Pennsylvania.[4] The Constitution transferred the role of arbiter to the Supreme Court, giving it original jurisdiction over all cases "to which a state shall be a party." This original jurisdiction was made exclusive by the Judiciary Act of 1789.

Despite the controversies under way at the time of the establishment of the Court, only three suits between states were brought before 1849. During the next 90 years at least 29 such suits developed. All the early suits involved boundary disputes; in fact, during the first 60 years of the Court they constituted the only cases between states coming before it.[5] More modern litigation involves water rights, pollution, debts, enforcement of contracts, efforts by two states to prevent a third from enforcing a law to restrict the interstate flow of natural gas in the event of a shortage, and the imposition of severance taxes on fuel.[6]

The Court construes liberally its own power to settle controversies between states, indicating that the particular subject of the controversy is irrelevant. Because the parties are states, they have a constitutional right to come into the courts of the Union. Nevertheless, the Court sometimes looks at the subject and declines original jurisdiction. It did this in suits brought by states in attempts to enforce their penal laws, holding that its original jurisdiction extends only to civil suits. The Court also has indicated that its jurisdiction to hear cases between states would be used only when necessary. In the case of *Alabama* v. *Arizona*[7] where Alabama sought to enjoin

19 other states from regulating or prohibiting the sale of convict-made goods, the Court held that the threatened injury to a state must be imminent and of great magnitude. It further held that the burden on the state bringing the case to establish all its elements is greater than that generally required for private citizens to recover in court. States must appear before the Court when summoned; otherwise the Court will proceed without them as it did when Georgia failed to appear in 1793 in the celebrated case of *Chisholm* v. *Georgia.*[8]

The Court has refused to hear cases brought by one state against another for the recovery of financial losses of its citizens. New Hampshire sued Louisiana in 1883 to collect on bonds issued by Louisiana and held by New Hampshire citizens. The Court declined jurisdiction in the case, ruling that a state may not invoke the original jurisdiction of the Court to enforce the individual rights of citizens.[9] In general, a state may not bring a suit in its own name for the benefit of particular persons. It may sue to protect its own rights or sometimes as a *parens patriae*—as a Parent—to protect the welfare of its citizens as a whole. The Supreme Court generally constructs strictly its grant of jurisdiction over these cases, which it shares with other national courts.

Compelling Compliance. The Supreme Court has no specified method of compelling compliance with its decision and interstate suits are typically lengthy affairs. The *Virginia* v. *West Virginia* cases are probably the best example of the time it can take to settle a dispute and the difficulties the Court may have in enforcing its judgment against a reluctant state. When West Virginia separated from Virginia and was admitted to the Union as a separate state, it agreed to pay a fair portion of the public debt that had been incurred by Virginia before 1861. Virginia began negotiations in 1865 for the amount due, but West Virginia was not inclined to pay. In 1906 Virginia brought the first of nine successive cases against West Virginia In the major cases the Court decided it had jurisdiction and that by 1916 West Virginia owed Virginia $12 million, but West Virginia ignored the demands for payment. Finally, in 1918, Virginia demanded that the Court direct the West Virginia legislature to levy a tax to pay the judgment. The Court was at a loss as to what action to take and set argument for the next term on the steps to be taken to enforce the judgment. At this point, the animosity of the two states having abated somewhat over time, West Virginia provided in 1919 for a bond issue and the debt was finally paid in 1939.[10]

INTERSTATE COOPERATION

Although the relations among the states are sometimes discordant, there is evidence that the states increasingly are acting in concert to solve the gigantic problems confronting them. The growth in the number of interstate compacts and contracts, the increase in the number and effectiveness of interstate organizations, and the more frequent conferences and consultations all support the idea of heightened cooperation. State efforts are not always successful because they are likely to be pragmatic attempts to solve particular problems rather than sustained movements to produce intergovernmental harmony. Nevertheless, recent activities have opened new channels of communication and smoothed old ones.

Interstate cooperation is obviously influenced by many factors, some institutional and some human. Constitutional provisions, congressional legislation, executive orders, national grants-in-aid, and the leadership of national administrative agencies stimulate some uniform laws, regulations, and practices. The Constitution makes specific provisions for the rendition of fugitives and for the adoption of interstate compacts, the latter requiring the consent of Congress. National legislation provides for the ratification of compacts, the establishment of regional organizations, intergovernmental personnel exchanges, and interstate functional agencies in fields such as transportation, to cite only a few cooperative efforts it stimulates.

National statutes, reinforced by executive orders and Office of Management and Budget circulars, require cooperation in such matters as planning for metropolitan areas of an interstate nature. National grants-in-aid sometimes go to interstate regional organizations or contain provisions such as requirement for an environmental impact statement involving interstate cooperation. National administrative agencies encourage uniformity in rules and regulations. Certainly the Environmental Protection Agency works toward general standards for environmental pollution control.

Probably even greater propulsion toward cooperation is provided by the staggering problems facing the states, difficulties not coinciding with state boundaries and requiring interstate action to solve. They are aggravated by tremendous population growth and technological developments that allow people greater mobility and increase the pressures on existing facilities. No one state is able to prevent the pollution of the Mississippi, Missouri, or Colorado rivers. Interstate action is necessary and, in fact, states do cooperate in projects of this sort. Eight states have worked together for many years to cut down on pollution of the Ohio River, to cite one example. Problems such as providing for the indigent or upgrading economically depressed areas are often regional or national in scope and require more than one state's successful handling of its share.

States employ various devices for cooperation. The most prominent are informal consultation and agreement, organized conferences, compacts, other contracts, uniform state laws and reciprocal laws, and interstate organizations. States also cooperate through the assignment of personnel to joint projects and through such activities as the interstate cooperation in law enforcement. The latter occurs when police from State A apprehend a criminal fleeing from State B and hold him for rendition, or when arrangements permit police from State A to follow him into State B upon his crossing the line if they are in "hot pursuit." States also devise contingency plans for use of personnel from neighboring jurisdictions in the event of emergencies such as fire or rioting. Sometimes these arrangements are made by compact.

It is most difficult to determine the extent of the informal interstate consultation and agreement that takes place or the matters involved because there are so many channels through which they could occur. Not only do governors visit, telephone, and write to each other, but other state officials also act similarly. There are numerous examples of governors agreeing informally to push a specific program, attend a meeting, or take a hand in a particularly knotty problem affecting another state. Administrators frequently consult, especially on matters effecting the peripheries of their states, such as highway location.

Some states stand out as sources of information for other states. The American State Administrators Project survey for 1978 reveals the administrators are most likely to contact California, and, to a lesser extent, Minnesota, Michigan, Texas, and Pennsylvania. Although New York's programs were highly regarded, it was sixteenth in rank insofar as being sought out by other state administrators for advice. The states most likely to seek advice from other states were Georgia and Washington.[11]

In addition to official action, many professional organizations such as the National Association of Accountants, the National Association of Social Workers, and the American Bar Association, as well as public interest groups such as the National or Regional Governors' Associations, and citizens' groups such as the Citizens Forum on Self-Government (formerly the National Municipal League) provide vehicles for the exchange of ideas. Much time at these meetings is spent in informal conversation, and arrangements to deal with problems can be made. The opportunity they create for bringing public officials face to face is probably more valuable than the programs they present, although these, too, can serve to stimulate thinking on mutual problems and facilitate exchange of information.

Uniform and Reciprocal Legislation

State concern with the problems created by variations in legislation on a particular subject is shown in efforts to enact uniform legislation and to grant reciprocity to each other. Uniform legislation involves the adoption by each state of substantially similar drafts of statutes on a specific subject, such as securing the attendance of out-of-state witnesses at a trial. Thus, although each legislature enacts a separate statute for its state, there will be a high degree of uniformity among the laws of all states on the subject. Reciprocity is an exchange of privilege. State A may lower its public-college tuition for students from all those states who do the same for students from State A. Or licenses to practice a particular profession, granted by State B, may be recognized in states C and D if State B allows professionals licensed by them similar privileges.

Active Groups. Many organizations promote the adoption of uniform legislation. The most notable of them in view of its singleness of purpose and its long record of activity in the field is the National Conference on Uniform State Laws. Other groups also work toward this end, but most have other major purposes. Over the years the Citizens Forum on Self-Government has proposed a series of model state constitutions, model city charters, model county charters, and model acts that have influenced state and local government structures and policies. State constitutional conventions, state legislatures, and the interest groups involved have used these documents as yardsticks for measuring the desirability of proposed legal provisions. National government agencies such as the Public Health Service and the Environmental Protection Agency, as well as various professional associations, put forward proposals that result in uniform arrangements if adopted. The Advisory Commission on Intergovernmental Relations designs a legislative program concerned with all levels of government, and the Council of State Governments suggests state legislation.

Commissioners on Uniform State Laws. The one agency dedicated solely to putting forward drafts of legislation for possible adoption by the various state legislatures substantially as written is the Conference of Commissioners on Uniform State Laws. The Conference, organized in 1892, consists of a maximum of five commissioners from each state designated by the respective governors. Most commissioners are practicing attorneys and law professors, with a few heads of legislative research and drafting agencies also included. The Conference appoints associate members from legislative research and drafting staffs.

Initiated by the American Bar Association, the Conference works very closely with it. Usually the two organizations hold meetings at the same time and place, and their committees cooperate as projects develop. Drafts of legislation proposed by the Conference are approved by the House of Delegates of the American Bar Association.[12]

Subjects Involved. Most of the legislation proposed concerns matters outside the normal fields of political contention; much of it deals with commerce. The Uniform Commercial Code illustrates the type of legislation likely to be successful. This code and the Narcotic Drug proposals have been adopted by all states. On the other hand, a full decade lapsed with no proposals approved for uniform legislation on death tax credits and nonresident individual income tax deductions. Also, after two decades uniform rules of criminal procedure had not been adopted by any state.[13] In matters where states compete, such as in economic development, uniform legislation is difficult to achieve because of the conflicts of interests concerned. Consequently, the number of policy areas in which uniform legislation is acceptable is limited. Legislation is most likely to be adopted when it is highly interstate in character, when it meets a recognized need, and when it is in the area of private law where controversy is less likely to accompany social change.

The success of the Conference in pushing uniform legislation rests mainly on the support that the drafts receive from groups equipped to pressure for legislation in the states. The conference has no difficulty getting the drafts introduced, but it does not function as an organized pressure group for their adoption. The state bar associations are particularly important in this respect. When the organized legal profession is united behind a proposal, the chances of Conference drafts receiving a favorable legislative reception are enhanced. On the other hand, uniform legislation has little chance of adoption if those involved—such as any industry concerned— disagree.[14] This is why uniform regulation of interstate motor carriers has not materialized.

A Case Study. The method of drafting and adopting uniform legislation is illustrated by the history of the Uniform Commercial Code, which almost completely rewrote the entire field of sales contracts and personal and commercial credit. Work on this code began in 1940. An initial draft was published 10 years later, and its final promulgation occurred in 1958. Committees from the Conference worked closely with the American Law Institute and the American Bar Association. Proposed drafts were introduced into several state legislatures for their comment, and legislative research agencies assessed their effect on existing statutes. Much discussion and criticism in both the legislatures and the banking and credit associations resulted in the drafters seeking to clarify existing law, and to fill in gaps such as that pertaining to the protection of consumers in credit contacts. New drafts were written. The New York Legislature authorized an interim committee study and its report was studied before final drafting. Discussions of its 1950 draft filled two issues of *Law and Contemporary Problems*, a journal published by Duke University Law School. In 1958, the final draft was approved by the House of Delegates of the American Bar Association. The American Banking Association supported the code before various legislatures.

In this case the Conference of Commissioners on Uniform State Laws served as negotiator between the state legislatures and the various professional groups concerned with technicalities of the law. In particular, it attempted to alleviate concerns expressed by the Council of State Governments and its affiliates, especially the Association of State Attorneys General. Its adjustment of the various interests concerned, as well as its attempts to work out the highly technical problems before the legislation was introduced, doubtlessly contributed to adoption of this uniform legislation in all 50 states. Negotiation of interest group conflicts outside the legislative chambers is a component of much legislation adopted in the United States.[15]

Interstate Compacts

Additional evidence of the increasingly strong inclination of the states to cooperate with other states can be found in the growing number of interstate compacts; however, these instruments still play a minor role in solving interstate problems. Compacts are formal agreements between states somewhat in the nature of treaties on the international scale. They are usually initiated by the states involved and then submitted to the Congress after approval by the state legislatures concerned. Once in operation, compacts are binding on all citizens of the signatory states, both as to public and private rights. Compacts, properly drawn and entered into, are within the protection of the contract clause of the Constitution, and the Supreme Court has original jurisdiction over their enforcement. Congress also has authority to compel compliance. States cannot escape their financial or other obligations under them.

Congressional Consent. The Constitution requires that compacts have the approval of the Congress. This is usually but not always the procedure, either before or after the agreement. There are instances of completed compacts that do not have congressional consent, such as the Southern Regional Educational Compact, but the line between the ones that require such consent and those that do not is imprecise. Generally, those transferring political control or power adversely affecting a constitutional grant of authority require congressional approval; others do not. The Supreme Court makes the final decision in each case, usually at the instigation of private interests.

The Supreme Court held in *Virginia* v. *Tennessee* (1893)[16] that consent could be implied as well as expressly given. It said that specific consent was necessary when a compact "affected a power delegated to the national government" or when it had ramifications for the "political balance" of the federal system. More recently, in a case dealing with a 19-state agreement to cooperate in taxation of interstate corporations, which was not submitted to Congress for approval, Supreme Court Justice Lewis F. Powell, speaking for the majority, wrote in 1978:

> Legal precedent indicates that the prohibition against interstate agreements without congressional approval was directed to the formation of any combination tending to increase the political power of the states, which may encroach upon or interfere with the just supremacy of the United States. . . .

Powell concluded that the Multistate Tax Compact "does not purport to authorize the member states to exercise any powers they could not exercise in its absence."[17]

Congress approved compacts rather routinely until the 1930s when it began to examine them more closely. Consent to the Oil and Gas Compact in 1935 was limited to four years and periodic resubmission has been required ever since. To date, Congress has not approved the Midwest Nuclear Compact or the Interstate Environment Compact. The latter, instigated by the Southern Governors' Conference, provides for supplemental agreements in environmental matters. Despite its ratification by nine states since 1971, Congress still has not seen fit to approve it.[18]

Congress may be concerned with preserving national control over interstate environmental matters. In 1942 President Franklin Roosevelt vetoed a bill consenting to an interstate compact among Colorado, Kansas, and Nebraska on the use of the waters of the Republican River. He did so because the compact appeared to restrict national control of a navigable stream and to limit national interest in the development of water resources. The compact was subsequently redrafted and approved. Recent acts of consent for many compacts reserve the right of Congress to alter, amend, or repeal them. Some statutes of consent provide that Congress or any of its standing committees may require submission of information by the compact agency.[19] Whether these provisions are enforceable or not has not been determined by the courts.

These congressional requirements grew out of a controversy between the House Committee on the Judiciary and the Port Authority of New York and New Jersey in which the Committee subpoenaed Austin J. Tobin, executive director of the Authority, to appear and bring with him records about the Authority's internal management. The Authority, supported by its parent states of New York and New Jersey, refused to submit documents on the ground that it was an agency of the two state governments and thereby immune from investigation of its internal affairs by a congressional committee. After losing the case in the United States District Court, Tobin won on an appeal to the Court of Appeals. Since the case was carried no further, *In re Tobin* is the prevailing opinion.[20] It should be noted that the opinion was on the ground that the Committee exceeded its grant of authority from the House of Representatives. The Court did not decide whether or not Congress could investigate compact agencies, although statements in the opinion indicated that there might be limits beyond which Congress could not go.

Participation. Figure 7-1 shows that until 1920 relatively few interstate compacts were ratified. There were 36 between 1783 and 1920. Since that date, the pace of agreement has accelerated, with 65 being adopted between 1921 and 1955. During the decade of the 1960s alone, 47 compacts were approved. This was more than were put into effect through 1930. By the date of the country's Bicentennial, a total of 177 had been ratified. The pace slowed during the decade of the 1970s and fewer than 20 were adopted in this period. State participation continues to grow, however, as states ratify the agreements. Two compacts, the Interstate Compact on the Supervision of Parolees and Probationers and the Interstate Compact on Juveniles, have been signed by all the states, and at least 10 others have in excess of 25 signatories.[21]

Structural Variations. Before 1920 compacts were bistate agreements, but since that time they frequently have included more than two states and occasionally Canadian provinces. A significant development is the *federal-interstate compact* in which the national government is a signatory party and participant and is not limited merely to approving or disapproving state actions.

A federal-interstate compact is enacted as a statute in each participating jurisdiction and applies to the states with the same effect as an interstate compact. When the national government enters, this unit, too, must enact a statute joining in the endeavor. This statute differs from the acts of consent for interstate compacts because it is regarded as a national statute while the consent legislation is not. Consequently, a federal interstate compact is binding on national agencies as well as on state governments. This gives it a potential for inspiring a much closer coordination of national and state law and administration than other legal devices. Congress can modify or negate the compact by taking contrary action at a later date.[22] Currently, three federal-interstate compacts are operational— the Delaware River Basin Compact, the Susquehanna River Basin Compact, and the Agreement on Detainers.[23]

A development of the near future could be the state-local compact. The legislatures of Minnesota and Wisconsin have passed enabling legislation to establish a commission to study the proposed Minnesota-Wisconsin Port Authority that would include the mayors of Duluth and Superior, as well as state representatives.[24]

Uses of Compacts. Weldon V. Barton classifies compacts into four categories differentiated by use—regulatory; metropolitan area; river basin development; and state service.[25] The first category includes those concerned with regulatory functions in an advisory or operational capacity, such as the Interstate Oil Compact or the Ohio River Valley Sanitation Compact. Both of these compacts created commissions with important powers to regulate matters affecting oil or water. Thirty-three states are signatories to the Interstate Oil Compact that Richard H. Leach says was "created almost as a desperate alternative to federal control, which the oil industry and the oil state both dreaded."[26]

Metropolitan area compacts afford a legal basis for the states involved to cooperate and establish permanent interstate agencies to plan and admin-

FIGURE 7-1 GROWTH OF INTERSTATE COMPACTS
1783-1979

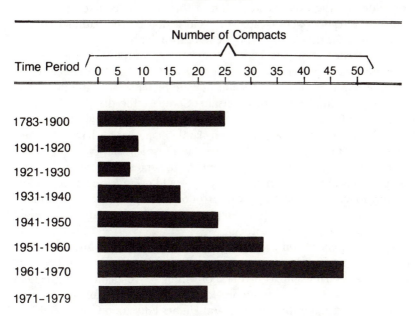

Council of State Governments, **Interstate Compacts, 1783-1970** (A Compilation)
(Lexington, Ky.: 1971), p. 3; 1971-76 data from the Council of State Governments.

ister urban programs. Examples include the Delaware River Joint Toll Bridge
Compact between New Jersey and Pennsylvania and the Palisades Interstate
Park Commission between New York and New Jersey. Most of these compacts are single purpose and their activities are fairly routine, involving
largely technical and managerial rather than political decision-making
functions. Three agencies established in this fashion are more deeply involved in politics. The Port Authority of New York and New Jersey, the
Delaware River Port Authority, and the Bi-State Development Agency
(St. Louis) are multipurpose commissions that plan unified economic
development and undertake varied operating functions. All enjoy considerable autonomy, largely as a result of their financial arrangements. They
are eligible for national grants-in-aid under the Urban Mass Transportation
Act of 1964.

The river basin compacts range in scope from one simply allocating
water among states to a national-state compact establishing an agency with
formal authority in water resource policy roughly comparable to that of the
nationally-created Tennessee Valley Authority. There has been a recent
surge in the adoption of river basin compacts; 20 were agreed to between

1927 and 1961. The national government is a participant in some of the more recent ones such as the Delaware River Basin Compact where it is represented on the Commission. Most of these compacts, like those in the regulatory category, were created to avoid action by the national government to solve the development problems of the river basins.

State service compacts exist in numerous functional areas such as crime control and prevention, education, welfare, and health. They attempt to reduce duplication of services and provide better services through interstate cooperation. Under the Interstate Compact for the Supervision of Parolees and Probationers, adopted by all states and the Virgin Islands and Puerto Rico, thousands of persons on parole or probation have been permitted to go to a state other than the one in which they were convicted. Their probation or parole is supervised in that state by its probation and parole officers in the same manner as they would oversee their own parolees or probationers. The compact provides a uniform legal procedure for meeting the needs of these people and replaces the rules of rendition that could make interstate cooperation difficult.

Interstate service compacts frequently serve as models for subsequent adoption of similar arrangements among other states. The Southern Regional Educational Compact of 1948, providing for cooperation in the field of higher education, was a model for the Western Regional Education Compact of 1951 and the New England Higher Education Compact of four years later. The Western Interstate Corrections Compact of 1958 was followed the next year by the New England Interstate Corrections Compact. Often service compacts are drafted with a view to nationwide adherence by all states. This was true of the Compact for Education (EDUCOM) and those on mental health, placement of children, and juveniles. EDUCOM's purpose is to "establish and maintain close cooperation and understanding [concerning education] on a nationwide basis." It provides a forum for discussion of ideas, opinions, and problems, and a clearinghouse for information on education.

Because the individuals who could profit most from these compacts are generally politically powerless, they are not very effective in promoting action under the compacts. The state officials who administer them consequently determine their effectiveness. States are often reluctant to commit their funds for interstate use so that often no compact agency is established to promote actual usage of the service compact. Where these agencies do exist the paucity of financing has hampered their effectiveness in planning and mobilizing support for interstate action.

Usefulness. Compacts are useful in many ways. They are important devices for settling disputes between states, although they sometimes elevate to the state level disputes between private claimants, such as in the instance of water basin development. It should be understood that many compacts, especially in the river basin category, result from activities of private economic groups with special interests in the resources involved— that is, farmers, private power producers, manufacturers, and processers. They use the compact device to block stronger national action or control because most of them feel more competent to deal with the states than with the national government. The use of interstate compacts to maintain state control of economic matters is not necessarily detrimental to the national interest; but it could delay coordinated national action in dealing with problems of nationwide concern. Barton writes, "Acceptance of a compact as a 'compromise' between national action and inaction may provide a tool to groups subject to regulation to play the states against each other in order to retain control in their own hands."[27]

Substantial evidence exists that the states use compacts to protect their power in the federal system, and such use is applauded by the strong supporters of the states. Compacts may also serve to disrupt direct national-local relations, as in the instance of the Compact for Education, and to alleviate the pressure for transfer of authority over some social problems to the national government. They are useful in coordinating efforts to solve problems and to reduce duplication. They help to bridge the gap created by jurisdictional lines which makes areawide solutions to areawide problems more difficult.

Deficiencies. In a penetrating analysis of interstate compacts in which Illinois is a participant, Marian E. Ridgeway cautions that the recent proliferation of compacts has taken place without adequate attention. While conceding that compacts are essential to any nonnational interstate undertaking of a binding nature and are advantageous in some instances, she points out that as a consequence of this lack of attention there is insufficient identification of their deficiencies and a failure to realize they are largely unproven. They may be attempted in improper spheres. Sometimes drafting is inadequate and frequently the proposals do not receive enough study during enactment. Once in effect, they are not systematically reviewed nor are they sufficiently evaluated by impartial observers.

Possibly more important is Ridgeway's assessment that once operating, with compact commissions and "non-profit" corporations, these instrumentalities tend to be independent of public and state control. This produces a lack of responsiveness to the general public and to the states. Furthermore, compacts are highly responsive to special interests. With time, there is diminishing control by the states and increasing control by the professional bureaucracies staffing them. Ridgeway writes:

> What has most clearly emerged from the research is a conviction that increasing involvement of states in interstate compacts heralds the beginning of a new shape for American federalism: a complex system being made even more complex, less clearly compartmentalized, more difficult

to control by law and popular action because less easily seen and less easily organized for the placing of responsibility and authority. In this new stage of federalism's evolution, the people of the United States appear to play a diminished role. Authority, planning, negotiation, decision-making, administration move into the realm of governors, special economic development interests, combinations of mayors and other locally elected officials, revenue bond purchasers, appointed technicians and specialists, and private planning consultants. In Robert Salisbury's terms, it is a "new convergence of power." State legislatures and the Congress assume the task and role once held in the state government by the voters; the giving or withholding of consent. The one remaining role for the people is taxpaying.[28]

The question of equal representation on the basis of population also is raised in the solutions of problems by compact because each state usually has one vote in the compact agency, thus underrepresenting the more populous states. Federal-interstate agreements have generated another type of objection. Some fear that they may be used to abolish state boundaries and create regional governments. Federal rather than state law would then prevail.[29] Despite these misgivings, use of compacts is likely to continue.

Other Interstate Contracts

In addition to the more formal compacts, other contracts between states are used to further mutual purposes. They have had a long history in education, for example. In southern states they were utilized in the past to provide higher education for blacks, particularly in specialized fields. Instead of admitting black students to the state university or law school, or establishing such schools for blacks, some states contracted with other states to accept eligible black students into their schools. The state where the student was a resident paid the state portion of the cost. This kind of arrangement is no longer legal when used to deny equal opportunity to all citizens of a state. It may still be used, however, to provide specialized training provided no discrimination is involved. State A, for example, may contract with State B to accept students from State A into its college of veterinary medicine, and makes a payment to the accommodating state in addition to the tuition paid by the student. This procedure is more likely to be used for education in programs not commonly offered. A wide variety of other services also may be provided by contract.

Why Are Some States More Cooperative?

We do not know exactly why some states cooperate to a greater degree than others. Nevertheless, recent research identified some factors associated with the willingness to enter into compacts and to adopt uniform legislation. In an analysis of nationwide compacts and uniform laws that have been approved by at least two-thirds of the states, David Nice found that cooperation in these efforts is positively associated with moralistic political culture as defined by Elazar, liberal party ideologies, greater public participation (voting turnout and interparty competition), and legal systems characterized by high professionalism in the legislature and high bar association influence in the selection of judges.[30] Both a moralistic political culture and liberal party ideology reflect a positive view of government and a belief in the value of reform. The same is true of high voting turnout and interparty competition. States with nonconforming neighbors are less likely to conform, according to Nice, a finding that indicates regional influences on cooperation.

An interesting finding of Nice is that conservative states that resist the expansion of national power are also less likely to cooperate in compacts and uniform laws, devices that could forestall national action. As Nice writes:

> The common thread, then, is hostility to action by *any* level of government: state, national, or jointly interstate. Lurking behind controversies over which level of government should handle a given policy responsibility are controversies over what the policy should be. State governments which decline to cooperate with other states, oppose national intervention, and have governmental institutions designed primarily for inaction object to all three for the same reason: the dominant constellations of political forces in those states oppose effective action.[31]

Nationwide Interstate Organizations

In addition to those mentioned above, many other interstate organizations operate with the express purpose of furthering cooperation among the states. They range from associations in which the state formally participates as a political entity (for example, the Council of State Governments) to groups involving state officials such as the National Governors' Association or the National Association of Attorneys General. Some are bistate, others are national or regional in scope. They vary widely in structure, membership, and function. A few of the most prominent are now discussed.

The Council of State Governments. Prominent among interstate organizations is the Council of State Governments, founded in 1925 as the American Legislators' Association and given a new name with broadened activities eight years later. It is a research, information, and service organization that provides assistance to state officials. It does this in a variety of ways including holding conferences and workshops, conducting training programs, and disseminating information through publications. Its Washington office monitors national government actions affecting states and presents the state viewpoint on policy issues when necessary. The Council also serves as secretariat to several national organizations of state officials such as the National Conference of Lieutenant Governors and the National Association of State Purchasing Officers. Its *Book of the States,* published biennially, is a storehouse of information on state government. It also publishes *State Government,* a periodical, and other materials that are good sources of information about state governmental affairs.

Government of the Council is vested in a governing board of about 175 members including all the nation's governors, usually two members of each state's legislature, and a chief justice. About one-third of this group constitutes the executive committee. The Council meets annually to establish organization policy and allocate funds. Each state contributes financially to the support of the Council.

Commissions on Interstate Cooperation. Each state has a Commission on Interstate Cooperation or similar official body. Organized in the manner of joint committees of the legislature with members from both the house and the senate, about four-fifths of the commissions also have representatives of the executive branch, including the governor. In some states the legislative council or the legislative research agency functions as the commission.

Little in-depth research has been done on the commissions. What there is reveals substantial variations in functions and accomplishments. The most successful ones, at least in the past, have had sufficient funds to employ executive secretaries or research staffs, a factor seemingly contributing to their effectiveness.[32] These commissions have made significant contributions to the enactment of uniform and reciprocal legislation, rules, and procedures. They have formulated and promoted interstate compacts and have facilitated the adoption of national-state and regional programs. Some have conducted substantial research and disseminated information. In some states, to the contrary, the commissions have been scarcely used. One factor depressing their importance in certain states has been the legislative council, which has assumed the leadership in developing legislative programs.[33] It may be that the work of the Council of State Governments, the National Conference of State Legislatures, or other interstate or state organizations puts the commissions in the shade. In any event, their substantial potential for influencing intergovernmental relations appears to remain largely untapped.

National Governors' Association. Governors of the fifty states, American Samoa, Guam, Puerto Rico, and the Virgin Islands participate in the National Governors' Association that meets biennially in different locales in the United States.[34] Regional Governors' Conferences also exist. Organized in 1908, the National Association seeks to serve as a medium for exchange of ideas, foster interstate cooperation, improve national-state and interstate relations, and work for greater efficiency in state administration. The Association undoubtedly provides a useful forum for the exchange of ideas and enables governors to meet face to face, thus establishing a base for future cooperation. In the past, it was criticized because its output often seemed meager in comparison to the time, effort, and money going into meetings as well as for its heavy emphasis on social activities. Perhaps it is unrealistic to expect a substantial work output from an organization of this sort, composed of busy executives with heavy responsibilities to their constituents at home. Recent meetings have seen more time dedicated to work, and between-session committees concerned with various interstate problems, such as energy, have enhanced the reputation of NGA. Under vigorous leadership, it has assumed more responsibility for putting forward the position of the states in the federal system and is now in the forefront in this respect. In addition, the establishment of a research arm and the opening of a Washington office gave the governors increased presence and credibility in the nation's capital.

Views of the Association are stated in the resolutions adopted at the annual meetings. Products of the work of standing committees, the resolutions are reviewed by the executive committee and then accepted or rejected by the membership. For one year's policy positions, the Conference approved or continued positions on 97 matters covering the broad areas of crime reduction; executive management and fiscal affairs; human resources, natural resources and environmental management; rural and urban development; transportation, commerce, and technology; and some miscellaneous matters including approval of presidential voting rights for citizens of Guam and the Virgin Islands.[35]

National Conference of State Legislatures. Headquartered in Denver, with a state-federal relations office in Washington, D.C., the National Conference of State Legislatures (NCSL) is one of the major groups representing state government. It is governed by an executive committee of 32 state legislators. Its funding comes from the states; however, in the past it has received some grant money from the national treasury.[36]

The major purposes of NCSL are to improve state legislatures, maintain a strong voice for the states in federal decisionmaking, and foster interstate cooperation. Its Washington office monitors national legislation, advises its members, and helps officers to lobby for adoption of the policy positions of the organization. These positions are developed by task forces that meet year round. Subsequently, the annual meeting adopts or rejects them. At one such meeting, for example, the Conference adopted 145 resolutions on such issues as public employee collective bargaining, medical malpractice, pollution, energy, mass transportation, gun control, and housing. In addition to influencing national policy, NCSL disseminates information to state legislators and others through its magazine *State Legislatures* and other publications and works to upgrade legislative operations in the states. It also provides training and development programs for legislators and their staffs.[37]

INTERSTATE REGIONALISM AND FEDERALISM

Regionalism is a spatial concept in which certain areas of the nation are grouped together because of homogeneous characteristics clearly distinguishing them from neighboring areas. Thus, when one speaks of the South, New England, the Midwest, or West, certain images immediately come to mind that make the particular region distinctive from the rest of the country. Regionalism understood in economic, cultural, and political terms has been very important in American history.[38]

Economic Regionalism

Regions often are perceived in economic terms. While the Northeast has a highly diversified and industrial economy, other sections of the nation have agricultural or mineral-based economies. More important, regions have definite economic development and income patterns that are major factors in the establishment of regional configurations in taxing, spending, and intergovernmental fiscal relations. For example, in 1980 personal income in the mideastern states ran 110 percent of the national average and that in the Farwest 107 percent. In the Southeast, in contrast, personal income equaled only 83 percent of the average for the nation as a whole.[39] These disparities were among the factors that led to the creation of special economic and social development regional organizations, such as the Appalachian Regional Commission or the Ozarks Regional Commission.

Economic aspects of regionalism also show up in taxing and spending patterns. Ira Sharkansky, a leading researcher on the topic, observed regional patterns in per-capita amounts spent for government services, distributions of expenditures by functions, and sources of revenue.[40] Major differences among regions are lessening, but sameness within regions is increasing as well. Consistent regional patterns appear in reliance on national grants-in-aid, distribution of functions to either the states or othe localities, and state-local intergovernmental financial assistance. State-local centralization, which also has regional characteristics, is an important determinant of taxing and expenditure responsibilities.

Non-economic, historical factors also affect current regional fiscal trends. As Sharkansky notes,

> the political attitudes and values of original settlers or large groups of subsequent migrants may have been critical. Locally oriented admin-

istration and the heavy use of local revenue sources is evident in New England and in several other regions (Great Lakes, Upper Middle West, and Plains) that received many settlers either directly from New England or from intermediate regions settled by New Englanders.[41]

Likewise, the strong debt restrictions in the constitutions of Great Lakes states probably resulted from earlier excessive spending for public improvement projects in that area. Also, reaction to the laissez-faire extremes of early lumber and mineral barons may have produced what Sharkansky calls "the generous public services and high level of state and local government expenditures" in the Mountain region.[42] Regardless of the relative weight of economic variables and non-economic historical factors, what is evident from Sharkansky's research is "the power of regional norms to persist over time and to influence current styles in state politics and public services."[43]

Economic disparities among regions sometimes produce interregional tensions as exhibited by the so-called Frostbelt-Sunbelt controversy and the Sagebrush Rebellion. The former pitted the northeastern and midwestern regions against the southeastern and southwestern states. The flow of population and industry to the warmer areas alarmed the frostbelt states and they began to form coalitions of regional congressmembers or governors to protect their interests. They demanded greater shares of federal funds and regionally differentiated economic policies. In particular, they wanted to be assured of adequate energy supplies. Sunbelt advocates, however, contended that their regions remained relatively poor despite their relative economic gains in the last decade. They argued that they should continue to benefit from favorable national policies.[44] The Sagebrush Rebellion pitted the western states, particularly the mountain states, against the rest of the nation in arguments over regulation of land usage, federal ownership of large tracts, and land use policies.

Cultural Regionalism

Regionalism also has important cultural or social aspects. In general, the average American thinks of a region in terms of specific perceptions about its collective social behavior. Many such perceptions of regional cultures may be nothing more than a stereotype held over from past years. Irrespective of the accuracy of the image, its existence gives a cultural identity to a region. The intergovernmental impact of regional cultural differences is evident daily. The conservative, states' rights, anti-centralization philosophies of many southerners, the individualism and strong local orientation of New Englanders, the cooperative Progressivism of midwesterners, and the maverick tradition of westerners all give parameters and biases for intergovernmental behavior. As the Advisory Commission on Intergovernmental Relations correctly notes, "the importance of cultural regionalism cannot be underestimated."[45]

The extremes of cultural regionalism can lead to attempts to dissolve a federal union. The major effort at dissolution failed in the United States after a bitter fratricidal conflict. Regional cultural differences have been the source of secession in many other federal systems.[46] Canada, for example, has had a constant struggle to maintain the cultural regionalism of its French-speaking population and yet avoid the extremes of secession. In the United States today, the awareness of cultural similarities often leads to regional cooperative actions and organizations and only rarely to inter-regional conflicts as in the early case of the isolation and hostility of the South over the position of blacks in American society.

Political Regionalism

The political aspects of regionalism come about largely from a region's economic and cultural uniqueness. Most observers of American politics can readily point to sectional political patterns. They include variations in participation levels, consistent one party dominance, and regional political philosophies. They also consist of ongoing attitudes toward the system (e.g., federalism or centralization) and toward specific issues (e.g., abortion or national aid to education), and perceptions of public trust or political alienation. The U.S. Senate Subcommittee survey utilized at various places in this book gives repeated evidence of regional attitudinal differences. In terms of philosophy, for example, only 22 percent of the respondents from the East agreed with the statement "the best government is the government that governs least," whereas 44 percent of those from the Midwest agreed. The South (28 percent agreeing) and the West (35 percent agreeing) fell between these two extremes.[47]

Regional patterns are evident for almost every aspect of American politics and, more specifically, intergovernmental relations. Concerning public trust toward levels of government, for instance, the survey asked "Do you feel you have more, less or same confidence in the Federal [National] government compared to five years ago?" A total of 62 percent of the western respondents had "less confidence," while only 50 percent of the traditionally more hostile South had lost confidence. The other regions were less than but close to the western responses (Midwest 59 percent and East 60 percent). There was significantly less loss of confidence toward the states and localities among all regions of the country.[48]

Diffusion of innovations among the states is the last political aspect of regionalism to be considered here. Jack L. Walker has analyzed how innovations such as new taxes, regulation of professionals, fair housing legislation, and home rule for cities, are spread, or diffused, among the states.[49] Walker notes that there are "innovative" states which have consistently pioneered the adoption of these types of changes. Over the years New York, Massachusetts, and California have been the most innovative states in the Union, while Wyoming, Nevada, and Mississippi have been the least receptive to innovation. More importantly for this discussion, the research shows that there are regional leaders, states such as New York, Massachusetts, Florida, and New Mexico, which can be seen as "regional pace setters" with followers, usually within their own region of the country, that "tend to adopt programs only after the pioneers have led the way."[50] Certain states provide leadership for more than one region. New York, as a result of its prominence, size, and geographic location, serves as a model for the New England, Mid-Atlantic, and Great Lakes regions.

In part, the regional patterns of innovation adoptions are caused by common needs, resources, and historical and cultural experiences of neighboring states. Also, it is important to note what Sharkansky calls a "copy your neighbor" syndrome.[51] When talking about or analyzing a state's problems and progress, the tendency is to compare the state with its immediate neighbors. Thus, a candidate for governor of Georgia is much more likely to compare that state's educational system with that of Florida or South Carolina than he is to look to California or New York for analogies. In Sharkansky's terms, this "legitimates one's own programs to those of nearby governments."[52]

Regional associations and meetings also encourage this type of diffusion patterns. A meeting of the Southern Governors' Conference is sure to stimulate discussion of new revenue-raising techniques or administrative changes such as the creation of a state department of local affairs. Professional civil servants show evidence of constant patterns of regional intergovernmental communications. For example, budget officers of major agencies in the states of Florida, Georgia, Kentucky, and Mississippi were asked: "Have you or any of your colleagues contacted officials in other states in an attempt to learn how they deal with a particular situation that you have encountered in your work?" Of those answering affirmatively, 87 percent listed states in the region[53] and 35 percent listed states bordering directly on the respondents' states. This is not unexpected, since as one study points out:

> The legitimacy of regional comparisons tends to feed upon past habit. Because officials have consulted with their counterparts in nearby governments, they have learned who can be trusted for credible information, candor, and good judgment. Unless an official is committed to an intensive program of research before making his own policy decisions, he may be satisfied after making a few calls to individuals with whom he has dealt amicably in the past.[54]

Lessening of Regional Distinctions

Economic, cultural, and political regionalism is slowly declining in importance. The onslaught of national television and radio networks, the increasing mobility of American families, and the impact of the national government's equalization programs have an homogenizing effect on the United States population. Over the decades we are becoming more alike as we lessen our emphasis on regional history and traditions, lose our dialects, and achieve incomes and life styles closer to the national average. For example, the gap among regions in per capita income has narrowed over the years as Figure 7–2 illustrates. As the income of residents of the southeastern and southwestern regions improved relative to the national average, that of citizens of the farwestern, mideastern, and New England regions experienced a relative decline.

Just as the importance of this financial type of regionalism began to decline during the 1950s and 1960s, the prominence of regional organizations began to increase. This increase persisted until the onset of the 1980s when national support for their development was withdrawn.

Regional Organizations

Regional organizations are not part of the constitutionally defined federal system. As in the case of local units of government, the United States Constitution does not explicitly refer to regional organizations as such, although in providing for interstate compacts, it defines a process through which they may be organized. The colonists experimented with regional arrangements more than 300 years ago when the New England Confederation was created to furnish a common defense against the Narragansett Indians and to provide for the peaceful settlement of common problems such as boundary disputes. Since that early beginning, use of regional organizations has been relatively infrequent.

Although the national government has used regional administrative organizations since 1788, the states have relied only sparingly on multistate organizations to solve regional problems. The Port Authority of New York and New Jersey Compact (1921) and the Colorado River Basin Compact (1929) are two of the earliest significant examples of such undertakings. A total of 56 interstate compact agencies now operate, but for the most part these are narrowly based or relate to a single function or project.

Multistate regionalism was given a major impetus in 1933 by the congressional creation of the Tennessee Valley Authority, a national agency, generally considered to be the first truly multifunction, multistate regional organization. The National Resources Planning Board gave considerable publicity to the idea of multistate organization during the New Deal, but

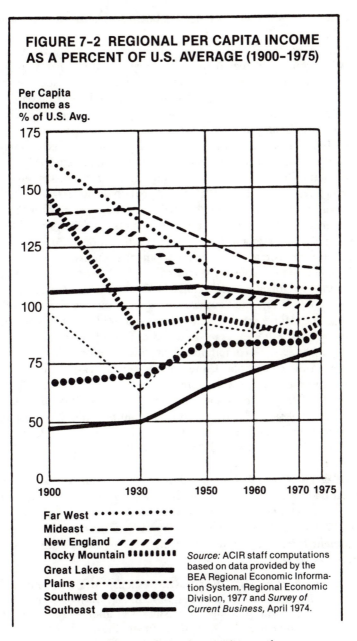

FIGURE 7-2 REGIONAL PER CAPITA INCOME AS A PERCENT OF U.S. AVERAGE (1900-1975)

Per Capita Income as % of U.S. Avg.

Far West ··············
Mideast – – – – – – –
New England ✱✱✱✱✱
Rocky Mountain ▌▌▌▌▌▌▌▌▌
Great Lakes ▬▬▬▬▬▬
Plains ··················
Southwest ●●●●●●●●●●●
Southeast ▬▬▬▬▬▬

Source: ACIR staff computations based on data provided by the BEA Regional Economic Information System. Regional Economic Division, 1977 and *Survey of Current Business,* April 1974.

Source: Janet Rothenberg Pack with the assistance of Gordon Folkman, "Frostbelt and Sunbelt: Convergence over Time," *Intergovernmental Perspective,* Vol. 4, No. 4 (Fall, 1978), p. 9.

at the time of its demise in 1943 the Board had not given birth to any regional creations.

From the end of World War II to the mid-1960s there was very little activity for multistate regionalism. The few structures that were set up were unifunctional, generally for economic development such as the Bi-State Development Compact (St. Louis, 1950), and the Delaware Valley Urban Area Compact (1961), or for water resource management, such as the Delaware River Basin Compact in 1961.

The 1960s saw a major change in the federal system with the emergence of many national-multistate organizations. Beginning in 1961 with the creation of the Delaware River Basin Commission, a rapid succession of these new structures emerged. In 1965 the Appalachian Regional Commission (ARC) was created. As part of the trade-off for the creation of the ARC, the Congress, under Title V of the Public Works and Economic Development Act of 1965, also authorized the Department of Commerce to establish national-multistate regional development commissions. Five regional development commissions were created by 1967—Ozarks, Four Corners, New England, Upper Great Lakes, and Coastal Plains. Later, the Pacific Northwest, Old West, and Southwest Border commissions were established. In 1979, the Mid-Atlantic, Mid-South, and Mid-America commissions were designated, but were never activated or funded. Thus, ocean-to-ocean regional agencies were contemplated to assist in economic development. All states in the continental United States were at least partially included in one of these regional organizations.

Title II of the Water Resources Planning Act of 1965 authorized the establishment of similarly-structured river basin planning commissions. Six river basin commissions were created under Title II by 1971—Pacific Northwest, Great Lakes, Souris-Red-Rainy, New England, Ohio, and Susquehanna.

The creation of 12 economic development commissions and the six regional basin commissions was the high water mark of regional organizations in the United States. Why were these organizations authorized? David Walker, assistant director of the Advisory Commission on Intergovernmental Relations, summarized the feelings that stimulated the new approach as follows:

> The shift in the sixties then was in response to a new and different cluster of problems, the most significant of which was the spill-over character of certain pressing policy issues. Common to all of these recent regional efforts was the view that the traditional interstate compact approach involving only the participating States was inadequate for certain program purposes and that the Federal-single State relationship did not cover adequately the interstate ramifications of these functional concerns. Put more positively, the Federal-multistate partnership

concept emerged as a popular formula for resolving some of the administrative, political and fiscal difficulties that had emerged—at least in certain regions—in the economic development and water resources planning and management fields.[55]

Some centralists see these national-multistate bodies as a means of circumventing the limitations of traditional interstate compacts and furthering national policy. At the same time for their more state-oriented defenders, they are sometimes viewed as statutory "means . . . of achieving additional impact on Federal policy and administrative decisions in their respective program areas."[56] Most observers agree that the strong points of these multistate bodies are: (1) they are means of securing additional national money, beyond the normal grant-in-aid programs; (2) they are likely to strengthen the hands of state governors in relations with the national government and other forces within the states; and (3) they aid in the solution of some difficult multistate problems.

For all these positive points, the national-multistate commissions are still new experiments in federalism with many unanswered questions. Are geographically fragmented problems to be united spatially, only to be divided functionally? Once removed from the electorate, how are these agencies to be held accountable? Are the commissions to become new power centers, eventually being relatively autonomous of both the states and the national government? The answers to these questions will have to await another upsurge in the fortunes of regional establishments.

The Reagan administration had hardly settled into office before it began to dismantle the regional commissions. As Bruce McDowell explained:

At the multistate level, as 1981 ended, the federal government "decommissioned" the eight active and three stillborn economic development regions established at the request of the governors under Title V of the Public Works and Economic Development Act of 1965. It also closed down the six federal-state river basin commissions that had been established under Title II of the Water Resources Planning Act of 1965. Then, effective September 30, 1982, it disbanded the staff of the region-supporting and state-supporting federal interagency Water Resources Council. In addition, the budget of the independently established Appalachian Regional Commission was substantially reduced for FY 1982 (and further reduced for FY 1983) as that organization was set to phase-out with the agreement of Congress and participating governors.[57]

The withdrawal of national support did not end the lives of all the commissions, although the financial loss had a deleterious impact on their operations. In some of the regions, state governments undertook to reconstitute the organizations and five of the Title V economic development commissions were incorporated as Councils of Governors. One joined an already established organization of states concerned with growth policies, and the other two active commissions are still in transition.[58]

Similarly, all but one of the Title II river basin commissions operate in other guises. Four have been reconstituted as nonprofit corporations composed of state water resources officials. A fifth is now part of a multi-state commission involved in transportation and commerce on the Great Lakes.

INDIVIDUALS AND INTERSTATE COOPERATION

Since the beginning of the Republic, America has been a mobile nation. As individuals and commerce move back and forth cross state borders, provision must be made for their protection and regulation. The "full faith and credit" and the "privileges and immunities" clauses as well as provisions for rendition, all first stated in the Articles of Confederation and carried over practically unchanged in the Constitution, are the means through which the states cooperate to regulate and protect the individual.

Full Faith and Credit

The Constitution provides that "Full faith and credit shall be given in each state to the public acts, records and judicial proceedings of every other state." The clear intention of this provision is to protect the individual as he or she moves from state to state. A man born in New York, married in Florida, and graduated from college in Wisconsin must be sure that his records are duly recognized as he settles in California. Similarly, this clause protects against a person moving to a different state to evade such responsibilities as debts.

The Constitution further sets forth that the "Congress may by general laws prescribe the manner in which such acts, records, and proceedings shall be proved, and the effect thereof." Congress has enacted such legislation, but it is still up to the states to grant the "faith and credit." For the most part, states willingly abide by the interpretation that the laws, records, and legal proceedings of one state, proven and authenticated, have the same effect in the courts of another state as they are presumed to have in their own.

The willingness notwithstanding, "full faith and credit" often becomes complex and drawn out because of legal problems known as "conflict of laws." Suppose, as an illustration, a will is written in Georgia for a resident of that state who then moves to Tennessee and dies. It is the responsibility of the state of Tennessee to probate the will according to the laws of Georgia, not those of Tennessee. Similarly, a civil judgment against a resident of New York who moves to California to avoid payment is enforced by the latter state's judicial branch. These provisions pertain, of course, only to civil proceedings. Interstate criminal questions are handled under the rendition provisions of the Constitution.

Privileges and Immunities

Individuals are further protected in the interstate system by the "privileges and immunities" clauses. Article IV provides that "The citizens of each state shall be entitled to all privileges and immunities of citizens in the several states." In addition, the Fourteenth Amendment mandates that "No state shall make or enforce any law which shall abridge the privileges and immunities of citizens of the United States." Thus, certain "privileges and immunities" are protected because a person is a citizen of both the United States and of a state.

The problem is the lack of clarity, even to constitutional lawyers, as to the meaning of these clauses. In general, the concept of privileges and immunities means that no state may discriminate against the citizens of another state in favor of its own. A state, for instance, must allow a citizen of another state the right to purchase property and must tax that property at the same rate as taxes on indigenously-held property. It must further afford the nonresident full police protection and use of the courts and guarantee his right to move in and out of the state.

The states need not grant immediately all political privileges to newcomers. For example, a citizen of Arizona must meet all the constitutional and statutory requirements of California before being able to vote there. Further, resources of institutions of a state may be reserved for the exclusive use of its residents or a state may charge higher rates for their use by nonresidents. Thus, there may be higher fees for nonresidents' use of state parks and, as is generally the case, a state may require additional out-of-state tuition at its colleges and universities. A person does not automatically bring his privileges and immunities from his home state. A doctor, therefore, has to meet his new state's professional standards before he is permitted to practice there. Lastly, these provisions do not extend to business corporations even though they are treated as individuals in almost every other question of law. A state thus may impose higher license fees for "foreign" corporations.

Rendition

The Constitution provides that "a person charged in any state with treason, felony, or other crime, who shall flee from justice, and be found in another state, shall, on demand of the executive authority of the state from which he fled, be delivered up, to be removed to the state having jurisdiction of the crime." This provision assures that since a state crime can be punished only in the state where committed, a person cannot evade his just punishment by fleeing to another state.

Rendition[59] is a relatively simple process. The governor of the home state simply presents evidence of indictment, criminal charges, or conviction, and requests the return of the fugitive for trial or imprisonment. The fugitive may ask the courts of the host state to determine the legality of the rendition papers, but he or she cannot seek to be found innocent or guilty of the actual crime. A returned prisoner may be tried for crimes in addition to those for which rendition was originally requested.

Although the Constitution says that the person *shall* be "delivered up," the courts have ruled that a governor may not be compelled to do so. On rare occasions states refuse to "deliver up." Reasons for refusing range from the observation that the fugitive has become a model citizen of the host state to questions of the justness of the law or expectations of an unfair trial for the accused. Expectations of unfairness occur most often when questions of race or so-called "political crimes" are involved. Even though the governors have the option, practically all requests for rendition are honored because no state wishes to become a sanctuary for the criminals of another. Furthermore, a rendition-denying governor of today may be the rendition-requesting executive of tomorrow. Because the rendition process is somewhat cumbersome in its formality and occasionally uncertain in its outcome, Congress has made it a national offense to flee across state boundaries to avoid prosecution or imprisonment.

RIVALS OR PARTNERS?

As members of a growing, dynamic nation, the states have become more and more dependent on each other. Their interactions have increased and become both more fractious and more cooperative. Many conflicts occur on a regional basis, especially between the Frostbelt and Sunbelt states, although other controversies erupt as well. Rivalries over business and industrial development constantly sour interstate relationships, and the addition of the disparities between energy-producing and energy-poor states aggravates the differences among them. Financial retrenchment and growing concern over pollution are likely to intensify the rivalries. After all, there is no Berlin Wall between them.

The long standing sibling rivalries have not precluded cooperation whenever state officials feel that it is in the interest of their constituents or whenever they perceive some personal political gain. Through interstate compacts and contracts, organizations, and other devices they seek to ameliorate the differences among them. In the early 1980s, when the national government withdrew its support of the interstate regional development organizations, governors in several regions of the nation cooperated to continue their operations. Cooperative ventures are plagued, nonetheless, by poor communication, popular fears of excessive or uneven costs, and leadership that in some instances is unwilling to devote resources to projects that often afford little political profit.

Years ago William Anderson raised the question as to whether the nation and the states were rivals or partners.[60] The same question could be asked of the states. And the answer is "both." As their officials go about their daily business of advancing the interests of their citizens, they find it necessary to play both the antagonist's and partner's roles. Anyone who expects otherwise believes in a utopia and ignores the realities of the political arena.

NOTES

1. David C. Nice, "Cooperation and Conformity Among the States," *Polity,* Summer 1983 *(forthcoming).*

2. Albert H. Rose, *Ohio Government: State and Local,* 3rd ed. (Dayton: University of Dayton Press, 1966), p. 14.

3. Samuel Krislov, *The Supreme Court and the Political Process* (New York: Macmillan Publishing Co., 1965), p. 145.

4. Alfred H. Kelly and Winfred A. Harbison, *The American Constitution: Its Origin and Development* (New York: W. W. Norton and Co., 1948), p. 103.

5. Charles Warren, "The Supreme Court and Disputes between the States," *Bulletin of the College of William and Mary,* Vol. 34, No. 5, pp. 7–11, 13–14 (1940). For a more extensive treatment see the same author's. *The Supreme Court and the Sovereign State* (Princeton, N.J.: Princeton University Press, 1924). See also *The Constitution of the United States Of America: Analysis and Interpretation,* prepared by the Legislative Reference Service of the Library of Congress, Edward S. Corwin, editor (Washington, D.C.: Government Printing Office, 1953), pp. 591–599. This discussion relies heavily on the last-named publication.

6. Commonwealth Edison v. Montana, 49 L. W. 4957 (1981).

7. Alabama v. Arizona, 291 U.S. 286 (1934).

8. Chisholm v. Georgia, 4 Wall. 475 (1793).

9. New Hampshire v. Louisiana, 108 U.S. 76 (1883).

10. Robert E. Cushman and Robert F. Cushman, *Cases in Constitutional Law,* 3rd ed. (New York: Appleton-Century-Crofts Education Division, Meredith Corporation, 1968), pp. 276–277.

11. Advisory Commission on Intergovernmental Relations, *State Administrators' Opinions on Administrative Change, Federal Aid, Federal Relationships,* Report M-120 (Washington, D.C.: December, 1980), p. 13. Future citations are to ACIR.

12. Phillip Monypenny, "Interstate Relations—Some Emergent Trends," *Annals of the American Academy of Political and Social Science*, Vol. 359 (May, 1965), pp. 54, 56.

13. Francis D. Jones, "Uniform State Laws," *Book of the States*, 1972–73 (Lexington, Ky.: Council of State Governments, 1972), p. 99

14. Monypenny, pp. 56, 58.

15. Ibid., pp. 56–57.

16. 148 U.S. 503 (1893)

17. U.S. Steel v. Multistate Tax Corporation, 434 U.S. 452 (1978).

18. Brevard Crihfield, "Interstate Compacts, 1783–1977," *Book of the States, 1978–79* (Lexington, Ky.: Council of State Governments, 1978), p. 582.

19. ACIR, *Multistate Regionalism.* Report A-39 (Washington, D.C.: U.S. Government Printing Office, 1972), pp. 157–58. This report contains an extensive discussion of regional organizations. See also Martha Derthick with the assistance of Gary Bombardier, *Between State and Nation: Regional Organizations in the United States* (Washington, D.C.: The Brookings Institution, 1974).

20. 306 Fd2 270 (1962), Certiorari denied 371 U.S. 902 (1962).

21. *Interstate Compacts and Agencies, 1979 Edition* (Lexington, Ky.: Council of State Governments, 1979).

22. ACIR, *Multistate Regionalism*, p. 156. For the effect of federal approval, see Delaware River Joint Toll Bridge Commission v. Colburn, 310 U.S. 419 (1940); Hinderlider v. LaPlata River and Cherry Creek Ditch Company, 304 U.S. 92 (1938).

23. Crihfield, p. 582. A study by the Comptroller General found federal-interstate compacts useful in dealing with river basin problems. See Comptroller General of the United States, *Federal-Interstate Compact Commissions: Useful Mechanisms for Planning and Managing River Basin Operations*, CED–81–34 (Washington, D.C.: General Accounting Office, February 20, 1981).

24. Crihfield, p. 583

25. Weldon V. Barton, *Interstate Compacts in the Political Process* (Chapel Hill: University of North Carolina Press, 1967), Chap. 1. The present discussion of these categories relies on Barton unless otherwise indicated.

26. Richard H. Leach, "The Interstate Oil Compact: A Study in Success," *Oklahoma Law Review*, Vol. X (August, 1957), p. 284.

27. Barton, p. 57.

28. Marian E. Ridgeway, *Interstate Compacts: A Question of Federalism* (Carbondale: Southern Illinois University Press, 1971), pp. 308–309.

29. John W. C. Kohr, "The Hidden Danger of These Bills: Interstate Compacts," *The Pennsylvania Crier*, Vol. 8, No. 2 (August, 1979), p. 1.

30. In describing moralistic political culture, Elazar writes that both the public and the politicians regard "politics as a public activity centered on some noting of the public good and properly devoted to the advancement of the public interest. Good government, then, is measured by the degree to which it promotes the public good and in terms of the honesty, selflessness, and commitment to the public welfare of those who govern." Daniel J. Elazar, *American Federalism: A View from the States*, 2d. ed. (New York: Thomas Y. Crowell and Co., 1972), pp. 96–97.Nice, *passim.*

31. Ibid. See also *Regional Conflict and National Policy,* ed. by Kent A. Price (Washington, D.C.: Resources for the Future, 1982).

32. Ibid., p. 4.

33. Patricia S. Florestano, *Interstate Cooperation Commissions* (Annapolis: Maryland Commission on Intergovernmental Cooperation, 1974). Frederick L. Zimmermann and Richard H. Leach, "The Commissions on Interstate Cooperation," *State Government,* Vol. 80 (1960).

34. For discussions of the governors' organization see: Glen Brooks, *When Governors Convene: The Governors' Conference and National Politics* (Baltimore, Md.: Johns Hopkins University Press, 1961) and Donald H. Haider, *When Governments Come to Washington: Governors, Mayors, and Intergovernmental Lobbying* (New York: Free Press, 1974).

35. *National Governors' Conference Policy Positions,* 1973–74 (n.p., n.d.).

36. "Representative Interstate Organizations Associated with the Council of State Governments," *Book of the States, 1976–77* (Lexington, Ky.: Council of State Governments, 1976), p. 567.

37. Ibid.

38. The literature on this topic is immense. Three important general works are Howard W. Odum and Harry Estell Moore's *American Regionalism: A Cultural-Historical Approach to National Integration* (New York: Henry Holt, 1938); Daniel J. Elazar's *American Federalism: A View From the States* (New York: Thomas Y. Crowell, 1966); and Ira Sharkansky's *Regionalism in American Politics* (Indianapolis: Bobbs-Merrill Co., 1970). The first-mentioned work suggests some important distinctions between the terms "regionalism" and "sectionalism" (pp. 35–51). Sharkansky's book provides an excellent bibliographic essay on the topic (pp. 163–183). In addition to these general works, well-known studies have been produced about specific regions, e.g., V. O. Key's *Southern Politics: In State and Nation* (New York: Alfred A. Knopf, 1949); and Duane Lockard's *New England State Politics* (Princeton: Princeton University Press, 1959).

39. ACIR, *Significant Features of Fiscal Federalism, 1980–81 Edition.* (Washington, D.C.: December, 1981), p. 77.

40. See Ira Sharkansky, *Regionalism;* and his *Spending in the American States* (Chicago: Rand McNally and Co., 1968), especially pp. 93–109. See also ACIR, *Regional Growth: Historic Perspective* (June, 1980); and ACIR, *Regional Growth: Interstate Tax Competition* (March, 1981).

41. Sharkansky, *Regionalism,* p. 143.

42. Ibid., p. 144.

43. Ibid.

44. Janet Rothenberg Pack with the assistance of Gordon Folkman, "Frostbelt and Sunbelt: Convergence over Time," *Intergovernmental Perspective,* Vol. 4, No. 4 (Fall, 1978), p. 8. See also Robert Jay Dilger, *The Sunbelt/Snowbelt Controversy: The War Over Federal Funds* (New York: New York Univeristy Press, 1982).

45. ACIR, *Multistate Regionalism,* p. 3.

46. Thomas M. Franck, ed., *Why Federations Fail: An Inquiry Into the Requisites of Successful Federalism* (New York: New York University Press, 1968).

47. U.S. Senate, Committee on Government Operations, Subcommittee on Intergovernmental Relations, *Confidence and Concern: Citizens View American Government. A Survey of Public Attitudes* (Washington, D.C.: Government Printing Office, 1973), Part II, p. 111.

48. Ibid. For local governments, 34 percent of the East, 33 percent of the West, 28 percent of the South, and 26 percent of the Midwest expressed a loss of confidence, Ibid., p. 93. The responses for state government were 34 percent for the East, 27 percent for the West, 23 percent for the Midwest, and 21 percent for the South. Ibid., p. 99.

49. Jack L. Walker, "The Diffusion of Innovation Among the American States," *American Political Science Review,* Vol. 63 (September, 1969), pp. 880–899. This summary discussion relies heavily on Walker's research. For a better understanding of the complexity of the innovation/diffusion approach, see Virginia Gray, "Innovation in the States: A Diffusion Study," *American Political Science Review,* Vol. 67 (December, 1973), pp. 1174–1185; and Jack L. Walker, "Comment: Problems in Research on Diffusion of Policy Innovations," ibid., pp. 1186–1191.

50. Walker, "Diffusion of Innovations Among the American States," p. 893.

51. Sharkansky, *The Routines of Politics,* pp. 86–105.

52. Ibid., p. 86.

53. The eleven states of the confederacy, plus the Border States of Delaware, Maryland, Kentucky, West Virginia, and Oklahoma. See ibid., p. 89.

54. Ibid., p. 89.

55. David B. Walker, "Interstate Regional Instrumentalities: A New Piece in An Old Puzzle," *Journal of the American Institute of Planners,* Vol. 38 (November, 1972), p. 359.

56. Ibid., p. 361.

57. Bruce McDowell, "Regional Organizations Hang On," *Intergovernmental Perspective,* Vol. 8, No. 4/Vol. 9, No. 1 (Winter, 1983), p. 15.

58. Ibid.

59. The term *rendition* is used instead of *extradition* because the latter also refers to a similar process between independent nations; rendition refers only to an interstate process.

60. William Anderson, *The Nation and the States: Rivals or Partners?* (Minneapolis: University of Minnesota Press, 1955).

CHAPTER 8

INTERLOCAL RELATIONS: RELUCTANT PARTNERS

E. E. SCHATTSCHNEIDER writes that the "outcome of all conflict is determined by the scope of its contagion. The number of people involved in any conflict determines what happens; every change in the number of participants, every increase or deduction in the number of participants affects the results."[1] This observation is now generally recognized as being a truism.

POTENTIAL FOR CONFLICT: PREMIUM ON COOPERATION

The sheer number of intergovernmental participants and intergovernmental transactions at the local level maximizes the potential for conflict there. The local level is the nexus of the intergovernmental system. Here converge the horizontal and vertical relations resulting from long-established patterns of interactions, both conflicting and cooperative, among the multitude of governments that dots the local landscape. National and state governments are increasingly involved, both because they were invited to interact and because they imposed their presence.

At no other point in the federal system is the harmonious working of the intergovernmental system more needed for survival of the participating governments than at the local level. Municipalities must coordinate with their neighbors to carry out most of the basic functions, such as police protection and planning. Practically any task begun by a city or county will involve interactions with a host of special districts. A county's intention to approve a zoning request for a new subdivision may require prior consultations and agreements with an independent water and sewer district to insure that these services are available to new residents. It may also require long-range planning with the independent school board to provide new classrooms or even new school buildings to meet expected enrollment increases. It may even require an agreement with a park and recreation special district to provide adequate open spaces, parks, and recreational programs for the new residents.

Further, all localities must interact with the state and national governments. With the local government's dependence on the state for its authority, particularly in non-home rule areas, and with an increasing financial reliance on the higher governments, intergovernmental interactions become crucial.

THE INTERLOCAL ENVIRONMENT

Students of the local government system must often be amazed that this system manages to function at all, much less function reasonably well. Local governments have more constitutional-legal limitations placed on them than do either of the other two levels. Yet, in terms of day-to-day basic services for the people, the localities carry far more of the burden than do the higher governments. These service demands produce tremendous and ever-increasing pressures on the most limited, most controlled, least flexible, and least elastic revenue systems in the entire American federal arrangement. The local system has the most fragmented arrangements of authority and decision-making, but faces the biggest challenges in providing areawide services.

It is also obvious that the citizens are often confused about which local government is responsible for what services. The citizens believe they know which responsibilities belong to the national government and which belong to the states, but when it comes to the local level, who is responsible for the missed trash pickup or the corner pothole? The city? The county? The township? A private company? Or, maybe an almost invisible special district, e.g., a tri-county garbage authority? Even with the difficulty of determining responsibility, the frustrated citizen, most often a homeowner, feels the impact of local taxes more than he does those of other levels of government. This results from the heavy reliance on property taxes for all local governments and from the geographical proximity of local units that makes it possible for the citizen more often and more vehemently to express his or her views to local officials.

With all these contradictions, obvious problems, temporary breakdowns, and setbacks—the bottom line is: *the system does work.* All these activities could be performed, without a doubt, in a much more satisfactory manner and yet as confused and disorganized as the local system of governance is, it does meet at least the more fundamental demands placed on it. As Daniel Elazar says, "If the system appears on the surface to be mildly chaotic, this does not mean that some order does not exist within its bounds."[2] The provider of that order is a reasonably smoothly operating intergovernmental system. On a daily basis pragmatic intergovernmental adjustments lubricate the numerous and obvious "squeak points" that might otherwise cause a burnout or breakdown of the local political system. An examination of the legal and the governmental-political environment will give insight into how the interlocal system works.

The Legal Setting.[3] While allocating powers to local governments and setting their legal limitations, state lawmakers must be consistently enamored with Cowper's famous dictum "Variety's the very spice of life, That gives it all its flavor." The best word to describe the local legal setting is "variety." There is no consistent pattern of legal arrangements.

In general, the various jurisdictions operate separately from each other, with the authority of each emanating from the state. Although counties are usually larger than municipalities (a major exception being New York City within whose boundaries are five former counties, now known as boroughs), they ordinarily have no direct control over the municipal governments within their borders. Moreover, their authority to perform certain functions may or may not extend to the area within the city limits. Usually the citizen is paying taxes to both the municipality and the county and each provides separate services.

Special mention should be made of independent cities. Although they may be surrounded entirely by county territory, as is the case with Baltimore City and Baltimore County, they operate entirely free of county supervision. Their citizens receive the services ordinarily provided by county government from the city.

County-township relations are another matter, however. Usually counties exercise substantial authority over these subcounty jurisdictions. They may operate as administrative subdivisions of the county.

State constitutions and state legislatures often play favorites among local governments. In some states, counties are the dominant form of local government to the point that they can practically dictate the pace and direction of intergovernmental relations at the local level. In other states, counties may be so weak as to be practically ignored or deliberately excluded from intergovernmental exchanges. Some state legislatures have shown a definite favoritism toward municipalities and have showered them with enough grants of authority, taxing powers, and state financial assistance to give them a dominant position in entering the interlocal arena. In these states, municipalities may often be able to prevent the counties, townships, or other local governments from extending jurisdiction into the city. For example, a large county containing a dozen municipalities may be prohibited from extending county police patrols into the municipal jurisdictions or it must exempt the municipalities from coverage of the county-wide master plan. Such arrangements make for neither adequate law enforcement nor adequate planning. In other instances, cities may be allowed to exercise *extraterritorial jurisdiction*, that is, authority outside their boundaries. Alabama is one state that permits municipalities of a certain size to extend services, charge service fees, and regulate in the county territory surrounding them.

A number of states give favored types of local government legal authority to create and control territorial growth of other types of localities. Some states permit counties to veto proposed new municipal incorporations—thus preventing the creation of new local governments—and some states even require county approval of municipal annexations. This means that a city or town may not extend its boundaries to take in new territory without county permission. Other states give authority in these matters to their larger municipalities. That is, an existing municipality of a legislatively-defined size may prohibit incorporation within its immediate environs—up to as much as five miles—and may easily annex surrounding territory, which generally means no referendum is required. The result of these "no incorporation/easy annexation" provisions has been to evolve a relatively unfragmented structure in the states with a combination of these laws, such as Georgia, North Carolina, New Mexico, and Texas. Conversely, a highly fragmented local structure is permitted in states that do not have this sort of combination, such as California, Illinois, New Jersey, and Pennsylvania. Different patterns, in part a result of these provisions, are shown in Table 8–1, which indicates the average number of local governments within counties for the selected states.

Considering Schattschneider's comment at the beginning of this chapter about the number of participants' impact on conflicts, it is evident that the "no-incorporation" laws, by limiting the number of local government participants, has affected the type and outcome of interlocal interactions. The net effect of the lower number of governments participating is uncertain; it probably varies from area to area and from time to time. It is certain, however, that in situations where local governments must cooperate with one another to solve areawide problems, compete with one another for scarce resources, and jealously guard their powers and prerogatives, the "rules of the game" for local interactions will be considerably different in Georgia with an average of eight local governments per county than in Pennsylvania with an average of 78 for each county.

Variations in legal powers of local governments are found within states as well as among states. Most states, for example, give different powers to

TABLE 8-1
IMPACT OF "NO INCORPORATION/
EASY ANNEXATION" LAWS

States with "no incorporation/ easy annexation" laws		States without "no incorporation/easy annexation" laws	
State	Average number of governments per county	State	Average number of governments per county
Georgia	8	Illinois	65
North Carolina	9	California	66
New Mexico	10	New Jersey	72
Texas	14	Pennsylvania	78

Source: Bureau of the Census, *Census of Governments:* 1977, Vol. 1, *Government Organization*, p. 10.

cities according to their population size. The "no-incorporation" powers are often granted only to the larger cities in a state. Similarly, larger jurisdictions are occasionally given revenue sources denied other local governments, such as a local sales or municipal income tax.

While a great variety exists in the legal environment in which local intergovernmental relations take place, notable regional patterns are present. Counties, for example, are usually stronger than municipalities in the South and the Border states. On the other hand, counties are very weak in New England where strong town and city governments are more important. Connecticut and Rhode Island do not even have organized counties.

The Changing Legal Setting

The legal setting that affects interlocal relations has been substantially modified in recent years by the great increase in new functions performed by local governments. Like the higher levels of government, localities are performing numerous functions that either were not performed at all or were carried out by the private sector until recent years. The innovative and experimental programs of a decade ago in areas as diverse as pollution abatement, manpower training, drug abuse education, day care, family counseling and spousal centers, are now commonplace. Further, jurisdictions that traditionally performed very limited functions are now providing a wide range of services, thereby making them practically indistinguishable from municipalities. In many suburban areas the counties now serve functionally as both city and county for their residents. These "urban counties," as they are often called, increasingly serve as rivals to municipalities, blocking the cities' expansion and competing with them for revenues and citizens' loyalties.

These new functions require grants of power and generally specific state legislative authorization. The states have in recent years readily given such authority, but have at the same time tightly retained control over their creatures. In some instances the states have been able to give new grants of functional power and simultaneously increase their local control. To the extent that this becomes more prevalent, the localities, in effect, will be exercising state powers and administering state programs.

Whether local governments are carrying out state policy or furthering their own interests can have important ramifications. In 1982 the U.S. Supreme Court ruled in *Community Communication* v. *City of Boulder* that municipalities are *not* exempt from federal antitrust laws unless they are furthering or implementing a "clearly articulated and affirmatively expressed state policy."[4] The decision grew out of a contested award of a cable television franchise by the city. The ruling implies that a locality must have a clear and specific grant of power from the state for each function as opposed to more generalized power designation often given by state constitutions and state legislatures. Would a municipality need a specific state act in order to grant trash collection contracts to private firms or to regulate fortune teller establishments? The wording of the *Boulder* case suggests such a grant would be necessary. If so, state control of local governments would be further enhanced in a major way. Subsequent Court rulings, federal legislation, and changes in state constitutions and legislation, however, are likely to limit the scope of this decision.

Lastly, the local legal scene has been modified by state actions designed to stimulate interlocal cooperation. Sometimes this has been limited to enabling legislation permitting interlocal cooperative agreements or contract purchase of services from another unit of government, e.g., a small municipality "buying" snow removal services from the county. The cooperative service agreements are not new; Indiana had an authorizing statute as early as 1852.

There has been a major growth in this type of interlocal relations in recent years. A survey by Joseph Zimmerman of municipalities participating in intergovernmental service agreements found that the major reasons for this type of activity were to: (1) take advantage of economies of scale; (2) provide needed facilities; (3) secure qualified personnel; (4) meet an urgent problem; (5) comply with citizen demand for a service agreement; (6) take the service "out of politics"; and (7) avoid civil service regulations. Further, this survey noted that the propensity to enter into agreements is a function of population size, with the larger units ratifying interlocal service contracts more often than their smaller counterparts. Great variations also existed among regions. In the West, 78 percent of the municipalities had at least one such contract. This was true for only 53 percent of the cities in both the East and the South.[5]

Most states today grant extensive authorization for cooperation among local governments. Included is permission for agreements across state boundaries and between localities, states, and the national government. The extent of this authority is shown in Table 8-2.

The states have authorized, or even ordered, the creation of cooperative agencies (for example, councils of governments, known as COGS) to facilitate program coordination, especially in planning. COGS, or regional councils, are voluntary bodies composed of representatives of the local governments within metropolitan areas. They work to find solutions to problems of the area and, in the past, reviewed projects to be funded by federal grants. Often they were created as a result of national planning review requirements under Office of Management and Budget (OMB) Circular A-95. In other instances they were created on the initiative of the local governments themselves. The Reagan administration eliminated the A-95 requirements.

On the more coercive side, state agencies sometimes step in to solve conflicts between two local jurisdictions in the provision of a service. A few years ago, the Kentucky State Board of Education ended years of wrangling between the city of Louisville and Jefferson County, in which this city is located, over the consolidation of the two school systems by ordering them merged.

States have responded to areawide problems by creating or permitting voters or officials of local areas to establish new multijurisdictional special district governments or agencies, especially for the functions of planning and water and sewage in urban areas, and resource development, fire protection, and economic development in rural areas. These district governments or agencies are generally relatively independent of all existing local governments and are often able to bypass or outright veto their actions.

Finally, in a few places, most notably in the Indianapolis and Minneapolis–St. Paul areas, the state legislatures have stepped in to give a major restructuring of local powers and responsibilities for some or many of the area's local governments.[6] In 1967 the Minneapolis–St. Paul Metropolitan Council was established by state legislative act. The Council has taxing authority, the power to plan and zone and to work in such fields as solid waste, air pollution, and noise abatement. Even with these powers, it is still a council of governments-type arrangement, rather than a "new government." In 1969 the Indiana Legislature enacted a bill that created "Unigov" for the Indianapolis metropolitan area by consolidating the city of Indianapolis and Marion County. This was the largest consolidation in the current century and the first one to occur during this time in the North. More

TABLE 8-2
GENERAL INTERGOVERNMENTAL COOPERATION
AUTHORIZATION, 1976

States	Cooperation power*	Contract power**	Across state lines	Local unit with home state	Local unit with U.S.
Alabama					
Alaska	X			X	X
Arizona	X	X	X	X	X
Arkansas	X	X	X	X	X
California	X	X²	X	X	X
Colorado	X	X	X	X	X
Connecticut	X¹	X¹	X	X	
Delaware					
District of Columbia					
Florida	X	X	X	X	X
Georgia	X			X	
Hawaii					
Idaho	X	X	X	X	X
Illinois	X	X	X	X	X
Indiana	X	X	X	X	X
Iowa	X	X	X	X	X
Kansas	X		X	X	X
Kentucky	X	X	X	X	X
Louisiana	X				
Maine	X			X	X
Maryland					
Massachusetts	X	X			
Michigan	X	X	X	X	X
Minnesota	X	X	X	X	X
Mississippi					
Missouri	X	X	X	X	
Montana	X	X		X	
Nebraska	X	X	X	X	X
Nevada	X	X	X	X	X

significantly, this is the only recent city-county consolidation to take place without a popular referendum. Such actions by the state legislatures are drastic, of course, but they may be the last resort open to states as the localities so often find themselves unable to function effectively in a politically and governmentally-fragmented system but cannot agree on a new structure for more effective governance.

The public apparently would like to see the power of local governments expanded. In a recent survey, 61 percent of a nationwide sample responded that they wished to see the local governments made "much stronger." Further, 27 percent preferred to see the localities made "only somewhat stronger," but only 8 percent wanted them to be less powerful. The least support for increasing local power came from the suburban respondents

States	Cooperation power*	Contract power**	Across state lines	Local unit with home state	Local unit with U.S.
New Hampshire	X	X			
New Jersey	X				
New Mexico	X		X	X	X
New York					
	X	X	X	X	
North Carolina	X	X	X		
North Dakota	X		X	X	X
Ohio					
Oklahoma	X	X	X	X	X
Oregon	X	X	X	X	X
Pennsylvania	X	X	X	X	X
Rhode Island					
South Carolina	X				
South Dakota	X	X	X	X	X
Tennessee	X	X	X	X	X
Texas	X	X		X	
Utah	X	X	X	X	X
Vermont	X	X			
Virginia	X				
Washington	X	X	X	X	X
West Virginia	X	X			
Wisconsin	X	X	X	X	
Wyoming	X		X	X	X

*Power to undertake joint or cooperative provision of services.
**Power of one unit to provide services for another.
¹The functions are limited—seem to include everything but general government.
²Cities and counties only.
Source: Adapted from Advisory Commission on Intergovernmental Relations, *Pragmatic Federalism: The Reassignment of Functional Responsibility*, Report M-105 (Washington, D.C.: July, 1976), pp. 11-12.

(57 percent), while the highest came from the central-city residents (64 percent).[7] The survey data do not show in which way the public feels that local governments should be strengthened. By greater grants of power from the state legislature? By internal administrative reform? Or, by external restructuring, for instance, the creating of an areawide metropolitan government? If past experience is a guide, the public may agree overwhelmingly to make local government stronger, but will surely be bitterly divided over how to do it.

The Governmental-Political Environment

As noted earlier in this chapter, the local system of governance is the most fragmented part of the federal system; there are more than 82,000 units of local government. This means for many people the maximizing of democratic ideals about local government, an assurance of many points of access, and perpetuation of neighbor-run, "grass roots" governments. For others, however, the fragmentation is seen as creating a situation in which adequate services cannot be provided because no areawide authority is present to deal with problems of that scope and human and financial resources are divided among numerous governments. One functional "city" is, then, divided artificially into many political and governmental subunits. This problem and its solutions are discussed later in this chapter.

More Municipalities

An important element in considering the governmental environment of interlocal relations is the increased number of nonschool district local governments. Although the total number of governments declined by more than 69,000 between 1942 and 1982, municipalities and nonschool special districts increased by approximately 22,000 during this same period. The number of municipalities, in fact, grew by 500 in the past 10 years. A large portion of these jurisdictions are suburban, "bed-room" type entities located on the fringes of larger central cities.

The trend to establish more small and medium-sized municipalities undoubtedly will continue as people flee the central cities. Of course, continuing energy crises and resultant higher gasoline prices and shortages may slow or even reverse this "flight." Indeed, a number of large cities actually gained population during the 1970–1980 decade as a result of immigration and annexation. Nevertheless, evidence points to more and more people in the future leaving the larger cities for suburban and small-town communities.

A recent Department of Housing and Urban Development survey found almost half of all Americans (47 percent) prefer to live in a rural area or small town that is not in the suburbs. Eight percent prefer to live in a nonsuburban medium sized city (50,000 to 250,000), while 27 percent chose suburban life. Only 16 percent prefer a large city.[8] An earlier Gallup study found similar anti-big city feelings.[9] In many ways this probably represents the idealized view Americans traditionally have had about small town life. There is substantial evidence, however, that this preference is based on strong and perhaps justified reasons for anti-big city feelings.

The largest single reason for which people leave the central city is a fear of crime and violence. The HUD survey found, for instance, that 72 percent of the central city residents saw crime as a "severe problem." Only 20 percent of suburban residents and 15 percent of rural residents identified crime as a "severe problem" in their communities.[10] Many of those who can afford to leave the larger central cities are doing so. Increasingly those who remain in such centers are the very wealthy and the very poor.

The emergent pattern is that people are increasingly disenchanted with the central city and are moving to suburbs and to other smaller towns.

Being accustomed to the amenities of city life, however, they often soon seek to secure urban services by creating a municipality, if one does not exist in the area, or by securing similar services from other governments (e.g., urban counties or special districts).

More Nonschool Special Districts

This migration with its accompanying public service demands has led to a great increase in the number of limited-purpose special districts. As efforts are made to overcome the growing local government fragmentation and to provide services in functional areas, such as water or sewage disposal, that are almost impossible to administer on a small government-by-small-government basis, a spur is given for the creation of more and more special districts. During the 1942–82 period, the number of nonschool special districts grew from about 8,000 to almost 29,000, with nearly 5,000 of that increase occurring in the final five years.

Most observers view this development with alarm. Horizontal fragmentation is being traded for functional fragmentation. Many special districts are nondemocratic because their governing bodies are appointed rather than elected and their activities are generally "hidden" from the public's view. Further, the special districts are generally beyond the control of general-purpose governments because the districts receive their legal authorization from the state, not the city or the county. Consequently the districts' governing boards are often appointed by the governor or chosen by some other method once removed from local elected officials. Furthermore, because they are multijurisdictional, the districts can play off one local government against another. Some of the most acrimonious and protracted intergovernmental conflicts at the local level occur between special districts and general-purpose governments. It is not uncommon, for example, for counties or municipalities to become involved in a five- or six-year struggle with a water and sewer district or with a multicounty planning authority. Often these conflicts are one of the few activities that can bring the cities and counties together in common cause. All the criticisms notwithstanding, the special district form of government consistently had the highest percentage of new creations over all other types of local government in the 1942–82 period.

Citizens Perceive Complexity

The complexity of the interlocal system takes its toll on the polity. A U.S. Senate Subcommittee survey asked interviewees to respond to a number of questions about government in the United States. Two questions and responses important for this discussion are shown in Table 8–3. The first set of responses shows attitudes toward the entire system, political

TABLE 8-3
ATTITUDES TOWARD COMPLEXITY OF GOVERNMENT
AND LOCAL GOVERNMENT DISORGANIZATION

Question 1: Sometimes politics and government seem so complicated that a person can't really understand what's going on.		Question 2: Local government is too disorganized to be effective.
Agree	86%	35%
Disagree	12	54
Not sure	2	11

Source: Adapted from U.S. Senate, Committee on Government Operations, Sub-Committee on Intergovernmental Relations, *Confidence and Concern: Citizens View American Government. A Survey of Public Attitudes* (Washington, D.C.: Government Printing Office, 1973), Vol. II, pp. 267–269.

and governmental, and for all three levels of government. The 86 percent agreement rate that government seemed "too complicated" was shared almost evenly by all regions of the nation and by all types of communities (central city, suburbs, towns, rural). The second question which specifically focuses on local governments, showed regional and community variations. Thirty-five percent of the interviewees agreed that local government is "too disorganized to be effective." The highest agreement with this statement comes from the East, which is by far the most fragmented region of the nation, with an average of more than 60 local governments per county. The lowest agreement is found in the Midwest (29 percent). Also, nationally 41 percent of the city residents agreed with the statement while about 32 percent of those interviewed from the suburbs, towns, and rural areas concurred.

A 1978 ACIR study likewise found 36 percent of the public believes that "state and local government is too fragmented and disorganized to be effective." Regional patterns almost identical to those reviewed above were clear.[11]

How the System Endures

Even with these misgivings about the existing structure of government, a variety of factors—including traditional political theory about the role of local government, ongoing political traditions and patterns of interactions for governments, groups, and individuals, and reasonably workable accommodation devices—converge to give the current interlocal system a surprising amount of durability.

Much of the durability of the local system comes from perceptions of what local government is all about. The political theory of Americans strongly supports the current structure—many small governments run by local, ordinary citizen-legislators. The well-known Jeffersonian concept of "grass roots" government run by the people—miniature republics—has firmly taken hold in the American mind. "Self-government," "rural America," "the government closest to the people," "neighborhood government," and "grass roots democracy," are all terms repeated and defended daily, affirming America's commitment to small local units that can float with considerable autonomy on the turbulent sea of local government.

This belief goes far to perpetuate the current chaotic local governmental system. Never mind that within urban areas governments compete, overlap, duplicate, and often fail to perform. They still are the local governments that one day will stand as the last bulwark in defense of democracy according to the modern-day Jeffersonians. And what is the alternative to the current local government arrangements? A "gargantuan" structure to equal the size of the metropolitan spread cities. The myth of local government being small and close rejects that alternative. Can New York City, Chicago, or Los Angeles really be called a *local* government, it is asked?

Leading scholars such as Paul Ylvisaker,[12] Roscoe C. Martin,[13] and Robert C. Wood[14] have argued that the Jeffersonian model never existed except in a few isolated atypical instances or as a historical construct. These writers generally argue that the Madisonian model of representative government is more in keeping with the American tradition. Wood, for instance, argues that a large areawide government is "more defensible in terms of the values the nation has accepted."[15] The problem is that such logical arguments are confronted by an emotionally held belief. The myth prevails in the face of many such eloquent and logical onslaughts, and it goes far in preserving the current local government system.

The political element overrides the legal setting, the governmental structure, and the parameters of action imposed by strongly-held political theories. The various roles played by individual and collective politics in the intergovernmental relations system has been stressed throughout this book. Also they will serve as the main focus of the next section and therefore need not be commented upon in depth here. It is important, however, at this point to stress that politics is the force that generally stimulates the interlocal system, just as it does in nation-state relations or in interstate actions. Politics causes the dynamic interactions and often the conflicts. And, as if to balance the ledger, it is politics that often overcomes constitutional barriers and ties the system together or facilitates interlocal cooperation.

The mayor of Hyattsville, Maryland, a city of 15,000 with a budget of only $2 million, repeatedly makes successful demands on the county government with its 700,000 population and $600 million budget. His success comes not from his power as the nonpartisan mayor of a relatively small city, but because of his influence with Democratic party leaders and Democratic officeholders on the county council and in the state legislative delegation. The success is not based on controlling the party, the county council, or the legislature, but merely on what everyone knows.: "Mayor Bass can hustle up a vote or two." Likewise, the local assessors of a state meet in a hotel lounge for a few drinks and work out a cooperative method for addressing grievances over municipal assessment procedures. This is done even though the state has not authorized any specific power to undertake interlocal cooperative agreements in this field. Also, the Republican congresswoman seeks national funds to help a local county executive (who also is a Republican) start a program for which the Democratic county council and governor had declined support. Chances are good that the program will help both the congresswoman and the county executive's upcoming reelection efforts.

And so it goes. The fragmented local governmental system moves onward rather dynamically and deliberately because, among other reasons, of a healthy dose of political inputs.

METROPOLITAN REORGANIZATION

The literature of intergovernmental relations has long been concerned with the problem of governmental fragmentation in our urban areas. Simply stated, a general awareness has developed that there are too many units of government in the large urban and metropolitan areas to permit effective governmental operations. Areawide problems are not being solved, in what Robert C. Wood has called the "governmental mosaic of the metropolis."[16] A consensus exists among most students of the metropolis that such fragmentation has produced major problems in policy planning and implementation and a general inability to deal with that social-economic complex referred to as "the urban problem."

Luther Gulick, speaking of attempts to solve areawide problems such as transportation, pollution, and water supply under the fragmented system, concluded that there is "accumulating evidence of failure everywhere, in spite of many heroic efforts."[17] He continued:

> Once an indivisible problem is divided nothing effective can be done about it . . . Spreading area-wide problems cannot be handled geographic piece by geographic piece. They must be tackled in their entirety, comprehensively, and are difficult even so.[18]

Proposals for Mitigating Fragmentation

Numerous methods of solving the problems associated with fragmentation have been proposed. They range from temporary and voluntary devices designed to alleviate an immediate difficulty resulting from fragmentation to a total reorganization of the metropolitan governance system by replacing the polycentric arrangement with one metropoliswide authority. Roscoe C. Martin identifies eight *procedural* adaptive devices and eight *structural* adaptive devies. They are:

A. Procedural Adaptation

    1. *Informal cooperation:* an agreement, neither authorized nor prohibited by law, between two or more local units of government to improve services.

    2. *The service contract:* a legal undertaking on the part of one government to supply and on the part of another to receive (and usually to pay for) the service or services named. N.B. The development of the Lakewood Plan.

    3. *Parallel action:* an agreement between two or more governments to pursue a common course of action. The decisions are agreed upon jointly, but their implementation requires individual action by the governments involved.

    4. *The conference approach:* the bringing together, at regular intervals, of representatives of the local governments within a given area for the discussion of common problems, the exchange of information, and the development of agreements on policy questions of mutual interest.

    5. *The compact:* A formal agreement under which two or more governments undertake certain mutual obligations.

    6. *Transfer of functions:* the transfer of one or more functions from one government to another more adequate in jurisdiction and resources —as from a village or city to a county.

    7. *Extraterritorial jurisdiction:* a legal grant by the state which permits the city to go outside its legal limits for certain fields of action.

    8. *Incorporation:* a process by which a given geographic area is transformed into a legal corporation which is recognized by law as an entity having particular functions, rights, duties, and liabilities.

B. Structural Adaptation

    1. *Annexation:* the simple legal device of expanding municipal boundaries to incorporate additional territory.

    2. *City-county separation:* the division or separation of the city from the county. The basic purpose of this device is to divide urban and rural populations so that each may have the kind and level of service it desires and for which it is willing to pay.

3. *Functional consolidation:* the consolidating or merging of functions in a particular metropolitan area without necessarily consolidating or abolishing any existing units of government.

4. *The special district:* a unit of government established to administer one or more designated functions. The new unit does not necessarily need to coincide with previous political boundaries.

5. *The authority:* a type of public administrative agency with quasi-governmental powers. This type of adaptation is not unlike the special district. The major difference is the normally larger geographic area of the authority and its power to issue revenue bonds.

6. *Geographical consolidation:* the merger or consolidation of two or more units of governments into one government.

7. *Metropolitan government:* a general government with jurisdiction over the whole of a particular metropolitan area.

8. *The regional agency or authority:* a unit of government which represents a regional approach to suprametroplitan problems.[19]

Most adaptations so far have employed combinations of the procedural devices listed in Martin's taxonomy. This is largely a result of the political difficulties accompanying major structural change. Martin's taxonomy can be viewed along two continua, that of effectiveness and that of political feasibility[20] (See Figure 8–1.) What is generally thought to be politically acceptable is often seen as too ineffective, too slow, or too temporary. What is perceived as most effective in dealing with fragmentation is generally simply not acceptable to the voters.

Efforts to Achieve Metropolitanwide Government

To say that attempted solutions to the problems of metropolitan fragmentation have concentrated on procedural and voluntary adaptations does not mean that efforts to achieve Wood's "one community—one government" have been abandoned.[21] A conservative estimate suggests that since World War II hundreds of communities have had some organized effort to adopt a form of areawide government, with many of these, of course, being repeat considerations for one area, as in the cases of repeated efforts for reorganization in St. Louis and Louisville. Further, a significant percentage of these attempts has actually reached fruition in the sense of a specific detailed plan of metropolitan governance being submitted to the voters or to the state legislature.

A system of metropoliswide government can be achieved in several ways. Included are large-scale annexation, the creation of a metropolitanwide general service district, the establishment of a local federal system, or the consolidation of local governments in the metropolis into an area-

FIGURE 8-1 EFFECTIVENESS/FEASIBILITY CONTINUA

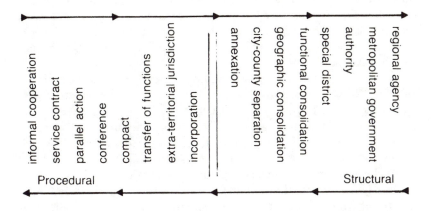

Source: Parris N. Glendening, "The Federal Role in Regional Planning Councils: Trends and Implications," *The Review of Regional Studies,* Vol. 1, No. 3 (Spring, 1971–72), p. 95.

wide government. In particular, consolidation has been attempted frequently in recent years. For a variety of legal and political reasons, however, the consolidations are almost always partial, leaving a number of local governments in existence and independent of the new areawide unit. Moreover, in numerous instances the voters have turned down the proposal.

Most efforts at geographic consolidation have utilized the county as the core of the proposed metropolitan government. For many years such a consolidation was viewed as all municipalities and special districts within the county being merged or consolidated with the existing or strengthened county government. In more recent years political realities have dictated that city-county consolidation may mean consolidation only between the largest city and the county, with the smaller suburban municipalities being permitted to remain outside the consolidated government but given the option to join later.

The history of the many proposals for metropolitanwide governance systems has been one of nearly universal rejection. Most proposals are killed by hostile interests or die from a lack of active support and are never presented to the voters. Those that survive and reach the voting booth are generally rejected. Successful adoptions are few. Rejection is the normal outcome of reorganization referenda.

Some far-reaching proposals have been accepted by the voters. Most notable was the successful adoption of a local federal system in the Miami-Dade County area in 1957. The more frequent but still very rare adoptions of city-county consolidation proposals have occurred primarily in the South, with the major consolidations involving Baton Rouge, Nashville, Jackson-ville, Columbus (Ga.), Lexington (Ky.), and the previously mentioned Indianapolis change. Thus, the South, which is that part of the country in which the metropolises are least fragmented and in which fragmentation is increasing much more slowly than in other geographical areas is the only section where a noticeable number of areawide structural reorganizations has been taking place.

In 1979, Portland, Oregon established a metropolitan service district known as "Metro," that is the first regional planning and service organiza-tion in the nation to have a council and executive officer elected by the public. Created by popular approval, Metro combines urbanized portions of three counties—Multnomah, Washington, and Clackamas. Although its functions are limited, they can be expanded at a later date. At the outset, the new district assumed the planning responsibilities of the Colum-bia Region Association of Governments and the solid waste and zoo man-agement activities of the former metropolitan service district. In addition, it is concerned with the metropolitan aspects of transportation, air and water quality, water supply, drainage and flood control, and liquid waste disposal. It also has authority to operate the regional transit agency. Other functions, such as regional human services, corrections, parks, recreation and cultural facilities, and libraries can be added if the voters approve.

VARIABLES AFFECTING METROPOLITAN REFERENDA DECISIONS

Not many years ago it was commonplace to blame rejection of metro-politan reform proposals on the ignorance of the voting public. "If only the people had understood the complexity of the problem and the logic of the proposal," it was often emotionally put forth, "they would have sup-ported it." Today we are beginning to understand better the many variables that come together in a unique combination to spell acceptance or, more predictably, rejection on any particular reorganization proposal. The more important factors—partisanship, race, and indigenous events—deserve consideration.

Partisanship

Since 1957, when Banfield wrote that "it will be difficult or impossible to integrate local government where the two-party system operates,"[22] partisan division between the normally Republican-dominated suburbs and the normally Democratic-dominated central cities has been seen as a major obstacle to the adoption of an areawide government. Barring the situation of nearly even population division between a central city and its suburban areas, almost certainly one party will run the new government on a continuing basis. Given the importance of viable local parties in the American party structure, the loss of the city hall or the county courthouse could prove disastrous. Banfield warned that "in effect, advocates of consolidation schemes are asking the Democrats to give up their control of the central cities or, at least, to place it in jeopardy."[23] This specter of partisan loss has been raised in many reorganization campaigns. In fact, no proposal has been adopted by voters in areas split by strong partisan antagonisms. The one adoption in a partisanly-divided metropolis (Indianapolis) was imposed by the state legislature.

Race

Racial cleavages have always played an important part in the politics of metropolitan reorganization. Generally, the variable of race was thought of in terms of white suburbanites who had fled the central city voting against consolidation to insure that they were not reunited with that which they fled. As Daniel R. Grant observes:

> More often than not, the politics of race has worked against the adoption of proposed metro governments. Lily-white suburbs have tended to vote against having anything to do with "those lower class city-hall types," and proponents of annexation, city-county consolidation, or metropolitan federation were denounced as tax-grabbing thieves who will invade the beautiful suburbs and spread core city blight and ethnic minorities out in the comfortably homogeneous and compatible suburbs. Seldom has the word "race" been mentioned specifically in the campaign advertisements and sloganeering, but this did not prevent its being one of the more important "silent issues" that was discussed only in "safe company."[24]

Much recent attention has focused on reasons for growing black opposition to reorganization. Many black leaders have taken the position that the deliberate intent of metropolitan reorganization or, at a minimum, the indirect effect of such a proposal is to dilute black voting strength. Studies on referenda in Cleveland, St. Louis, and Nashville point to the importance of black opposition based on this stated fear. There is, of course, a certain irony in racially-based opposition of both blacks and whites.

Some blacks stress that dilution of black voting strength is not a side effect of reorganization; instead it is the reason for it. For instance, LeRoy Johnson, a Georgia state senator, charged that the proposed consolidation of Atlanta and Fulton County was written not as "an effort of extending the tax base of the City but from an effort of curtailing and limiting the Negro voting strength."[25]

Regardless of the intent of city-county consolidation the effect has been to dilute the earlier concentrations of black voting power. Nashville in 1960 had a population that was 38 percent black. The black population of the consolidated government there is only 19 percent. Jacksonville dropped from 42 percent black before the 1967 consolidation to 23 percent after reorganization. Likewise, black population went from 24 percent in Indianapolis before consolidation to 18 percent after Unigov.

Lastly, some black leaders are accepting the view of writers such as Grant that political control of a dying central city might be meaningless.

> Situations which make it possible for black citizens to elect their own city council are undoubtedly a long overdue contribution to the self-respect and pride of blacks. It is exceedingly difficult to make a value judgment on the relative merits of racial balance in American society and a racial imbalance in communities that permit blacks to elect black officials and whites to elect white officials for separate governments.
>
> But such value judgments must be made in American society, and this writer suspects that it will be only a Pyrrhic victory if black mayors and black city councils inherit all of the problems and misery of the core cities in our metropolitan areas without the resources of white America to cope with these problems. The National Urban Coalition recently predicted that [within a decade] most American cities would be "black, brown, and bankrupt."[26]

Special Indigenous Events

Several analysts have concluded that the normal pattern is to reject a reorganization plan unless an unusual special indigenous event is present to alter the natural inclination toward rejection. A major scandal, a total breakdown in one or more public services, or a unique political leader or political event are the stimuli for major governmental change. Thomas M. Scott, for example, argues that radical reorganization, such as city-county consolidation, is possible only when special or unusual political factors cause politicians and citizens to "respond abnormally" in their voting behavior. Scott concludes:

> Radical reorganization plans tend to be approved only in areas with unusual social-economic-political characteristics. . . . These cases are unique and must be explained as deviations from the normal patterns. . . .
> Practically speaking, this analysis suggests that in the near future radical metropolitan change will continue to win voter approval only under unique circumstances. In the meantime "normal" metropolitan areas (as most are) will forestall crises by dealing with their problems in a piecemeal manner.[27]

A case-by-case review of the successful reorganizations generally supports the argument that a unique situation is needed. A most notable illustration is found in the Jacksonville-Duval County referendum. A group known as the Citizens for Better Government actively campaigned for the new plan by pointing out excessive governmental duplication and inefficiency, one of the nation's highest crime rates, severe water and air pollution problems, extremely high city debts and, most important, repeated cases of graft and corruption. Ten months before the referendum, the grand jury indicted two city commissioners, four council members, the recreation director, and the city auditor. In addition, the tax assessor resigned after a grand jury investigation. Further, 15 city senior high schools were disaccredited because of inadequate financial support and physical facilities. The disaccreditation came shortly before the August referendum. It was in this unique environment that the consolidation was approved by a margin of 24,725 votes.

Other Variables

A review of the many case studies on metropolitan reorganizations suggests many other variables that at one time may play a key role in the success or failure of a proposal. Important issues in at least one campaign include (1) class and class perceptions, (2) alienation and sublimation, (3) apathy, (4) service perceptions, (5) lack of knowledge of the proposal, (6) fear of tax increases, (7) leadership inadequacies, (8) legal requirements, and (9) political philosophies.

RELUCTANT RELATIONSHIP

This chapter has pointed out that relations among local governments are not necessarily close or frequent and that many of them have no interactions at all. To some degree, relationships are determined by state constitutions and statutes that prescribe legal patterns among their local jurisdictions, patterns that not only vary from state to state but exist within states in infinite varieties. It has stressed, also, that if intergovernmental cooperation is necessary anywhere, certainly it is among neighboring jurisdictions at the local level. The large number of governments—many quite small—the fragmentation of government in metropolitan areas, and the major problems of environmental pollution, crime, housing, and other aspects of urban life often preclude single-jurisdiction treatment of difficulties.

The problems were presented as structural, but they are really political. Because of political considerations, cooperation often is hard to obtain. Officials in each jurisdiction want to protect the interest of their own communities, not only because their political fates may depend on it but because they, too, live there. Consequently, they are reluctant to yield any local advantage for the good of the entire area. There is nothing to be gained in agreeing to accept someone else's solid waste, for example, unless some trade can be effected. Mayors or county officials who do this may appear to be top diplomats to the metropolitan area but be regarded as villains at home.

Major remedies to the fragmentation problem are rarely adopted. Some segment of the population always believes itself threatened and refuses to accept metropolitan government. For it to be popularly approved, the advantages of consolidation must be clear to the entire community and not just to the group that will profit from the move. Moreover, a crisis or other unique situation may be required. The result is that solutions tend to veer toward the politically feasible—often partial and insufficient—rather than following the more comprehensive approach of areawide government.

NOTES

1. E. E. Schattschneider, *The Semi-Sovereign People* (New York: Holt, Rinehart and Winston, 1960), p. 2

2. Daniel J. Elazar, "Local Government in Intergovernmental Perspective," in Daniel J. Elazar, R. Bruce Carroll, E. Lester Levine and Douglas St. Angelo, editors, *Cooperation and Conflict: Readings in American Federalism* (Itasca, Ill.: F. E. Peacock Publishers, 1969), p. 417.

3. The legal powers and limitations and the forms of government were discussed earlier, primarily in Chapter 4. This section limits its comments to certain additional legal matters that have more direct bearing on interlocal relations.

4. 102 Supreme Ct 835, 1982.

5. Joseph F. Zimmerman, "Meeting Service Needs Through Intergovernmental Agreements," *Municipal Year Book, 1973* (Washington, D.C.: International City Management Association, 1973), pp. 79–88.

6. For a discussion of the Indianapolis plan, see York Willbern, "Unigov: Local Government Reorganization in Indianapolis," in Advisory Commission on Intergovernmental Relations, *Regional Governance: Promise and Performance. Substate Regionalism and the Federal System, Volume II Case Studies,* Report A-41 (Washington, D.C.: Government Printing Office, 1973), pp. 45–73. For an analysis of the Minneapolis-St. Paul change, see in the same volume, Ted Kolderie, "Governance in the Twin Cities Area of Minnesota," pp. 111–138. (In subsequent notes the Commission will be cited as ACIR.)

7. U.S. Senate, Committee on Government Operations, Subcommittee on Intergovernmental Relations, *Confidence and Concern: Citizens View American Government. A Survey of Public Attitudes* (Washington, D.C.: Government Printing Office, 1973), Vol. II, p. 121. Survey conducted by Louis Harris and Associates, 1973.

8. U.S. Department of Housing and Urban Development, *The 1978 HUD Survey on the Quality of Community Life: A Data Book* (Washington, D.C.: HUD, 1978), p. 554.

9. *The Gallup Opinion Index,* Report 90, December, 1972, p. 22.

10. Department of Housing and Urban Development, p. 220.

11. ACIR, *Changing Public Attitudes on Governments and Taxes* (Washington, D.C.: The Commission, 1981), p. 35. Report S–10.

12. "Some Criteria for a 'Proper' Areal Division of Powers," in Arthur Maass, ed., *Area and Power* (Glencoe, Ill.: The Free Press, 1959).

13. *Grass Roots* (2nd ed.: University, Ala.: University of Alabama Press, 1964).

14. *Suburbia* (New York: Houghton Mifflin, 1958).

15. Ibid., p. 295.

16. Robert C. Wood, *1400 Governments: The Political Economy of the New York Metropolitan Region* (Garden City, N.Y.: Doubleday and Co., 1964), p. 56.

17. Luther H. Gulick, *The Metropolitan Problem and American Ideas* (New York: Alfred A. Knopf, 1962), p. 23. This view of near complete failure is not universally accepted. See, for example, Robert C. Wood, "Metropolitan Government, 1975: An Extrapolation of Trends," *American Political Science Review*, Vol. 52 (1958), pp. 108–122. Warren emphasizes the positive aspects of public choice in a market situation. See Robert Warren, "A Municipal Services Market Model of Metropolitan Organization," *Journal of the American Institute of Planners*, Vol. 30 (August, 1964), pp. 193–204; and Vincent Ostrom, Charles Tiebout, and Robert Warren, "The Organization of Government in Metropolitan Areas: A Theoretical Inquiry," *American Political Science Review*, Vol. 55 (December, 1961), pp. 831–842. A few authors have argued that the problem is not one of structure, but of a lack of political will to do the task. See Frances Fox Piven and Richard A. Cloward, "Black Control of the Cities: Heading It Off by Metropolitan Government," *The New Republic* (October 7, 1967), p. 18; and Parris N. Glendening and Mavis Mann Reeves, "The Future of State and Local Government and American Federalism," in Mavis Mann Reeves and Parris N. Glendening, *Controversies of State and Local Political Systems* (Boston: Allyn and Bacon, 1972), pp. 481–483.

18. Gulick, p. 24.

19. Roscoe C. Martin, *Metropolis in Transition: Local Government Adapatation to Changing Urban Needs*, a report prepared for the Housing and Home Finance Agency under the Urban Studies and Housing Research Program (Washington, D.C.: Government Printing Office, 1963). Martin's study is now out of print. For a summary of his 1963 report, see Roscoe C. Martin, "Action in Metropolis—1," *National Civic Review*, Vol. 52 (1963), pp. 302–307; and ibid., Part II, pp. 363–367, 371. For a slightly different taxonomy see ACIR, *Alternate Approaches to Governmental Reorganization in Metropolitan Areas*, Report A-11 (1962). For a comprehensive analysis of metropolitan reform effors, see John C. Bollens and Henry J. Schmandt, *The Metropolis: Its People, Politics, and Economic Life*, 4th ed. (New York: Harper and Row, Publishers, 1982).

20. Parris N. Glendening and Patricia S. Atkins, "The Politics of City-County Consolidation," *County Year Book, 1977*, p. 63. See also Parris N. Glendening, "The Federal Role in Regional Planning Councils: Trends and Implications," *The Review of Regional Studies*, Vol. 1, No. 3 (Spring, 1971–72), p. 95ff. Thomas M. Scott employs a similar approach when he talks of a "continuum radicalness of metropolitan government change." See his "Metropolitan Governmental Reorganization Proposals," *Western Political Quarterly*, Vol. 21 (June, 1968), pp. 254–255.

21. Robert C. Wood, "Metropolitan Government, 1975," p. 111.

22. Edward C. Banfield, "The Politics of Metropolitan Area Organization," *Midwest Journal of Political Science,* Vol. 1 (1957), p. 86.

23. Ibid.

24. Daniel R. Grant, "Metropolitan Area Government and the Politics of Racial Balance: Some Public Policy Issues." A paper presented at the Southern Political Science Association meeting. Gatlinburg, Tennessee, November 12, 1971, pp. 2–3.

25. Quoted in the *New York Times,* November 9, 1969, p. 65.

26. Grant, p. 10. See also Willis D. Hawley, *Blacks and Metropolitan Governance: The Stakes of Reform* (Berkeley: University of California, Institute of Governmental Studies, 1972).

27. Scott, p. 261.

CHAPTER 9

THE FUTURE OF THE INTERGOVERNMENTAL SYSTEM: CHANGE AND UNCERTAINTY

ARGUMENTS about American federalism have gone on for more than 200 years. Even before the Constitutional Convention of 1787, Americans debated the relationship between the states and the central government. In the convention itself, delegates considered alternative types of association before recommending the Constitution for approval. And during the ratification campaigns, the exchanges on the subject—highlighted by Hamilton, Madison, and Jay's *Federalist Papers*—set a standard for scrutiny of the federal arrangement unequaled in contemporary times.

Over the years, numerous events have focused the debate on various aspects of federalism and its future and increased the decibel level of the arguments. Among these were early court decisions that "settled" many patterns of intergovernmental relations: among them were *Fletcher* v. *Peck* and *McCulloch* v. *Maryland*. In addition, arguments over commerce, tariffs, and slaves before the Civil War and that war itself stimulated close examination of the system. More recently, the civil rights–integration struggle of the 1950s and 1960s and the problems of education, the environment, and the cities during the 1960s and 1970s, again directed attention to national–state relations. During the past 15 years, discussions emphasized the continuing fiscal problems of all levels of government, particularly those of the national government from the late 1970s and into the 1980s. The financial pressures gave rise to President Reagan's New Federalism, sometimes referred to as "Austerity Federalism,"[1] because its major stimulus is viewed by many as a thrust toward reducing the size of the national government, if not, indeed, all governments.

The direction of and enthusiasm for emerging intergovernmental patterns depend on whose ox is being prepared for roasting, to continue the culinary analysis so prevalent in the study of intergovernmental relations. The successes civil rights leaders obtained through the national judiciary surely whet their appetites for greater centralization and national judicial intervention. Similarly, the flavor of the times, with increased national governmental activities to guarantee equal opportunities for all citizens, just as surely dulls the taste buds of many racial separatists for that type of federalism.

ASSESSMENTS OF AMERICAN FEDERALISM

Objective commentators on American federalism often are pessimistic about its future. Two examples from well-known students of intergovernmental relations and one from the ACIR will suffice. W. Brooke Graves, whose *American Intergovernmental Relations* has been cited often in this book, concluded his 1964 mammoth study with these comments:

> Americans . . . face unprecedented problems of national security—possibly even of survival—in a divided world, but they face critical problems at home in the preservation of American federalism, problems which few of them seem to realize. It is quite conceivable that the nation might survive, and its federal system of government be irretrievably lost.
>
> The American federal system has served the people well for nearly 200 years. It has great elements of strength. It has survived crises in the past and will, in all probability, survive others in the future. But there is no assurance that it will always continue to do so unless statesmanlike solutions are found—and found quickly— to meet new problems arising out of an almost completely different set of social and economic conditions under which it must operate now and in the future. . . .
>
> The time may be later than we think.[2]

Richard H. Leach, another well-known authority on federalism, evaluated the future of the American arrangement in a 1972 essay replete with pessimistic statements about the continuation of a viable system. He wrote:

> There is . . . considerable evidence that the country has already become so nationalized that continuation of a localistic system of government is already an anachronism. . . . In this view, state and local governments are superfluities, largely irrelevant to an attack on America's pressing problems; the national government alone can launch a successful attack.

Not that some sort of local or regional agents of the national government would not be necessary to carry out many facets of that attack. They would be necessary. The point is, however, that they would be agents, even as counties have always been of state governments.[3]

Nevertheless, Leach's overall theme is that certain relatively mild changes will likely forestall radical restructuring of the federal system, at least for the near future.

More recently, the ACIR concluded in a 1980 study that "contemporary federalism is an serious disarray. Like the economy, and like the political system generally, intergovernmental relationships have lost their pragmatic virtue: in many respects, they no longer work."[4] Although immediate demise was not foreseen, the Commission regarded the situation as serious enough to propose a number of major changes in national, state, and local responsibilities.

PRAGMATISM AND FEDERALISM

These types of conclusions are increasingly common throughout the literature. We are not quite so pessimistic, however. We think that a viable federalism will be operating in the United States during any future we can envision. We recognize the problems facing American government today, but we believe that internment of the present constitutional structure or the search for another governance arrangement is premature.

In part, our optimistic view is based on faith in what we call pragmatic federalism—a federalism accompanied by constantly adjusting intergovernmental relations, fashioned to current needs, with an emphasis on problem solving and a minimal adherence to rigid doctrine. These relations provide the flexibility that enables the system to endure.

The compromises of the Constitutional Convention of 1787 were the seeds of a pragmatic federalism that places responsibilities on each successive generation to make similar practical adjustments in the structures and processes of federalism to keep alive the balance struck between centralization and decentralization. The men who framed the Constitution had substantial disagreements about the most desirable arrangements to adopt, just as another group of 55[5] individuals would disagree if a similar convention were held today. Their divergent views were worked out in a series of practical accommodations designed to meet the conflicting needs for a central authority and for an uncentralized political autonomy. The Connecticut Compromise relating to representation in the Congress, the establishment of the Electoral College, and the delay in restricting the importation of slaves, for example, were all pragmatic efforts to make a union work.

The federalism set up 200 years ago was not a dogmatic embodiment of any particular philosophy, nor was it an excessively legalistic undertaking.

Indeed, the heritage passed along to posterity was a bare skeleton that had to be fleshed out by successive generations, including ours.

And flesh it out we have, first one way and then another. Americans have engaged in a kind of civic experimentalism that never seems to reach *the* answer but always seems to reach *an* answer. The early adjustments that were made did not become an unyielding corset that provided strict perimeters for bodily development. Each situation had to be worked out anew. Consequently, officials made practical decisions aimed at solving the problem that faced them at the time, nurturing first one part of the federal configuration and then another. As a result, the contours of federalism changed from time to time.

Our early forebears, enmeshed in a reverence for constitutionalism, debated many issues on philosophical grounds. As the dual federalism that marked American federalism until the 1930s gave way to a cooperative federalism, however, decisions seemed more and more to be guided by considerations of how problems *could* be solved rather than how functions ideally *should* be assigned, performed, and financed.

During the Great Depression of the 1930s, the governmental system incorporated developments of the Progressive Era of 1901–1920 and expanded national authority to cope with the states' impotence to solve economic problems international in scope. Nevertheless, many of the New Deal emergency programs initiating national involvement in activities theretofore performed by state and local governments and commencing direct national-local relationships later were rescinded when the economic conditions of World War II solved the problems these programs were established to alleviate.

Since World War II—particularly since 1960—the rate of change has accelerated. All governments grew, performing a wider range of services for more people, regulating more, taxing more, and spending more. Decisions by officials on all levels as they sought to deal with the problems of an urban society shifted functional responsibilities dramatically. Almost all activities were intergovernmentalized and the major providers of many services changed. The national government assumed functional responsibility for services previously rendered by states or local governments or both of them (occupational health and safety, for example), and states enlarged their role in the provision of former local services (education and court financing, for instance). National officials increasingly relied on state and local governments for implementation of national programs. States became major intergovernmental managers. At the same time, the national government sought to solve many problems created by state diversity by moving to regulate state and local governments, preempt their functions, and issue direct orders to control their actions.

Responding to problems generated by the proliferation of categorical grants-in-aid, each created to solve a particular problem, Congress turned to new intergovernmental aid mechanisms—general revenue sharing and block grants—as partial solutions. It created, combined, and, on occasion, discontinued federal assistance programs as it perceived the current need. And it used the grant programs to strengthen its influence over official behavior in the subnational jurisdictions.

Attempts to deal with problems faced by some citizens brought unprecedented national intervention in state handling of civil rights, criminal justice, and apportionment of legislative bodies. Courts became managers of legislative redistricting, prisons, and school systems when it seemed the only way to ameliorate an otherwise intolerable situation.

Starts, stops, and reversals were made on regional matters with both substate and interstate regional organizations created, abolished, reconstituted, and modified. In the course of revising this book, Table 1–2 that depicts regional organizations was changed nine times in the course of two years to keep abreast of actual events.

The changes made in the federal system did not result from constitutional revision. There was no constitutional convention to redraw the basics of government. There was no single catastrophic event to stimulate public acceptance. Instead, the new web of intergovernmental relations that emerged resulted from accelerated and rampant incrementalism, to use what William Safire calls an "oxymoronic phrase" because "the adjective at first glance appears to fight the noun it modifies."[6] The words are not really incongruous, however. "Accelerated and rampant incrementalism" describes a continuous series of relatively minor or incremental, and generally unrelated, events that came together to modify substantially America's brand of federalism.

It is not clear what final form of government will emerge from the changes in the post-World War II period. It is surely correct, however, to say that no lasting, static form is being created because the system is constantly changing and evolving. Even if the shape of the emergent government or the crystallization of new patterns of intergovernmental relations are unclear, most observers are certain that the events of recent years have moved the American federal system far along the road marked "centralization."

CENTRALIZATION AND DECENTRALIZATION

The history of American federalism is one of rather steadily increasing centralization. The movement of power to the center government can be traced as a force moving inexorably forward, occasionally slowing, maybe even temporarily hesitating or halting, but almost never retreating. Walter H. Bennett's study on American federalism concludes with what has become a truism of the intergovernmental system:

The sweep of events in this century and the general character of American industrial society would make it naive to assume that there will be a wholesale reversal of the trend toward governmental centralization. Problems which were once local but have become national in scope are not to be expected suddenly to become local again.[7]

It is possible to identify periods in which centralization surged onward, such as during the Civil War and its immediate aftermath, during the height of the Progressive movement of the early twentieth century with its business and finance regulation—generally meaning national regulation—proposals, during the Depression and its resultant New Deal, during the World War II and the postwar international commitments, and during the activist programs of the 1960s in the areas of racial equality and urban development. It is also possible to identify periods when the centralization trend was relatively quiescent, such as that between the end of Reconstruction and the beginning of the Progressive period, or during the administration of Presidents Hoover, Eisenhower, and the most recent ones—Nixon, Ford, Carter, and Reagan.

Approximately 20 years ago William H. Riker identified the degree of centralization for major time periods during the nation's history.[8] The ACIR recently updated that study (Table 9-1). Since Riker's 1964 assessment the average degree of centralization moved toward the federal government from a measure of 2.8 to 2.5 according to ACIR staff judgments. The 2.5 assessment means that on the average the 17 functions lie almost exactly between national and state responsibilities as contrasted with a slight edge toward the states (2.8) earlier and a clear state dominance for prior time periods.

With the movement of the national government into the functions of morality (issues of abortion, ethics in government, fair campaign practices, truth in lending, violence on television), the state and local governments no longer are exclusively responsible for any of the 17 functions. The national government retains exclusive control in only two (external affairs and the monetary system). Most programs are therefore partnerships in the American federal system, albeit partnerships in which the central government plays an increasingly important role. The national government is the senior partner in eight areas, equal partner in three, and junior partner in four functions.

An examination of federal expenditures for a particular domestic function as a percent of all government expenditures for that function indicates the range of the national government's involvement. On the high end, the central government funds 90 percent of all natural resource expenditures, 90 percent of subsidized housing and urban renewal costs, and 76 percent of public welfare. On the other end, certain expenditures clearly are dom-

TABLE 9-1
THE DEGREE OF CENTRALIZATION IN THE UNITED STATES, BY SUBSTANTIVE FUNCTIONS AND AT POINTS IN TIME

Functions	Circa 1790	Circa 1850	Circa 1910	Circa 1964	Circa 1979
1. External affairs (military/diplomatic)	4	1	1	1	1
2. Public safety	5	4	4	4	4
3. Property rights	5	5	4	4	4
4. Civic rights (liberties and voting)	5	5	5	3	2
5. Morality (social values and norms)	5	5	5	5	4
6. Patriotism (instill allegiance and pride)	3	3	3	3	3
7. Money, credit, and banking	3	4	3	1	1
8. Transport and communication	4	4	2	2	2
9. Utilities (services and regulation)	5	5	5	4	3
10. Production and distribution	5	5	4	2	2
11. Economic development (subsidies)	3	4	3	2	2
12. Natural resources	—	—	2	2	2
13. Education	—	5	5	4	4
14. Indigency (aid, including the handicapped)	5	5	5	2	2
15. Recreation and culture	—	4	4	3	3
16. Health (services and regulation)	—	—	4	3	2
17. Knowledge (research, patents, copyrights, etc.)	1	1	1	2	2
Average	4.1	4.0	3.5	2.8	2.5

1. The functions are performed exclusively or almost exclusively by the national government.
2. The functions are performed predominantly by the national government, although the state governments play a significant secondary role.
3. The functions are performed by national and state governments in about equal proportions.
4. The functions are performed predominantly by the state governments, although the national government plays a significant secondary role.
5. The functions are performed exclusively or almost exclusively by the state governments.
— The functions were not recognized to exist at the time.

Source: William H. Riker, *Federalism: Origin, Operation, Significance* (Boston: Little, Brown and Co. 1964), p. 85. The 1979 assessment was prepared by Bruce D. McDowell for the Advisory Commission on Intergovernmental Relations, *The Federal Role in the Federal System: The Dynamics of Growth. A Crisis of Confidence and Competence.* Report A-77 (Washington, D.C.: July, 1980), p. 90.

inated by the state-local sector. National expenditures, for example, account for only 9 percent of total library outlays, 8 percent of education costs, and an infinitesimal portion of fire protection expenditures.[9]

Reacting to the growing pull toward the national level, recent presidents —most notably Nixon, Ford, Carter, and Reagan—attempted to stop the tug of centralization and to move toward a more decentralized system. President Nixon's New Federalism, announced in August, 1969, was a major effort to achieve these ends. It placed an emphasis on administrative decentralization and functional devolution. The latter was based on the view that as many activities as possible should be turned over to the states and localities, conditioned only by their willingness and capacity to perform. Federal funds should be used to strengthen the fiscal capabilities of states and general purpose local governments. These efforts at decentralization, particularly functional reassignment to state and local governments, had their origins in themes developed in the 1950s. The states, it was argued, were responsible partners in the federal system and further centralization was unnecessary, undesirable, and dangerous.

Although Presidents Ford and Carter continued the decentralization thrust of their predecessor's New Federalism, major changes did not occur and the effort was judged by most observers to be a failure. The ACIR, for example, concluded its 14-volume study of the intergovernmental grant system by noting harshly that ''. . . the major trends that have emerged during the past decades . . . combine to support the summary generalization that never has the maze of fiscal, functional, regulatory and administrative links between and among the federal [national] government, the states, and all substate units been more complex, costly and convoluted than it is now.''[10]

Failure occurred for a number of reasons. Congress, for example, contributed to the failure by establishing federal assistance programs for activities theretofore thought to be state and local concerns, not national. An aggregation of similar problems—such as snow removal or pothole repair—in a number of local communities was treated as a national problem. Carl W. Stenberg, commenting on such developments, observed that ''intervention on such a massive scale also created confusion and uncertainty over which level of government or group of public officials was ultimately responsible for service delivery. There were simply too many fingers in the intergovernmental service delivery pie.''[11]

As the number of intergovernmental aid programs continued to mushroom, the executive branch's efforts to decentralize were, for the most part, as Stenberg notes, ''sporadic and shortlived.'' He continued:

> . . . the structure of the intergovernmental system became more complex, confusing, and costly. Thousands of bodies were created largely as a result of federal initiatives or resources to perform various roles in connection with assistance programs. These included ten Federal Re-

gional Councils, several multistate economic development commissions, over 500 clearinghouses for handling areawide review and comment procedures under OMB Circular A–95, and more than 2,000 single and multipurpose substate regional planning bodies. Most of these bodies were established to plan, coordinate, and facilitate communications— functions that were especially vital to intergovernmental relations in the 1960s. Their implementation capacity, however, has been severely curtailed by their voluntary nature and lack of operational authority.[12]

President Reagan's sweeping victory in 1980 gave new life to the decentralization efforts. Picking up the "New Federalism" term of earlier years, the new President vigorously and successfully pushed policies designed to (1) reduce federal expenditures for state and local intergovernmental aid; (2) make extensive use of block grants with concurrent reduction in the number of categoricals, and (3) eliminate much of the intergovernmental regulatory "red tape" developed during the past two decades.

The President's New Federalism decentralization effort met with considerable success during the new administration's first year. Intergovernmental aid in current dollars declined for the first time since the 1930s, dropping from a peak of $94.8 billion in fiscal 1981 to $88.8 billion in fiscal 1982, a decline of 6.3 percent.[13] Further, the Omnibus Budget Reconciliation Act of 1981 consolidated 77 categoricals and two block grants into nine block grants. This was a massive change designed to give state and local governments more discretion. Moreover, the Title V national–multistate regional development commissions (e.g., Ozarks, Great Lakes) were terminated as federal entities, and the Appalachian Regional Commission was severely curtailed. Federal support—financial and administrative— for substate regionalism was withdrawn and the A–95 review process discontinued. Finally, the administration began to relax informally many of the regulations that had made the intergovernmental process so complex. The *Washington Post* reported that the Reagan administration had "stopped tough regulatory enforcement. From the Department of Agriculture and the Environmental Protection Agency to the Department of Transportation and the Department of Labor, agencies are relaxing their once vigorous oversight of business and local government compliance with federal regulation."[14]

These significant steps backwards on the centralization path all occurred during the first 10 months of the new administration's term. Bernard F. Hillenbrand, then executive director of the National Association of Counties, wrote that the changes "set the tone for the most exciting national debate since the Civil War." Further, the New Federalism "for sheer magnitude and comprehensiveness dwarfs any proposed governmental reorganization in our 200 year history."[15]

Hillenbrand's hyperbole notwithstanding, the impact of these changes cannot be overestimated. Counterattacks by affected interest groups and by financially hard pressed state and local officials did, indeed, slow down the pace of change—so much so that one national newspaper actually editorialized about "the Late New Federalism."[16] To the extent, however, that these efforts for decentralization reflect not just the popularity of a single president, but rather an anti-tax, anti-big-government-in-Washington public opinion, the fight to halt further centralization is likely to have sustained vigor for years to come. Even so, these explicitly stated philosophies and programs designed to slow or reverse the centralization trend may prove to be little more than a temporary detour. As indicated earlier, it is almost impossible to identify any sustained period in which decentralization has taken place.

PROPONENTS OF CENTRALIZATION

While the centralization trend produced misgivings, fears, and opposition from most public leaders, the public and many students of federalism, there are proponents who cheer on that trend, and who look forward to the final demise of all decentralized centers of power. Herbert Croly, a leading publicist of the Progressive movement, argued that "American government demands more rather than less centralization merely and precisely because of the growing centralization of American activity."[17] Three decades later the influential Harold J. Laski was advancing the centralization argument in this manner:

> My pleas here are for the recognition that the federal form of state is unsuitable to the stage of economic and social development that America has reached. I infer from this postulate two conclusions: first, that the present division of powers, however liberal be the Supreme Court in its technique of interpretation, is inadequate to the needs America confronts; and, second, that any revision of those powers is one which must place in Washington, and Washington only, the power to amend that revision as circumstances change. I infer, in a word, that the epoch of federalism is over. . . .

> The view here urged, of course, looks toward a fundamental reconstruction of traditional American institutions. It is not impressed by the view, associated with the great name of Mr. Justice Brandeis, that the "curse of bigness" will descend upon any serious departure from the historic contours of federalism. . . . What, at least, is certain is this: that a government the powers of which are not commensurate with its problems will not be able to cope with them. Either, therefore, it must obtain those powers, or it must yield to a form of state more able to satisfy the demands that it encounters. That is the supreme issue before the United States today; and the more closely it is scrutinized the more obviously does its resolution seem to be bound up with the obsolescence of the federal system.[18]

The statements of Croly and Laski were written during periods of great systemic difficulty and adjustment. Their views, however, are not merely of historical interest. They state a recurring theme that surfaces whenever federalism faces stress. Harry V. Jaffa, well known for his writings on American political thought, gives a more contemporary (1960) statement of the pro-centralization position. Jaffa's main concern is for greater centralization in the interest of defense and national security, which demonstrates the topicality of the attitudes toward centralization and decentralization. His conclusions, however, are identical to Croly, Laski, and other centralization proponents.

> The case for a stronger national government rests upon one simple proposition: The problems which face the American people, to an extent unprecedented, are national problems and can be dealt with effectively only by the common direction and close coordination of the efforts of all Americans. The only agency which can marshal all the resources of the nation, and order all its efforts to the overriding purposes which all share, is the government of the United States.[19]

Not all the centralists make their case on the basis of broad increases in power to deal with general social and economic problems. Some have a much narrower focus. William H. Riker, for example, noting that the decentralized power arrangement of the federal system has been effectively utilized by racists and segregationists, comes to the sweeping conclusion that "if in the United States one approves of Southern white racists, then one should approve of American federalism."[20]

Not only are the pro-centralization arguments generally rejected by most people who study federalism and by the American public and its leaders, but a certain solace can be had in the system's ability to deal with their focal points of complaint. Brooke Graves, responding to Laski's argument, noted that "to these criticisms, one is justified in answering that under the federal system as it now operates, there is sufficient constitutional power to deal with virtually any problem of national proportions. . . ."[21]

The key to Graves' rejoinder is in the phrase "as it now operates." There undoubtedly were major shortcomings in the system's ability to deal with the problems of the 1920s and 1930s to which Laski was addressing himself. Nevertheless, the system was able, through pragmatic change and accommodation, to handle the problems. Likewise, the federal arrangement has been modified enough to provide socioeconomic regulations sought by Croly, to alleviate the security and defense concerns expressed by Jaffa, and to overcome the subunits' protection of segregation that Riker feared. To illustrate, what was needed in regard to integration was a broader interpretation of protections afforded by the Fourteenth Amendment and a national commitment to get on with the business of desegregation. A national restructuring, including the abandonment of federalism, was not necessary.

ALTERNATE MODELS

Since the beginning of the American Republic, alternate associational arrangements have been suggested. The Constitutional Convention considered several possibilities before agreeing to compromises that gave birth to the current structure. Alexander Hamilton, for example, proposed a highly centralized model in which all sovereignty would reside in the central government and the subunits would be like "corporations for local purposes." Later, John C. Calhoun, looking to the maintenance of state sovereignty, advocated the concepts of concurrent majority and the mutual negative. For the latter, he argues, as had John Taylor of Caroline, that the state and national governments each possessed the power to veto the acts of the other. Such actions would be used only sparingly and then only to protect the basic interests and powers of the respective jurisdictions. The two concepts definitely would have restructured power distributions within the federal system.

The historical models are periodically resurrected and reexamined during periods of systemic crisis. During the aftermath of the *Brown* v. *Board of Education* decision, many apologists for the South focused on Calhoun's model for federalism. Leach in 1972 refers to Hamilton's model as "one option open to America in the future." He states further that the continuing failure of the states "could rapidly sour the traditional affection Americans feel for them and thus open the door at last to the Hamiltonian model."[22]

Federal systems as utilized in other parts of the world are increasingly serving as models for the examination of alternatives to the American structures and processes. In this age of federalism more than 20 nations are organized on a federal basis. Because large heterogeneous countries most often seek out this associational device, the federal nations cover more than half the land area of the world and include more than one-third of its population.

The comparative models offer illustrations of many different patterns of intergovernmental relations. In addition to recent excellent general studies on comparative federalism, there has been an outpouring of detailed studies on particular aspects of federal systems.[23] Comparative studies of theories of federalism,[24] judicial review in the federal process, and as a device for maintaining the federal balance,[25] fiscal federalism,[26] and causes of failures of federal systems[27] give a wealth of information on alternate ways of adjusting the federal mechanism. Most foreign models have generated discussions that have been restricted almost exclusively to the academic community. Nevertheless, evidence exists that they are beginning to be of utility to broader-based policy considerations. During the debates on revenue sharing, for example, alternate methods of federal fiscal adjustment, especially experiences of other nations with revenue-sharing programs, were reviewed by many of the debate's participants.

Finally, there have been consistent calls for the total abandonment of the states in favor of creating large regional units of government with more rationally drawn boundaries. This plan is not new. The first issues of both the *Political Science Quarterly* (1886) and the *Annals of the American Academy of Political and Social Science (1890)*, for example, carried articles condemning the states and calling for the establishment of rational regional units of governance.[28] In more recent times the best-known plans for such a total restructuring are those advanced by Rexford Guy Tugwell and Leland D. Baldwin.[29] These proposals generally spring from concerns about (1) the delays and inactions caused by the division of power between the states as currently structured and the national government; (2) inadequate size with regard to both resource potential and service areas; and (3) irrational boundaries that artificially divide natural geographic areas, cities, and other jurisdictions. The proposals envision consolidation of existing states into approximately a dozen regional organizations with very flexible boundaries. (See Figure 9-1 for Baldwin's suggested plan.) The regional entities would be far more subject to national review and control than are states under the existing Constitution.

Barring a catastrophic upheaval, these totally restructured models are not likely to be adopted. Nor, in fact, is there likely to be a rush to pick up the strikingly different alternatives of other systems throughout the world. Americans are conservative about their forms of government and are reluctant to change them.

THE FUTURE

What does the future hold for American federalism?

Prophesying the future of political, economic, and social systems is always inexact.[30] The variables affecting it appear infinite. They and the unanticipated crises that can occur and the unexpected outcomes of past choices all stand in the way of clear vision. Moreover, the complexity and interrelationships of our massive social, political, and economic systems further complicate the predicting process.[31] Nevertheless, decisions as to what should be done at the moment are based to some extent on beliefs as to what tomorrow is likely to bring. Because the operation of the American government depends heavily on the intergovernmental relations that undergird the system, perhaps some light can be thrown on federalism's prospects by first anticipating developments in specific sectors of these relationships.

FIGURE 9-1 BALDWIN'S PROPOSED NEW STATE ALIGNMENT

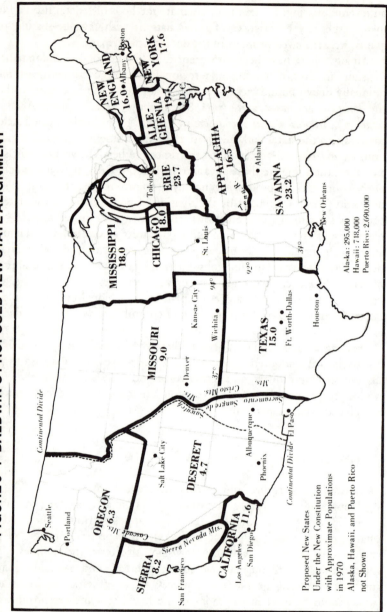

Source: Leland D. Baldwin, *Reframing the Constitution: An Imperative for Modern America* (Santa Barbara, Calif.: Clio Press, 1972), p. 61.

Continued Centralization in National-State Relations

As far as national-state relations are concerned, the trend toward centralization is likely to continue, although at a slower pace. Technological developments, population growth and shifts, and cataclysmic events make a retreat from the nationalization of American social and economic systems impossible. The political system must then respond to these trends. The pressures of those who in the past have profited from national action—minorities, nationally organized interest groups, members of Congress whose manipulation of national programs afford them electoral advantage at home, and those honestly believing in the virtues of nationalization—will continue to influence decisions. The fragmentation of state interests, the decline of state political parties and the consequent loss of state political power, the lack of general public concern for who solves a particular problem, and the political ambitions of governors, judges, and members of Congress will enfeeble the efforts states can harness to challenge the national goliath.

Contrariwise, the transformation of state governments into competent, responsive, and responsible entities that has occurred in the past quarter century, the establishment of the State and Local Government Academy to provide better legal representation for these jurisdictions in court contests with national authorities, the philosophical preferences of Americans for smaller units of government, the pressures on national officials to trim the deficits and reduce spending, and the disillusionment with national efforts to solve every problem—all of these brake the centralization trend.

Every generation or so, Americans will debate national-state relationships, an issue ordinarily raised by the party out of power in Washington, D.C. and advanced under campaign rhetoric such as "cooperative," "creative," or "new" federalism, designed to remind the voters of federalisms's virtues. After the debate has run its course, the pendulum that swings back and forth between the national and state positions in the system will continue to operate. But it will swing less toward the states and slightly further in the direction of the national government.

Conflict and Cooperation Among the States

No doubt relations among the states will remain fractious and competitive. States seeking new industries will look covetously at those located in sister states and try to entice them to their areas. Tax systems will be designed to burden state residents as little as possible and, where feasible, to export their impact to other states through the imposition of severance taxes on fuels, tourist-paid levies on hotels and restaurant meals, and tolls for the use of highways.

The distribution of political rewards, the existence of deep reservoirs of state chauvinism, and the withdrawal of national government encouragement for interstate cooperation all point toward the continuance of the frictions and sibling rivalries that have marked interstate relations even in the best of times. State political systems infrequently reward leadership encouraging interstate cooperation; gains go to those who favor the home-folks. To some extent this is imbedded in the deep residue of pride in state citizenship, a pride not limited to Texans. Virginians and Tennesseans are just as proud of their heritage as Texans are of theirs, and New Yorkers have only occasionally discovered anything west of the Hudson River. Californians, although often natives of "Elsewhere, U.S.A.," pride themselves on living in America's "promised land." The cutoff of national support for multistate regional organizations will add to the difficulties of concerted actions. If nothing else, the established organizations provided opportunities for face to face encounters, discussion of common problems, and comprehension of shared concerns while serving as established mechanisms for cooperation.

Despite the forces aligned against improvements in interstate relations, the forecast is for continuing and greater cooperation, simply because it will be necessary. The spread of urbanization, the mobility of American society, growing environmental difficulties, and, in general, a shrinking of the nation as a result of technological developments will make joint actions imperative. Other influences also are at work. Better educated and less provincial governors, legislators, and administrative officials can perceive the interdependence of the states and agree to some accommodations for the general good. Having learned the value of interstate cooperation through interstate compacts and regional organizations, state officials can be expected to join with their counterparts in other states to solve some regional problems. The reconstitution of the former Title V commissions at the instigation of the governors concerned is evidence of this. Nevertheless, cooperation will not be undertaken enthusiastically and will be accompanied by fractious and competitive behavior very little different from the past.

Maintenance of the Status Quo for States and Localities

The crystal ball does not reveal what it would take to alter state relations with the local governments within their boundaries, so, barring some cataclysmic event, they are likely to remain substantially the same. That is, they will be state-determined with increasing centralization and local dependency. Little by little, over time, changes will be made, especially when state constitutions are revised. But the political forces operating to produce greater local discretion are not strong enough in most states to effect major changes. Nevertheless, local governments in some states can look forward to a loosening of state control in some areas of activity. Hand in hand with more autonomy will come additional mandates as states attempt to upgrade their local systems. Increased state financing and assumption of local functions also can be expected as local governments, faced with decaying infrastructures, citizens accustomed to certain levels of services, and public resistance to higher taxes, become more dependent on the states. The one trend that is clear is that because of local financial difficulties and the growing prominence of the states as managers of major intergovernmental programs, state-local relations will receive more attention in the coming decade than they have in the past.

Inter-Local Adaptations

Local governments show little promise of becoming neighbors. Most will continue to operate as isolated entities, neither noting nor caring about problems of the jurisdictions next door unless they themselves are affected. When local governments in metropolitan areas seek to combat the problems of fragmentation, they will rely on procedural, voluntary, and ad hoc adaptive devices. This rather unimaginative view of the future is a realistic assessment of the political and legal difficulties accompanying major structural change. It also recognizes that for all the rhetoric on the failing of the current arrangement, one must conclude—even if somewhat begrudgingly—that the system *does work!* Wood's similar conclusion, written in 1958, is still valid today.

> Despite our predictions, disaster has not struck; urban government has continued to function, not well perhaps, but at least well enough to forestall catastrophe. Traffic continues to circulate; streets and sewers are built; water is provided; schools keep their doors open; and law and order generally prevail. Nor does this tolerable state of affairs result from an eager citizenry's acceptance of our counsel; we know only too well that our proposals for genuine reform have been largely ignored.[32]

There will continue to be some major adoptions of areawide governments in coming years. Many jurisdictions are giving serious considerations to metropolitan reorganization. The largest number of these considerations, however, is concentrated in the South, Southwest, and West. Most of the successful adoptions in the near future are likely to be in these regions, particularly in the West.

Many states will be changing the "rules of the game" to facilitate metropolitan reorganization. Some states have already abolished requirements for extraordinary or concurrent popular majorities. A few states, e.g, Florida, are encouraging comprehensive review by offering state technical and financial assistance for local government study commissions. Many states, especially in the South, Southwest, and Far West, are trying to minimize future problems by heading off fragmentation with "no-incorporation, easy-annexation" laws. Some of the impact of these changes is shown in the often repeated statistic of approximately six million people affected by annexation during the 1960s. Almost two-thirds of the urban municipalities were involved in some annexation action during that period.

One of the most significant changes in the "rules of the game" is the proposal for ending the requirement for popular referendum approval of a local government change. Some of our largest cities, e.g., Boston, Philadelphia, New Orleans, and New York City, were created by nineteenth century city-county consolidation actions of state legislatures. That approach is likely to be revived in the future. The 1969 Indiana Legislature merged Marion County and Indianapolis. Other state legislatures are considering similar actions. For example, the Alabama Legislature failed to approve by only one vote a consolidation of part of Jefferson County with the city of Birmingham. And in 1975 the Nevada legislature consolidated Las Vegas and Clark County, an action that was subsequently overturned by the state supreme court.

One has mixed reactions about reorganization by state legislative action. It does, of course, eliminate many causes of past rejections. Nonetheless, that approach plays havoc with the strongly-held tradition of popular approval of forms of local government and opens the door to possibly new and dangerous gerrymandering of governmental structures. The Republican-controlled Indiana legislature was, for example, accused of partisan action to help both the party and the state's newest Republican "star," Richard Lugar, mayor of Indianapolis, who subsequently became a U.S. senator.

When the states and localities are unable to deal adequately with the problems resulting from fragmentation, the national government in the past took actions designed to encourage a more rational order to the metropolitan scene. A combination of grant-in-aid funding with metropolitanwide comprehensive planning and review requirements—the famous 204, 701, and A–95 procedures—already has exerted an important influence on local government organization, especially as a stimulus for the growth of some strong councils of governments. Efforts of this type have declined dramatically in the past few years, especially under President Reagan's "New Federalism."

Much more direct action on local government organization is the rule, rather than the exception, for other nations. While drastic national governmental action of the type undertaken in nations such as Great Britain, Canada, or Germany is very unlikely for the United States, some form of national presence in interlocal relations, especially in the metropolitan area, is likely to be felt for the forseeable future.

The States' Vital Role

Overall, the future of American federalism depends in large part on what the states do. Not only do they largely determine the future course of state-local, interstate, and interlocal relations, but their strength and vigor will shape emerging national-state and national-local relations. If they continue to grow in stature, assume their responsibility for the shape of the federal arrangement, and resist selling their birthright as vital partners in the American system for 30 pieces of silver, they can restore the federal balance. If they do not—if they refuse to face up to the loss of political power, to follow through with the strengthening of their structures and processes already begun, and to plead poverty to get national assistance— the country will proceed step by step along the path to greater centralization. Although there are promising signs that the states will shoulder their responsibilities, the political weaknesses induced by various developments over the years—direct election of United States Senators, adoption of the Sixteenth Amendment and the national income tax, political party convention reforms and court decisions that weakened state parties, and a supreme court that moved from referee to player on one of the teams— will make the task more difficult. Even so, Americans can anticipate active state participation in the federal system for the forseeable future.

ONWARD AND UPWARD PRAGMATICALLY

Whatever Americans decide about adopting the courses of action just predicted for various facets of American intergovernmental relations, their choices will not likely be based on deliberate decisions to pursue an explicit philosophy for the development of American federalism. Nor will they be apt to follow a calculated course of "what's best in the long-run" for the American system. Based on past practices, their decisions will reflect the fact that while the workings of American federalism will change incrementally day by day, the practices of decisionmakers in effecting those changes are unlikely to undergo fundamental alteration. They will continue to practice pragmatic federalism—to keep on tinkering with the structure, changing it here and there as problems arise. The end result may show a new emphasis, a shift in priorities, but it will not be a major overhaul of the system. Observers can view the developing federalism much as time sequence photography of a mushroom patch—always in motion.

NOTES

1. John Shannon, assistant director of ACIR, "New Federalism in the 1980s," Testimony before the Joint Economic Committee, U.S. Congress, July 20, 1982, p. 2.

2. W. Brooke Graves, *American Intergovernmental Relations* (New York: Charles Scribner's Sons, 1964), p. 911.

3. Richard H. Leach, "The Future of American Federalism," *Politics, 1972,* (March, 1972), pp. 77–78.

4. David R. Beam, "Forecasting the Future of Federalism," *Intergovernmental Perspective,* Vol. 6, No. 3 (Summer, 1980), p. 6.

5. Actually, 74 delegates were originally appointed to the Constitutional Convention. For a variety of reasons, 19 of them never appeared and of the 55 participating in the deliberations in Philadelphia, only 39 signed the final document.

6. "Publius" (William Safire), "New Federalist Paper No. 1," *Publius: The Journal of Federalism,* Vol. 2, No. 1 (Spring, 1972), pp. 98–99. "Accelerated and rampant incrementalism" was concocted in that same linguistic kitchen that gave us phrases such as "loyal opposition," and Safire's own "national localism."

7. Walter Hartwell Bennett, *American Theories of Federalism* (University, Ala.: University of Alabama Press, 1964), p. 220.

8. William H. Riker, *Federalism: Origin, Operation, Significance* (Boston: Little, Brown and Co., 1964), p. 85.

9. U.S. Bureau of the Census, *Governmental Finances in 1980-81,* Series GF81, No. 5 (Washington, D.C.: Government Printing Office, 1982), p. 31.

10. U.S. Advisory Commission on Intergovernmental Relations, *The Intergovernmental Grant System: An Assessment and Proposed Policies.* Report A–62 (Washington, D.C.: June, 1978), pp. 67–68.

11. Carl W. Stenberg, "Federalism in Transition: 1959-79," *Intergovernmental Perspective,* Vol. 6, No. 1 (Winter, 1980), p. 11.

12. Ibid., p. 12.

13. ACIR, "Federal Aid to States Registers First Decline," *News Release,* April 28, 1983.

14. November 15, 1981.

15. "A Federalism Blockbuster," *County News* (NACo), Feb. 1, 1982, p. 3.

16. *Washington Post,* April 8, 1982, p. A–26.

17. Herbert Croly, *The Promise of American Life* (New York: Macmillan Co., 1912). A summary of the ambivalent attitudes of the Progressives toward centralization and federalism is found in Graves, pp. 781–816.

18. Harold J. Laski, "The Obsolescence of Federalism," *The New Republic,* Vol. 98 (May, 1939), pp. 367–369. This classic statement is reprinted in Mavis Mann Reeves and Parris N. Glendening, *Controversies of State and Local Systems* (Boston: Allyn & Bacon, 1972), pp. 92–98.

19. Harry V. Jaffa, "The Case for A Stronger National Government," in Robert A. Goldwin, ed., *A Nation of States: Essays on the American Federal System* (Chicago: Rand McNally, 1963), p. 106.

20. Riker, p. 155. See also Leach, p. 74; Graves, p. 787.

21. Graves, p. 787.

22. Leach, p. 78.

23. See, for example, Ivo D. Duchacek's *Comparative Federalism: The Territorial Dimension of Politics* (New York: Holt, Rinehart and Winston, 1970); Carl J. Friedrich, *Trends of Federalism in Theory and Practice* (New York: Frederick A. Praeger, 1968); and Riker, *Federalism.*

24. See, for example, Friedrich, *Trends of Federalism in Theory and Practice;* and Sobei Mogi, *The Problem of Federalism: A Study in the History of Political Theory,* 2 vols. (London: George Allen and Unwin, 1931).

25. Richard E. Johnson, *The Effect of Judicial Review on Federal-State Relations in Australia, Canada, and the United States* (Baton Rouge: Louisiana State University Press, 1969).

26. R. J. May, *Federalism and Fiscal Adjustment* (London: Oxford University Press, 1969); ACIR, *Studies in Comparative Federalism: Australia, Canada, the United States and West Germany* Report M–130 (Washington, D.C.: November, 1981). Richard H. Leach is the author of this report.

27. Thomas M. Franck, ed., *Why Federations Fail: An Inquiry into the Requisites for Successful Federalism* (New York: New York University Press, 1968).

28. John W. Burgess, "The American Commonwealth," *Political Science Quarterly,* Vol. 1, No. 1 (March, 1886), pp. 9–35; and Simon N. Patton, "Decay of State and Local Government," *The Annals of the American Academy of Political and Social Science,* Vol. 1, No. 1 (July, 1890), pp. 26–42.

29. Rexford Guy Tugwell, *Model for a New Constitution* (Palo Alto, Calif.: James E. Freel and Associates, 1970); and Leland D. Baldwin, *Reframing the Constitution: An Imperative for Modern America* (Santa Barbara, Calif.: Clio Press, 1972).

30. Seymour Martin Lipset, "Predicting the Future of Post-Industrial Society: Can We Do It?" *The Third Century: America as A Post-Industrial Society,* ed. by Seymour Martin Lipset (Chicago: University of Chicago Press, 1979), pp. 1–35.

31. See Beam.

32. Robert C. Woods, "Metropolitan Government, 1975: An Extrapolation of Trends," *American Political Science Review,* Vol. 52 (1958), p. 112. Woods added that "we may not face catastrophe, but this is no reason for countenancing one-hour commuting schedules, for permitting blight, for condoning the repellent sprawl of cheap commercial developments, inadequate parks, congested schools, mediocre administration, traffic jams, smog, pollution, and the hundred and one other irritations which surround us. . . ," p. 113.

NAME INDEX

349

SUBJECT INDEX

This thoroughly revised second edition of *Pragmatic Federalism* provides a rich historical background for its analysis of contemporary intergovernmental issues, including the impact of programs of the Reagan administration. Written in a highly readable style, the book appraises the adaptive ability and resilience of the American federal system.

PALISADES PUBLISHERS
Pacific Palisades, CA 90272

ISBN 0-913530-36-0

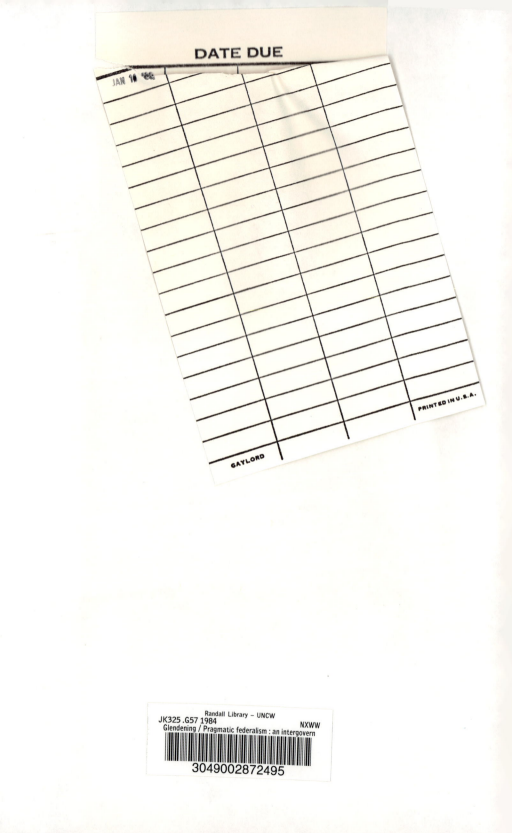

DATE DUE